D1527439

African-Brazilian Culture and Regional Identity in Bahia, Brazil

New World Diasporas

UNIVERSITY PRESS OF FLORIDA

Florida A&M University, Tallahassee
Florida Atlantic University, Boca Raton
Florida Gulf Coast University, Ft. Myers
Florida International University, Miami
Florida State University, Tallahassee
New College of Florida, Sarasota
University of Central Florida, Orlando
University of Florida, Gainesville
University of North Florida, Jacksonville
University of South Florida, Tampa
University of West Florida, Pensacola

African-Brazilian Culture

and Regional Identity in Bahia, Brazil

SCOTT ICKES

University Press of Florida

Gainesville · Tallahassee · Tampa · Boca Raton

Pensacola · Orlando · Miami · Jacksonville · Ft. Myers · Sarasota

This book may be available in an electronic edition.

18 17 16 15 14 13   6 5 4 3 2 1

Ickes, Scott.
African-Brazilian culture and regional identity in Bahia, Brazil / Scott Ickes.
p. cm.—(New world diasporas)
Includes bibliographical references and index.
ISBN 978-0-8130-4478-1 (alk. paper)
1. Blacks—Brazil—Bahia (State)—History. 2. Bahia (Brazil : State)—Social conditions.
3. Bahia (Brazil : State)—Race relations. 4. Bahia (Brazil : State)—History.
5. Social classes—Brazil—Bahia (State) I. Title. II. Series: New World diasporas series.
F2551.I25 2013
305.800981′42—dc23   2013007073

University Press of Florida
15 Northwest 15th Street
Gainesville, FL 32611-2079
http://www.upf.com

Contents

Illustrations

Map

Tables

Figures

Acknowledgments

Looking back, I realize I chose the topic of this book in part because of the people I would meet. I have not been disappointed! A number of them made contributions to this book both large and small. I would like to thank Eric Carlson and Rob Wright for their wisdom and support at the outset. I am grateful to Daryle Williams for his ongoing contributions and for long ago taking on advising the project so early in his own career. I would like to thank Carla Peterson for her early support of my work and to acknowledge research and travel grants from the History Department and the Committee on Africa and the Americas at the University of Maryland (now merged with the David C. Driskell Center for the Study of the Visual Arts and Culture of African Americans and the African Diaspora). A U.S. Department of Education Foreign Language and Area Studies fellowship for Portuguese language training was crucial to getting the project off the ground after several years focusing on the history of Central America.

In Bahia, a number of people have been important to me personally and professionally. I would like to thank Ricardo Castro Piedade and Gisele Reis for many long years of support and friendship. Joêlia Brito, Vera Silva, Simone Nascimento, Jorge Antônio Batista, Luisa Huber, Mark Swift, Meire Reis, and Valter Silva, too, have made important contributions to my life and work. Joêlia Brito and Vera Silva helped in the archives, as did Maoro Menezes de Oliveira Dias, Alane Fraga do Carmo, and Cínthia da Silva Cunha. Vera Silva was central to a successful oral history project, assisting with interviews and transcriptions. My "legal team" of Michael Loeb and Vivienne Kahng were always there to help things run smoothly during time in Rio de Janeiro and São Paulo.

I would like to thank Professors Jeferson Bacelar, Ubiratan Castro de Araújo, João Reis, and Jocélio Teles dos Santos at the Centro de Estudos Afro-Orientais and the Universidade Federal da Bahia for their time, suggestions, and institutional support. My thanks also go to Kátia Düring for access to some of her work-in-progress for S.A.M.BA, the Sócio-Antrop-ologia da Música na Bahia research group, for the years 1930–37. Hendrik Kraay and John Collins were also generous with material that improved the arguments here. I would like to express my gratitude to those many Salva-dorans listed among the interviewees at the back of the book and others who trusted me with aspects of their life history, and also to those individu-als too numerous to list who helped me find appropriate interviewees. The time and contributions of Cid Teixeira, Solange Bernabó, Maria Tavares, and Clarindo da Silva also made this a better project. During my time at the Universidade Federal Fluminense in Niterói, my work benefited from the experience and encouragement of Hebe Castro, Magali Engle, Marta Abreu, and Rachel Soihet. I would like to thank the Fundação Pierre Verger for permission to reproduce photographs from their collections and Sol-ange Bernabó and the Instituto Carybé for permission to reproduce illus-trations by Carybé from the Coleção Recôncavo.

Numerous readers, commentators, and interlocutors have improved the content of the manuscript. In particular, I would like to thank Daryle Williams, Barbara Weinstein, Stephan Palmié, Mary Kay Vaughan, Phyllis Peres, Rebecca Lord, Doug Bristol, Amy Masciola, Nick Frances, Michael Hussey, John Wood, Gerry Leavey, and Paul Gready for their contributions to early versions of the work. Later versions were improved by the sug-gestions of Case Boterbloem, Eric Duke, Adriana Novoa, Jolie Dyl, Greg Milton, Mary Currie, Dan Belgrad, Bernd Reiter, Brian Connolly, Mitchell Glodeck, Willys Santos de Andrade, the sharp eye and shaper pen of Kate Babbit, and two very helpful and hard-working reviewers at the University of Florida Press.

Support of my immediate colleagues at the University of South Florida (USF) has been crucial throughout the process, with special mention to Bernd Reiter, Phil Levy, Case Boterbloem, Frannie Ramos, Fraser Ottanelli, John Belohlavek, and Kevin Yelvington. Rachel May at the Institute for the Study of Latin America and the Caribbean has been especially supportive of research and teaching on Brazil. The institute provided me with a 2009 Summer Research Grant to help complete the project, and the USF History Department also provided travel funds for archival research. At the Uni-versity of South Florida, Sandra Law and her team in Inter Library Loan are a great asset, and I would like to thank the numerous and often anony-mous staff of the libraries and archives where I did my work. The staff at the Fundação Pierre Verger have been especially helpful. I also extend my thanks to the *Bulletin for Latin American Research*, *Revista Afro-Ásia*, and the *Americas* for allowing me to reproduce material that appeared there.

I would like to acknowledge the contributions of my family. My children have been a great source of joy, relief, and motivation and have been very positive about the research and writing. Sol has always been politely curious about my progress. Ash was certain he could "fix the book." (He meant over breakfast, with masking tape.) Rhia invited me to read it to her at bedtime. I am a very lucky father. In return, I am glad the research has encouraged them to take learning additional languages seriously (as has living in Tampa) and to keep practicing their capoeira. Their grandparents, Judi and Roy Ickes and John and Clare Currie, have been important sources of strength and support throughout. Finally, I happily dedicate this book to my partner Mary Currie with love, affection, and a deep appreciation for everything she has done to help this project come together.

Abbreviations

AHMS   Arquivo Histórico Municipal de Salvador

APEB   Arquivo Público do Estado da Bahia, Seção Republicana, Salvador

CPDOC   Centro de Pesquisa e Documentação de História Contemporânea do Brasil, Rio de Janeiro

FPV   Fundação Pierre Verger, Salvador

HFN   Melville J. and Frances S. Herskovits Field Notes, Schomburg Center for Research in Black Culture, New York Public Library, New York, New York

NARA II   National Archives and Records Administration, College Park, Maryland

PRO   Public Record Office, Kew, UK

Introduction

Brazil's Black Rome and the Remaking of Bahian Regional Identity

Brazil's northeastern city of Salvador, capital of the state of Bahia, stands out as one of the most prominent points of reference within the African diaspora. The city, also often referred to as "Bahia," is known for hosting a vibrant, complex, and historically rich African-Bahian culture. Salvador's carnival draws more than two million people into the streets and showcases Afrocentric carnival clubs such as the *blocos afros* and *afoxés*, including the four-thousand-strong, all-male *afoxé* the Sons of Gandhi (Filhos de Gandhy), comprised almost exclusively of men of African descent. Salvador has nearly as much claim as Rio de Janeiro to samba, the music and dance quintessentially associated with both Brazil and African Brazilians. The heavily percussive fusion known as samba-reggae, a racially politicized offshoot of samba, has captured the imagination and diasporic sensibilities of Michael Jackson, Paul Simon, and Quincy Jones, all of whom traveled to Salvador in the 1990s. The most well known ensemble of samba-reggae, the street performing group Olodum, consists largely of African-Bahian teenagers. Capoeira, an African-Brazilian martial art, the practice of which is both competitive and playful, also evolved in Bahia.

The cultural-spiritual foundation of African-Bahian culture, including samba-reggae, capoeira, and many aspects of Salvador's distinctive carnival, is Candomblé, an African-Brazilian religion akin to Voodoo or Santeria. Candomblé's cosmology, iconography, and ritual draw heavily on West and west-central African traditions. The temples of Candomblé worship (*terreiros* or *casas* in Portuguese) have since the early nineteenth century provided institutional support to African slaves, free blacks, and generations of African Bahians, allowing them to reshape their cultural heritage and identity around cultural references to Africa. Links between Candomblé and other expressions commonly understood as *cultura negra* (black culture), such as samba, capoeira, and the *batucadas* (all-male percussive carnival clubs) remained strong through the twentieth century and into the twenty-first. This African-Bahian heritage is particularly on show during Salvador's numerous popular religious festivals. Moreover, the food associated with Bahia's African-Bahian community and the women who cook it, known as Baianas, have come to characterize Bahia both within Brazil and internationally. Traditionally the Baianas (frequently women of some standing within the hierarchy of Candomblé) dressed distinctively in styles based on West African fashions and peddled food as their primary source of income. Nowadays a small number of these Baianas accept commissions from the Bahian state to work in the historical city center, posing for photographs with tourists for a fee. So close is Bahia's association with traditions typically described as African that Brazil's diplomatic corps and even former president Lula da Silva have employed this regional heritage in carefully scripted diplomatic efforts to woo African trading partners.[1] In very meaningful ways, Bahia has been associated with African-Bahian culture. Consequently, Bahia occupies a place of honor and privilege within the African diaspora. As Candomblé has been a vital institutional support at the center of this diasporic cultural richness, it fits that Salvador is known as Brazil's "Black Rome," as Candomblé priestess Mãe Eugênia Ana dos Santos (1869–1938) proclaimed in the 1930s.[2]

This contemporary association between Bahia and African-Bahian culture, however, boasts a more nuanced—and more fraught—nineteenth- and twentieth-century lineage than the city's tourist board would have one believe. With this book I return to the historical moment, roughly the years between 1930 and 1954, when a discourse of cultural inclusion was created and when the foundations for Salvador's subsequent configurations of cultural politics were established. Before 1930, Bahian elites cultivated a largely antagonistic position toward African-Bahian practices, and the press, politicians, and the police criticized, repressed, and persecuted public expressions of African-Bahian culture. However, a close analysis of Salvador's major popular festivals (from the Portuguese phrase for these events, *festas populares*), including carnival, reveals how a number of factors came together after 1930 to foster the incorporation of markedly African-Bahian practices into newer formulations of Bahian regional identity and "Bahianness" (in Portuguese, *baianidade*). Focusing on the festivals and the components of African-Bahian culture within them reveals the extent to which Salvador's African-Bahian working-class men and women (which includes those who worked in the informal economy) were involved in this process of reformulation, largely through their insistence on the ownership and legitimacy of their cultural heritage through ritualized performances in public spaces. Bahians of African descent continued to organize and practice their festive traditions during this period, pressing their claims for acceptance and recognition within Salvador's social and cultural life.

The festivals also drew the attention of journalists, intellectuals, and politicians who came to embrace African-Bahian culture, including both public and private ceremonies linked to Candomblé, samba, and capoeira, and contributed in central ways to reshaping the dominant discourse on African-Bahian cultural traditions.[3] By 1954, shapers of ideological opinion within the dominant class regularly honored African-Bahian popular culture as constitutive of and even central to Bahian regional identity, celebrating Candomblé ritual and performance within Salvador's public festivals in print media, via the radio, and occasionally in government discourse. Samba and related African-Bahian practices became a defining feature of the city's carnival, while the Baiana, too, became a venerable symbol of Bahia, appearing in song lyrics, photographs, and artwork.

Nevertheless, studying the festivals and the discourses surrounding them also reveals the extent to which this cultural inclusion provoked conservative reactions against the positive recoding of African-Bahian cultural practices. Even as the celebration of African-Bahian culture became widely accepted as central to commonsense constructions of Bahian regional identity, the inclusion of African-Bahian culture came up against both practical and discursive limits. In a very meaningful way, then, the popular festivals were important sites of "contestation and negotiation" over the meanings of African-Bahian culture.[4]

Bahian Cultural Politics

Since the early colonial period, a central question of social organization in Salvador from the point of view of the elite had been how to control, exploit, and live alongside the city's majority population of slaves, former slaves, and free blacks. Salvador's nonwhite population, in turn, had a complex history of individual and collective attempts to accommodate, contest, negotiate, resist, or flee altogether the impositions of the dominant class of the colony (1500–1822) and empire (1822–89). Culture was and continued to be fundamentally important within the relations of power between the dominant and subordinate classes in the city.[5]

During Brazil's First Republic (1889–1930), Bahian elites feared that their largely African-descended population prevented or at least decreased the possibility that Salvador could achieve the level of progress Europe or the United States had attained. They felt they had to make a choice, and they chose the European model of "civilization" over African culture. According to one typical newspaper article, Europe was at least "3,000 years ahead of Africa."[6] Scientific racism informed the discourse of Bahian elites on African Bahians, variants of which were promulgated locally by academics associated with the Bahian Faculty of Medicine, where social Darwinism combined with medical theory to establish a diverse range of causative, although not necessarily irreversible, connections between race, criminality, and degeneration.[7] African-Bahian culture in particular was considered to be antithetical to reigning notions of civilization and came under attack in public forums. Candomblé and capoeira were routinely savaged in the press: Candomblé was understood to be a haven for black magic, barbarism, and unhygienic conditions. Its medicinal traditions were judged to be unsafe and even life threatening. Capoeira was portrayed as the brutal practice of a shiftless and lazy yet menacing underclass, a practice that threatened to disturb not just the peace but also the existing social order. Both Candomblé and capoeira suffered episodic but concerted campaigns of police repression and persecution, a persecution that was institutionalized in the rewriting of the republic's penal code in 1890. The harassment was especially intense in the 1920s, when the infamous police chief Pedro de Azevedo Gordilho spearheaded a campaign of violent raids and intimidation that terrorized Salvador's working class.[8] Public hygiene campaigns targeted the open-air markets and informal dining in public spaces. As the popular periodical *Crispim da Bóia* lamented in 1906, Salvador was "a land of trash and blacks."[9]

"Race science" imbued jurisprudence and elite thought with notions of black inferiority. Labels such as *mulata* and *crioula* were used to indicate sexual licentiousness and compare nonwhite women unfavorably with the city's chaste and honorable *moças da nossa sociedade* (society girls). The African-Bahian woman street vendor—the Baiana—was dismissed throughout the First Republic as the *mulher de saião* (woman of the big skirt), a pejorative expression for the poor black working woman, who was portrayed as coarse and unclean, sullied by her continual presence in the street. It was even argued that the Baiana tarnished the image of Bahia beyond the capital.[10] African-themed carnival clubs were banned in 1905.[11] Even the forward-thinking, modernist editors of *Samba*, a short-lived 1928 local literary magazine, ignored or were antipathetic toward much of Salvador's African-Bahian culture and notions of Bahian regional distinctiveness.[12] Samba music in 1929 still had its vocal detractors, such as the anonymous contributor to *A Tarde* who wrote "Down with Samba!" and condemned the practice as "incompatible with progress." This lack of interest in African-Bahian culture contrasted starkly with the attitudes of the modernists in 1920s São Paulo and Rio de Janeiro who had come to embrace the nation's culturally heterogeneous past.[13]

As in the nineteenth century, however, there were moments during the First Republic that reveal some potential for compromise and accommodation between the dominant and subordinate classes over the acceptance of African-Bahian traditions. The image of Bahia's First Republic elite as uniformly aggressive toward African-Bahian culture should not be over-drawn. Samba, for instance, had been welcomed into the dance halls of the upper classes, just as its musical precursors the *maxixe* and *lundu* had been for at least a generation.[14] African-Bahian cuisine was widely accepted as a marker of regional singularity.[15] Even the ban on African-themed carnival clubs was lifted in 1914, and some politicians and other officials allied themselves with particular temples of Candomblé for personal and political reasons.[16] Clearly there were examples of alternative positions on African-Bahian culture and even degrees of acceptance other than simple, at times brutal repression.[17]

After 1930 came a dramatic shift in the relationship between elite thought and African-Bahian culture, an ideological reversal that saw increasingly widespread acceptance of African-Bahian practices and their inclusion in a set of defining characteristics of Bahianness. This shift has primarily been discussed in relation to the changed dynamic of resistance and accommodation between Salvador's police, press, and government and the *terreiros* of Candomblé and the wider Candomblé community, meaning both those who were deeply involved—the *povo-de-santo*, or "people of the saint"— and those who were less deeply involved but who shared in some of the practices or cosmological orientations of Candomblé, many of whom also participated in samba, capoeira, and the city's carnival *batucadas*.[18] This followed a marked trend that was underway in Rio de Janeiro in the 1920s and early 1930s that was initiated by modernist artists and intellectuals such as composer Heitor Villa-Lobos, poet and writer Mario de Andrade, and sociologist Gilberto Freyre, who saw Brazil's popular culture and racial and cultural mixing as the key to *brasilidade*, or "Brazilianness." This cultural trend provided part of the intellectual foundation for arguments that Brazil was a "racial democracy."[19] A number of scholars have explicitly or implicitly treated the shift to a discourse of African-Bahian cultural inclusion as a Bahian variant of the national discourse of racial democracy. The emphasis in Bahia, however, was on cultural amalgamation (or *mestiçagem*) rather than racial inclusion.[20]

This book examines the relationship between the Candomblé community, the dominant class, and print media, but it shifts the focus and argues that the Candomblé-related aspects of the city's major popular festivals, including carnival, had just as much influence as the Candomblé of the *terreiros* in providing the bases for the discursive embrace of African-Bahian culture as a central marker of Bahianness. Although most of these popular festivals were predominantly Catholic, they also included major elements that were specific to or that overlapped with the practice of Candomblé. For instance, the ritual washing of the steps of the Church of Nosso Senhor do Bonfim was for those within Catholic traditions in honor of Jesus Christ on the cross. For those within Candomblé traditions, however, the ritual washing was an obligation to Oxalá, the powerful Yoruban *orixá* (deity) of creation. Moreover, the Candomblé community provided vital institutional support for and overlapped socially with the other publicly performed manifestations of African-Bahian culture. These other manifestations included capoeira and the music and dance of samba and the city's carnival *batucadas*, all traditionally performed during the festivals.

In addition to the contributions of the performers of these practices, the reversal of opinion on African-Bahian culture was driven by the choices of members of the dominant class. First, political elites such as appointed governor Juracy Magalhães (1931–36), and even the governors appointed to run Bahia during the politically repressive, fascist-inspired dictatorship of Getúlio Vargas (known as the Estado Novo, 1937–45), fostered a climate favorable to the acceptance of African-Bahian cultural practices. Second, figures within the middle and upper middle class, such as newspaper editor Odorico Tavares, or modernist authors such as Jorge Amado or Odorico's brother Cláudio Tavares, saw the embrace of African-Bahian cultural practices as a progressive political act and this shaped the increasingly official acceptance of those practices as central to Bahian regional identity.

The political and economic policies of the Vargas era (1930–54) encouraged these transformations. Bahian elites were antagonistic toward the centralization of the federal government promoted by Getúlio Vargas as president (1930–37) and dictator (1937–45), and they mobilized regionalist sentiment as a proactive defense against the political encroachment of

Vargas. Vargas's policies finalized the long process begun in the eighteenth century by which control of the national agenda passed from the northeast to the southeast. For Bahian elites, the question became on what basis they could argue for (or demand) the right to govern themselves and for greater influence over policy making in relation to the southeast. In the 1930s these demands could have been made on the basis of industrial potential, but that argument threatened the agro-export oligarchs, who rejected this route. For many it made more sense to embrace Bahia's so-called agricultural vocation and its traditions, meaning the actual ritual acts, values, mores, and so forth associated with Bahia that harkened back to a glorious Bahian past.[21]

There was another option. Getúlio Vargas in the 1930s wanted a strong centralized state that could promote and regulate industrial economic activity and organize Brazilian society according to a corporativist vision of an organic, hierarchically ordered, and harmonious social body. Bound up with these priorities was the desire of the Vargas state to use cultural nationalism to generate a more coherent national identity. Part of this process included a self-conscious reworking of what it meant to be Brazilian through a favorable examination of its past, most of which, in the case of Brazil's northeast, centered on sugar plantations, colonial government, and the Catholic Church, principally in Bahia and Pernambuco. Vargas and his ministers also encouraged the embrace of Brazil's popular cultural traditions as the material and quasi-spiritual bedrock for notions of Brazilianness and offered the resources of the state to artists and intellectuals in Rio de Janeiro and São Paulo who agreed to work with these emphases. Most relevant to Bahia, the federal state embraced samba and carnival and later, although less spectacularly, capoeira, as central to Brazilian identity.[22]

Both facets of this project of national identity creation suited Salvadorans. Bahia was central to the economic heyday of Brazil's early colonial past. It hosted many of the African-Bahian traditions prevalent in Rio de Janeiro, which owed those traditions partly to migrants from Bahia in the nineteenth and twentieth centuries (as well as to its own lengthy history of contact with Africa via the slave trade and cultural exchange between the two continents). Salvador's dominant class set out to play it both ways. On the one hand, throughout the 1930s and 1940s, they continued to reject Vargas's political intrusions. They wanted as much autonomy as possible and reacted strongly to economic and political policy agendas that privileged industry in the southeast at the expense of their agro-export interests in the northeast. On the other hand, Bahian elites, and especially the urban liberal professionals who had been influenced by the nation's modernists of the 1920s, saw the advantage in aligning Bahia favorably with cultural and intellectual trends in the southeast.[23] As discourses on "Brazil" emerged and solidified, Bahians reshaped their own discourses and regional identity to better insert or insinuate themselves into the national narratives. Journalists billed the city as the "maximum repository of the traditions of [Brazilian] nationality" and the "old Brazilian '*mater*.'" Watching the Festival of the Senhor do Bonfim, one newspaper claimed, was like witnessing "the very history of Brazil."[24] By 1950, various dailies had declared the Senhor do Bonfim, Bahia's unofficial patron saint, to be "the principal Saint of Brazil."[25] As Salvador's mayor, Hélio Machado (1955–59), put it in his preface to Carlos Ott's *Formação e evolução étnica da cidade de Salvador*, Bahia's historical and cultural roots were in truth "those of the very Brazilian nation."[26] By employing the cliché that history is relevant if a nation is to move triumphantly forward, Machado made a clear case for the importance of Bahia as a custodian of Brazil's colonial past within the larger project of the nation's capitalist modernization. Consequently, Bahian regionalist discourse both opposed a centralizing federal state and claimed greater spoils for Bahians within that federal framework.[27] Most aspects of these claims were not new. However, the inclusion of African-Bahian cultural practices in regionalist rhetoric played a novel and significant role in these formulations after 1930.

Moreover, Bahians themselves came to believe in these discourses, which had important consequences for race and class relations in the region. Historian Anadelia Romo has provided a nuanced appreciation of how the dominant class in Salvador sought to "folklorize" African-Bahian culture and create a "cultural preserve," partly as a wider critique of a modernity for which, in the words of José Valladares, "much was sacrificed of the genuine soul of the earth in exchange for a progress whose virtues, evident in other places, still have not attained among us the grade of perfection that makes them desirable."[28] Romo's metaphor of a preserve, or museum, speaks to the limitations of that cultural inclusion and captures how some elites wished to see Bahia's "Africanness"—fixed in the past, on show yet contained. Romo has also done important work in establishing a motive for the dominant-class embrace of African-Bahian culture in Salvador. Her assessment of several influential government figures and intellectuals—José Valladares, Anísio Teixeira, and Thales de Azevedo—leads her to conclude that there was a conscious fear among the dominant class that Bahian modernization would have negative consequences for the region's relations of race and class. In particular, they worried that Bahia would no longer resemble its "more idyllic past." Instead there would be an increase in racial and class tensions (as had already occurred in Rio de Janeiro and São Paulo, in their view). I build on these contributions but foreground the agency of Bahia's African-Bahian working class and the performative power of Salvador's popular festivals within Salvador's cultural politics. The festivals were central to the discursive reevaluation of African-Bahian culture and its inclusion within Bahian regional identity. They were also sites of contestation over the meanings of this inclusion.

Hegemony, Agency, and Performance

To better appreciate the changing relationships between culture, discourse, and power in Bahia after 1930, and to think about the historical consequences of these changes for African Bahians, I have found it useful to apply the notion of hegemony to my findings on the reformulation of Bahian regional identity. Developed initially by Antonio Gramsci as a way of breaking down the separation of the base and superstructure in orthodox Marxism and addressing questions of authority, legitimacy, and consent to rule, hegemony has over the last four decades developed something of a "contemporary spectrum" of academic usages.[29] One subset of usages, which typically appears in the social sciences, employs conceptualizations of hegemony that imply a "finished and monolithic" ideological consensus between the ruling class and the ruled.[30] These have been rightly criticized for being too static.[31] Another subset of scholars, including Laclau and Mouffe and even Jean and John Comaroff, emphasizes the discursive and functionalist power of hegemony, but I pull back from the discursive finality of their positions.[32]

Despite its limitations, hegemony remains a compelling tool for analyzing Bahian cultural politics. Mallon, Roseberry, and others who have formulated an understanding of the applicability of hegemony that is closer to its Gramscian intentions have done so in a way that allows for greater human agency and for the pluralities of culture, class, and ideology in relation to the "formations, institutions and organizations of the state and civil society in which subordinate populations live."[33] Hegemony in their view is much less about consent and much more about the formulation of a framework (however unstable) for the terms (cultural, ideological) through which subordinate classes negotiate the relationships of their domination. Especially useful for the mid-twentieth-century Bahian context is Mallon's distinction between hegemonic process and hegemonic outcome.[34] For Mallon, a hegemonic process is the molding of a "common material and meaningful framework" through the interaction of agents (Gramsci's organic and traditional intellectuals), who borrow from previous discourses and/or create new ones through the (ideological) introduction of new codings of old practices.[35] This molding takes place within a context of contestation and negotiation (even dialogue) between subordinate and dominant groups and/or individuals, potentially leading to the creation of a Gramscian "historical bloc." This historical bloc, or cross-class alliance, pushes for the incorporation of (some but not all) of the demands of the subordinate group (or groups) into a wider political project that is overseen by the dominant group in an effort to promote ongoing legitimacy and support for their control of power.[36] This to my mind clearly fits the recoding of African-Bahian culture in Salvador and the reformulation after 1930 of Bahian regional identity to associate Bahia with *cultura negra*.

It is difficult to say, however, that the transformation of Bahian regional identity also represents a hegemonic outcome. Here I follow Mallon: A hegemonic outcome is the moment or endpoint when the dominant class rules on the basis of both repression and subordinate-class consent. As repression or force are ever present in dominant-class control, the important issue centers on the degrees of consent. An agreement exists—still finely balanced, perhaps—between the two parties on the basis of the inclusion of subordinate-class notions of fairness or shared notions of political or social morality, which allows those in power to rule in ways that primarily serve their interests.[37] In theory, this scenario of a hegemonic outcome could describe the political cultural dynamic in Salvador, especially for the years after 1945, but I do not go this far for several reasons.

Mallon insists that a key feature of a hegemonic outcome is that the dominant class buries the contributions of the subordinate group. This disavowal of subordinate agency enhances the legitimacy of the dominant class and diffuses subordinate-class pressure for greater concessions within the hegemonic framework. This, in part, is what makes the subordinate class "subalterns."[38] In Salvador, such efforts to disavowel subordinate agency, to the extent that they happened at all, were never successful (or successful for very long). The Candomblé community, capoeira leadership, samba performers, and others continued to make their presence and contributions obvious, not least within popular festivals, and have continued to do so up to the present.

Moreover, I can establish no moment when Salvador's subordinate class, or the Candomblé community dispersed throughout it, can be said to have accepted the legitimization of elite rule on the basis of their cultural inclusion. The source base on which such an assertion might rest and that might allow one to rule out other explanations for subordinate-class behavior, is distressingly thin.[39] This is true even if one could decide what "consent" actually meant in this historical context (bearing in mind that Brazil for part of this period, 1937–45, was a dictatorship). Also important, the Candomblé community, or even all Bahians who practiced or engaged with some aspect of African-Bahian culture, should not be interpreted as speaking or acting in monolithic ways. Available sources and scholarship on the working class during the Vargas era in Salvador (in terms of its relationship to the modes of production, income levels, and class consciousness) make it clear that although working-class politics ranged well beyond issues of culture, we are still limited in our ability to appreciate working-class diversity or assess the importance of factors related to class that might lay behind their levels of grievance or disengagement or, conversely, their support for ruling coalitions.[40]

Nevertheless, as this study repeatedly shows, a significant section of working-class African Bahians were involved in reshaping Bahian regional identity, both consciously and unwittingly, directly and indirectly. That they did so in a cross-class alliance helps to further establish the point that the reformulation of regional identity (Roseberry's and Mallon's creation of "a common material and meaningful framework") should still be seen as a hegemonic process (but not having reached a clear endpoint) in which the inclusion of subordinate-class demands was leading to some form of normative subordinate-class allegiance to the established political order between 1930 and 1954. Seeing it in this way moves the analysis beyond overly simplistic interpretations of the process of cultural inclusion as "cultural co-optation" of a reified, complicit subordinate class by a reified dominant class. Roseberry's and Mallon's notion of a hegemonic process helps reveal the complexities and nuances of social and political relationships in mid-twentieth-century Salvador as well as the relevance to these relationships of the city's major public festivals and their performances of African-Bahian culture. Distinguishing between notions of hegemony formation and hegemonic outcomes reveals something of the power and potential of cross-class alliances in Salvador and perhaps as well in other multiracial, multicultural societies in the African diaspora. Yet the example of Salvador also illustrates in a specific historical context the limitations of this approach for the political and social inclusion of people of African descent.[41]

Central to my exploration of Bahian cultural politics is the point that Salvador's public festive rituals made decisive contributions to the discursive refashioning of Bahian regional identity. Anthropologists and historians since Victor Turner and LeRoy Ladurie have argued with increasing clarity and sophistication that festivals do more than simply reflect a community's cultural values or its social hierarchy. Festival performance is now seen as a "transformative realm," and festivals are powerful staging points for reinforcing or altering cultural values and even social structures.[42] In the oft-cited words of Richard Bauman, public performances "are cultural forms about culture, social forms about society, in which the central meanings and values of a group are embodied, acted out, and laid open to examination and interpretation in symbolic form."[43] Rituals, including the many formal and informal acts that comprise Salvador's popular festivals, are for Roberto da Matta central to the processes by which "a society reveals itself as a differentiated collectivity, as a unity that perceives itself as unique and different from other groups."[44]

This may be especially true in Salvador, where public festivals were frequent enough that they cannot be dismissed as exceptions. Not only were the festivals public performances, but many of the cultural practices now associated with Bahia were performative—including capoeira, samba, carnival, the *batucadas*, and the *afoxés*.[45] Candomblé, too, had a public performative side.[46] For instance, it was performed for scholars, public servants, and politicians at the Afro-Brazilian Congress of 1937 and of course has been many times since. The Baiana, too, is performative in her role as a public persona. Indeed, the very notion of performance is associated with Bahianness, as captured in the popular aphorism "*Baiano não nasce, estreia*" ("Bahians aren't born, they debut").[47]

Recent studies of twentieth-century Latin American festivals emphasize the dynamic nature of the festival event and that its meanings and interpretations are continually subject to contestation and negotiation.[48] Ritual and performance are best understood as part of negotiated social processes as they are criticized, contested, or reinterpreted. The power to define which symbols, ideas, meanings, and values are performed or that as a consequence of performance become, as Peter Wade has put it, "dominant and tacit and commonsensical" is not equally distributed. It is "the work done in particular projects by particular sets of people . . . which give [certain] readings moral authority" and not others. A discourse within a hegemonic process—one such as the discourse of Bahian regional identity—whether performed or negotiated through the written word, includes symbols, ideas, and values from a variety of sources and takes shape within a context of unequal relations of power and serves as a basis by which disparate social groups, or individuals within those groups, pursue their interests.[49]

These formulations of the power and centrality of performance enhance our appreciation of African-Bahian agency within the process of the reformulation of the meanings of Bahianness. Cultural discourses are lived as well as constructed through media, samba lyrics, or museum exhibits. Indeed, it is through action (not always overtly conflictive) that discourse is both negotiated and actualized within a specific social field. Within the festivals, the Candomblé community performed their culture and thereby asserted that their own rituals, cosmology, and values were as legitimate as those of the dominant Catholic religion, which provided much of the framework for the festival event. The waterborne processions described in chapter 3, for instance, and related activities—such as drumming, dancing to African-derived rhythms, fulfilling collective obligations to West African *orixás*, or even playing capoeira in the plazas during the festivals—were important to the production and reproduction of alternative ethnic identities in the capital city.

As Kim Butler has stated, organizing and participating in such practices was "a political act of self-determination in that it counteracted the restrictive ideologies of the dominant culture." These practices were also motivated by the explicit or barely articulated exigencies of the role that, say, religious belief played in people's lives as "culture."[50] To emphasize the richness of working-class cultural life and contribute to a better understanding of what Nájera-Ramirez calls the "politics of identity embedded in the festivals," or how the festivals contributed to the ongoing formation and lived experience of working-class, especially African-Bahian, identities, I have included significant descriptive ethnographic material throughout the chapters, but especially in chapters 3 and 5.[51] The festivals were an opportunity for the Candomblé community to apply pressure from below as they grew more insistent in their push for public acknowledgement, respect, and a greater discursive space for themselves. Eugênia Ana dos Santos, or Mãe Aninha (whose description of Salvador as "Brazil's Black Rome" was part of this process of pressure from below), may have died in 1938, but other leaders took up the same cause as Candomblé worship gained increasing public visibility. The resilience and extent of working-class African-Bahian cultural practices lent a crucial degree of pressure to the reshaping of Bahian regional identity, as African-Bahian practices became partly synonymous with Bahianness.

Nevertheless, working-class African Bahians and their allies were not the only actors to contest the meanings of Bahianness. The chapters that follow reveal the existence of alternative discourses on African-Bahian culture and regional identity. Examples include the position of conservatives inside the Catholic Church who strongly objected to mixing aspects of Candomblé with ostensibly Catholic ceremonies and the very public position taken up by Bahian public intellectual Pedro Calmon against samba in 1939 as an inappropriate national symbol.[52] The fact that some members of the Candomblé and capoeira communities directed attempts to purge elements that the dominant class found to be "an offense to morality" reveals the extent to which the dominant class continued to determine the limits of the acceptance of African-Bahian practices. The elevation of practices such as the percussive *batucadas* to the status of the "carnivalesque soul" did not mean that they were valued the same as dominant-class cultural practices. An ideological hierarchization of values still pertained within the cultural sphere, even in cases in which the incorporation of practices coded as African Bahian were unequivocal, such as with samba during carnival.[53] In the discourse of the dominant class, African-Bahian practices were still represented as inferior to other aspects of Bahianness associated with the dominant class and drawn from the state's European heritage—reason, science, medicine, and law. These "European" aspects legitimated the continued political rule and economic control of the dominant class. This hierarchy within the ideological construction of Bahianness was reflective of and reinforced the hierarchical structuring within society more broadly, which approached a relative segregation between the dominant and subordinate cultures. I return to these performative and discursive limitations in the chapters that follow.

Chapter 1 provides important background information on Salvador's social dynamics and organization and the wider economic context of the city and Salvadorans. In chapter 2, I recount the story of the revitalization of African-Bahian culture from 1930 to 1937, as leading African Bahians, especially within the Candomblé community, cooperated with progressive middle-class intellectuals to take advantage of the political opening created by Vargas's appointed governor Juracy Magalhães. This alliance asserted African-Bahian claims to public space and pushed for greater acceptance of African-Bahian traditions. This process was foundational for the reversal of the dominant-class position on African-Bahian culture and the recalibration of Bahian regional identity after 1930.

The descriptive exploration in chapter 3 of Salvador's major public festivals emphasizes the cultural contribution of the city's largely African-Bahian working class and its Candomblé community. This group used festivals to shape the wider acceptance of African-Bahian practices and created pressure that I suggest was central to the ideological reevaluation of those practices after 1930. This chapter also contributes to knowledge about the festivals, on which there is very little scholarship for the period 1930 to 1980. In chapter 4, I look at how Magalhães's political successors and the press used festivals as opportunities to formulate and disseminate a public discourse of inclusive Bahianness that came to embrace the city's African-Bahian heritage. Chapter 5 explores Bahian carnival during the Vargas era. Taken together, chapters 3, 4, and 5 show the importance of African-Bahian agency, the power of public performance and ritual, and the extent and limitations of the dominant-class reshaping of the meanings of Bahianness from 1930 to 1954.

Chapter 6 looks at the years 1945 to 1954 and argues that this period was central to the consolidation of the notion that "Bahia" was synonymous with African-Bahian culture. The process during this period takes on the contours of a regional identity project in which actors, social groups, institutions, and ideas that first emerged in the mid-1930s came together and became mutually reinforcing. In the Conclusion I take up the point that the Vargas era in Salvador bequeathed a legacy for the rest of the twentieth century. This legacy was the creation of a particular dynamic of political-cultural struggle over the meaning of Bahian regional identity and the degree to which Bahia would be associated with African-Bahian cultural practices. Both these vectors of conflict and negotiation fed into wider political contestation over what the cultural inclusion of those practices should mean for justice, discrimination, equal opportunity, and quality of life for Bahians of African descent.

Note on Terminology, Currency, and Spelling

My use of the term "African Bahian" is analogous to the usage of *negro-mestiço* (black and mixed race) in Bahian social science.[54] This in turn stands in for official terminology used in the Vargas era (in police reports, for instance), including the categories of *preto* (for a person of apparently full African ancestry), *pardo* (for a person of pronounced African ancestry but apparently also of some European ancestry), and *mulato* (for a person of mixed European and African ancestry). Official terminology also included *moreno* (for a person close to if not entirely of apparently European ancestry) and *branco* (for a person of European descent or a person who was able to pass as such). Despite a wide variety of informal terminology and usage, these basic distinctions were in operation in everyday social contexts in Salvador.

Prior to 1942, the Brazilian currency was the mil-réis, which was written "1$000." Sums smaller than 1,000 were written as réis, the plural of the singular real. Much larger sums were expressed as contos de reis. One conto equaled 1,000 mil-réis and was written as "1,000$000." In 1933 the mil-réis was pegged to the U.S. dollar at a rate of 12$500 réis = 1 dollar. In 1942, the mil-réis was replaced by the cruzeiro at a rate of 1 mil-réis = 1 cruzeiro. From 1942 to 1953 the official exchange rate was 18.5 cruzeiros = 1 U.S. dollar.[55] I have modernized most Portuguese spellings except for titles (of books, for instance), quotations, and some names.

1

◿ Salvador, Bahia, 1930–1954

Brazil's First Republic (1889–1930) witnessed extraordinary transformations associated with urbanization, immigration, and industrialization in the southeastern states of Minas Gerais, Rio de Janeiro, and, especially, São Paulo. In 1930, Salvador, by contrast, remained very much unaffected by the factors and consequences of modernization. The only significant visual differences in the city between 1850 and 1930 were the gradual "urban improvements" made under Governor J. J. Seabra in the 1910s, the tramlines that had sprung up along the principal streets, and the disappearance of the more obvious markers of urban slavery (which had been abolished in 1888). The long decline of Bahia's sugar industry and the rise of coffee in the southeast cemented the shift in the national balance of power away from Salvador, which had been Brazil's colonial capital until 1763. The Revolution of 1930 reoriented Brazil's federal politics toward a centralized program of nation building based on industrial growth in the southeast. In Salvador and its hinterland, however, the old colonial social and economic structures continued largely intact until the slow development of Bahia's petroleum reserves from the mid- to late 1950s. Bahian elites lost most of their political influence as Salvador struggled to attract benefits from Rio de Janeiro's and São Paulo's progress and growth. Brazil's northeast lacked its own internal dynamism. The emergence of a cacao industry in Bahia in the late nineteenth century was some consolation, but it by no means matched the transformative power of coffee in the southeast.[1]

This socioeconomic stagnation and decline of political influence provides the backdrop for the changes in Salvador's cultural politics and the reformulation of its regional identity after 1930. Given the weak economic basis for cross-class cooperation (based, for example, on a belief in the shared benefits of modernization and economic progress) and given the small size and relatively low levels of organization within the Salvadoran working class, it would have made sense for African Bahians to channel their political initiatives into cultural politics. It also would have made sense for political and cultural elites to emphasize a project of cultural inclusion. Consequently, a closer look at Salvador's economic and political developments and attendant social structures after 1930 is worthwhile both for context and to better appreciate the historical relationship between an incomplete process of modernization and the incorporation of African-Bahian cultural practices within Bahian regional identity.

Economic and Political Developments

During the first half of the twentieth century, Salvador's political and economic realities profoundly influenced the lives of the working class. The city where Salvadorans were born, worked, played, raised families, and died was the principal urban center of a vast agricultural hinterland that produced tobacco, sugar, salt, *piaçava* fiber, leather goods, and cacao, the state's big earner.[2] This extractive rural economy was characterized by manioc, tobacco, and sugar in Bahia's Recôncavo region, the hinterland of Salvador and the Bay of All Saints. To the south of Salvador were the principal cacao- and coffee-growing regions, while to the north and west of the capital lay drought-stricken scrub, brutal poverty, and semifeudal social relationships. Salvador, as the state capital, the region's financial center, and its only significant port, benefited greatly from linking the agricultural production of the state with the industrializing economies beyond Bahia, in Brazil's southeast and the United States and northern Europe. To illustrate the city's dominance in this respect, even as late as 1954, 80 percent of the state's commercial tonnage went through the ports of Salvador.[3] That the financial negotiations that governed the cacao industry (and every other sector of the economy) were transacted in Salvador sealed the city's dominance over the hinterland. Both the regional headquarters of the national bank (which set prices and exchange rates) and the Bahian Cacao Institute (established in 1931) worked out of Salvador. Moreover, export houses in Salvador also functioned as banks, binding rural producers to the dictates of the metropole by lending money from the capital at high rates.[4]

Bahia in 1930 was still a provider of commodities to industrialized and industrializing economies of the North Atlantic and the southeast of Brazil. Even though late-nineteenth-century Bahia had experienced moderate industrialization—the region had even briefly been at the forefront of national railroad expansion, and in 1881 Bahia boasted the highest number of textile enterprises in the country—its elite chose not to, or could not, build on these foundations.[5] The initial problem lay in mobilizing enough capital at this crucial time to promote further industrial diversification. The sugar industry in the early twentieth century was already in steep decline and the cacao industry still in its infancy, dominated by small family farms. Neither brought in sufficient capital to build on this growth, and the internal market was too weak to catalyze it. Although in the late 1920s cacao production and commodity prices reached exhilarating heights and after 1930 the federal government put in place programs that, while aimed at stabilizing agro-export, had the unintended effect of stimulating industry in the southeast, neither supported industrialization in Bahia. Rather than take advantage of these favorable conditions for diversification into industry, Bahian investors continued with their "agricultural vocation." Moreover, new agricultural sectors expanded, attracting any additional capital. These new sectors produced sisal, *mamona*, and carnauba and *ouriçuri* wax, all exports for industrial use beyond Bahia.[6] Immediate incentive clearly lay in continuing to produce primary goods, and the Bahian middle class of the 1930s seem to fit the dependency theorist's model of a weak bourgeoisie unable to pursue the industrial diversification that would have benefited the region in the long run.[7]

Not surprisingly, despite export-led per capita growth after 1900, Brazil's northeast rapidly lost ground to the industrializing southeast. By 1930, the die was cast. The northeast needed federal intervention or its industry would stagnate, but President Getúlio Vargas's vision for the region, as described by representatives from both the U.S. State Department and the British Foreign Office, was that northeastern agriculture and cheap labor would subsidize the industrialization of the southeast. Eventually the northeast would provide a market for the southeast's industrial goods. The northeast's dependence on the external markets of the North Atlantic shifted to a reliance on the internal markets of Brazil's southeast, and land tenure in the northeast remained, in the words, of the American consul in Bahia, "largely primitive and feudal."[8]

Internal factors contributed to Bahia's industrial inertia, stalling the pace of industrialization and modernization. The high concentration of wealth in the hands of the elite inhibited the growth of a significant internal market. The region's transportation infrastructure was outdated and dilapidated: Efficiency was low and costs were high. Only the ports were relatively modernized, having received an infusion of capital in the 1910s.

The lending practices of banks were heavily weighted toward the short term and charged high interest rates, forcing entrepreneurs to concentrate on activities most likely to give a fast return, thus inhibiting sustained growth. Most of the banks operating in the region were either foreign owned or based outside Bahia (especially in São Paulo and Minas Gerais) and did not necessarily reinvest profits in Bahia. Profits that did remain in the region were typically spent on symbols of class distinction and hierarchy, namely, finished goods from abroad. Government institutions were weak and untrustworthy, and very little tax was either paid or collected. Politicians gave frequent lip service to change, clearly recognizing the problems but making little substantive effort to solve them. The few industries that did develop, which produced cigars, hats, glass, and textiles, continued to compete with imports.[9]

Early-twentieth-century Salvadorans, rich and poor alike, held fast to and even seemed to embody traditional Brazilian mores and behaviors, which perhaps also held back industry. Colonial attitudes and relationships continued well beyond the end of slavery in 1888. Manual labor continued to be undervalued as *coisa de cachorro e negro* (something for dogs and blacks). What distinguished an important man was that he did not have to work with his hands; even the artisanal trades were in low repute. Patron-client relationships were still the vertical glue that bonded social relationships, as was deference to one's social "superiors" and acceptance of one's fate.[10] Salvadoran elites, in fact, worked hard at celebrating the region's traditional values as virtues. Dain Borges points out how public men lauded Bahia's "vocation for agriculture," or reified their provincialism as regionalism. Newspaper editorials praised Salvador's many traditions and claimed a special place for the city within Brazilian civilization. Such self-justificatory and self-congratulatory attitudes reinforced traditional relationships and ways of doing things, bolstering agricultural interests against the development of industry. For decades there was much talk of education, investment, democracy, and a "modern" Bahia of railways, automobiles, tall buildings, and public works, but Bahian elites did not embrace a practical agenda for industry until well into the 1930s, and by then it was too late to capitalize on earnings from cacao exports.[11]

Although Vargas's policies between 1930 and 1954 led to dramatic changes in Brazil's southeast, they did very little to transform Salvador's economic base or political structures. In fact, in important ways they actually entrenched them. The first Vargas regime (1930–45) strove to build a strong centralized state, which was to play a prominent role in the promotion and regulation of economic and especially industrial activity. Vargas's reform agenda reflected his conviction that the country needed a centrally conceived and administrated economic strategy to prevail over the interests of members of local agro-export oligarchies (which included Bahia's traditional elite) who had hitherto dominated national policymaking. Through astute legislation and a series of carrot-and-stick economic measures, Vargas won the support of business interests in key economic sectors in the southeast of Brazil. These industrial elites approved of a key element of Vargas's strategy for industrial production—the subordination of labor to the state.

Vargas and his key ideologues, especially from 1937 to 1945 during the dictatorship of the New State or Estado Novo, also sought to organize Brazilian society according to a corporativist vision of an organic, hierarchically ordered, and harmonious social body. Speechwriters and government ministries set out to inculcate appropriate values such as hard work, self-sacrifice, self-respect, and the importance of family and religion. The state expanded its administrative reach through increased bureaucracy and federal intervention in education, health care, and the domestic sphere.[12] In the arena of cultural policy, the Vargas administrations used both patronage and censorship to encourage intellectuals and artists to shape ideas that contributed to national pride and inspired patriotic feelings. Vargas and his advisors also encouraged the process of national identity formation by elevating diverse forms of popular culture to symbols of Brazilianness.[13]

Vargas's projects of political centralization, economic modernization, social reorganization, and ideological "renovation" (moving away from liberalism) were not uniformly successful, and their impact varied from state to state throughout Brazil. The economic projects of the Vargas regimes, for instance, were much less a significant force for change in the northeastern state of Bahia and its capital Salvador than they were in the southeast of the country. Additionally, most of the political, economic, and social initiatives Vargas encouraged remained either largely superficial in practice or reinforced the agro-export social and economic structures already in place in Bahia.[14] Perhaps even worse, especially after 1946, federal monetary policies intended to foster industrial development in the southeast actually retarded growth in Bahia's agro-export sector.[15] The consequences for Bahia were significant. Economically, Bahia fell further behind the southeast. The Bahian elite were painfully aware that the political prestige and influence of Bahia was waning and would continue to wane under Vargas.[16] Yet the focus of Vargas's cultural policy—creating a national identity in part through the embrace of popular culture—held out the possibility that Bahia could claim greater relevance within the project of national identity formation.

Given the political and economic threat that the Vargas program posed to Bahia's landed oligarchy, it is not surprising that the oligarchy and the urban elite remained antagonistic toward the Vargas regime and mobilized to resist the centralization of the federal state and the perceived loss of local control. As Paulo Silva describes in detail, the dominant class rallied around the flag of regional political autonomy, putting a significant amount of energy into making the case that Bahia deserved its autonomy based on its past glories and contributions to the nation. The headline of the newspaper *O Imparcial* in August 1934 summed up their position: "Bahia will fight to the end to win its autonomy!"[17] These efforts were rewarded with some initial success; the oligarchy rebuffed Vargas's first three appointed governors, called interventors. Vargas succeeded on the fourth attempt, however. Governor Juracy Magalhães (1931–36) would go on to use federal patronage to outflank his opponents and win sufficient support from rural bosses or lesser oligarchs. By 1936 he had brought Bahia into the fold of federal policy. The oligarchs railed at Magalhães in their newspapers to little effect, and when Vargas dispensed with democratic politics from 1937 to 1945, the Bahian elite had to content themselves with making the best compromises they could with the Vargas state. This in the end was not very difficult, as none of Vargas's appointees in Bahia threatened to reshape the economic or social order dominated by the oligarchs.

In 1945, Vargas was forced to abandon his dictatorship. During the period 1945–54, Bahian politics were split between the Vargas party machine put in place during the dictatorship and the party of the oligarchs, the União Democrática Nacional (UDN). Neither could get the upper hand. The Vargas machine was still effective in harnessing the rural vote through ties of patronage, while the UDN rode a wave of pro-democracy sentiment and regionalist drum beating. The slogan of the UDN in Bahia was *"Restituir à Bahia a posse de si mesma"* ("Give control of Bahia back to Bahia").[18] Even the politicians of one of the two Vargas parties, the Partido Social Democrático (PSD), incorporated regionalist rhetoric into their campaigns. In 1947, although the UDN candidate, Otávio Mangabeira, won the election rather handily, there was not much ideological difference between the UDN and the opposition PSD.

For the next few years, an "interparty accord" between the UDN and PSD was a model of bipartisan democratic compromise that was distinct from what most of the rest of the country was experiencing. Mangabeira's secretariat was bipartisan, and he appealed to the patriotism of members of other parties to persuade them to work together for the good of the state and the governor's program of improvements. Mangabeira was a very skilled politician with generally democratic sentiments, and his administrative efforts on behalf of modernizing Bahia turned out to be far-reaching. The press, apart from the Communist daily, was pro-Mangabeira and supported the political accord. They were also supportive of President Eurico Gaspar Dutra (1946–51),[19] in no small part because Bahia was receiving more largesse and subsidies from the central government than it had in decades. Mangabeira's prominence at the national level was paying dividends. Other Bahians were also prominent enough to attract federal resources for the state, including Clemente Mariani (federal minister of public health and education, 1946–51) and Juracy Magalhães (federal congressman, 1946–51; president of the state mining company Vale do Rio Doce, 1951–52), and the bloc of Bahian congressional deputies in Rio de Janeiro. The region's slow but steadily growing oil production also had something to do with federal attention, although the press gave the credit to Mangabeira.[20]

In 1950, Vargas recast himself as a populist and won the presidency. For the next four years he sought to extend his legacy through social welfare legislation while continuing to integrate labor organizations into political structures. He relied increasingly on populist rhetoric and propaganda, but his popularity waned, and in April 1954, as figures in the military began to conspire against him, Vargas took his own life. His suicide generated a mass outpouring of support for him and for policies that in the waning years of his regime had seemed bankrupt. Vargas's political and economic heirs were able to take advantage of this support after 1954.

In Bahia, the two governors who followed Mangabeira belonged to one of Vargas's two political parties. Regis Pacheco (1951–55) was elected on a PSD ticket, and Antônio Balbino (1955–59) on Vargas's Partido dos Trabalhadores Brasileiros (Brazilian Worker's Party, the PTB). Balbino in particular took advantage of posthumous enthusiasm for Vargas.[21] Neither Pacheco nor Balbino were populists, however. Pacheco rose to the nomination as the candidate least likely to offend anyone in the PSD-PTB coalition. That coalition was much less antagonistic to the landed power of Bahia's old oligarchy than Vargas's rhetoric would lead one to believe. In fact, while the PSD and PTB may have had stronger ties with the popular elements in Bahia, especially the labor unions, their leadership was similar to that of the UDN and were drawn from or loyal to the ranks of the large landowners, many from the cacao region of southern Bahia. The UDN also remained strong after 1950. Landulfo Alves, a former Estado Novo interventor, won one senate seat for the PSD-PTB, and Clemente Mariani of the UDN won the other. The Bahian landed elite continued to dominate the state. Its program of modernization was very conservative; it sought economic growth but made sure that political power remained in the hands of the oligarchy. This political and economic reality contrasted starkly with the populist rhetoric of Getúlio Vargas's final term in office and with conditions in the southeast of Brazil, where there was far more political agitation and volatility than in Bahia.[22]

The postwar and post–Estado Novo period of democracy was dominated by two noteworthy economic trends. The first was the localization and exploitation of existing oil reserves, which led to rapid, if still incomplete, industrialization after 1954. Expansion of the oil industry during the war years was slow—drilling averaged only ten wells per year—although the propaganda of economic nationalism was decidedly accelerated. During a trip to Bahia in 1948, President Dutra visited AT-1, the deepest oil well in Brazil, and inaugurated a new road to the reserves. The potential of Bahia's petroleum industry was significant. By 1951, the flow of oil from the fields at Candeias had the National Petroleum Council's newly built refinery at Mataripe working at full capacity, forcing the capping of new discoveries at Pedras and Entre Rios until refining capacity could be increased.[23] The Brazilian constitution of 1946 no longer prohibited foreign concerns from investing in the arena of oil exploration and the U.S. embassy was keen to keep abreast of developments. In those early years, U.S. technicians lent their expertise to many aspects of Bahia's petroleum industry, from prospecting to refining.[24]

Despite the promise of oil-driven development in Bahia, the second trend of the postwar period was the continuation of the economic disequilibrium between the industrial southeast and the agricultural northeast. Although the end of the Estado Novo contributed to a resurgence of Bahia's mercantile and financial bourgeoisie—which was led by Clemente Mariani and the Banco da Bahia, who applied what pressure they could on the central government to resolve the *"problemas baianos"*—national economic policies continued to benefit the southeast. Postwar exchange-rate policies designed to protect financial reserves and protect against imports worked to the detriment of Bahia's agro-export economy, while federal tax mechanisms, especially the infamous *confisco cambial,* hurt the agro-export regions even more severely. Bahians were now contributing to the subsidization of industrialization elsewhere in the country, while Bahian elites did little to encourage industrialization in Bahia itself.[25] A few Bahian elites, such as Rômulo Almeida or Mariani, called for a regional plan for industrialization, but arguments that the economy should focus on agriculture still held sway in Salvador right after the war.

For example, the Tosta Filho report of 1948 on the state of the Bahian economy, written by the first director of the Bahian Cacao Institute at the invitation of Governor Mangabeira, suggested in no uncertain terms that Bahia should concentrate on its comparative advantage—agro-export— rather than get caught up in overly expensive and ultimately uncompetitive industrialization schemes. As the U.S. consul reported after private conversation with the author of the report, "Mr. Tosta believes that first attention should be directed towards agriculture and that industrialization . . . can only come many years from now." It is not clear to what degree this report influenced the direction of Bahian state-led development in the late 1940s and early 1950s. Tosta Filho was certainly influential within Mangabeira's administration; the governor had invited Tosta Filho to relocate to Bahia from Rio de Janeiro to shape Bahia's economic policy. At the very least, his report illustrates that regional elites before 1950 were still sharply divided on whether agricultural or industrial investment was the most advantageous way forward for Bahia.[26] Yet within ten years—by the end of the 1950s—Salvador's political class had for the most part committed itself to economic growth through industrialization and not agriculture (although the landed elite would continue to influence the policy debate). A 1958 Bahian state Economic Planning Commission report stressed the need for protectionist policies for local industry and the need to channel resources from the agro-export sector into industrial development. Governor Juracy Magalhães (1959–63) made it a priority to renegotiate an increase in the royalties the federal government paid to Bahia for its oil; his intention was to divert the money into an expansion of industrial capacity.[27]

Well into the 1950s, Bahia's stuttering process of industrial diversification seemed to have little to offer the national agenda of industrialization, modernization, and economic independence. Bahian elites appreciated federal programs that supported Bahian agriculture but initially regarded the federal government's prioritization of industrialization as detrimental to their economic interests. At the same time, they feared being left behind. Prior to the discovery of oil reserves outside of Salvador, the history and cultural traditions of Bahia seemed to provide the best opportunity to remain relevant to the southeast of Brazil. Once oil was discovered and was made a national economic priority, Bahia gained an additional means of asserting its relevancy, this time as part of Brazil's industrial economic development. There were local benefits as well, and Bahian politicians pushed for what many traditional elite families still considered their birthright—influence at the federal level to shape policies that benefited themselves and Bahia. Moreover, the dual discourses of cultural inclusivity and economic development could work in tandem to quell dissatisfaction over the indisputable fact that Bahia was a region that remained beset by harsh disparities of wealth and power between the region's elite, who were largely of European descent, and the working class and working poor, who were largely of African descent.

Society in Salvador

In the 1930s, Salvador's urban development reflected the city's position as an agro-export entrepôt. The business district, or Comércio, was adjacent to the ports and encompassed several blocks of three-story buildings that housed import-export firms, banks, law and accounting offices, and warehouses. The backdrop to the business district, when seen from the bay, was a natural 250-foot-high escarpment running parallel to the shoreline. A most striking topographical feature, the ridge of the escarpment extended for several miles in each direction and divided Salvador's urban center into a Cidade Baixa (Lower City), which included the ports and warehouses and financial institutions, and a Cidade Alta (Upper City), which ran along the top of the ridge. The Upper City was where the first colonial governments in Brazil had established their offices and their residences, monopolizing the views over the bay and the cooling breezes. The colony's only Episcopal see had been here as well (although it had been demolished in 1933), as were the later municipal and state governments.[28] Linking the Upper and Lower Cities was an elevator (known as the Lacerda Elevator), the refurbishing of which in the 1930s had been financed by U.S. capital. As the city grew, the wealthy and middle class spread along the ridge (and increasingly along the adjacent ridges), while the less well off and the poor squeezed in as best they could, usually on the hillsides or in the less salubrious valleys. The population of 290,000 in 1940 was little changed from 1920. The population increased dramatically from this point, jumping to more than 415,000 by 1950. Salvador today is a city of approximately 3 million.[29]

The origins of Salvador's cultural richness lay in the Atlantic slave trade, which transported wave after wave of human beings and cultural material to the Americas, material that was recombined and transformed within the

Table 1.1. Population of Salvador, 1900–1960.

Census year	Total population	Percentage growth
1900	205,813	—
1920	282,422	37.20
1940	290,443	2.50
1950	417,235	43.70
1960	655,735	57.20

Source: Instituto Brasileiro de Geografia e Estatística, Anuário estatístico do Brasil, 1973.

context of New World slavery and the wider economic and social contexts of colonial Brazil during the period 1500–1822.[30] Over 1.5 million Africans forcibly disembarked at Salvador, making it the second most trafficked port of entry for African slaves in the Americas, after Rio de Janeiro. For centuries these were predominantly Bantu-speaking peoples, and Bantu subcultures provided much of the economic and social backbone of Bahia's colonial history. Moreover, much of the cultural richness of colonial Brazil was west-central African. It is clear that this region—Angola and the Congo, in particular—provided the cultural material for the earliest forms of what would eventually establish the musical platform for samba, although the "blackness" of such practices is often oversimplified.[31] The first men to practice capoeira in Brazil, it is generally agreed, were originally from this region, although it is difficult to establish with certainty whether capoeira itself came from this region or whether it developed in Brazil.[32] West-central African culture also contributed to many early African-Bahian religious expressions, dress, diet, world views, and value systems.

From the early nineteenth century the number of West African peoples arriving in Salvador increased, especially from the Bights of Benin and Biafra. Consequently, over the last decades before the abolition of the Brazilian slave trade in 1851, Yoruban culture rose to prominence in and around Salvador alongside or incorporating other increasingly creolized subcultures. Yoruban was not the only new culture added to the mix in the early nineteenth century: Muslim identity played a role in a number of uprisings during the unstable 1820s and 1830s.[33]

Over the final decades leading to the abolition of slavery in 1888, the greater autonomy of urban slaves in Salvador, a large and mobile free black population, the urban background of many West African arrivals, and the continuation of commercial ties with West Africa created the possibilities for the institutional development of the terreiros (or temples) of Candomblé as durable social and cultural institutions of local import. Often Yoruban in influence, these *terreiros* also incorporated elements of Bantu, Fon, and Brazil-Indian religious and linguistic material. The absence of a significant influx of European immigrants and the slow pace of modernization in Bahia further strengthened these emerging institutions and their prominence among the poor. The transition out of slavery in Bahia was characterized by a revival of African cultural expression rather than by European immigration and urbanization.[34]

Paradoxically, and not unrelatedly, the abolition of slavery and the advent of Brazil's First Republic (1889–1930) one year later sharpened the national and state elites' focus on order, progress, and a "civilization" that was strongly defined as European, and in particular Parisian. In the southeast of Brazil, São Paulo was transformed by European immigration after 1890 and by the attendant urbanization and eventual industrialization. The nation's capital, Rio de Janeiro, underwent an ambitious urban renewal and regeneration project from 1902 to 1906.[35] Salvador underwent its own small-scale urban renewal and sanitization efforts during the first of Governor José Joaquim Seabra's administrations (1912–16).[36] Through the 1910s and 1920s, modernizers under Governor Seabra (1912–16 and 1920–24) and Governor Góes Calmon (1924–28) sought to impose their vision of an economically and technologically progressive Bahia purged of its popular African-Bahian cultural practices. During this period, Bahian elites emphasized their role as the Brazilian Athens, claiming to have originated or at least been partly responsible for whatever degree of European, western civilization Brazilians could claim to have.[37] However, they increasingly feared that the modernizing center-southeast, particularly the Rio de Janeiro–São Paulo axis, was leaving Bahia behind, especially as the hoped-for European immigration to Bahia failed to materialize.[38]

Even as Salvador's direct ties to Africa through slavery diminished, commercial and cultural ties between Bahia and West Africa remained strong throughout the nineteenth century and into the twentieth.[39] Additional racial and cultural contributions from the Portuguese and from Brazilian Indians further enriched and complicated the city's ethnic, racial, and cultural diversity, often through immigrants from the countryside, and the continued mixing, borrowing, and replenishing resulted in a twentieth-century working-class community in Salvador that was extraordinarily varied and complex. In the 1930s, up to 70–75 percent of Salvadorans were of African or mixed-race ancestry. Most belonged to the poorer classes, although a small percentage belonged to the lesser elite.[40] According to Milton Santos, migrants from the countryside represented as much as 70 percent (87,500 people) of Salvador's total population increase from 290,000 in 1940 to 415,000 in 1950.[41]

In the 1930s, the continued dominance of the agro-export sector determined Salvador's social hierarchy. Elite families were relatively homogenous. Their wealth was overwhelmingly tied to landed estates or to the finance and export of agriculture, despite some ventures in industrial enterprises. They were for the most part the descendants of the traditional Bahian sugar aristocracy, which was still the dominant force in Salvador, having extended their influence into banking, exports, and the liberal professions. They were nevertheless politically reliant on alliances with the backlands bosses who controlled the rural vote, some of whom made their presence felt directly in the political life of the capital. Other segments of the landed elite, especially the absentee landowners of the cacao region but also sisal growers and cattle ranchers, lived in Salvador and formed an important political pressure group. Their children increasingly came to make the capital their home, living in the wealthy neighborhoods such as Vitória, Canela, and Barra, especially as political power seemed to be shifting from the countryside to the city after 1937.[42]

These landowners shared power with and were occasionally related through marriage to the merchant families, who were often first- or second-generation Portuguese immigrants.[43] As the century wore on, the Church and especially the military provided avenues of advancement into the elite, albeit narrow ones. The ruling classes of Bahia were more conservative on social issues than they were on economic policy. Regarding matters of religion, family, education, gender, class, and race, the Bahian were among the most traditional urban elite in Brazil. They were united as well in their conviction that they had the right to lead (or drag) Bahia into modernity. Few believed the "masses" could become a modern, democratic body politic. Having embraced the notion that European descent corresponded with progress and civilization, Bahia's elites had a long history of distrusting the darker-skinned, troublesome, and often resentful masses and were hesitant to introduce any progressive measures that they feared might open up space for social rebellion. At best, the European elites patronized the nonwhite masses. Tenets of liberalism found their way into elite rhetoric, but very few put it into practice.[44]

The small Salvadoran middle class, "largely understandable as an appendage to the aristocracy of the Recôncavo and the *coronéis* of the backlands," never challenged the agro-export elite, except half-heartedly for a brief period from 1933 to 1937.[45] Instead, they identified with the upper classes. This was especially true of the clerks, accountants, managers, and others whose livelihoods stemmed directly from the commercial business of the ports, as well as public functionaries and most practicing liberal professionals. During the 1920s and 1930s, there was also an influx of Old World immigrants, largely from Iberia (Portugal and Galicia) and to lesser extent from the Middle East and Asia. These newcomers drew on pooled resources, family labor, and a readiness to work incredibly long hours and quickly established themselves, particularly in retail. Equally as quickly they entered the public imagination as greedy corner-shop creditors and became the targets of frequent outbursts of working-class frustration.[46]

Fundamental markers of solidly belonging to the "middle class" were a secondary education degree, a liberal professional position, close relationships or political ties to an important family, and respectable behavior. *Boa aparência* ("good appearance," typically meaning European descent) was important as well.[47] Nevertheless, while the elite were almost entirely of European descent or, if they were of mixed-race descent, were light skinned, much of Salvador's middle class were *branco-mestiço* (white or lighter-skinned *mulatos*), although a significant portion of the middle class in Salvador was darker skinned.[48] This was the consequence of demographic necessity in a city nearly 80 percent nonwhite as well as a tribute to individual talents and aspirations. In most working-class neighborhoods, Salvadorans of color could be found who were rising to middle-class prominence thanks to their hard work, personality, business acumen, favorable patron-client relations, thrift, and/or good fortune. Doctors and educators were occasionally African Brazilians, as were writers and engineers, such as Teodoro Sampaio, who designed much of Salvador's urban sewer system. Many middle-class African Bahians were of lighter skin—*mulato* or *pardo*—or even *branco da Bahia* (so light-skinned that they considered themselves and were considered "white" in the context of Bahia's preponderance of African ancestry), thus reinforcing a generally accepted correlation between skin color or hair texture and economic standing in Brazil, whose continuum was much more fluid than that in the United States. This lack of strictly defined racial categories or a definitive color bar meant that a higher social standing "whitened" a family. For example, an individual might not be identified as black (*preto*) if they had a good job or a good education, even if their physical traits were markedly those of a person of African descent.[49]

Some members of the African-Brazilian middle class surely saw themselves as a "black middle class," although sources that document this are hard to come by.[50] Men such as Maxwel Porphirio de Assumpção, Manuel Querino, and later Edison Carneiro spoke out on racial or (more often) cultural discrimination, but more typically social problems among people of African descent were understood or at least articulated as problems associated with poverty and not discrimination.[51] Others held firmly to assimilationist values. As near as we can tell, even those who were sympathetic to or actually participated in African-Bahian cultural practices, Candomblé, for instance, or understood the mechanisms of prejudice or discrimination, chose not to make an issue of the racism that was operational in the city. Those who spoke out on racial discrimination were often self-employed liberal professionals or those with relatively secure civil servant posts, such as Cosme de Farias, who practiced law, typically as a public defender. Still others found themselves in leadership roles, or at least positions of patronage, among the working class and especially within the Candomblé communities, thereby fulfilling important linking roles between predominantly working-class activities and the more "respectable" echelons of Bahian society. Miguel Santana was one such figure; he worked as an employment agent in the commercial district while also holding a powerful position in one of Bahia's most visible Candomblé *terreiros*.[52]

At the level of everyday interactions, African Bahians knew that race at least partly explained poverty and discrimination. In the 1930s, Martiniano do Bonfim, Edison Carneiro, and Mãe Aninha all employed *raça* as a delimiting category for people of a distinct historical *and* contemporary experience, as did other leading Candomblé figures of the day. They also contributed to codifying Candomblé and other aspects of working-class culture as "black"—differentiating between the "religion of the blacks" and "religion of the whites" (Catholicism).[53] The organizers of the first umbrella organization of temples of Candomblé, such as Martiniano do Bonfim and Carneiro, specifically emphasized the race of the new organization's members by naming it the Union of Afro-Brazilian Temples of Candomblé of Bahia (União das Seitas Afro-Brasileiras da Bahia; emphasis mine).[54] Kim Butler has suggested that the Candomblé community's long history of ethnic division during slavery gave way to a revived, inclusive pan-African identity in the wake of abolition. Even taking into account that the Bahian *terreiros* could be fractious and competitive and prone to overemphasize their differences, many African Bahians shared a collective sense of racial identity with regard to job discrimination and dominant-class prejudice.[55] This may have been especially so during the 1920s, when persecution against practitioners of Candomblé was particularly intense, providing an oppositional "other" against which the Candomblé community could identify as a group. Furthermore, *terreiro* affiliation among the laity was not overly divisive. Individuals moved around over time and depending on their individual circumstances. *Mães-* and *pais-de-santo* (priestesses and priests of Candomblé) as well as initiates frequently attended ceremonies of temples with which they were unaffiliated.[56] Ultimately, an articulate ethnic identification existed among Salvador's Candomblé community, and a distinct racial awareness and identification existed more widely among *pretos, pardos,* and *mulatos,* particularly so among the working class.

This should not imply that there was a stark and straightforward distinction between a light-skinned dominant class and a darker-skinned working class. Culture and particularly class were important variables in how one or one's family was treated, and culture and class influenced both racial ascription and self-identification. A middle-class, mixed-race, and light-skinned lawyer probably would not have felt much of a sense of solidarity with poorer, darker-skinned migrants from the countryside on grounds of race, class, or culture. The Brazilian Black Front of the early 1930s provides an illustration of how class could supersede race: While popular with working-class African Bahians, the front, Brazil's first major civil rights organization, was rejected on the whole by middle-class Bahians of African descent. Consequently, the organization turned its efforts to working-class concerns and was eventually absorbed into an umbrella working-class organization associated with the Bahian government.[57]

Salvador's working class should not be understood, however, to have been a homogenous or a unified collective vis-à-vis Salvador's elites (a much more, but not entirely, homogenous group). This would do an injustice to working-class heterogeneity in both socioeconomic terms and along lines of race and gender, to their diversity of thought, and to our understanding of the actual processes of interaction and historical change from 1930 to 1954. Nevertheless, the terms "working class" and particularly "worker" overlap significantly with how both white and nonwhite Salvadorans identified themselves, whether they worked in artisan trades, factories, or as manual laborers. This was especially true, one suspects, as the Vargas era wore on.[58]

Most of Salvador's urban population during the Vargas era was working class, as determined by income level. It was among the working classes that one found the vast majority of people of African descent, although the diversity within this social group was appreciable and the status of a person's occupation could matter enormously. For example, an individual might have earned a significant income in the trades and still have considered himself, or have been considered, a worker, while another individual operating a small shop out of her house in a poor neighborhood may have considered herself middle class. Income levels within the same trade varied between apprentices, assistants, and masters. Of course, class is very much relative and contextual. If a fisherman owned several boats and had others working under him, did his managerial skills and business savvy warrant his inclusion within Salvador's middle class? Perhaps. He was more likely to have been considered and have considered himself a successful leader or patron within Salvador's working class. Nevertheless, the owner-operator might share a middle-class identity and interests elsewhere in other contexts. Cultural values mattered, too, alongside race, gender, family connections, and even personality. Many (but not all) dominant-class Bahians would have disqualified this owner of several boats, who was of notable African ancestry, from being middle class, particularly if he fulfilled daily Candomblé obligations to enhance his business. In addition, a person could be working class in certain contexts and lower middle class in others.[59]

Certain occupations, however, were typically working class and shared specific characteristics—underemployment, seasonal employment, minimal job security, or meager incomes relative to the cost of living. While most working-class African Bahians had a profession with which they identified themselves, they did any number of things over the course of their life in the informal economy when they could not find work in their field.[60] According to the 1950 census, 53 percent of the population over ten years of age was not officially economically productive. This statistic illustrates the extent of unemployment or the importance of the informal economy or, most likely, some combination of the two. A further 25 percent worked in domestic service, a typical form of underemployment for the working classes; the salaries were miserly and the mainly female work force labored largely for room and board. Moreover, those Salvadorans who had work also had "a veritable army" of dependents and relatives to look after, often from the countryside.[61]

Much of the available employment for working-class men, young and old, centered on the docks and the transportation of goods from ship to ship or to warehouse and market. The Bay of All Saints daily hosted a picturesque fleet of small- and medium-sized sailboats that transported agro-export commerce from the interior and the staples—fish, fruit, meat, beans, cassava, rice—that filled the stalls of the urban markets and fed the city. (After 1950, more efficient roads and trucks made the region's waterborne transportation network obsolete.) The boatmen, sellers, and haulers at the markets and throughout the city's streets and street corners were overwhelmingly male, although as we shall see, many women were food vendors. Most male working-class skilled laborers (apart from those who worked in fishing and sailing) could be found in small shop trades such as carpentering or tailoring or working as mechanics, stonemasons, shoemakers, or bakers. If work was done in a shop, it was usually done alongside the owner and master craftsman himself. It could be argued that certain of these occupations could be considered middle class, when their practitioners were very successful and catered to an elite clientele, especially when one factors in the status that accrued to the owner or master craftsman. While a small number of such "middle-class" tradesmen existed, in Salvador trades like these were for the most part badly remunerated and the economy was rarely sufficiently buoyant to accommodate a high number of such successful tradesmen.[62]

Other common working-class jobs involved menial tasks in the service of the clerks and bureaucrats of Salvador's commercial district or in bars, cafes, or restaurants. Other occupations included cleaners, drivers, night watchmen, gardeners, stock boys, errand and message boys, porters, and assistants. Work might also be found in the larger concerns, such as the British-owned Moinho da Bahia (a food-processing operation); in the small factories stretching northward along the bay and colonizing Salvador's working-class suburbs on the Peninsula de Itapagipe, such as the beverage makers Fratelli Vita; or with the local utility and transportation companies, such as the Linha Circular. Working-class men also sought lesser positions with the local or state governments as police, sanitation workers, and public transportation or construction workers. The private sector's inability to absorb in-migration left Salvador's local government with little choice but to expand its ranks. Occasionally, working-class men and women could work their way into lower-middle-class occupations, becoming, for example, secretaries or taxi drivers. But again, many of these jobs were typically so underpaid, undervalued, and unstable that they would be considered working-class occupations, although they were highly coveted. A number of working men supplemented their income by playing in bands for private festivities, often based around specific saint's days. Joining the military was another option.[63]

Gender played an important role in determining different work experiences and life chances for working-class women and men.[64] While many women's socioeconomic position was determined by the employment of their spouse, *amasiado* (long-term partner), or father or brother, anecdotal evidence shows that some chose to, and could, remain economically independent for long periods of their lives. This was especially true of women who had no children or could rely on relatives to act as caregivers. If their children were over ten years old, boys could be apprenticed and girls could be placed with a seamstress. (After two or three years such placements could bring in a small supplement; prior to this the typical payment covered commuting costs.)[65] There were, however, only a limited number of occupational possibilities for adult working-class women. The best earnings for women fell to those women who were priestesses at the top of the Candomblé hierarchy. "*Candomblé não faz nada de graça*" ("Candomblé does nothing for free") is a relatively common aphorism in Salvador.[66] In addition to their income as *olhadores* (those who give advice or resolve problems through divination),[67] some also controlled, or at least organized under them, the labor of their *filhas-de-santo* (initiates). The help of her initiates allowed Tia Luiza, for example, to increase her sales by managing the work of others. During the day she sold slaughterhouse off cuts (*cabeça de boi*).[68] More typically, however, women, no matter what their degree of involvement in the community of Candomblé, sold foodstuffs prepared at home (or often cooked on the street) or worked as laundresses, seamstresses, and especially domestic housekeepers. Women might also have stalls in the various markets around the city. The Herskovitses noted that almost all working-class women supplemented household income on a daily basis in some small way or another, even if this meant simply putting a plate of couscous for sale on the windowsill. There were also several textile and food factories, such as the Fábrica Boa Viagem, that employed a percentage of women, but little has been written on this aspect of Bahia's early industrialization.[69]

Not all working-class African Bahians, however, were partial to ceremonies of Candomblé, either spiritually or socially, or liked samba or played capoeira. Nor were these practices only the preserve of people of African descent. Nevertheless, Candomblé (especially the *terreiros* that were purportedly closer to their African roots), samba, and capoeira merit their catchall label of *cultura negra*, as most Bahians at the time probably would have agreed that these practices were "black" in terms of the origins, influences, and the degree of African ancestry of the majority of their practitioners. Moreover, many individuals within the community also identified as Catholics and saw little contradiction in this. This does not make them any less part of the "Candomblé community."[70]

The world of Candomblé was not homogenous.[71] A principal subplot within the story of Salvador's cultural politics throughout this period, which has been well addressed in the scholarly literature, is the so-called Nagô-ization of Candomblé, a process by which specific *terreiros* within the Nagô-Ketu tradition from the 1910s to 1930s (re-)introduced (or claimed to introduce) West African and specifically Yoruban ethno-religious practices (of which Nagô was a subculture) such as language, liturgy, and rituals into their local practices. At the same time, these *terreiros* used their invigorated "authenticity" to claim greater spiritual power vis-à-vis their rivals, a position that was reinforced by social scientists who were, as early as the 1890s but primarily in the 1930s and 1940s, fascinated to find "Africa" in Brazil.[72] This process was appreciated at the time, perhaps especially by Candomblé practitioners who were losing out as a consequence of this analysis.[73] Beatriz Dantas was the first of recent scholars to address how popular leaders aligned themselves with top local, national, and international scholars to establish Nagô-Ketu *terreiros* as the most authentic and legitimate in Salvador. Indeed, this Nagô-Ketu hegemony continues to the present day.[74] The Nagô-ization process gave impetus to the wider discursive shift within Bahian regional identity, of which the popular festivals were also a part.

Finally, at the bottom of the working-class hierarchy, if you will, subsisted Salvador's significant underclass: the chronically indigent and those who were unemployed or underemployed due to lack of skills, lack of influence, old age, or ill health. Street children were also already a longstanding visible social problem for Salvador, and prostitution seemed a ubiquitous fixture of Salvador's less salubrious central tenement neighborhoods and adjacent nightspots.[75] Despite the added impetus of Vargas's emerging industrial welfare state, Salvador's public institutions typically (and at times shamelessly) failed to keep pace with the sharp demographic increase after 1940, which added dramatically to the problems of inadequate housing, health care, transportation, and food distribution. In fact, Salvador's housing and employment crises seem to have statistically worsened since 1940.[76]

From the standpoint of the man or woman in the street, the most notable feature of Bahia's economic performance was the high cost of living or, put another way, low wages. Both men and women frequently juggled several occupations according to season, availability, and talent for finding work and keeping it. Women were of course also responsible for childcare and domestic duties, and often tended to their grandchildren as well as their own children, although men on their own or with very young children took on domestic duties too. Rent and food took up most of the household's earnings. The staples were rice, beans, manioc flour, corn, pasta noodles, potatoes, bread, butter, oil, sugar, and bananas, with daily meat or fish (fish especially on Wednesdays and Fridays) if they did not stretch the budget too far.[77]

Another lamentable feature for most of Salvador's working class was their difficult living conditions. In the centrally located neighborhoods such as the Pelourinho or along the winding Baixa dos Sapateiros street, there was an acute housing shortage. Two- to five-story decrepit tenements were broken up into one-room habitations that sheltered entire extended families and were sometimes even shared between more than one family. A miserable toilet or two served for the entire building. The corridors and stairwells functioned as common areas that were extensions of everyone's private quarters. Rents were high. Eviction dramas involving entire extended families frequently made the newspapers. Housing farther out, especially in the *invasões* (land invasions) that began in earnest in the mid- to late 1940s, was almost always rudimentary, with earthen floors and clay walls at best. Roofs might be made of palm fronds or clay tiles.

Increasingly, some middle-class neighborhoods farther from the center of the city became working class, such as Garcia, Federação, Engenho Velho, Mata Escura, and Matatú Pequeno. Or rural outskirts would become new neighborhoods on the Peninsula de Itapagipe (such as Roma) or running north parallel to the bay (Calçada, Liberdade, and Largo do Tanque). After 1940, these communities developed much more quickly, and without the benefit of any kind of central planning. As the population moved into certain areas, a new neighborhood would emerge. The first to arrive sought to live as close as possible to employers and patrons, hoping to find work as domestic workers, errand boys, or gardeners or to sell fresh fruit, coconut water, or fish and shrimp from the bay door to door. The more entrepreneurial set up small services such as locksmiths or mechanics, and artisans set up shoe and furniture workshops and the like. Food and dry goods were sold out of the front of peoples' homes until dedicated shops were set up. The same applied to local bars. Providing local color, many small plots of land remained amongst the houses and workshops, where bananas and papaya would seemingly self-sow, helping the poor through leaner times. People cultivated other staples, medicinal or sacred herbs, and flowers for prettying up homes and yards. As Salvador spread, these *rocinhas* still featured on the city's outermost limits. Occasionally some survived the building of newer housing. One can still come across these small plots of rare greenery today.

Table 1.2. Literacy according to race and sex, 1940.

Racial category	Men (% literate)	Women (% literate)
White	93.3	89.5
Pardos	72.4	61.8
Pretos	56.4	44.9

Source: Instituto Brasileiro de Geografia e Estatística, Características demográficas do Estado da Bahia, 203.

Those who moved beyond the center of town had the problem of finding transportation to places of employment. As late as 1967, almost two-thirds of the sidewalks and roads of the working-class neighborhood of Liberdade, where nearly 20 percent of Salvador's total population lived, were unpaved. Mudslides were a threat during the rainy season. Everywhere plumbing, water, and electricity infrastructures were undermaintained or nonexistent, giving rise to constant petitions to the municipal government by neighborhood committees and newspapers. Half of the city's residences were not connected to the city's water and sewage systems.[78]

The education system for ordinary Salvadorans was perpetually in crisis. In 1940, one-third of the population over five years of age was illiterate. For adults over twenty, the percentage would have been somewhat higher.[79] For women it was higher still, roughly 40 percent. As the 1940s wore on, Salvador's rate of illiteracy may have in fact risen slightly with the arrival of so many migrants, despite the dying off of the segment of the population with the lowest levels of literacy (the elderly) and the fact that more literate adolescent segments were reaching statistical adulthood.[80] For people of color in Salvador, rates of illiteracy were significantly higher than rates for whites. In 1940, illiteracy among whites over the age of ten years was 9 percent. For pardos it was 34 percent, and for pretos, 50 percent. Women were always less literate than men.[81]

Salvador's mortality rates were among the highest of Brazil's major cities, twice as high as those in São Paulo. Miserable living conditions, poor diet, low levels of public health, lack of education, and deplorable medical facilities were the main reasons. Infant mortality was high, and the average life expectancy for newborns, based on government data collected from 1939 to 1941, was 34.86 years (32.49 years for men and 37.38 years for women).[82] Diseases such as tuberculosis and malaria took many lives. Medicine for the poor consisted mainly of herbal remedies and prayer. Over a third of Salvadorans who died from 1939 to 1941 did so because of "infectious or parasitic diseases." Tuberculosis was the major killer, and malaria and syphilis were the second and third most devastating illnesses, respectively. At almost every age, the mortality rate for males was higher than that of females. The exception to this was a higher mortality rate for females in the age group of fifteen to nineteen years, and that most certainly was due to the "very high" rates of death related to childbirth.[83]

If the principal features of twentieth-century modernity were bourgeois democracy, an industrial base, the reorganization of social relations to accommodate a capitalist economy, and a moderate degree of consumerism, Salvador in the mid-1950s was still some way from being "modern," even if it had begun an uneven process of political, economic, and social modernization. Although President Vargas's project of industrial growth and social inclusion transformed certain aspects of life in the urban southeast, his policies barely interrupted, let alone restructured, Bahia's traditional social and economic hierarchy based on land ownership, agro-export production and commerce, and patron-client relations. The Vargas era did, however, increase the power of the federal government to play a role within this traditional dynamic. Moreover, as the chapters that follow will indicate, the Vargas-era emphasis on a national cultural identity encouraged the elevation of African Bahians and African-Bahian culture in the national cultural arena. Limited sources make it difficult to establish a firm causal connection between Salvador's stunted economic and political modernization and the cultural transformations that began after 1930. Nevertheless, it is important to set out the economic context of these changes to have a better point of comparison with how the processes of cultural inclusion and regional identity formation continued to play out in Bahia after 1954, in other regions in twentieth-century Brazil, and indeed within the African diaspora.

2

The Revitalization of African-Bahian Culture

On the sixteenth of September 1931, Juracy Magalhães arrived by steamer in Salvador, Bahia, to take up the office of interventor, or appointed governor. The Brazilian Revolution of 1930, which had catapulted Getúlio Vargas to the (provisional) presidency in the hope that he would break the grip of the old oligarchs, was still not a year old. Yet Magalhães's appointment was already Vargas's fourth attempt to establish political control over the most important state in northeast Brazil. The three previous interventors Vargas had appointed had been unequivocal failures. It did not look promising for Magalhães, either. A twenty-six-year-old *tenente*,[1] Magalhães had no political or administrative experience. Worse, he was an outsider; he had been born in the state of Ceará and lacked any connection to Bahia's traditional oligarchic families. Ominously, as his boat entered the port, not a single important political figure awaited his arrival at the docks to meet him, just several dozen people "rounded up by my *tenente* friends." A welcoming speech was made by a "*mulato inteligente*," whose language should have given the young military officer a fair inkling of the strength of regionalist intransigence the oligarchs would marshal against him. According to Magalhães, the speaker's metaphor for Bahia was "the Herculean heroine with the gigantic breasts [who] never gives in or sells out."[2]

Sure enough, after a brief honeymoon period Bahia's traditional elite brought out the knives. Expressing themselves largely through their own newspapers, the opposition to Magalhães employed the predictable regionalist rhetoric of past glories, past greatness, and the dignity and honor of Bahia as the colonial capital, or *mater*, of Brazil.[3] In the early 1930s, this was the standard public discourse on Bahia, a discourse jealously guarded by the state's self-appointed custodians, who disseminated it through speeches and print media. The Bahian elite based in Salvador also sought to promote this longstanding image throughout Brazil and, in particular, in Rio de Janeiro, the nation's capital and the locus of federal power, prestige, and largesse. In this discourse, what made Bahia worthy of distinction and privilege was its contribution to Brazilian civilization—its history of producing great orators, poets, statesmen, archbishops, educators, judges, and colonial administrators, individuals whose achievements were not just the pride of Bahia but also the glory of all of Brazil. Nevertheless, as the anecdote of Magalhães's arrival reveals, there was already another discursive representation of Bahia that associated the city and region with blackness. The phrasing of the welcoming speech by the "*mulato inteligente*" referred to the classical figure of Hercules, but it also referred to the state's African-Bahian population. The heroine with the gigantic breasts was undoubtedly intended to conjure images of the Mãe Preta, the black nursemaid who was one of the few significant early-twentieth-century symbols of racial inclusiveness in Brazil.[4] The black nursemaid was hardly a symbol of racial equality; although it acknowledged certain contributions of Africans and African Brazilians, it did so in a way that situated them in a subordinate position within the national narrative. Given the subalternity of the African-Brazilian wet nurse, it is likely that Bahia's traditional elite would have preferred to bury the reference to her altogether and stick with the comparison to Hercules.

Magalhães, however, refused to be intimidated. He went on to become one of the most successful interventors from the point of view of the Vargas regime. Magalhães's political accomplishments allowed him the leeway and political capital to begin the process of reshaping social and cultural relations in Salvador. Using similar initiatives to those of Getúlio Vargas in Rio de Janeiro, Magalhães redefined the relationship between official regime politics and workers in the city by introducing a number of administrative and populist measures that promoted bonds between Bahia's working classes and himself.[5] His early Vargas-era project of reaching out to the urban working class increased the support of government for popular cultural practices within the public domain, thereby underwriting the valorization of African-Bahian culture. Magalhães's position on popular culture dovetailed with trends that were already gaining momentum in Brazil, such as the wider reassessment of the African-Brazilian contribution to the nation that was taking place in the artistic, intellectual, and political circles of Rio de Janeiro and São Paulo and the rising interest within the national scholarly community in the ethnic cultures of the African diaspora. Salvador, too, had its own local intellectual currents, as the work of writers Jorge

Amado and Edison Carneiro illustrates. Magalhães's administration was characterized by the interventor's proclivity for cooptation and compromise, and it was the first to allow enough political and ideological space that a number of artists and intellectuals on the Left could make alliances with African-Bahian popular leaders and intellectuals. The result was an invigoration of African-Bahian culture that set in place the foundations for the public legitimization and ultimately the celebration of African-Bahian cultural practices. Indeed, to some degree African Bahians' efforts shaped Magalhães's positions as well and provided opportunities for his government to form relationships with institutions and individuals at the heart of the African-Bahian social and cultural world. Individual leaders within the Candomblé community played key roles in this regard, as did numerous faceless Bahians who insisted on maintaining their ethnic practices. For instance, capoeira masters and sambistas were insistent on their right to practice their arts. Middle-class intellectuals in Salvador also played crucial roles in reframing the discourse on African-Bahian culture, almost always in some sort of partnership with the cultural practitioners themselves.

This chapter discusses three examples of such cooperation. The first was the official acceptance of capoeira, culminating in a capoeira exhibition at the governor's mansion in 1936 (or possibly 1937; the exact date is uncertain). The second and third examples are events that took place in 1937. In January of that year, popular and dominant-class pressure convinced the Archbishop of Salvador to waive the prohibition on the washing of the steps of the Church of Nosso Senhor do Bonfim as part of the popular Festival of the Senhor do Bonfim. The ritual washing was a significant public act that honored both the Catholic saint Senhor do Bonfim and the Candomblé *orixá* known as Oxalá. It was therefore both a symbol of and a contribution to the process of reappraising the importance of African-Bahian culture. That same month, Salvador hosted the Second Afro-Brazilian Congress, a week-long conference that brought together middle-class intellectuals, scholars, and leaders from the Candomblé community to discuss African-Bahian culture. The congress delivered an explicit political message that African-Bahian culture was legitimate, important, and of value to Bahia and Brazil.

Aspects of this story of the cultural shifts that were under way during Magalhães's time in office have been addressed in the literature.[6] Here I emphasize the importance of the combined agency of a variety of actors from different social groups who had differential access to power in the project of invigorating and revitalizing and legitimating African-Bahian culture. Their efforts made the years just after 1930 a crucial early phase in the reshaping of the meanings of *baianidade*, or Bahianness, for local, national, and ultimately global consumption. This chapter also addresses aspects of the Magalhães government's relationship with the working class, a dynamic that places the story of the revitalization of African-Bahian culture in a wider regional and national context.[7]

The Magalhães Effect: Salvador's Changing Political and Cultural Climate

After the Revolution of 1930, Magalhães's first priority was to outflank the opposition arrayed against him and against President Vargas. Magalhães chose not to alter the clientelist nature of Bahian politics. Instead, he realigned the state's patron-client networks so they bypassed the traditional elite and ran straight to the interventor's office. This encouraged the backlands bosses (known as the "colonels") to withdraw their support from the traditional Bahian elite families and ally themselves with Magalhães. Magalhães became, in the words of one historian, Bahia's *supercoronel* (super-colonel).[8]

Magalhães also built an urban power base through brokering and then institutionalizing a quasi-populist truce between the state and labor, using social welfare institutions to attract the working classes to the regime and to better incorporate the Bahian work force into political and economic initiatives. These were tactics that Vargas himself was implementing through his Ministry of Labor, Industry and Commerce, particularly in the industrializing southeast of Brazil. In Bahia, Magalhães embarked upon a looser and less expansive but still systematic attempt to organize certain segments of the state's workers. The interventor's task was to encourage unions where none existed and to draw all unions under the aegis of the regional Directory of the Ministry of Labor. Only unions that adhered to official rules that prohibited strikes could continue to operate legally. In return, the official unions might reap occasional benefits, such as intercession and support during their negotiations with management and access to social services. Federal social and economic legislation enacted during the Vargas era seemed to have made some impact toward bettering working conditions and workers' job security, as those who belonged to the government unions frequently earned higher wages and better insurance benefits. One prominent group in Salvador who managed to protect their wages through controlled access to their trade was the stevedores (although such employment could be notoriously unsteady). While this shoring up of an urban populist political base was intended ultimately to benefit Vargas and his federal agenda, in Bahia the young interventor shrewdly encouraged a personal loyalty to himself as well. He did so with singular success, if the number and tone of telegrams from unions across the state sending their "proletarian regards" and wishing Magalhães "great accomplishments and perennial happiness" are anything to judge by. Just as he had done with the backlands colonels, Magalhães was turning himself into the super-patron, this time of the working classes.[9]

A brief curriculum vita of a working-class leader, Pinto Moreira, reveals the early connections between Bahian workers and the Vargas state. Moreira was a stonemason who actively supported the Revolution of 1930. He was an energetic member of the October Third Club (named after the date of the revolution) and an aggressive labor organizer. In the early 1930s, he founded and reorganized several unions, including the University Association of Bahia, bringing them in line with Magalhães's government.[10] Magalhães also included workers on his advisory council, such as the typographer and labor leader Teodomiro Batista. Magalhães acknowledged the importance of Moreira and Batista and other popular leaders when he pointed out that the support of Salvador's urban proletariat won his party the majority of votes in 1934 in both the state's capital and its interior. Magalhães also gained the support of many of Salvador's urban professionals, who were frustrated with First Republic politics.[11]

Interventor Magalhães worked hard to win over the working class in Salvador and in the rest of the state. Time after time from 1931 to 1937, he wed his convivial personality, a trait much appreciated by Bahians, to several of Vargas's tactics for seizing and controlling political power. These included building schools, medical facilities, and crèches and forming the Social Assistance Advisory Board (Conselho de Assistência Social) and Bahian Department of Child Welfare (Departamento Estadual da Criança). He also directed government funds to private or religious social welfare institutions. An adept communicator, Magalhães attended well-publicized meetings with neighborhood associations about infrastructure improvements during election campaigns, initiated a weekly radio program that allowed him to directly address the populace (at least those few who could afford a radio), and even used the opposition press to get his ideas out to the public.[12] It is difficult to be sure how Salvador's African Brazilians felt about Magalhães. He made no race-based appeals to win support, yet the city's working classes overall remembered him favorably, as was suggested by Magalhães's successful political campaigns in 1945 for federal deputy from Bahia—in which he won the highest percentage of votes of all the candidates—and again in 1959 for the governorship of Bahia.[13]

Magalhães's political-administrative modus operandi was consistent. At almost every juncture he preferred conciliatory cooptation that masked his intention of controlling those who entered patron-client relationships with him. His skill in this regard was almost unerring. This is patent in his handling of the rural coronéis (colonels) and in his relationship with labor. It also defined his cultural populism, especially his relationship to popular culture. Indeed, Magalhães's unprecedented steps (in Bahia, at least) to cement political relationships with working-class intellectuals and cultural leaders proved to be vital to the reworking of the old cultural order in Bahia. There is evidence that Magalhães had some sympathy for the practice of Candomblé, such as his personal friendship with Manoel Bernardino da Paixão, a pai-de-santo of the terreiro Bate-Folha.[14] This sympathy may have been a factor in the increased leniency toward Candomblé on the part of the police that was evident during Magalhães's time in power, especially after 1935. For example, instead of outright repression of the practice of Candomblé, as had taken place in the 1920s, the police under Magalhães followed a licensing system that regulated the ceremonies (although raids still occurred, perhaps when the police felt their regulatory prerogatives were not being respected, particularly with regard to the use of percussion instruments).[15]

Magalhães's leniency may have had something to do with his political ambitions. From 1931 to 1935, he was an appointed official and his title was interventor. In 1935, he was elected as governor of Bahia for the first time, albeit through an indirect vote from the Bahian legislative assembly. At that time, his official title changed from interventor to governor. This was a first step in the restoration of direct gubernatorial elections after the coup of 1930. Magalhães's political ambition to continue as governor may have had some influence on the timing of his more lenient positions toward African-Bahian culture after 1935.

The way the licensing system worked in Salvador was typical of the Vargas-era government's increasing institutionalization of its relationships with Brazil's working classes. All temples of Candomblé that wanted to have major ceremonies honoring their orixás had to obtain written permission from the police, especially if the ceremonies were to include drumming. Drumming, of course, was often central to the ritual obligations that terreiros and their members had to their orixás. Under this system they also had to pay a fee, effectively buying their religious freedom. This system efficiently brought Candomblé within the administrative sphere of the state and strengthened the relationship (albeit one of unequal power) between politicians and those who practiced Candomblé.[16] It meant, potentially at least, that Vargas's interventors and the police force were partly responsible for protecting Candomblé from the wrath of the dominant classes, as long as the temples played by the rules. This power over the temples could also be abused, of course, but this was true of most similar institutional arrangements at the time. The relationship between the state and the *terreiros* would depend upon the will of the men in office and the agents of the state. It certainly helped the Candomblé community that a number of police officers attended ceremonies or were members of *terreiros*.[17]

Magalhães's influence on the new leniency toward Candomblé was no doubt abetted by the nation's historical distance from the abolition of slavery in 1888 and faith of local elites in the twentieth-century "civilizing process." North American sociologist Donald Pierson, who spent two years in Salvador, in 1935 and 1936, recalled that by the mid-1930s, many of the city's elite felt that they could afford a patronizing rather than persecutory position toward Candomblé, treating it more "as a matter for levity than as a cultural threat." The prevailing wisdom among hopeful elites was that Candomblé was destined to die out as Salvador's delayed but inevitable modernization gathered strength.[18]

The greater leniency toward Candomblé after 1930 was part of a broader political openness at the top of the Bahian political hierarchy toward workers and working-class and African-Bahian culture. On its own this would not have been enough to so radically alter the dominant public discourse on Candomblé, capoeira, or samba. It did, however, create openings that middle-class and working-class intellectuals and the wider Candomblé community took advantage of. While support from Juracy Magalhães was undeniably important, a driving force behind the changing political climate on African-Bahian culture was the efforts of the practitioners themselves and their middle-class allies.

Pressure from Below

For many decades—indeed for many generations—before 1930, the Candomblé community had been looking for ways to improve its status within Bahian society. As Kim Butler has noted, the community wanted to lay the "foundations for cultural and religious pluralism to prevail over the principle of acculturation to European norms."[19] These efforts took on a special salience during the 1920s, when the *terreiros* sought to protect themselves from the intense police persecution of that decade. As Angela Lühning and others have described, the *terreiros* strengthened ties with their traditional patrons, or *ogans*, who could serve as protectors and public relations representatives vis-à-vis the police. Occasionally, an *ogan* was actually a member of the police or a military officer.[20] Frequently, *ogans* were white or light-skinned local notables, members of the middle and even upper class who were often affiliated with the temples through honorary titles and therefore logical choices for negotiating for favorable treatment of the *terreiros*. This would be especially true of the larger *terreiros*, with more, and often more socially prominent, *ogans*. During the late nineteenth and early twentieth centuries, *ogans* increasingly were scholars and writers, including the first few public intellectuals in Salvador to partly defend the legitimacy of Candomblé and capoeira—Raymundo Nina Rodrigues in the 1890s (although he still argued that Candomblé was atavistic primitivism) and Manuel Querino in the 1910s and 1920s.

Relocation was another strategy for self-protection, perhaps more critical for smaller *terreiros* without important patrons, which were the majority. As Edison Carneiro could observe by the mid-1930s, a great many leaders of *terreiros* had already made the decision to move away from the central neighborhoods to the outlying areas of the city that were less settled and less well policed. Perhaps this exodus also contributed to the improved relations between Magalhães's government and the Candomblé community, since it no doubt removed much of the social friction caused by long nights of drumming and the presence of ritual offerings (including occasional dead animals) in the streets.[21]

The most striking features of the revitalization of working-class African-Bahian culture after 1930 were the combined efforts of leaders within the wider community of Candomblé—such as Martiniano do Bonfim, Eugênia Ana dos Santos, and Manuel dos Reis Machado—to carve out a discursive public space for Candomblé and capoeira. The alliances they established with a small but energetic group of scholars and public intellectuals in Salvador lent prestige to African-Bahian culture as an object of study and took the lead in efforts to change Salvador's dominant discourse on African-Bahian culture.

The role of Martiniano do Bonfim in the elevation of Candomblé to a legitimate object of scholarly attention is well known.[22] Martiniano was already a major figure in Candomblé circles by the 1930s, a *babalaô* (high-ranking diviner) in Salvador and one of the last to have a direct knowledge of Africa. At a young age, Martiniano had left Brazil to live in Lagos, Nigeria. He stayed there for eleven years and made several return visits after he moved back to Brazil. In Salvador he was feted and relied upon for the respect he brought to individual *terreiros*. His importance and authority within the world of Candomblé extended beyond the confines of the *terreiros*. From the 1890s to the 1930s, Martiniano was a key informant for every scholar, local and international, who came to Salvador to study African-Bahian culture. The list is impressive: Nina Rodrigues, Manuel Querino, Jorge Amado, Arthur Ramos, Edison Carneiro, Donald Pierson, Ruth Landes, E. Franklin Frazier, Lorenzo Dow Turner, and Melville and Frances Herskovits, among others. Martiniano thus had a significant impact on how early twentieth-century ethnographers represented Candomblé in Salvador. Scholars' emphasis on the systemic cultural complexity of Candomblé practices was fundamental to the early efforts to legitimize Candomblé. Their presentations of Candomblé suggested that it should be ranked much further along the evolutionary continuum (then in vogue) than had previously been acknowledged. Later in the 1930s this complexity was used to contrast Candomblé with other, simpler forms of "black magic," a separation that lent legitimacy to the claims of Candomblé leaders to a constitutionally guaranteed freedom of religion. Martiniano was thus invaluable for his deep knowledge of "authentic" Candomblé. Meanwhile, the proliferation of national and international scholarly attention to Candomblé served to validate the practice as worthy of greater public esteem.

Of particular relevance here is Martiniano's affiliation with Yoruban culture, which, since the work of Nina Rodrigues in the 1890s, scholars and public intellectuals had come to see as the most advanced of African cultures in Brazil. In Salvador, Candomblé *terreiros* evolved from historic traditions that dated back to the transfer of individuals and cultures from various points on the African continent. These points of origin had reified into the notion of the *nação*, or "nation," to which a *terreiro* belonged (at least primarily), notwithstanding the fact that there had been much cultural borrowing, overlap, and innovation.[23] The *terreiros* with links to Yoruban culture were part of the Nagô or Ketu nation/tradition. In his various relationships with scholars or laypersons, Martiniano invariably stressed the superiority of the traditions of Nagô-Ketu *terreiros* because of their close correspondence to African ritual and levied criticisms at other traditions. Others in the Nagô-Ketu tradition voiced similar opinions. There was little the other traditions could do to counter this; as Anadelia Romo has shown, scholarship during this period was oriented toward ethnic African traditions, not creolized cultural traditions.[24] Indeed, as Lisa Castillo points out, even Nagô-Ketu *terreiros* had to be quick to embrace the new alliance with the printed word of scholarship and the media if they did not want to lose out. The once-venerable Nagô-Ketu *terreiro* Alaketu faded quickly in relation to its immediate competitors because it did not establish its reputation with ethnographers and journalists.[25]

Other factors probably played a role in this Nagô-ization process, including the demographics of the late slave trade. People from the Nagô-Ketu cultural areas were disproportionately represented in the last group of slaves to enter Brazil. In addition, enduring commercial links between Salvador and Yoruban areas of Africa and Martiniano's extended stay in West Africa also contributed to the dominance of the Nagô-Ketu *terreiros*. By the time Brazilian and North American scholars turned their attention to Salvador, Nagô-Ketu was well on its way to being understood as the most "African" and therefore the most authentic and legitimate of the Candomblé traditions. Other Candomblé traditions lost ground in the religious marketplace because they were increasingly seen as weaker. This was a real disadvantage in a context in which much of the attraction of Candomblé is the ability of the *orixás* to intervene in personal and professional relationships on behalf of the practitioner. As a result, for many outside the Candomblé community, the Nagô-Ketu traditions and their supposed African authenticity came to represent what Candomblé practice actually meant. Even within the Nagô-Ketu tradition, the *terreiros* competed with one another over whose practices were more legitimate.[26]

My point here is to emphasize that this Nagô-Ketu ascendency was central to the wider discursive shift on African-Bahian cultural practices after 1930, as that tradition became the most acceptable and appreciable face of Candomblé. At first this may seem counterintuitive, given the emphasis within the Nagô-Ketu tradition on its closeness to African traditions. Although this was of interest to scholars and intellectuals, it flew in the face of the disdain of the dominant classes for African culture. It was also contrary to the emerging discourses on Brazilian national identity that privileged cultural mixing, or *mestiçagem*. There were alternative traditions in Candomblé, such as *caboclo* Candomblé, which could easily have been constructed and celebrated as a uniquely Brazilian hybrid of indigenous, African, and European traditions. (The *caboclo*, or the Brazilian Indian, was already a long-established symbol of Bahian independence and, according to both Kraay and Albuquerque, represented an early form of popular civic consciousness.)[27] Nevertheless, Nagô-Ketu's close association with the "authentically African" within Candomblé did not disqualify the wider religious practice from becoming a central marker of Bahianness. This was due largely to the energetic public relations work organized by Edison Carneiro and the literary contributions of Jorge Amado. Martiniano, too, was no doubt aware of the dual role he was playing. Whether he was implicitly or explicitly arguing for the greater authenticity of the Nagô-Ketu tradition, he was also hoping to elevate the discursive status of Candomblé practice. Near the end of his life, Martiniano wrote that his involvement in scholarly work on Candomblé in Salvador was done in the belief that it would lead to greater sympathy and justice for "the black race."[28] Edison Carneiro summed up Martiniano's agency in 1936, perhaps with some overstatement, arguing that his "entire life was devoted to the social and human rehabilitation of his long exploited race."[29] Over several decades, particularly in the 1930s, Martiniano consciously attempted to contribute to the vindication and legitimization of African-Bahian cultural practices within regional public discourse.

A small but influential number of journalists, intellectuals, writers, and artists in Salvador contributed to the revitalization of African-Bahian culture within the discourse of Bahian regional identity. Of these, Edison Carneiro was certainly the most politically and intellectually active ally of the Candomblé community after 1930. Carneiro was born in Bahia in 1912 and raised in a house known for its bustling intellectual atmosphere. Carneiro's father, Professor Souza Carneiro, encouraged his children's intellectual curiosity and that of many of the children's intellectually inclined friends and neighbors. The professor presided over the youngsters' forays into writing, poetry, and philosophy.[30] In the 1930s Carneiro, who was African-Bahian, began to study and write on a number of topics, including history and African-Bahian culture and ethnography. While he was completing his law degree, Carneiro's perspectives were shaped by his relationships with like-minded young men. Some of these men were, like Carneiro, members of the Communist Party in Salvador. Almost all embraced the modernist movement emanating from Brazil's southeast after 1922, a movement that privileged Brazilian culture or at least Brazilian innovations over European culture and included Bahians such as novelist Jorge Amado and poet Godofredo Filho. They had their own pioneering modernist journal, the *Moment* (*Momento*), not to be confused with the post–World War II communist-supporting newspaper of the same name.[31] After 1930, the Vargas government embraced similar positions with modernist intellectuals in the southeast of the country as part of his populist national-identity-building agenda. Moreover, in 1933 Gilberto Freyre published his influential revisionist history of colonial Brazil that emphasized the contributions of Brazil's African descendants. A dramatic shift in Brazilian social thought with regard to the country's African legacy was gaining strength. Brazil's positivist intellectual traditions, which had "rejected the African heritage as one of many dangerous and polluting social menaces," were being reappraised, as first the modernists and then social essayïsts, novelists, *folcloristas*, and government policymakers of the 1930s began to endorse the contributions of African Brazilians to Brazilian culture.[32] This general shift may very well have contributed to increasing the number of middle- and upper-class Bahians who were willing to tolerate and possibly even accept African-Bahian culture. It certainly influenced Carneiro, and Carneiro gave it a uniquely Bahian focus.

Evidence of this "new posture" in Salvador was the publication in 1936 of a series of articles in *Estado da Bahia* that sympathetically addressed African-Bahian cultural practices in Salvador, including interviews with important figures within the Candomblé community and coverage of events leading up to the Second Afro-Brazilian Congress in January 1937.[33] Carneiro organized these articles, and the decision of the editor of the newspaper to publish them marked a decisive moment in the history of Salvadoran journalism and its relationship to Candomblé in particular. There were over twenty contributions, and, as Lisa Castillo emphasizes, the intent was to promote a positive image of Candomblé to the public and to convince the Candomblé community that a more modern public relations campaign could be to its advantage.[34] Several *pais-de-santo* as well as Martiniano do Bonfim were interviewed or made contributions to the series. Prior to this moment, mainstream newspapers routinely carried complaints about ritual practices, published articles that ridiculed and derided Candomblé, and frequently spearheaded campaigns to abolish the practices and arrest the practitioners. This did not disappear entirely after 1936, but the Carneiro-organized articles' respectful approach to Candomblé was novel and came to characterize the dominant journalistic discourse on Candomblé through the 1940s and right to the present day. This shift was not limited to print media, although this is where the most important advances were made. A public recital in January 1937 associated with the Afro-Brazilian Congress showcased "Candomblé music" as performed by Pai-de-Santo Joãosinho da Gomeia and a number of his initiates. Local newspapers covered the event, complete with a photograph of the performers, but also, and very significantly, a local radio station broadcast the recital, characterizing it as a "legitimate black orchestra."[35]

Carneiro also published his first books during this period. *Religiões Negras* (Black Religions) came out in 1936 and *Negros Bantus* (Bantu Blacks) in 1937. These books, together with works of national importance such as Nina Rodrigues's *Os Africanos no Brasil* (Africans in Brazil, 1902, 1932), Gilberto Freyre's *Casa-Grande e Senzala* (The Masters and the Slaves, 1933) and Arthur Ramos's *O Folclore Negro do Brasil* (Black Folklore of Brazil, 1935) clearly signal that Brazilian social sciences were privileging studies of African-Brazilian history and culture as valid contributions to the study of Brazil, as did the First Afro-Brazilian Congress of 1934 in Recife.[36] Although African descendants in both Bahia and Brazil still had many more detractors than supporters among the dominant class during the 1930s, the public's valuation of their cultural practices had increased very quickly in a short time.

It was the prolific author Jorge Amado, however, who was the first to portray African-Bahian culture in a positive light for a wider audience. Amado was a principal driving force behind the popularization of the association of Bahia with African-Bahian culture, particularly abroad. His early works—*País de Carnaval* (1931), *Suor* (1934), *Jubiabá* (1935), *Mar Morto* (1936), and *Capitães da Areia* (1937)—were written within the traditions of "socialist realism," as befitted a young progressive Communist and member of the youthful, self-styled Rebels' Academy, an artistic and literary group that included Edison Carneiro. In these relatively hard-hitting "proletarian novels," Amado focused on Salvador's working-class world and its African-Bahian cultural practices. Martiniano do Bonfim, for instance, was one of his sources for *Jubiabá*.[37] Through the character Jubiabá, Amado opens a window into various subcultures related to Candomblé and the place of the religion in the life of poor people in Salvador. Amado stressed the importance of Candomblé and samba to people of African descent in Salvador, carefully weaving culture into his wider critique of capitalist labor relations and exploitation. For good measure he also ridiculed the pretension and prejudices of the city's conservative traditional families. Amado's work was pioneering and revisionist: For the first time, African-Bahian characters, values, and cultural practices were sympathetically incorporated into successful works of fiction.[38] Amado was catalyzing the process of reshaping Bahian modernity to include Bahia's popular traditions and "the Negro." Unfortunately, Amado's lyrical prose and characterization had the perhaps unintended effect of romanticizing and exoticizing (not to mention eroticizing) Bahian popular-class life. Somewhat predictably, it was this romanticization of working-class culture that newspapers picked up on, especially after 1936, thus undermining Amado's critical position, and to some degree that of working-class Bahians. Nevertheless, Amado's depictions of Bahia had a long-lasting effect.[39]

The influence of Amado's work came in part from the close relationship between his fiction and reality. Importantly, Amado's novels generated, or contributed to, a public debate about the meanings of African-Bahian culture and to what degree that culture should be accepted. This debate involved the practitioners themselves in several ways. In addition to Martiniano's consulting on *Jubiabá*, a public episode revolved around the affront taken by Severiano Manoel de Abreu to Jorge Amado's depiction of the character Jubiabá, a *pai-de-santo*. The problem was that Abreu was a well-known Candomblé *pai-de-santo* of the *caboclo* tradition who went by the name of his saint, which was Jubiabá. So there were grounds for an accusation that Amado had based his fictional character on Abreu. (In fact, as noted, Amado had based his character on Martiniano do Bonfim.) What is relevant here are the arguments of Abreu, who took pains to critique Amado's fictional representation. The real-life Jubiabá had had several run-ins with the police in 1921 and 1931 that had made the newspapers, and possibly for this reason he took a measure of offense at Amado's descriptions. Abreu felt that Amado had portrayed him as too poor and marginal a character, as a "mediocre witchdoctor earning a living from exploiting people's ignorance" ("*macumbeiro qualquer que vive tapeando o povo ignorante*"). In a newspaper interview Abreu insisted that he was middle class and that he rejected practices that the wider public considered to be "black magic" (*feitiçaria*).[40]

Within this context the contributions of another leader within the Candomblé community to the reshaping of public discourse on African-Bahian culture becomes important. Eugênia Ana dos Santos, or Mãe Aninha, was of the Nagô-Ketu tradition. In 1910, Aninha founded and became the *mãe-de-santo* of Opô Afonjá, which was to become one of Salvador's most prominent *terreiros*. From 1910 to 1938, Aninha was one of the most significant figures within the world of Candomblé. Aninha's authority stemmed, like that of Martiniano, from her high standards and accumulation of the deep knowledge and ritual power of Candomblé. It also grew out of her ability to bring through new initiates who would go on to achieve impressive degrees of influence and prestige. She had the capacity to attract and organize supporters who were spiritually bound to her *terreiro* yet were also important people in secular walks of life in Salvador. In the 1920s she moved temporarily to Rio de Janeiro to set up a branch of Opô Afonjá; she moved to Salvador in 1935. Much of her authority and the esteem in which she was held stemmed from her argument that the rituals of her *terreiro* were more African than the rituals of other *terreiros* and that she had resuscitated a large part of the African traditions that others had forgotten, some of which occurred under the direction of Martiniano do Bonfim. By all accounts, Aninha had a formidable personality. The importance of Candomblé as a social and spiritual institution at the heart of the cultural identity of many poor people of African descent cannot be underestimated. Merely keeping the *terreiros* going was an act of cultural resistance to the dominant order. Insisting on the cultural and religious freedom to worship, as she began to do in the 1930s, was a radical act.[41]

In the final years of her life, Aninha used her power and prestige to good effect beyond the confines of the Candomblé community. According to Edison Carneiro, she staunchly supported the Second Afro-Brazilian Congress held in Salvador in 1937, contributing a paper on traditional (sacred) African food in Bahia and opening the doors of her *terreiro* for a scheduled tour of participants and a festival in honor of the congress. Aninha also lent her influence to the efforts of the Union of Afro-Brazilian Temples of Candomblé, which was founded in 1937 to push for the religious freedom to practice Candomblé. Lisa Castillo describes Aninha's belief that one could be both a practitioner of Candomblé and a university-trained scholar as radical and transformative for the time.[42]

The formidable *mãe-de-santo* was an advocate for Candomblé in other venues as well. Donald Pierson tells of an encounter between Aninha and an unnamed Catholic priest in which Aninha defended her claim to spiritual authority by pointing out that Moses was never "ordained by the pope," adding, according to Pierson, that the first man "must not have been a white man but instead a colored man." She also said that "Jesus must also have been an African, or at least very dark. 'For did not his parents once hide him in Egypt? And is not Egypt in Africa? If Jesus was not dark, how could they have hidden him among the people of Africa?'"[43] Her response clearly reveals an Afro-centric discourse that was critical of dominant narratives in mainstream Christianity and was designed to defend the religious authority of the leadership of Candomblé from attacks by the Catholic Church. Aninha would go on to make a theological argument in defense of Candomblé's ritual animal sacrifices: "We [the Candomblé *terreiros*] follow the Law of Moses. He commanded that sacrifices be made of sheep, goats, oxen, chickens, pigeons, and so forth. Is it not so? We merely obey his commandments." Aninha is credited with seeking to disseminate the notion that Salvador was Brazil's "Black Rome"—a spiritual haven for all Brazilians of African descent. Aninha had a clear sense of how cultural and racial hierarchies in Salvador operated and the determination to speak out against and rectify at least some of the injustices she saw. Largely through her own energy, initiative, creativity, and charisma, Aninha made several important contributions to the public acceptance of Candomblé during Magalhães's time in power. When she died in 1938, her funeral was covered in the newspaper *Estado da Bahia*, which estimated that two thousand people accompanied the funeral cortege to the cemetery.[44]

During the 1930s, the final years of Aninha's life, other figures within Candomblé also contributed to the struggle for greater visibility and acceptance of Candomblé and the assertion of the African-Bahian cultural identity. Maria Escolástica da Conceição Nazaré, or Mãe Menininha of Gantois, and her husband, Álvaro MacDowell de Oliveira, campaigned for the public legitimization of Candomblé. Miguel Santana played a key role in building bridges between the Candomblé community and the dominant class. João Alves Torres (João da Pedra Preta, later João or Joãosinho da Gomeia) and others such as Manuel Bernardino da Paixão (Bernardino do Bate Folha), Manoel Paim, and Manuel Victorino da Costa (Falefá) also made conscious efforts to follow the lead of Martiniano and Edison Carneiro and use links with scholars and the media to improve the public image of Candomblé. There is also some evidence that after 1930 the tradition of leaders of *terreiros* establishing relationships and striking deals with politicians was alive and well, if not on the increase. The aforementioned Severiano Manoel de Abreu (Jubiabá), for example, claimed in a newspaper article in 1936 to have "handed more than a thousand votes to Dr. Americano da Costa in the municipal elections at the request of Dr. Martinelli Braga," one of Magalhães's political organizers.[45] In exchange, the *terreiro*, and by extension the neighborhood where it was situated, was to receive improvements and presumably more protection from the police. Similar stories are common in Candomblé lore and oral history. Magalhães himself is said to have frequented *terreiros* for a bit of advice on the future and to garner support for his policies, although this story may be apocryphal.[46] But Abreu's public assertion that votes were gathered through the *terreiros* is hard to completely discount, especially given the typical practices of the time. Moreover, others besides the leaders within the hierarchy of Candomblé developed strategies to emphasize the legitimacy and increase the visibility of African-Bahian practices.

Capoeira

Intimately connected to the Candomblé community was the subculture of capoeira, a martial art practiced in small groups in the streets and squares of Salvador. The practitioners of this art in the 1930s were largely working-class African Bahians.[47] The elite discourse on capoeira, as with Candomblé, changed significantly after 1930 from the view that it was an activity associated with marginalized social behavior and rebellious aggression against the dominant order to the view that it occupied a notable and celebrated place within Bahian regional identity. A brief look at a few of the factors behind this shift further illustrates the revitalization of African-Bahian culture under Juracy Magalhães and the degree to which these changes were a consequence of a propitious political atmosphere, wider national shifts, and the proactive efforts and influence of two working-class African Bahians—Manuel dos Reis Machado, known as Mestre Bimba, and, later in the period, Vicente Ferreira Pastinha, known as Mestre Pastinha.

Capoeira brings together martial arts, sport, dance, music, gamesmanship, and performance. It is performed in rotating pairs inside a ring of participants. The action is accompanied and to a degree determined by music, hand clapping, and/or song, which makes it a hybrid of dancing, acrobatics, and fighting. In the early twentieth century, capoeira games, or *rodas* (literally "rings"), came together spontaneously or were loosely organized primarily among young men as a form of training or as ends in themselves. These often took place in squares or near the docks, on weekends or during work breaks. *Rodas* were also part of a wider sociability that took place at birthday parties, family gatherings, samba parties, or public festivals. They fluctuated between the festive and the competitive. Capoeira's origins probably lie in west-central Africa, although most of its twentieth-century form evolved in Brazil and acquired elements from West Africa and from Brazil itself, both before and after the abolition of slavery in 1888.[48] In 1890 capoeira was declared illegal, and for decades it was largely ostracized in dominant-class discourse and its practitioners were persecuted by the police. Nevertheless, as Antonio Pires underlines, capoeira remained a fundamental institution of African-Bahian working-class life.[49] The degree to which it was persecuted varied depending on the mood of the police, access to patrons or influential practitioners (some practitioners *were* police), bribes or simple requests for exceptions to be made, or luck or timing. After 1930, however, the dominant-class discourse on capoeira shifted dramatically, and the first license to legally practice capoeira was issued in 1937.[50]

The early impetus for these shifts came from liberal professionals in Rio de Janeiro at the end of the nineteenth century, who sought to regularize capoeira through a series of codifications of the game and a patriotic characterization of it as a "national sport." Against a backdrop of the aggressive persecution of capoeira, especially in Rio, the intention behind this "sportification" (*esportização*) was to remove the practice from its social context and relieve it of the stigma of being associated with Rio's African-Brazilian working class. It was largely unsuccessful, but the campaign revealed one way that the dominant class would accept capoeira—through reform and sanitization.[51] In 1916, Manuel Querino suggested that some members of the dominant class in Salvador also practiced capoeira as a "sport." But the majority of practitioners were still working-class African Bahians, and this is the group that suffered a period of particularly intense police repression in the 1920s.[52]

After 1930, the actions of Manuel dos Reis Machado, known as Mestre Bimba, catalyzed a change toward public acceptance of capoeira and its inclusion as a marker of Bahian regional identity. As an adolescent, Mestre Bimba worked on the docks, where he learned his capoeira, the area around the docks having been something of a center of formal and informal instruction and play. In 1932, Bimba set up the first instructional academy in Salvador for training students of capoeira, although he had led numerous organized training sessions prior to this, always on the margins of the law and public acceptability. Bimba had begun to evolve and teach a particular style of capoeira, which he called capoeira *regional*, a hybrid form largely of his own creation (but inspired by a trip to Rio de Janeiro) that incorporated moves from other martial arts and boxing. It was a hybrid in another important way. Middle- and even upper-class Bahians of European descent—especially medical students such as Ângelo Decânio, later one of Mestre Bimba's biographers—began to pay for formal lessons in the academies. According to former students, biographers, and his own later interviews, Bimba was proactively reshaping capoeira in line with contemporary trends in Brazilian society, a move that contributed to a change in how the mainstream public saw capoeira. Formerly an activity associated with the streets and criminality, it was becoming legitimate and socially acceptable.[53]

Bimba chose a propitious time to undertake these transformations. First, a wider acceptance of capoeira had recently begun. For example, in October 1931 *A Tarde* reported that an informal capoeira gathering between acquaintances turned nasty one afternoon. Several people were hurt, passersby were alarmed, and the police were called. The article made no suggestion that this was inevitable with capoeira or *capoeiristas*, as would have been the case in earlier years. The protagonists had taken the day off from work, but they were not portrayed as delinquent. Moreover, the journalist pointed out that the injuries occurred only after the practitioners had ceased to obey the "rules of the sport," thus highlighting the all-important distinction between a vagrant, marginal activity and a regulated sport. As a sport, capoeira was becoming acceptable to the dominant class.[54]

Second, it is possible that Mestre Bimba was encouraged to make his transformations by Juracy Magalhães's openness to popular culture and his interest in courting working-class political support for his and Getúlio Vargas's agenda. In fact, Magalhães invited Mestre Bimba, probably in 1936, to put on an exhibition at the gubernatorial palace that was attended by the governor and guests.[55] Also during 1936, Bimba was invited to lead a capoeira exhibition during the celebrations for Bahian Independence Day.[56] Shortly thereafter, in July 1937, Bimba received the first official license from the Department of Vocational and Secondary Education in Bahia to teach the "sport." These events are clear evidence of the official acceptance of capoeira in Bahia, and the Independence Day capoeira exhibition indicates that capoeira had become a marker of regional identity.

Bimba's decision to regularize his own brand of capoeira and market it to the dominant class was certainly a major factor in its wider and increasing acceptance. Juracy Magalhães, too, clearly played an important role by giving capoeira official state sanction. The exhibition at the gubernatorial palace may have been private, but the impact was public. Although in 1936, *A Tarde* still complained that a capoeira exhibition had no place in the commemorations of Bahian Independence, the shift was under way.[57] By the late 1930s, newspapers had begun to cite capoeira as a popular, folkloric feature of Bahian life. Moreover, the reconceptualization of capoeira as "physical education" enhanced its acceptability to both the liberal modernizers, who were obsessed with the notion of sanitization, and the emerging, fascist-inspired political faction in Brazil, which longed for a disciplined individual and social body. These adjustments to the practice and image of capoeira were echoed by the director of the Physical Education Division of the federal Ministry of Education and Health in 1944, when he declared capoeira to be "a sport of our folklore."[58]

What is remarkable about the inclusion of capoeira as a marker of Bahian regional identity, however, is that it did not become a sanitized middle-class sport in this process of change. Although sportification certainly helped ease the process, capoeira nevertheless remained an aspect of African-Bahian working-class life. Here again the role of Bimba was important. As capoeira grew quickly in national stature during the Vargas era, Bimba emphasized its historical associations with Bahia and more specifically African Bahians. Bimba himself was a member of the Candomblé community, having grown up close to the practice. His mother was a *filha-de-santo*, and Bimba remained spiritually close to the *orixás* and held an official position in the percussion orchestra of his wife's *terreiro*.[59] Thus Bimba's style of capoeira, for all its technical innovations, was still easily associated with African Bahians and African-Bahian culture, and Letícia Reis argues that this may have actually helped it gain its national status. She points out that Estado Novo functionaries saw Bahian capoeira as a more "pure" form than the form practiced in Rio de Janeiro, not least because in Rio de Janeiro it was still almost entirely associated with *malandros* (hustlers) and delinquents. This is not to say that only middle-class Euro-Bahians were playing the nicer version of capoeira that was acceptable to the Estado Novo state. (Indeed, wealthier youths' may have been attracted to the rougher versions in the first place or at least to the fantasy of participating in the rougher versions.) Yet Bimba had applied a deeper historical meaning to Bahian capoeira as an art form that could help define the uniqueness of the historical formation of the Brazilian nation and celebrate its mixed cultural heritage.[60]

It was largely under these terms that capoeira (whether capoeira *regional* or, later, capoeira *angola* under Mestre Pastinha, which is discussed briefly in chapter 6) was incorporated into notions of Bahianness, and in turn, that an African-Bahian practice became a symbol of Brazilian national identity after 1930. As Teles dos Santos and others have shown, however, a struggle over the meanings associated with the practice continued into the twentieth century. Folklorists, military officers, and writers chose at various times to appropriate a version of capoeira stripped of its African heritage, typically characterizing it as a creolized "national gymnastics."[61] This reformulation was clearly under way even by the 1930s, and to some degree Bimba himself capitalized on and contributed to this reformulation. Nevertheless, for Bahian regional identity, capoeira's primary associations would continue to be with African-Bahian working-class culture, and after 1930 the significant shift would be the acceptance and even celebration of these associations and the incorporation of capoeira into Bahian regional identity.

The Revival of the Washing of Bonfim

I will now turn to the first of two additional events from 1937 that further illustrate the coming together of Magalhães's cultural populism and pressure from below—the revival of the Washing of the Church of Nosso Senhor do Bonfim, which takes place in mid-January. Since the late eighteenth century, the Festival of the Senhor do Bonfim (Our Lord of the Good End) had included a public ritual washing of the inside of the church (particularly its floor), its *adro* (gated front patio), and even its front steps. This Washing of Bonfim, which takes place on the second Thursday after Epiphany, brought together elements of high and popular Catholicism in a climactic moment of splashing water, white flowers, sweeping, mopping, singing, shouting, and entering into trances. In addition to its Catholic components, the washing was also part of the ritual calendar of many of the *terreiros* of Candomblé. For the Candomblé community, the Washing of Bonfim was an obligation to Oxalá, the Candomblé *orixá* associated with the Senhor do Bonfim.

In the 1920s, the archbishop of Salvador, Augusto Álvaro da Silva, was still enforcing a standing prohibition (one that was unevenly enforced) on the washing of the inside of the Church of Nosso Senhor do Bonfim that dated back to 1890.[62] Particularly after 1926, the archbishop and conservative priests in charge of the Church of Nosso Senhor do Bonfim made it so difficult for devotees to carry out the washing that the *Diário de Notícias* stated in 1937 that it "had not occurred in some eight to ten years, more or less."[63] Figures within the Church had been attacking the washing for decades as a sacrilegious offense to good Catholic practice, targeting it with vitriol in the Catholic press as a scandalous assault on Salvador's standards of civilization.[64] Over the first decades of the twentieth century, the ritual seems to have had fallen victim to the concerns of the dominant class about popular practices, particularly those associated with African Bahians.

The elements of the washing that offended the conservative Catholic hierarchy fell into two categories. The first included behaviors considered "unchristian," including the shouting, pushing, and shoving associated with the spiritually overexcited and out-of-control crowd involved in the ritual and behaviors considered "excesses" such as rowdiness, drunkenness, or practices that could be considered ecstatic. These features had often played some part in many of Salvador's public festivals and were initiated by the people themselves. It was particularly offensive, however, when these behaviors occurred inside the church itself.[65] The second category of behaviors the Church found problematic, according to the newspapers, were those associated with Candomblé and those that were considered "fetishistic."[66] These included the presence of the Baianas and the mere fact that they were fulfilling their obligations to Oxalá. The act of washing created a powerful spiritual/ritual linkage between the Catholic figure of Christ on the cross and Oxalá, for the cosmological origins of Oxalá involved his emergence from primordial waters as well as parables that involved the deity being cleansed.[67] Here again the "problem" was aggravated by the extension of these "unchristian" aspects of the ritual washing into the very precincts of the Church of Nosso Senhor do Bonfim itself. The Washing of Bonfim was therefore targeted as the most prominent example of the sorts of popular devotional practices and activities (many associated with Candomblé) that the archbishop had regularly denounced as "unchristian" and that the Church in Bahia had sought to reign in after 1889.[68]

These attitudes seem to have decreased the incidence of the washing in the 1920s and early 1930s to the point that its survival was at stake, although there is evidence that some form of washings took place during this period.[69] The newspapers in 1937, however, are consistent in their affirmation that this year the washing underwent a dramatic revival within the Bonfim festival. Imprecision in the sources obscures exactly how this occurred, yet the main players who marshaled popular support and participation against the conservative position of the Catholic Church are easily identified. These were the Lay Brotherhood of Bonfim (known as the Irmandade Devoção ao Senhor do Bonfim); Vargas-era politicians; middle-class liberals, intellectuals, journalists, and scholars; and popular Salvadorans, especially members of the Candomblé community.

The Brotherhood of Bonfim, which counted among its members some of Salvador's most illustrious and powerful citizens, including Juracy Magalhães in 1936 and 1937, was accorded much of the credit for the revival of the washing ritual by the newspapers.[70] While the available sources do not reveal any official stance Magalhães may have taken on the washing, we have already seen enough of Magalhães's position on popular culture to suggest that he would have favored lifting the ban. Additionally, in 1934, the *Diário de Notícias* in 1934 stated that the mayor's office (the mayor, José Americano da Costa, had been appointed by Magalhães) was keen "to support the Washing," suggesting that politicians at that level of state administration were pushing back against the Church.[71] Any hesitancy on Magalhães's part in taking a public position supporting the washing may have been out of respect for Archbishop da Silva, one of Magalhães's few early backers among the elite upon his arrival in Salvador. Even if Magalhães did not take an active role in having the prohibition lifted or within the activities of the brotherhood, his membership in the brotherhood was an endorsement of its efforts to have the ban lifted.

As a group, the Brotherhood of Bonfim contributed to the revival of the washing in several ways. In 1936 and 1937, they did much of the organizational work for both the procession and the washing. This was done, in particular, through their support of the Organizing Committee of the Washing of Bonfim. This committee, led by José Luis Barreiros, consisted of several energetic public figures, although as far as can be determined these were not members of the elite. The committee was described in one newspaper as "popular," although this term referred more to the middle class and to progressive ideas than to the working class. One of the members of the committee, "Major" Cosme de Farias, for example, was not a major in the armed forces but a crusading and often unpaid public defender.[72] It was either the organizing committee or the brotherhood, or perhaps both, that encouraged elite Salvadorans, especially elite women (the *senhoras de nossa sociedade*), to participate in the washing of the church floor as part of the agreement to lift the ban. If Salvadoran elites participated in the washing inside the church, even if a certain number of Baianas were included, then the majority of working-class Bahians could be restricted to washing the *adro* and possibly the steps leading up to the *adro*. This distinction seemed to be crucial to the lifting of the prohibition, as in theory it promised to limit behavior that church authorities considered to be sacrilegious to a space outside the church (although efforts to keep the *povo* [the masses] at bay were not always successful). It is also likely that members of the brotherhood drew on personal networks as they lobbied the city's middle- and upper-class residents and civil authorities to pressure Salvador's Catholic hierarchy to have the ban lifted.[73]

In addition to the efforts of the Brotherhood of Bonfim and presumed good will of Juracy Magalhães, journalists on the city's secular daily newspapers increased the pressure on the Church to waive or lift the ban by championing and celebrating the ritual. In 1936 and 1937, journalists repeatedly described the washing as a "venerable tradition," a "*ceremônia tradicionalíssima*" (super-traditional ceremony), and "an ancient habit."[74] Journalists from the *Diário da Bahia* felt it important to anchor this depiction historically, and the paper claimed to have interviewed Maria Melania Ribeiro, a 110-year-old African-Bahian (*preta*) woman with "a broom in her hand [for the Washing]," who told the reporter of her memories of participating in the washing as a young girl. Newspaper reports also celebrated the washing as a manifestation of Salvador's true "Catholic soul," the implication being that this included popular Catholic practices and associations with Candomblé.[75] In fact, against a backdrop of the Catholic Church's strong criticism of the washing, the journalists' articles and editorials give the impression of an almost ideological crusade in its defense. The popular daily *O Imparcial*, for example, which was known for its reactionary chauvinism during this period, went so far as to depict the ban on the washing as an assault on "our Bahian traditions" by "foreign elements" (*elementos estranhos*), a reference to the Dutch-born Redentist priest at the Church of Nosso Senhor do Bonfim.[76] The press campaign to revive the washing was in part coordinated by the Organizing Committee of the Washing, as a letter from its president, José Luis Barreiros, to the *Diário de Notícias* in 1938 attests. Barreiros called attention to the fact that although everything was prepared, the final permission for the washing was yet to be given by the Catholic hierarchy in the person of the archbishop. The obvious intent was to keep the pressure on to make sure the archbishop would waive the ban for a second consecutive year.

The final and admittedly most amorphous contributor to the revival of the washing in 1937 was Salvador's working classes, especially the Candomblé community. For many of the *terreiros*, especially those in the Nagô-Ketu tradition, the Washing of Bonfim was the culmination of a set of ceremonies to honor Oxalá. For the temple of Mãe Aninha, for example, the Washing of Bonfim was the public extension of the rituals comprising the Waters of Oxalá. There is ample evidence to suggest that the insistence of the *mães-de-santo* (priestesses), *pais-de-santo* (priests), and *feitas-* or *filhas-de-santo* (initiates) on participating in the processions (and on some sort of washing ceremony devoted to Oxalá) kept the washing alive during the period of prohibition. For instance, according to one newspaper article, in the years leading up to 1937, the Candomblé community continued to transport water to the church, only to find its doors shut and guarded. In clear defiance of the spirit of the position of the Archbishop of Salvador, they nevertheless engaged in a poor substitute, a washing of the patio. If the gates to the patio were shut, they washed the steps in front of the church.[77]

Within the Candomblé community, specific religious leaders and intellectuals were also influential in the reestablishment of the washing, although the evidence for this is indirect. The highly regarded *mãe-de-santo* Eugênia Ana dos Santos—Mãe Aninha—seems to have been at the forefront of this influence in the mid-1930s. According to a newspaper article from 1940, Aninha created the Repasso, which involved a smaller, almost private washing of the altars of the Church of Nosso Senhor do Bonfim on the Friday rather than the traditional Thursday.[78] Unfortunately, it is not clear when she began this tradition, but it was almost certainly in 1935, 1936, or 1937.[79] It seems that Aninha successfully brokered permission to perform a ritual washing devoted to the Senhor do Bonfim (and Oxalá) inside the church during the festival even as the Church still refused to sanction a public event before 1937. This would have shown remarkable initiative and very possibly contributed to preparing the groundwork for the revival of the tradition in succeeding years. Even if the Repasso was inaugurated only in 1937, it still illustrates the initiative of a certain sector of the Candomblé leadership in negotiating space for its own rituals within the institutions of the dominant culture. Moreover, once the Church lifted the ban in 1937, it continued to refuse to allow the public to wash the inside of the church. Practitioners of the ritual were restricted to the stairs and the porch outside, meaning that it was significant that Aninha had organized the opportunity for a more private, controlled access to the interior of the church for the Candomblé community.

More concrete evidence that the Candomblé community was an active agent in the revival of the washing comes from the presence in 1939 and 1940 of Miguel Santana, a high-ranking *ogan* in Mãe Aninha's *terreiro*, as the president of the Organizing Committee of the Washing of Bonfim. Miguel Santana was very successful in his position as an employment agent in Salvador's port district and was therefore a notable figure in Bahia's secular world. Although hardly a member of the political and economic elite, Santana was something of a crossover figure who was able to liaise with the Lay Brotherhood of the Senhor do Bonfim and with Salvador's Candomblé community. He was suitably placed to ensure that Salvador's Candomblé community was represented by at least one African Bahian. Santana's efforts most likely involved pressure for the right to hold the washing in the first place and then the organization and management of the participation of the Baianas through the hierarchies of their respective *terreiros*.[80]

The lifting of the ban in 1937 was not the end of the struggle over the right of Salvadorans to hold their washing ritual. The Candomblé community continued to apply pressure. Antônio Monteiro, who founded the middle-class Comissão Permanente da Lavagem Simbólica (Permanent Commission for the Symbolic Washing) in the late 1940s, gave an interview in the 1990s in which he emphasized the contribution of the Union of Afro-Brazilian Temples of Candomblé to the consolidation of the lifting of the ban on the washing.[81] The union worked in the late 1930s to regulate and control abuses within the Candomblé community and to win acknowledgement of legal rights for African-Bahian religious practices. One of its key organizers was Edison Carneiro. Another was Álvaro MacDowell de Oliveira, also mentioned above, a lawyer who was married to Mãe-de-Santo Menininha. After 1937, according to Monteiro, part of the purpose of the union was to encourage more practitioners of Candomblé to participate in the procession and the washing and to emphasize publicly that this participation was linked with the practice of Candomblé. Research in the Catholic newspapers supports Monteiro's point. The *Semana Cathólica* railed against the "Bolshevik" and "anarchist" union because of its activities in 1939 in favor of the washing. Such activities included a public invitation in the newspapers to the *pais-de-santo* and *mães-de-santo* and their initiates to participate in the washing. Adding insult to injury, the Union of Afro-Brazilian Temples of Candomblé adopted the Senhor do Bonfim (Oxalá) as their patron saint.[82]

Ultimately, then, this overview of the pressures that were marshaled to convince the Catholic Church to lift its ban on the Washing of Bonfim in 1937 illustrates how the changes under way in Salvador with regard to African-Bahian cultural practices stemmed from the efforts of actors from a number of different social sectors in Salvador, from the politically powerful Juracy Magalhães to the adherents and practitioners of Candomblé. The Candomblé community, however, was involved in other efforts to revitalize African-Bahian culture and make it acceptable to the dominant class, as revealed by their contributions to the Second Afro-Brazilian Congress.

The Second Afro-Brazilian Congress, 1937

The climactic moment of the early shift toward public acceptance of African-Bahian studies in Salvador came with the Second Afro-Brazilian Congress of January 1937.[83] Principally the result of Edison Carneiro's hard work and that of a number of his fellow young intellectuals, the congress was held in the prestigious Instituto Geográfico e Histórico da Bahia, a regional bastion of the local intellectual elite and of traditional scholarship in the vein of "official history." The congress ran over three days and brought together national and international scholars of African-Brazilian culture for a series of public scholarly presentations, lectures, and solemnities. It was more than just an homage to African-Brazilian traditions; this was the event that convinced a skeptical public that African-Bahian culture was a legitimate object of scholarly attention.[84] A number of Salvador's popular leaders and intellectuals made important contributions. *Babalaô* Martiniano do Bonfim was the event's honorary president. Mãe Aninha contributed a piece on the uses of traditional (sacred) foods within Candomblé. Several other leading figures of the Candomblé community were involved. For instance, the members of the *terreiro* of João da Pedra Preta put on an exhibition of samba and *batuque* for the congress participants, who were also treated to a capoeira exhibition, and the organizers claimed that forty *terreiros* actively supported the congress.[85]

The state government provided half the funding for the congress and provided some official hospitality for the visiting intellectual luminaries. Salvador's mayor, José Americano da Costa, attended the inauguration of a shrine to a Candomblé *orixá* put on for the participants. The three co-organizers—Edison Carneiro, Áydano do Couto Ferraz, and Reginaldo Guimarães—considered their primary mission to be the winning of the liberty and right of African Bahians to practice their religions freely.[86] Their tactics included appeals to both regionalism and nationalism by conceiving the study of African-Bahian practices as part of a larger project of writing the history of Brazil, a project that had haltingly been started by Bahians Manoel Querino and Nina Rodrigues in the nineteenth and early twentieth centuries and had been given fresh impetus by the publication of Gilberto Freyre's *Casa-grande e senzala* (*The Masters and the Slaves*) in 1933. The research of psychiatrist and ethnographer Arthur Ramos and his work in academic publishing was also central to this revalorization of the cultural contribution of the African Brazilian. In a similar vein, Carneiro and his associates placed African-Brazilian religion alongside highbrow Western cultural practices such as those of "novelist Jorge Amado, musician Fructuoso Vianna, poet Júlio Paternostro" and painter José Guimarães. The organizers also took pains to point out the impressive amount of international support for the congress, citing the participation of eight renowned scholars from the metropoles of North America and Europe and from the São Paulo Department of Culture. The press covered the congress favorably, and its closing ceremonies at Gantois, a famous *terreiro* de Candomblé, were reportedly broadcast by Radio Commercial da Bahia.[87]

Clearly the congress was *the* moment of the 1930s that brought together the various protagonists involved in the process of reevaluating African-Bahian cultural practices: the government, the practitioners themselves, and their middle-class allies, including regional, national, and international scholars. Carneiro moved quickly to capitalize on the success of the congress to further legitimize Candomblé within something akin to a quasi-legal framework. Under Carneiro, the congress became a springboard for the founding of the Union of Afro-Brazilian Temples of Candomblé, whose explicit aims were to monitor and regulate Candomblé practices. Carneiro believed he could win legal recognition and protection for Candomblé (which was in any case theoretically sanctioned by the 1934 constitution then in effect) by ridding Salvador of its practitioners of what was pejoratively referred to as superstition and *feitiçaria*.[88]

Carneiro's broad initiative to present a more acceptable and legitimate face of African-Bahian culture gave further impetus to the establishment of Nagô-Ketu Candomblé practices as the most authentically "African" branch. As the most outspoken public intellectual in Bahia, Carneiro consciously contributed scholarly legitimacy to this hierarchizing of different religious practices based on the authenticity of links to Africa and the supposed superiority of Nagô-Ketu "civilization" over other non-Western cultures (both Brazilian Indian and African). In doing so, he was following the lead of the nationally influential Arthur Ramos, based in São Paulo, who was updating a line of thinking originally proposed by Bahian psychiatrist Nina Rodrigues.[89] Thus the "purer," more "traditional," or more "African" institutions—namely, those of Yoruban (Nagô-Ketu) traditions—could be, and were, constructed as less threatening and more sophisticated than those of other Candomblé traditions. These proponents argued that practitioners of the Nagô-Ketu traditions were worthy of the same protection enjoyed by practicing Roman Catholics and that they were distinct from those practices the dominant culture saw as black magic. Not surprisingly, the Nagô-Ketu *terreiros* were taken more seriously than other *terreiros* by

the congress of 1937, although other Candomblé traditions were represented. Significantly, the Nagô-Ketu *terreiros* also assumed the leadership
within the *união* and used their standards to define what acceptable Candomblé was and what lay outside these parameters. This practice continued the consolidation of the idea that Nagô-Ketu *terreiros* and associated
practices represented the most legitimate and authentic version of Candomblé.[90] More important here, however, is that the Nagô-Ketu leadership
and Edison Carneiro made significant contributions toward improving the
image of Candomblé among the wider public. We can surmise from Carneiro's efforts that he believed that a significant portion of Salvadorans still
held prejudices against Candomblé. However, it would seem that the public
was willing to accept a distinction between acceptable and unacceptable
Candomblé practices.[91]

Carneiro, the organizers, many participants in the congress, and the
leadership of the *união* exploited this distinction to deepen public acceptance of a cleaned-up version of Candomblé that was acceptable to scholars. If Salvador was to have a respectable working class, then Candomblé
could be considered part of that respectability. This was how a cultural
practice can rise within the hierarchy of the public discourse. Moreover,
it is important to note that these efforts were supported, at least indirectly,
by state funding. Interestingly, the state subsidy perturbed Gilberto Freyre,
who had conceived and organized the first Afro-Brazilian Congress in Recife in 1934. For Freyre, government funding implied government influence
and threatened to compromise the scientific pledge of objectivity, although
there is no evidence that such influence took place. The subsidy is one of the
clearer signs of the Bahian government's willingness to embrace African-
Bahian culture. The congress as a whole, as Romo has described in some
detail, was a remarkable moment that brought together the leadership of
the Candomblé community and their allies, supported by figures within the
international scholarly community and local government, to push for the
recognition of the legitimacy of African-Bahian cultural practices.[92]

Conclusion

Important shifts, changes, and reemphases in the years after 1930 laid the
foundations for the emergence of a new dynamic of cultural politics in Salvador. Despite the fact that Magalhães was a youthful outsider with no family connections to Bahian politics, the new interventor astutely bypassed
the state's most prominent and powerful elite families (who vehemently

opposed his appointment) and harnessed the political power of much of the rest of the state's rural and small-town landed elite to a political machine that supported the aspirations of Getúlio Vargas. This allowed Magalhães to subdue the intractable antagonism of Bahia's traditional elite toward the federal government. His six years in office also contributed to an atmosphere that encouraged the rejuvenation and revitalization of African-Bahian culture within Salvadoran public space.

This coincided with and contributed to an increasing assertiveness on · the part of various practitioners of African-Bahian cultural practices, such as Mãe Aninha, Martiniano do Bonfim, Mestre Bimba, and João da Gomeia. This assertiveness and the efforts of progressive middle-class intellectuals set the foundation for a seminal shift in the public perception of African Bahians' contributions to Bahian regional identity. These changes represented the crucial steps in the reformulation of the cultural-political relationship between Salvador's dominant and subordinate classes.

The revival of the Washing of Bonfim and the Second Afro-Brazilian Congress illustrate the contribution to this process of figures among Bahia's dominant class as well as within the Candomblé community. The agency of the Candomblé and capoeira leadership lay in their willingness to push for greater cultural-political space in Bahia and their ability to seize the opportunities provided by Magalhães and the media to push ahead with their agenda. Their influence derived from their personalities and the esteem in which they were held by the more or less faceless poor and largely African-Bahian working-class community.

However, the events and changes in the period 1930 to 1937 did not mean that the embrace of African-Bahian culture was certain to be permanent or irrevocable. Conservative elites and in particular the Catholic Church pushed back against these shifts and would continue to do so. The ecclesiastical prohibition on the masses' participation in the washing of the inside of the Church of Nosso Senhor do Bonfim was not actually formally rescinded, but it seemed to have entered a phase of annual renegotiation. The degree to which African-Bahian culture would be embraced more widely was also limited and controlled. An element of qualification and compromise was a salient part of the strategies African-Bahians implemented during this period. The Union of Afro-Brazilian Temples of Candomblé endeavored to "clean up" Candomblé by codifying certain practices as inappropriate. Bimba, too, "modernized" the practice of capoeira by including moves from other martial art forms and established an academy system where he trained members of the dominant class.

Moreover, in this new discourse on regional identity, African-Bahian culture did not replace or supersede cultural practices that were defined or understood as "European" or "modern." Finally, exactly what this nascent cultural inclusion might mean for African Bahians was yet to be determined. Clearly the politics of culture in Salvador had shifted and *cultura negra* was playing a more significant role. The specific nature of this new emerging discourse of *baianidade* would continue to be negotiated beyond 1937 as part of a wider shift in Bahia's politics of culture, class, and race. If African-Bahians and their allies wanted to deepen and extend their influence they would need additional leverage. They would find this leverage, particularly from the mid-1930s onward, in the performative power of the city's popular festivals as public ritual acts. The festivals would prove vital in the process of reconstructing the meanings of African-Bahian culture for Bahian society. It is to a closer look at Salvador's popular festivals that we now turn.

3

Performing Bahia

Public Festivals, Samba, and African-Bahian Agency

At dawn on Thursday morning, the ninth of January 1941, up to one thousand Salvadorans from all walks of life converged on the space in front of the Church of Nossa Senhora da Conceição da Praia in Salvador's commercial district. They had come wearing mostly white to participate in the procession for Bahia's "patron saint," the Senhor do Bonfim (Our Lord of the Good End, or Christ on the Cross), and to witness or participate in the climactic ritual washing of the steps of the Church of Nosso Senhor do Bonfim.[1] Gradually they organized themselves, and at the sound of clarions or a mortar salute, they set off on a long, snaking procession of over four miles that ended at the steps of the church on the Peninsula of Itapagipe, which jutted out into the blue-green waters of the Bay of All Saints. Among those participating were politicians, politicians' wives, and journalists (all typically in a car); a military band; and any number of "humbly decorated," mule-driven carts, while many poor, devout Salvadorans walked. The procession took up to three hours at the height of the Brazilian summer, which entailed both a physical and symbolic hardship that many Salvadorans regarded as fundamental to the passion for the Senhor do Bonfim. The procession illustrated the depth of their devotion and recalled the sacrifice and suffering that Christ endured on the cross, the most potent symbol of Christianity. Moreover, as a penitential procession, the march resonated emotively with the community's deeply rooted traditions from Iberia, where such processions were organized in times of distress such as during droughts or epidemics.

Yet for many involved in the procession and those who would participate in the ritual washing of the church steps, these public rituals were not done (or were not only done) to commemorate Christ on the cross. They were also ritual obligations to Oxalá, a Candomblé deity and an important and powerful figure within the hierarchy of Candomblé cosmology (especially within the Nagô-Ketu tradition). Tellingly, no Catholic priests led in organizing the procession from the Church of Nossa Senhora da Conceição da Praia to the Church of Nosso Senhor do Bonfim. Most of the spiritual focus and leadership for the procession instead came from the *mães-de-santo*, *filhas-de-santo*, and a few *pais-de-santo* of the Candomblé community. The women in particular were dressed in their all-white ceremonial finery, some transporting vases of water and flowers to the church for the ritual washing. Thus the procession that made its way from the commercial district and down the peninsula of Itapagipe was syncretic, deeply imbued with traditions and meaning from both Catholicism and Candomblé.[2]

Meanwhile, hundreds of onlookers gathered along the route of the procession and hundreds more at the Church of Nosso Senhor do Bonfim awaiting the arrival of the procession and the Baianas. Rockets or mortars were fired to mark the progress of the procession over the last leg of the journey, further exciting the crowd. As the procession arrived at the church and the Baianas climbed the steps to place their flowers at the altar (or at the top of the steps, if the priest refused to open the church doors, as sometimes happened), the crowd closed in, clapping their hands and shouting, "Long live the Senhor do Bonfim!" A passage by the exiled Austrian writer Stefan Zweig, who witnessed the Washing of Bonfim in 1941, is worth reproducing here to complete the description of the ceremony:

> At last the long-awaited moment had arrived. . . . Several policemen pushed the crowd back from the nave to clear the floor whose tiles were to be scrubbed. Then, under a continuous barrage of applause from the crowd, water was poured from the jugs onto the floor, and a moment later the brooms were seized. . . . The impatience of waiting, coupled with the incessant shouting and the jubilation, had made them wild. And suddenly it seemed as though a riot of a hundred black spirits had been let loose in the middle of the church. One snatched a broom from another; a second later two, three, then as many as ten were holding on to a single handle at the same time, scrubbing rhythmically and more and more rapidly. Others, without brooms, threw themselves on the floor and began scrubbing it with their naked hands, while men, women and children cried ecstatically their "Viva Bomfim! Viva Bomfim!" Soon the riot had developed into a mad ecstasy, the most fantastic example of mass hysteria I have ever

seen. . . . Its improbability was further accentuated by the fact that it happened in broad daylight in church, without the assistance of alcohol, music, or any other stimulant.[3]

The passage provides a window onto the emotional intensity of this public ritual act and its power to shape meaning and discourse. One must keep in mind the syncretic nature of the ritual. The "mass hysteria" that so impressed Zweig combined elements of both religious traditions. For its participants, the Washing of Bonfim was a conscious act of popular Catholicism and Candomblé-related worship and spirituality.

Salvador's annual festival calendar included a number of these major city-wide public festivals as well as many smaller neighborhood-based festivals. In addition to the Festival of Senhor do Bonfim (which began on the second Thursday in January, after Epiphany), there were several other festivals of similar stature: Santa Barbara (4 December), Conceição da Praia (8 December), Senhor dos Navegantes (31 December), Segunda-Feira Gorda da Ribeira (the Monday after Bonfim), and Yemanjá (2 February). These are the festivals on which I draw for most of my analysis, although I also include information from the Festival of the Three Kings (6 January) and the Festival of Boa Viagem (1 January).

The principal rituals of Santa Barbara, Conceição da Praia, and Senhor dos Navegantes were primarily Catholic—they celebrated Catholic saints, were accompanied by the standard practices of high Catholic mass and liturgy, and were centered on devout processions of effigies of these saints that occurred within and around Catholic churches. Nevertheless, as seen with the ritual Washing of Bonfim, in Salvador there was always an undercurrent (and frequently explicit expression) of Candomblé worship within or alongside the festivals. Catholic saints in Salvador had long been associated with African deities, both covertly and overtly, and during the period 1930 to 1954 the city's Candomblé leadership and wider community took pains to ensure that Salvador's popular religious festivals included the celebration of both saints and deities. In several cases, as we shall see, the public Candomblé rituals rivaled the Catholic elements in importance and dwarfed them in scope. For instance, the waterborne processional offerings to Yemanjá (the Yoruban Mother of the Water and patron of fishermen and sailors) during two ostensibly Catholic festivals—the Festival of Conceição da Praia and the Festival of Rio Vermelho—were, judging from photographs, similar in size to the processions for the Catholic saints. (Of course many Salvadorans participated in both.)

Table 3.1. Salvador's major festivals and dates.

Festival	Date
Santa Barbara	December 4
Conceição da Praia	December 8
Senhor dos Navegantes	December 31
Boa Viagem	January 1
The Three Kings	January 6
Washing of Bonfim	Second Thursday in January
Ribeira	Monday after the Washing of Bonfim
Yemanjá	February 2
Carnival	Sunday, Monday, and Tuesday prior to Ash Wednesday

Consequently, Salvador's multifaceted and polyvalent festivals were a prime site for contestation and negotiation as individuals from the city's subordinate and dominant classes and cultures sought to influence the meanings of these important public events. Building on the reappraisal of African-Bahian culture under Juracy Magalhães, the festival performances brought assertion and impetus to the shift toward the embrace of African-Bahian cultural traditions within a culturally inclusive Bahian regional identity. This chapter describes the role Salvador's *festas populares* played in this process of reappraisal, and indeed the ongoing revitalization, of African-Bahian culture in the middle to late 1930s and after. The pages below describe the changing anatomy and shifting dynamics of Salvador's largest popular festivals from 1930 and continue to emphasize the agency and influence of the city's largely African-Bahian working class and the Candomblé community in perpetuating certain aspects of the festivals and in shaping their wider social meanings. Salvador's working-class support of the rituals on behalf of or in relation to Candomblé *orixás* was particularly on the increase from the middle 1930s. Leading figures within the Candomblé community played greater roles in organizing the rituals and mobilizing people to take part in them. These figures played roles negotiating with the dominant class in a process that reveals the importance of African-Bahian agency in the perpetuation and growth of the aspects of the popular festivals related to Candomblé. Their actions should be recognized as efforts to shape the broader meanings of these deeply symbolic public events, meanings that by 1954 had become dominant and commonsensical in Bahia and across Brazil.

The Festivals: History and Revival

Salvador's major Catholic and Candomblé-related public festivals were part of an annual ritual calendar that began in early December and ran well into the following year, climaxing in carnival (but not effectively ending until the "June Festivals" of St. John, St. Anthony, and St. Peter). In their principal contours they were quite similar, each adhering to the criteria that ranked them as Festas de Largo (the *largo* being the public space or square adjacent to a church) or Festas Populares (popular festivals). Each festival was centered on a particular church or churches and was organized and paid for by *irmandades* (Catholic brotherhoods or sisterhoods) affiliated with the saint. Each festival relied on official Catholic liturgy, involved a major public procession, and was accompanied by several days of loosely organized festivities in the street or the church square.

The origins of Salvador's public festivals dated back to Brazil's Portuguese colonial heritage and reveal something of the social and political roles of religion during the early modern colonial enterprise. For instance, Our Lady of the Immaculate Conception (Nossa Senora da Conceição da Praia) was one of the first saints to be identified with Salvador. Within a century, in 1646, King John IV of Portugal proclaimed Our Lady of the Immaculate Conception to be Portugal's patron saint, further cementing spiritual and administrative links between the colony and the motherland. For Salvadorans, Our Lady of the Immaculate Conception came to be known as the patroness, or *padroeira*, of Salvador's lower city and eventually of the entire city. The Church of Our Lady of the Immaculate Conception was erected in the lower city next to bustling ports, markets, and the city's business district, where it took on the role of protector of the activity of the city's merchant sector and later of the business of finance, import, and especially export. In the 1930s the church was still situated almost on the beach itself (before land-filling schemes widened the distance between it and the rocks and sand of the shoreline) and consequently played host to all manner of requests to the *padroeira* for bountiful fishing and a brisk day's market trading or for a good cocoa crop to arrive from the interior of the state to process and sell (in Europe or West Africa) or perhaps even for advantageous terms of trade for imports and exports.

Another example of transplanting Iberian festival traditions in Salvador is the migration of the cult of the Senhor do Bonfim. This occurred in the 1740s, when Theodósio Rodrigues de Faria, a high-ranking Portuguese naval officer, brought an image of the crucifixion from Lisbon to

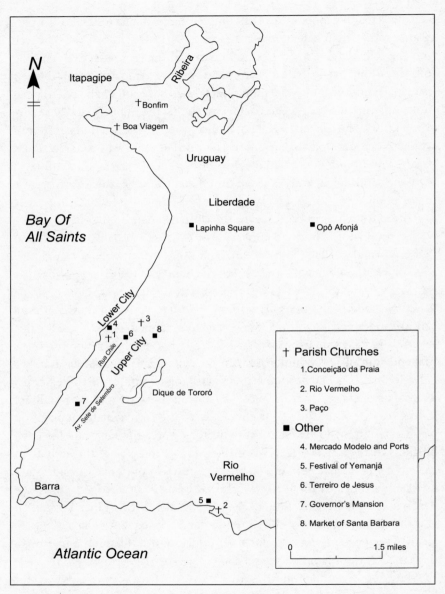

Map 3.1. Map of Salvador and locations of churches, festivals, and neighborhoods.
Credit: Laurie Andrews.

Salvador, which at the time was Brazil's colonial capital. The image of Christ Crucified must have resonated powerfully in the colonial setting, because finances were forthcoming and construction of a chapel to house the image commenced almost immediately. Within ten years, a lay brotherhood founded by Rodrigues de Faria celebrated the completion of the chapel. The brotherhood also constructed a public square and various residences and laid out the direct-approach road from the main city to the chapel, the Avenida Bonfim. Situated as it was on the only elevated bit of land on the Peninsula of Itapagipe, it was readily seen by ships in the bay, and the Lay Brotherhood of Bonfim had devotees among sailors and fishermen. But it drew its main support largely from Salvador's middle sectors, among which Rodrigues de Faria himself could be counted. Eventually, a washing of the chapel originated as an expression of devotion or gratitude, stemming from Portuguese and Brazilian customs of washing churches in the days leading up to the days of festivity. The ritual was to be performed on the holy day of Our Lord of the Good End, or the Senhor do Bonfim, and at some point in the nineteenth century the washing attracted the Candomblé devotees of Oxalá.[4] The ritual procession and washing of Bonfim, then, were products of transplanted Iberian Catholicism that were blended with local customs and circumstances. Salvador's other major and minor public festivals have similar histories.

Establishing the dates and the manner in which African and African-Bahian practices became a part of the popular Catholic practices associated with these religious festivals is a tricky task due to the incomplete nature of the sources. However, studies of African-Bahian religions in colonial and nineteenth-century Salvador reveal that this syncretism was a widespread phenomenon.[5] In addition, Africans and their descendants relied on their *terreiros* to develop their own public rituals in which the emphasis was on the African-Bahian *orixá*. Because most *orixás* were already associated with a Catholic analogue, the Catholic festivities of the dominant class provided opportunities for syncretic rituals. The Senhor do Bonfim, for instance, was associated with Oxalá (the Yoruban deity of creation) because of the comparable positions of the two entities within their respective cosmological hierarchies. For the Candomblé community, the washing resonated with aspects of the mytho-history of Oxalá. The location of the Church of Nosso Senhor do Bonfim, on a small hill above low-lying wetlands, fit the profile of Oxalá's residence, while parables emphasizing the role of water to Oxalá's mytho-history coincided with the Portuguese tradition of washing churches in the days leading up to the annual festival. Candomblé *terreiros* also had their own ritual obligations to Oxalá—called the Waters of Oxalá—that involved metaphorical and actual cleansings.[6] Two other such occurrences involving various degrees of syncretism were the celebrations for Iansã (the Yoruban deity of fertility and violent weather—lightning and strong winds) during the festivals of Santa Barbara (a saint associated with storms and protection from storms) and the celebrations for Yemanjá (the Yoruba deity of motherhood and the sea, associated with all variations of the Virgin Mary) during the celebrations of the Festival of Rio Vermelho.

Prior to 1930 and even into the early 1930s the city's festivals seemed to have been "in decline," to use the language of contemporary newspapers.[7] Gauging by the number of participants, the limited number of scheduled events and related activities, the lesser degree of public subsidy, and even the paucity of press coverage, it seems that this observation was accurate and not just a case of journalistic melodrama. One contributing factor was likely to have been the poor economic climate after 1929, although the journalists and folklorists from the 1940s and 1950s stated that the decline of the festivals had been occurring prior to the economic downturn. In the view of these writers, the festivals were suffering because "modernity and progress" were wiping out their traditional aspects. The newspapers pointed out that much of the revelry in the early 1930s had moved out of the streets, giving way to dances at elegant social clubs and recreational societies (*sociedades recreativas*).[8] But it is not clear if this was a cause of the overall decline or a consequence of it.

It is easier to construe what led to a revival of Salvador's public festivals toward the end of the 1930s, although the revival seems to have left out a number of the more colorful features of early-twentieth-century festivals described by João da Silva Campos—women throwing flowers from second-story windows during processions, for instance, or children dressing as angels.[9] One important factor in the revival was the encouragement the festivals received from political figures at the municipality and state levels, not least in the form of greater public subsidies that seemed, with a few exceptions, to increase annually. Moreover, the enthusiasm with which the press covered the festivals grew each year: The short notices of the early 1930s gave way by the 1950s to entire front-page spreads with photos and numerous supplemental pieces and lead-up coverage that began days if not weeks before the events. This was partly in response to the zeal of both the revelers and the politicians and was part of a wider process of maturation and consolidation of Brazil's radio and newspaper media outlets.

Media coverage of course fed the growth of the festivals and probably sometimes exaggerated their size or the degree of public enthusiasm. At times it is difficult to know for certain whether a festival had grown from year to year or if only the manner or focus of the reporting had changed. It is also difficult based on newspaper coverage to distinguish between increased participation in the Catholic processions and increased participation in the street festivities. Nevertheless, the street festivals seemed to grow larger and feed off the proliferation of carnivalesque revelry, as carnival music and associated behaviors were increasingly a part of certain festivals. Newspaper coverage of the Festival of Our Lord of the Navigators and the Festival of Rio Vermelho suggests that the carnivalesque was taking over popular space traditionally given over to other forms of festive ritual. Perhaps this is what commentators were referring to when they decried the loss of "traditional" forms giving way to the "modern." The revival of the festivals seems after the 1930s to have been driven by a combination of mass media coverage, political and even commercial imperatives, and the spiritual dedication and initiative of local people. Yet during these changes, religious devotion remained central to the experience.

A cautious assessment of the festivals after 1930 shows that almost certainly there was a revival of a number of festivals and that the size, scope, and importance of these festivals grew impressively in significant ways. As João da Silva Campos wrote in 1940, "The best attended and most enthusiastic disembarking [of Our Lord of the Navigators] of recent times occurred in 1937."[10] All major aspects of the festivals experienced this dramatic growth, including the formal public and performative aspects of the festivals, such as the processions, the Candomblé-related activities, and the informal street parties and celebrations. The two key phases of growth were in the mid- to late 1930s and then again in the late 1940s and early 1950s, with a lull during World War II (especially from 1943 to 1945). For example, the festival of Nosso Senhor do Bonfim grew in important ways after the revival in 1937 as the hybrid ritual Washing of Bonfim became fully absorbed as the climactic moment. Subsequently, a second period of consolidation and growth of the Festival of Bonfim took place in the early 1950s, after another brief ban on the ritual washing was lifted.[11]

Demographic growth after 1940 and even increased private incentive played important roles in the revival and overall growth of the festivals. As the midcentury approached, Salvador's city center and particularly its outlying suburbs grew rapidly, largely due to in-migration from the countryside (at an estimated rate of fifteen thousand per year by 1950).[12] These outlying neighborhoods began to hold their own festival commemorations in the local squares or principal streets, sending announcements to the newspapers and holding competitions to attract the more established musical groups of the various genres that were popular during festivals. These commemorations were often organized by a neighborhood sports club or social club. The organizers, eager for their neighborhood to participate in the devotion and festivity and keen to attract revelers to local commercial establishments, typically offered medals and even cash prizes to the best performers, and some eventually offered small subsidies to any group of organized revelers or musicians who showed up. This facilitated the emergence of newer, probably younger musical performers and groups from the neighborhoods with higher population growth, both middle and working class.

The Brotas district, for example, grew quickly after the extension of a streetcar line, and by 1950 it had begun to compete for several of Salvador's most popular bands to perform at their local commemorations on a stage along Rua Padre Daniel Lisboa, under the auspices of the Pirajá Athletic Club.[13] In addition to Brotas, other neighborhoods such as that of Ribeira, Liberdade, Massaranduba, and Tororó, as well as the area around the centrally located plaza, the Terreiro de Jesus, were increasingly mentioned as sites of organized commemorations for the city's festivals. Further stimulation for growth came from the directors of local community groups. The Society for the Progress of Mont'Serrat (Sociedade Beneficente Progresso de Mont'Serrat), for instance, provided a stage and space for games and food and drink, most likely for the new middle class that was passing the summer at or settling on this part of the peninsula. Similar points can be made about the Festivals of Our Lord of the Navigators and Boa Viagem, which were celebrated (largely) in the neighborhoods on the Peninsula of Itapagipe and were undoubtedly growing after 1940, not least due to population growth on the peninsula since the 1920s. Members of the middle class had bought or built homes along the Avenida Luís Tarquinho, which ran parallel to the peninsula's beaches. Additionally, much of Salvador's industry was increasingly located on the peninsula, and working-class families were populating the neighborhoods farther in from the beaches, such as Massaranduba and Uruguay.[14] Finally, workers and rural migrants began a series of land invasions on the peninsula beginning in 1946 that added to the swelling of the local population. As the city's population growth after 1940 began to enlarge working-class neighborhoods, Salvador's popular festivals experienced a commensurate growth not only in numbers but also in an accentuation of their working-class character.

The Festivals: The Sacred and the Profane

As the city's festivals revived in the 1930s, they retained their characteristic hybridity. The festivals continued to exhibit what journalists repeatedly celebrated as their sacred and profane qualities. "Sacred" in this context referred to the aspects of the festivals that derived from Catholic traditions and liturgy, such as the novenas, the masses, and the processions, while "profane" referred to the festivities in the streets and squares that accompanied the festivals. The latter word was also used to refer to the Candomblé-related aspects of the festivals.[15] This section will describe these aspects in some detail, emphasizing the importance of subaltern agency in shaping the content, form, and meanings of these public ritual events.

Each of Salvador's major festivals centered on public processions that led to their climactic moment. Special committees were convened to organize the processions that typically consisted of the parish priest and individuals from the lay brotherhoods or sisterhoods associated with the specific church. After a series of *novenas*, or devotions, that began nine days earlier, a steady flow of worshippers, penitents, bequests, and requests built to a climax on the final day. The brotherhoods, sisterhoods, and parishioners took charge of decorating the churches—"with enthusiasm and contrition"—and preparing them for the visits of the praying devotees. During the Festival of Our Lady of Conceição da Praia, on the morning of the procession, masses were said at 4:00 a.m., at 5:00 a.m., and then every half-hour until high mass at 10:00 a.m.[16]

The procession itself began at 4:00 p.m. on the eighth of December, when the sun was well past its zenith. An image of Our Lady of Conceição da Praia was paraded throughout the commercial district along a route mapped out in advance. In the late 1940s, Danish travel writer Hakon Mielche wrote that it was a

> wonderful sight to see Nossa Senhora come out of her church borne on the shoulders of eight of the town's stoutest citizens . . . decked in her finest garments in honor of the day. Her crown of pure gold had been fetched from its secret repository . . . her shoulders were draped with a dark-blue cloak of velvet sprinkled with diamonds.

The procession was headed by

> priests in scarlet capes and choirboys in white embroidered smocks. Holy water had been sprinkled on all sides, and the whole procession stopped every other minute so the people in the streets could get

the full benefit of Nossa Senhora's blessing. . . . Nuns, monks, school children in uniform, the fire brigade in full gala uniform . . . the civic authorities in their Sunday best with lace scarves over their shoulders and backs [were all in attendance] . . . and along the pavements stood the people . . . to pay homage.

As the procession returned to the church ninety minutes later, the "sunset was glowing over the centuries-old steps. Priests came out with flickering candles screened against the evening breeze from the bay." Violin music sounded from inside the church and a final blessing was pronounced. "One after the other the doors of the church were closed and from its belfry the bells rang their evensong." This ceremony concluded more than a week of Salvadorans paying their respects, requesting favors, or fulfilling vows of pilgrimage to the Virgin.[17] This was the general pattern of all the Catholic processions at the heart of each of the city's popular festivals.

Most of the city's popular festivals were also celebrated by the adherents of Candomblé. These "profane" aspects of the festivals were central to the wider cosmological world and annual ritual calendar of the Candomblé community. As described in the previous chapter, the Candomblé community was involved in the revival of the Washing of Bonfim in 1937. The Candomblé community, however, did not take this collective success for granted. They marshaled a significant amount of initiative and organizational energy to keep the pressure on the Catholic Church to continue to waive the ban on the washing ritual. In 1941, for instance, in the midst of the Festival of Senhor do Bonfim, the *Diário da Bahia* ran an article praising the work of Antônio Monteiro, Miguel Santana, and Edmundo Almeida for their efforts in mobilizing the Candomblé community and the broader public in support of the washing. Miguel Santana, it was mentioned, had also been the president of the Washing of Bonfim's organizing committee in 1939 and 1940. The paper also ran a staged group photo of Baianas "from the *terreiros* Gomeia, Cruz do Cosme, and São Caetano" posing on the front steps of the Church of Nosso Senhor do Bonfim and carried photos of that year's "Beauty Queens" chosen from the Baianas, known by the Afrocentric title of "Taitús" after the Ethiopian Empress Taytu Betul (ca. 1851–1918). The photographs and captions and the tenor of the article were very much an homage to the central role played by the Baianas as women of Oxalá. These photos help us appreciate how the agency and initiative of the Candomblé community was essential to the discursive reworking of regional identity after 1930.[18] Others from within the Candomblé community who were notable for their efforts during this period were Jorge Manoel da Rocha, an *ogan* of Opô Afonjá, and João da Gomeia (Joãosinho), a young *pai-de-santo* in charge of one of Salvador's more visible *terreiros*, both of whom actively recruited and organized Baianas to participate in the Washing of Bonfim.[19]

The Washing of Bonfim, however, was only one of a number of examples of Salvador's African-Bahian public ritual traditions. Just as the Festival of Conceição da Praia marked the beginning of Catholic Salvador's summer cycle of popular festivals, it also marked an increase in the ritual activity of the various temples of Candomblé dotted around the capital. During the period of Catholic novenas for Our Lady of Conceição da Praia, the Candomblé community also danced, sang, and completed their *obrigações,* or ritual obligations, to Yemanjá, who was associated with Our Lady of Conceição da Praia. According to information provided by Melville and Frances Herskovits, during the week of the festival of Conceição da Praia, the police granted thirteen licenses to temples of Candomblé to play drums during ritual celebrations. Eleven of the thirteen licenses were specifically for 7 December, which fell on a Sunday in 1941.[20] Many other temples had unlicensed ceremonies, several of which the Herskovitses attended, but in place of the drumming, the celebrants accompanied the rituals and dancing with singing, handclapping, and the playing of lesser percussion instruments such as calabashes and *agogôs* (cowbell-like instruments). In general, the drumming was not exclusively or even primarily for Yemanjá but varied for different deities depending on the obligations of each *terreiro* and the particular dynamics of the evening.[21] The exact night of the major Candomblé celebrations for Yemanjá varied from year to year, but as in 1941, most temples probably celebrated the night before the major Catholic procession on 8 December. This was what the Herskovitses observed in 1941; their field notes mention that the 4:00 a.m. mass was popular with the *filhas-de-santo* of Candomblé, who went to church straight from the previous night's ceremonies at the *terreiros*, still clad in their ceremonial finery, emphasizing the overlap between the ritual worlds of Candomblé and Catholicism. The chilly 4:00 a.m. service was preferred mostly by women who lived or worked locally and later in the day faced the daily round of earning a living, minding children, and doing housework.[22] Women for whom distance or finances precluded a trip to the Church of Nossa Senhora da Conceição da Praia in the center of town could still participate in the day's observances, as most of the churches in working-class parishes also held services on 8 December.

The entire first week of December was a busy one for popular religion in Salvador's working-class community. On the night of the fourth of December, there were many smaller commemorations, or *obrigações*, for Santa Barbara, who was associated with the Candomblé deity, Iansã. In addition to services at the principal *terreiros*, many gatherings took place in private homes. These events involved the preparation of specific *comida-de-santo* (holy food) for Iansã. Friends, relatives, and neighbors arrived throughout the evening with various offerings for the table and for the *orixá* (who needed energy to grant requests). These events, which were characterized by conversation, news and gossip, and, later in the evening, ritual dancing or samba, illustrate how Candomblé-related practices were diffused across the festive social fabric of Salvador.[23] On the morning of 4 December, many from the community would participate in the smaller procession that paraded the statue of Santa Barbara between the working-class market on Baixa dos Sapateiros street and the Paço Church (there was no church of Santa Barbara in Salvador). The square at the Paço Church was decorated with leaves from palm and pitanga trees. Santa Barbara did have her own market, however. The market on Baixa dos Sapateiros was called the Market of Santa Barbara, and Santa Barbara was an important saint for the men and women who worked the market stalls. The procession was accompanied by the band of the Fire Department, due to the fact that Santa Barbara was also the patron saint of firemen.

By the 1930s the public celebrations for Iansã at the marketplace were enjoying a notable degree of popularity. That they were thriving well into the twentieth century was due to the efforts of a *mãe-de-santo* named Balbina, who reportedly died in 1900. According to an article in *Estado da Bahia*, Balbina sold merchandise at the old Santa Barbara market before it was relocated to Baixa dos Sapateiros. She had generated a wave of enthusiasm within the market for devotion to Iansã. When the entire market was relocated in the late nineteenth century because of a fire, the new landlord offered Balbina a stall rent free. The article suggests that the landlord did so to support the collection of small donations for Iansã. These donations would go toward the festive offerings to the *orixá*, including no doubt the plates of the African-Bahian *caruru* (okra stew) that were the designated holy food for Iansã. Several decades later in the 1930s and 1940s, and perhaps not coincidentally, the Catholic saint's day of Santa Barbara along Baixa dos Sapateiros had become a public celebration for the Candomblé *orixá* Iansã. The epicenter of the festivities was the marketplace, especially the fish section, as Iansã was a patron saint of fishermen.[24]

Meanwhile, the more traditional Catholic emphasis within the festival continued in a church in the old commercial district. In 1951, *Estado da Bahia* applauded the efforts of Conego Manuel Barbosa and over twenty "society girls" to restore the formal Catholic aspects of the Festival of Santa Barbara. Was this a reaction to the popular Catholic and Candomblé character of the festivities in the market and along the Baixa dos Sapateiros? Either way, these were clearly parallel festivals, albeit with perhaps some overlap of attendees. The events in the commercial district were not likely to have rivaled their more working-class counterparts for enthusiasm for Iansã or its displays of samba and capoeira.[25] The parallel festivities for Santa Barbara clearly illustrate the degree to which Bahians from various socioeconomic groups and subcultures contributed to both the sacred and the profane aspects of the city's popular religious festivals.

The spread of the commemorations for Iansã within the Festival of Santa Barbara foreshadowed changes within the Candomblé community, particularly after 1930. Vivaldo da Costa Lima and others have written of the politicization of the *terreiros* during this period and their public "defense of their cultural identity."[26] Candomblé leaders reached out to allies and patrons outside their religious community, patrons whose positions in the dominant culture lent support and legitimacy to the *terreiros*' right to practice their beliefs. Of course, potential allies outside the Candomblé community had to be willing to be patrons. By the 1940s, Salvador boasted over one hundred *terreiros* dotted across the urban landscape. Moreover, enterprising young *mães-de-santo* and *pais-de-santo* constructed new *terreiros* during this decade on land bought in the city's expanding suburbs. These institutions became important community centers—at times the only community centers.[27] North American sociologist E. Franklin Frazier observed after a visit to Bahian in 1940 that "the Candomblé is not only a center for religious festival and worship; it is also the center of the social life of the neighborhood in which it is located."[28] This role of the *terreiros* reached well beyond their more committed members. As Edison Carneiro observed regarding the pervasiveness of Candomblé within Salvador's working class in the 1930s, even those who were not practicing members of *terreiros* "have a general idea of what's to be done or of who can do it for them, as they are all related to somebody connected with Candomblé."[29]

On 9 December 1941, four days after the celebrations and commemorations for Santa Barbara and Iansã, the processional rituals of official Catholicism for Our Lady of Conceição da Praia on the Bay of All Saints gave way to a processional ritual devoted to the Candomblé *orixá* Yemanjá.

Fortunately, the Herskovitses were on hand to witness one of Salvador's more dramatic popular religious spectacles and left an account in their field notes, as the Bahian press was silent on this waterborne tradition of Salvador's *povo-de-santo*. When the Herskovitses arrived in the commercial district of Salvador in the lower city, the square in front of the Church of Nossa Senhora da Conceição da Praia was full of empty booths from the previous days' festivities, "but under a tree at the corner nearest the market were the group playing drums and dancing batucada [here, any general festivity involving drums]. There were two barrel-drums, with snake-skin heads played with one hand and one drum-stick; three or four miniature barrel-drums . . . [and] a tambourine, which was very important." A crowd had gathered to watch, and left "little space for the dancers." From there, the Herskovitses proceeded to the market building where fish were sold. Here many more people had gathered to wait for the ceremonies to begin. The Herskovitses emphasized the extent to which the Candomblé community was present, as among those "standing about, or sitting, waiting, and listening to the batucadas," many of the women "wore the Bahiana [sic] costume, and many were obviously *feitas* [Candomblé initiates]." Most of the important *mães-de-santo* and *pais-de-santo* were present. Typical of these events, judging from later reports in the newspapers about a similar festival in early February, music and dancing were the main attraction either side of the waterborne procession. The Herskovitses wrote that "people were enjoying the batucada play enormously, especially since most [of] the dancing was being done by the old people. One old man was an especially fine dancer, and got repeated cheers, while an elderly and very fat woman brought down the house with her suggestive flipping of the voluminous skirts she wore."[30]

The ceremonial procession for Yemanjá consisted of a small fleet of sailing and fishing vessels that sailed out into the Bay of All Saints to leave presents for Yemanjá on the waves.[31] The initiated female members (*feitas*) of the participating Candomblé temples prepared the offerings ritually in a secluded food stall left empty after the festival of Conceição da Praia, amassing them alongside an ornately decorated vase of flowers. "Gifts included soap, perfume, mirrors, ribbons, bits of silk, combs, barrettes, and other things that would please a woman accustomed to giving much time to her toilette. The job of preparing this jar took about 20 minutes, and it was almost 4 o'clock [in the afternoon] when the *mãe-de-santo* carrying it retraced her steps to the market building, again followed by a crowd."[32]

The Herskovitses were guests of honor of a sort and had places in the principal boat, which was carrying the offering. This was a boat of a very successful master fisherman who was very high up within the Candomblé community.[33] The Herskovitses' account emphasizes the size of the event, stating that "the railings of the embankment about this inner harbor were black with people—there must have been several thousand." Beyond this "at least 500 people participated in the ceremony out in the bay" on the sixteen or so sailboats that constituted the procession. Overloading the boats was enough of a concern that a policeman (of the Guardia Civil) "ordered a few people into another boat to prevent overcrowding." This single policeman accompanied the procession out and back.

The field notes of the Herskovitses reveal aspects of the sacred nature of the event:

> Running before the wind, we sailed out into the outer harbor, past the breakwater and into the bay—we must have gone 10 miles or more, before the captain of our boat . . . a *pai-de-santo* . . . reached the spot where he thought the offering should be given. All the way out the drums (batucada) played and ritual songs were sung. . . .
>
> One *mãe-de-santo* got quietly possessed. She was near the bow of the boat, and sat back, her eyes half-closed, head lolling from side to side, with the familiar twitching of the neck and shoulder muscles. Farther toward the stern, a woman in Bahiana costume got quite happy, but never went completely under; none of the men (who were much in the majority) got the slightest possession, though one [of] them simulated it, in fun, much to the enjoyment of the others.
>
> At about 4:50 we pulled about, and waited for the following boats to reach us; then, when we were at the proper spot, over went the jar, the flowers floating a few moments before they, too, sank—a good omen. There were great shouts from everyone, and the race for home began. The singing became much louder, the gift had been accepted and everyone was happy. . . . We got ashore at 6:15, and as we went to our car could hear the batucada going strong inside the packed fishmarket, and could see the ring about the dancers.[34]

This offering to Yemanjá in early December was not the only one of its kind in Salvador. The extent of Candomblé worship alongside or in the context of Salvador's ostensibly Catholic festivals can be illustrated through a brief description of another waterborne ritual procession. This procession occurred during the Festival of the Our Lord of the Navigators (known alternatively in Portuguese as the Senhor dos Navegantes, or Nosso Senhor da Boa Viagem, Boa Viagem being the name of the neighborhood and the host church for the likeness of the Our Lord of the Navigators). The annual festival occurred on the thirty-first of December as the *imagem* (carved likeness), in this case of the Our Lord of the Navigators, was transported by a special vessel (called a *galeota*) from the Church of Boa Viagem (located on the coast on the Peninsula of Itapagipe) to the principal small vessel ports of Cayrú in the commercial district of the lower city. There it was greeted by "a great number of the faithful," politicians, church leaders, and the image of Our Lady of Conceição, who had "hosted" the Our Lord of the Navigators overnight in the Church of Nossa Senhora da Conceição da Praia. Meanwhile, the area around the docks and the Church of Boa Viagem hosted public festivals, decorated with paper streamers and flags, leaves of the pitanga tree, and an enormous cross erected on the principal dock. For nearly forty-eight hours most commercial activity around the docks ceased.[35]

The next morning, at ten o'clock on New Year's Day, a crowd gathered to attend a formal ceremony marking the beginning of the image's return trip to Boa Viagem aboard the *galeota*, called *Gratitude of the People* (*Gratidão do Povo*). This took place only after the image had sailed off in the opposite direction to the mouth of the bay at Barra before retracing its route back to its starting point at Boa Viagem. This day's events were known as the Festival of Boa Viagem. During the Estado Novo, a tradition of unfurling the national flag began (or was revived). Civil, military, and ecclesiastical authorities attended the embarkation ceremony, which was overseen by the mayor. The local *irmandades*, or lay brotherhoods, and sailors and fishermen and others who earned their living on the bay were much in evidence. Many who earned their living on the water belonged to the Candomblé community and had already paid homage to the *santo* by contributing flowers to the elaborate headpiece that had adorned the vessel while it was hosted overnight in one of the port's warehouses. There were also "many *filhos-de-santo* about" as "the images [of both Our Lady of Conceição and the Our Lord of the Navigators] were brought out of the church in procession." The port was filled with sailboats, "most of them full of people, singing to the beating of drums."[36]

According to the Herskovitses, "several thousand people" witnessed the embarkation, some having come straight from the New Year's Eve festivities of the previous night, fortified by cups of sweet manioc, corn, or tapioca drinks that were sold hot out of kettles by women on the principal streets of residential areas, accompanied by a slice of cassava cake or hominy cake.

Figure 3.1. The *galeota* with the image of Nosso Senhor dos Navegantes arrives at the beach of Boa Viagem, 1 January 1948. In the background the procession over the water begins to break up. Photo by Pierre Verger. By permission of the Fundação Pierre Verger. © Fundação Pierre Verger

One of the Herskovitses recorded that "as the boats sailed off . . . I counted over 125 of them—all packed, plus two larger steam vessels, a number of launches, a four, and two eight-oared shells, all very gay in their decorations."[37] Although during the early 1940s newspapers reported on the maritime ritual in only the barest of detail, the Herskovitses' description and comments reveal that the general organization and intent of this procession made it a Candomblé ceremony within or alongside a Catholic one. For instance, the same master fisherman and Candomblé figure who took the Herskovitses onto the bay during the offerings to Yemanjá in early December and was involved in this procession offered to take them out again during the Festival of Boa Viagem (although this time they declined). The role of Candomblé is further suggested by the drumming that accompanied the waterborne procession, although part of this drumming was part of a festive tradition of samba that took place aboard the boats. According to Jorge Alberto, who reported on the procession in 1953 for the magazine *Última Hora*, *atabaque* drumming alternated with religious songs and string instruments. Alberto pointed out that the majority of those participating in the Festa do Senhor dos Navegantes "adored" Yemanjá, who, as the "Mother of the Water," was the Candomblé protectress of those who made a living from the sea. For these stevedores, sailors, and fishermen, the waterborne procession was as much for Yemanjá as it was for the Our Lord of the Navigators. The stevedores were particularly well known for their ties to the Candomblé community.[38]

The return trip to Boa Viagem generally took all day. By the evening, Boa Viagem Square was full of revelers. The newspapers from the mid-1930s reported that the size of the festivities on the strip of beaches along the peninsula grew each year. The image of the Our Lord of the Navigators was disembarked on the beach and paraded to its reinstallation in the Church of Boa Viagem, signaling that the festivities would be approaching the final phase around the time of midnight mass.[39] The festivities back in the lower city near the ports typically went on until the next day. There, the festival involved over forty-eight hours of "batucadas, rodas de samba and much animation sustained by the sugar cane alcohol (*branquinha*) of the dockworkers."[40]

Last but not least, a third waterborne procession took place on February second during the Festival of Rio Vermelho.[41] This procession was entirely the work of the community of Candomblé and was inspired by the spiritual and occupational needs of the local fishermen. The Herskovitses recorded that in 1942, several thousand people watched as the *mães-de-santo* and *filhas-de-santo* led the ceremonies to the sounds of drumming, hymns, and the background sounds of carnivalesque revelry. An enormous volume of presents for Yemanjá was collected—"flowers, and perfume, and combs, and other things vain ladies like." The collection was taken on board the principal sailboat, and a fleet of sailboats and rafts "looking as though they would capsize any moment" took the offering out to sea. If the presents sank, and they almost always did, Yemanjá had accepted them. The gratification of her vanity portended good things for fishermen especially but also for those seeking success in other areas of life.[42]

These examples from the city's major festivals show the variety and extent of popular festive life in Salvador and how these festivals were marked by both sacred, Catholic components and profane, Candomblé-related aspects. A close look at the anatomy of the events suggests an impressive degree of initiative and organizational capacity on the part of members of the Candomblé community in Salvador, who, taken together, were a formidable influence on the festivities in the streets and public squares of the city during the years 1930 to 1954. Their insistence on including and performing their own rituals and related cultural practices reveals their belief in the legitimacy of their African-Bahian identity. Beyond this, their efforts certainly made significant contributions to shaping the meanings of these events as part of a broader reconstruction of the overall meaning of being Bahian.

Festivities in the Public Squares

There was another set of events, behaviors, and performative rituals beyond the Catholic- and Candomblé-informed processions that provided opportunities for working-class African Bahians to express their culture. These were the Festas de Largo, ongoing, generalized popular festivities that took place next to churches. These informal street festivities almost always began in the days leading up to the procession, paralleling or accompanying the novenas within the churches and the Candomblé preparations. These gatherings grew more animated once the processions had finished. In the *largos* of the churches, enterprising Salvadorans set up *barracas* (temporary stalls or booths) where they sold drinks, food, and ices, while other stalls or kiosks raised funds for the lay brotherhoods or sisterhoods. The food and drink sold in the *largos* during the festivities was something people looked forward to and were a common topic of conversation. A multitude of local fruits—pineapples, mangos, and oranges—was available for sale, owing to the fact that many of the festivals coincided with the fruiting season, which spoke to the longstanding connection of urban traditions to agricultural cycles throughout Brazil. As Raul Lody has emphasized, the food sold at the Festas de Largo added to what was already a sensual experience, combining with the drink, the heat, the music, the smells, the press of bodies, the dancing, the flirting, and the camaraderie or enmity. Taken together, the festival experience inscribed itself on peoples' bodies. Serra calls attention to the theatric aspects of these public moments, when individuals simultaneously played the roles of actor (or participant), audience member, and stagehand.[43]

Largely working-class and lower-middle-class men and women, most of whom were African Bahians, worked the booths as small entrepreneurs.[44] Many of the owners of the *barracas* set out tables and chairs for their customers, giving the *largo* an informal air while adding to the crowdedness and seeming muddle of the scene. Many vendors sold "traditional" Bahian fare cooked over kerosene burners and very West African in influence— deep-fried black-eyed-pea fritters or *acarajé*, okra stews, and the spinach-based *efó* all flavored with herbs, greens, peanuts, dried shrimp, seasonings, hot chilies, and/or palm oil. For those whose tastes ran to Portuguese and northeastern Brazilian traditions, specialties such as *sarapatel* (stew made with pig tripe) and *mocotó* (stew made with cow's hooves) were also on offer; *mocotó* was typically sought out after a particularly late night.[45] This festival fare was not taken for granted. Its quality was carefully assessed and debated. Many of the women were regulars and worked hard at winning the loyalty of their clientele with quality food and idiosyncratic touches that set them apart from the competition. Some relied on force of personality, others on attention to detail. Customers chose their favorites. Those without much spending power might save, borrow, or scrounge in preparation for the festivals.[46] Other individuals would help the local businesses near the festivals set up their drinks stalls in exchange for a snack or free beer and easy sociability later in the evening. For men in particular it was important to have at least some purchasing power, especially to be able to buy a meal for a woman. When a person was caught without money, he or she might pretend to have already eaten and certainly had an opinion about the quality of the food.[47]

For the African-Brazilian women of Candomblé (the Baianas) and others, the festival was an opportunity to earn money through catering. The hours were long; the work stretched over the entire week. Mielche was sufficiently impressed to comment on the work that took place before the Festival of Conceição da Praia: "Since early morning worthy Bahian women in their best clothes had been sitting in the shade of the trees down by the harbor busily preparing the sugary cocoa liqueurs and spiced meat balls [*acarajé*, possibly *kibe*], which later in the day they were to sell by the hundreds. . . . Elsewhere men had been busily preparing golden pineapples into juicy slices, peeling sugar-canes and splitting coconuts. Cases of bottled beer and soda water had been piled up in huge stacks." As one Baiana pointed out when asked by a journalist about the festivities, "For me, the festival began days ago. It's this hard work you see here. Selling *caruru, acarajé*."[48] Female family members, especially younger ones, often helped out during the festivals, so it was not unusual to see children sleeping behind the food stalls on mats or whatever was handy. The *barracas* were named after Catholic saints such as "Saint George," "Saint Roch," or "Barraca Saint Benedict," or carried names such as "Faith in God" or the "Just Redeemer." There were also names reflecting the importance of Candomblé, such as "Janaína Lives Forever" or "Goddess of the Sea." Individual owners chose names to honor their personal saints or *orixás*, and they hoped that in so choosing, the saint or *orixá* would offer protection and endorse the business.[49] Calling upon protectors for success was not an idle act, since in 1940 one paper put the costs of keeping a temporary *barraca* in the largo at a significant 80$000 per day.[50] This obviously limited the ownership of *barracas* to those with some access to capital. Most were well-established vendors or had other reliable means of income such as an ongoing business in a street market. Others worked as vendors only during the festival season and were employed in other occupations the rest of the year. These *vendedores ambulantes*, or itinerant peddlers, paid a tax of 11$600 per day that covered the extra expenses of the police and the municipal government.[51]

Evenings and nights were busy times in the *largo* during festivals. Salvadorans—mainly dressed in white—socialized, ate, drank, met friends, and strolled about with family members or a boyfriend or girlfriend. Some played games of chance or took in the displays and amusements that were set up in the *largo*. Wheels of fortune and merry-go-rounds were popular. In 1940, the new attraction was the *roda-gigante,* or Ferris wheel, evidence of the slow but steady progress of the modernization of Salvador's leisure industry. For many festival-goers, the evenings were very much about seeing and being seen. Music featured prominently. From the mid-1930s the lay brotherhoods provided illumination as the festivals continued well into the night and the municipal government provided loudspeakers for music and announcements. Ever present in the streets throughout the period was the dancing and singing to the latest hits and old favorites.

Capoeira and Samba

Capoeira and samba also played important roles in the years 1930 to 1954 in both the politics of ethnicity and the changing definitions of Bahianness. Capoeira was closely associated with the Festival of Conceição da Praia and was practiced just outside the *largo* and sometimes within it.[52] At any time

Figure 3.2. A woman dances in a *roda de samba* in the late 1940s, flanked by musicians and onlookers. Photo by Pierre Verger. By permission of the Fundação Pierre Verger. © Fundação Pierre Verger

of year in the lower city, near the old Mercado Modelo (central market) in particular, men played during the cooler times of day while taking a break from transporting goods at the market or during a lull at the ports.[53] Samba, too, was part of the workday ritual around the Mercado Modelo.[54] That capoeira and samba became prominent features at the Festival of Conceição da Praia stemmed from these already established working-class routines in the lower city. The *rodas* of capoeira during the festivals were an opportunity to perform before large crowds and consequently attracted the best capoeira players from across the city, even from around the wider Bay of All Saints. And the best percussionists came to play the key instruments of the *roda*, especially the *berimbau* and *pandeiro*.[55] The capoeira frequently transformed into *rodas de samba* and back again, depending on the dynamic of the crowd. The players and musicians added to the atmosphere of spontaneity, excitement, fun, and performance around the *largo*.[56] Bahia's autochthonous genre of samba, known as *samba de roda*, in particular allowed working-class women to participate and perform publicly, an activity recalled with fondness and pride by both male and female interviewees.

Although these activities took place during the Festival of Senhor do Bonfim, they were most prominent on the Monday after Bonfim weekend, during the daylong festival known as Segunda-Feira Gorda da Ribeira, or Ribeira Monday, which involved a mini-carnival procession. The samba *rodas* formed away from the main vehicle traffic, but they still attracted many passersby as well as those who actively sought them out. They were often located next to a Baiana with her *tabuleiro* (or tray of food for sale). Musicians played their *pandeiros, violões de doze cordas, atabaques, cuícas,* and *tamborins,* while individuals took turns dancing—performing—within a circle of clapping, laughing, singing, applauding onlookers. The stamina of the crowd and musicians was such that the *pandeiros* (which are similar to tambourines) were said to actually wear out. Male interviewees especially made a point of (re-)telling how a small fire would be made from banana leaves to warm the parchment of the instrument, thus retightening it on its frame.[57]

A focus on capoeira and samba as part of the festivities, however, captures only a small aspect of how deeply these practices were enmeshed within the city's African-Bahian working-class culture. In the case of capoeira this was primarily so within male-dominated occupations, such as that of stevedores or other occupations involving manual labor around the docks. There were a small number of places in the city where capoeira was practiced with some frequency, such as the *rodas* hosted by Mestre Waldemar in the neighborhood of Liberdade or by Mestre Cobrinha Verde in Amaralina and of course near the docks.[58]

While the overlap between the practice of capoeira and the Candomblé community was significant, it was even stronger between the Candomblé community and samba, which was practiced much more extensively than capoeira. Judging from the field notes of Melville and Frances Herskovits for the period November 1941 to May 1942, many of the private commemorations to saints held in homes or the *terreiros* included a samba session. In addition, public ceremonies at the *terreiros* often ended with samba.[59] When outside researchers such as Camargo Guarnieri of the São Paulo Music Library in 1937 or Lorenzo Dow Turner in 1940 wanted to record sambas or popular music, they went to the *terreiros* to record them.[60] There were traditional sambas, quite distinct from commercial sambas, and were written and performed specifically for Catholic saints' days that were also celebrated by the Candomblé community, such as those for the twin saints Cosmas and Damian or for Our Lady of Candeias (who was associated with Oxum within the *terreiros*).[61] Birthday celebrations, baptisms, and weddings created venues for samba or had a samba component. Private commemorations of Catholic saints, too, such as Saint Anthony, were very popular venues for samba.[62] Performing live music, singing, and dancing were more than entertainment for working-class Salvadorans. They were central to African-Bahian culture and to the fabric of African-Bahian working-class sociability.[63]

Salvador and its hinterland had their own urban and rural musical traditions that converged in the capital, which, as the economic hub of the region, drew in people and musical traditions into its orbit.[64] This was especially so around the ports and the Mercado Modelo. Salvador was unconnected to its own hinterland by roads or rail until the 1950s, and the ports were the only serious points of entry and exit. Stevedores, warehousemen, sailors, and fishermen liked their samba, especially in the spring and early summer (and the festivals to their patron saints during these seasons). According to an article in *A Tarde*, every Friday there would be "a samba-ing without end."[65]

In and around the Mercado Modelo a number of Salvador's local samba performers in the 1930s and 1940s engaged one another in musical "duels," composing extemporaneous sambas one after the other. Percussionists and others brought their instruments to this or other known spots or organized gatherings at various points in the city, such as the Largo da Piedade (especially prior to 1932), not just during the festivals.[66] It is likely that the rise of the percussive *batucada* groups during carnival in the late 1930s and 1940s was an excellent encouragement for songwriters, performers, and percussionists, and vice versa. As the *batucadas* were in fact never strictly limited to carnival, or to playing commercial sambas, their relationship to samba lyricists, musicians, and performers remained fertile for much of the year. The diffusion of the emerging samba industry from Rio de Janeiro via the radio was another vector of influence on the different genres of samba in Bahia, providing inspiration and even the promise (rarely actualized) of financial incentive for local talent as well as an extensive repertoire of lyrics, melodies, and rhythms to choose from and recombine.

Local newspapers began encouraging Salvador's local talent with competitions in the mid-1930s. From the late 1920s, locally composed *marchas* (military marches rhythmically adapted for carnival) and samba lyrics were increasingly included in newspapers such as *A Tarde*. These lyrics constituted pioneering references to Candomblé, to people of color (usually the *mulata*), and even to samba itself, as in the lyrics to "Feitiço de Mulatas" ("Candomblé Spell of the Mulatas").[67] In 1935, the first major contest for locally composed *marchas* and sambas was organized by journalists. These were *nossos sambas* (our sambas), and seventeen composers entered the competition (several with multiple entries).[68] Radio stations were a bit slower on the uptake. They were dominated by the productions of the recording industry in Rio de Janeiro, though by the mid-1940s local talent such as Batatinha (Oscar da Penha) and Riachão (Clementino Rodrigues) had broken through and had a consistent radio presence.[69]

Both within the Candomblé community and outside it, capoeira and samba played important roles in establishing a sense of history and shared culture for the African-Bahian working class. This could be particularly so during the popular festivals, but the process extended deeply into everyday life throughout the year. Even though "samba" by the 1940s was quite varied (in particular commercial sambas were in most instances very different from the sambas that were popular among slaves, freed people, and free blacks), there were still very popular subgenres or rhythms that were understood by practitioners to have been "brought over by the Africans."[70] During the Vargas era, various genres of samba in Salvador were a way of celebrating rites of passage and expressing both history and tradition. Samba lyrics were a way of chronicling (and critiquing) the trials and tribulations of being poor or working class in the city and expressing joys, successes, and the values that mattered to at least a subset of African Bahians. Consequently, samba—as actually played and danced by Salvadorans rather than the samba that came from the nation's capital over the radio—was a preeminent feature of African-Bahian working-class sociability.

Conclusion

Salvador's major popular religious festivals clearly underwent a revival during the 1930s, and the degree to which the Candomblé community and its allies insisted on being an explicit and integral part of the festival experience is remarkable. In fact, they were partly responsible for the extent of the revival mentioned by contemporary observers. The initiative, energy, and organization of the Candomblé community—its leaders, its people, and its allies—sustained the Candomblé-related aspects of the festivals, which were part of a larger process of cultural politics and ethnic identity formation. Through their often implicit assertion of equal citizenship within the cultural arena, the Candomblé community influenced the form, content, and meaning of the festival events. For instance, the ritual procession and the Washing of Bonfim in honor of Bahia's "patron saint" were two of the most significant events in the city's annual festival calendar. The waterborne processions for *orixás* were prominent expression of African-Bahian religiosity that involved hundreds of practitioners and were witnessed by thousands. These were all preeminent public occasions for the symbolic negotiation of the content and expression of Bahianness and the social and political meanings of Bahian regional identity. In addition to the religious significance of Catholic and Candomblé worship, the festivals provided excellent venues for more locally circumscribed performative rituals such as capoeira and samba. As such they played important roles for many Salvadorans by contributing to the structuring of community identity. The agency of the Candomblé community was central to Salvadoran festive culture. Through the power of performance, this festive culture both influenced and reflected the increasing acceptance of the city's and region's African-Brazilian cultural heritage as central to notions of Bahianness.

The festivals would continue to play a part in Salvador's cultural politics, contributing to creating the framework for negotiation between the dominant and subordinate class over the degree to which African Bahians would be included as citizens with equal access to cultural as well as political and economic power. The next chapter will examine how members of the dominant class supported and encouraged these efforts after 1930 and, partly responding to pressure from below, brought African-Bahian cultural forms to the fore and associated such practices with Bahianness and Bahian regional identity. Yet these were not the only available readings of the festivals. There were still those who regarded African-Bahian culture as problematic at best. Their attitudes reveal the contested and negotiated nature of the reformulation of Bahian regional identity.

4

⬖ Rituals of Inclusion

▽ Evolving Discourses of Bahianness

⬖

▽

During the time U.S. anthropologists Melville and Frances Herskovits re-searched Salvador's African and African-Bahian religious heritage, from November 1941 to May 1942, they noted the tense atmosphere in the city. The war in Europe dominated the news, Salvadorans were contending with shortages, and Brazil was feeling pressure from both the Allies and the Axis forces to relinquish its neutrality. In addition, the country was four years into Getúlio Vargas's increasingly unpopular dictatorship, the Estado Novo, and Bahia's state legislature had been in recess since 1937. The regime censored the press, harassed the political opposition, and ran the country by decree.

The political situation did not much interest the Herskovitses. They were principally concerned with studying the complex belief systems associated with Candomblé and exploring Candomblé's cultural links to Africa. They needed access to ceremonies and cooperative informants associated with the Candomblé *terreiros*. After 1930, Candomblé community leaders had continued their longstanding practice of courting relationships with out-side patrons, including those who could influence public opinion such as academics and journalists. Yet the political situation had the potential to compromise the Herskovitses work. They were foreigners, Candomblé was still regulated as it had been under Juracy Magalhães, and there was still pressure from the Catholic Church—which supported the dictatorship—to eradicate or restrict popular expressions of Candomblé worship.

In the end none of this affected the Herskovitses' research. They were able to rely on a broad range of informants from within the *terreiros*. In fact, the Estado Novo regime in Salvador facilitated their work. Shortly after they arrived, the interventor's secretary took Melville to one of his first Candomblé ceremonies in an official car (in this case the ceremony was that of João da Gomeia). That first night, with little or no prompting from Herskovits, the government official gave permission for the biggest drums to be played so the full ceremony could unfold. In the end the drums were not actually used. But clearly a pragmatic relationship existed between Vargas's otherwise repressive state and the better-connected *terreiros*.[1] The local press covered the visit of the North American couple under the headline "To Be Heard in Washington [D.C.] the Melodies of the Black Candomblés of Bahia," expressing a degree of pride that "black" Bahian culture was to be validated by members of the cultural intelligentsia in the U.S. capital.[2]

The reception of the Herskovitses in 1941 and the local media support for their "new, original studies" suggest how far the political leadership and the press had come since 1930 in their approach to Candomblé and African-Bahian culture. Salvador's dominant class seemed well aware of the power of the public festivals to transform the city's social structures and cultural values and of the importance of controlling public discourse on the central meanings of the ritual acts. This awareness was not new. In years past, elites had fretted about the revelry associated with the processions, and at least once conservative elite voices had suggested that public celebrations and even the processions should be banned.[3] From the middle to late 1930s, politicians and journalists largely sought different ways to control the meanings of the processions and popular festivals. They had come to embrace both sides of the festivals as vital components of Bahianness, what journalists characterized as the sacred (Catholic) and the profane (Candomblé and/or, street revelry).

Vargas's two principal interventors in Salvador after Juracy Magalhães—Landulfo Alves (1938–42) and Renato Pinto Aleixo (1942–45)—used the festivals as opportunities to marshal political support for their agenda, which, consonant with Estado Novo corporativism, included an obsession with greater social cohesion, especially under Alves and his brother, Secretary of Education and Health Isaías Alves. To this end, the political elite sought, with some success, to harness the pressure from Salvador's African-Bahian working classes while still maintaining the centrality of Catholicism to the dominant culture. In this they were building on Juracy Magalhães's proactive cultural politics and his populist nod to working-class culture. Even though they could not match Magalhães's magnetism and personalist engagement with working-class culture, Alves and Pinto Aleixo contributed to a relatively faceless but no less important institutionalization of government support for African-Bahian culture and the shaping of a more explicitly inclusive Bahian regional identity. After 1945 and the return to democracy in Brazil, Governor Otávio Mangabeira (1947–51) and several elected mayors of Salvador from 1947 to 1955 included the revival of the festivals as part of their agenda to revive the region's economy and restore its pride. This meant increasing financial support for the festivals, albeit slowly, and explicitly relating the festivals to tourism.

The secular press, particularly after 1936, began to use the festivals as opportunities to formulate and disseminate a public discourse of inclusive Bahianness that embraced the city's African-Bahian heritage. Festival reporting became a principal means by which the dominant class sought to shape and maintain a popular consensus on the meanings of the festivals. The degree to which the city's top four newspapers reflected the reigning dominant-class discourse can hardly be overstated. They were effectively political organs, informally (and occasionally formally) affiliated with political factions, political parties, and political candidates. The editors and owners were often politicians or political candidates themselves. This was especially true prior to the intrusion of Assis Chateaubriand's media empire into the Bahian media market in 1938. By the end of World War II, Chateaubriand owned two of Bahia's three largest newspapers. The fourth, the *Diário da Bahia*, was barely circulating. At this point, the "big three," as it were, had grown relatively independent of their editors' political ambitions, although all three were supportive of the political and economic interests of the center right.[4] Moreover, as Paulo Silva Santos relates, nearly every Bahian intellectual, scholar, or man of letters (or woman of letters, in a few cases) spent a significant early part of his or her career as a journalist.[5] This was true of a number of politicians and other public figures as well. For example, Otávio Mangabeira, the old-school patriarch who later became the first elected postwar governor of Bahia started out in journalism as a young man.[6]

This chapter builds on the idea that the newspapers reflected dominant-class positions on African-Bahian practices and argues that the newspapers served as tools or conduits for the self-conscious attempt to transmit these positions and manipulate the social meaning of African-Bahian culture for Bahian society. In this, they were encouraged by changes taking place in the federal capital, Rio de Janeiro (and to lesser extent in São Paulo). Of most relevance for Bahia was the elevation of samba to a central role in Vargas's government-sponsored process of cultural integration for the nation. A subplot within this process from the late 1920s was the increase, especially after 1930, in the number of sambas (penned and recorded in Rio de Janeiro) that embraced elements of African-Bahian culture, such as its cuisine or capoeira. Sambas celebrated the everyday importance of Candomblé for the city's working-class African-Bahian population. Particularly relevant within this context were the early careers of musicians Carmen Miranda and Dorival Caymmi, which fell squarely in the middle of the period 1930 to 1954. The lyrics and performances of Miranda and Caymmi made important contributions to the remaking of Bahia's dominant discourse on African-Bahian culture.

This political and journalistic support, however, was not a wholesale embrace of African-Bahian practices. Occasionally articles or news items that cast African-Bahian traditions in an unfavorable light would appear in the press. Moreover, the newspapers never rejected the Catholic culture of the dominant class, nor did they seek to place the practices of Salvador's working class above or even on an equal footing with those of the city's political elite, the owners and editors of the newspaper, or most journalists. Nevertheless, the shift in the political and media discourses on Salvador's festivals was crucial to reformulating the cultural and political relationship between Salvador's dominant and subordinate classes.

The State Engages Festive Culture

Juracy Magalhães was the first of Getúlio Vargas's appointees to systematically embrace Salvador's popular culture, including African-Bahian culture, to further his—and Vargas's—political agenda. As newspaper coverage of the festivals during his time in office was limited, it is difficult to know how much he was involved with the festivals or if most of his engagement with popular culture occurred apart from them. We can surmise, nonetheless, that Magalhães's posture on popular culture at the very least encouraged organizers and the press to enliven and extend the city's festival culture, even when festivals strayed from or in fact threatened the dominant Catholic Culture. We also know that Magalhães was the honorary president of the Organizing Committee of the Washing of Bonfim, which played a significant role in the reinstatement of the washing ritual.

We know somewhat more about Magalhães's two successors during the period 1937 to 1945, who made a number of appearances at Salvador's major popular festivals and whose regimes were more involved in the events in various ways. Landulfo Alves and Colonel Renato Pinto Aleixo were clearly encouraged by the political culture Vargas had orchestrated to move toward an increasingly populist engagement with the festivals.[7] This would help win popular legitimacy for a regime that in Bahia was initially under siege by local elites for having usurped their political power. The embrace of Bahian traditions may also have been a way of winning over elites and perhaps minimizing elite resistance to the Estado Novo. Landulfo Alves in particular may have emphasized Bahian cultural traditions to partly co-opt the issue of regionalism around which those who opposed Magalhães, and Vargas's agenda of political centralization, had been able to rally.

Part of this agenda included the important early steps toward institutionalizing Salvador's popular culture within a government-sponsored framework, including, for the first time, its African-Bahian traditions. The administration of Interventor Landulfo Alves took up this mission to a significant degree when Alves chose his brother, professor Isaías Alves, to head the Bahian Ministry of Education and Health in 1938. This portfolio included the directorship of the newly formed Bahian Office of Culture and Promotion (Diretoria de Cultura e Divulgação). One of the stated goals of this office, as Anadelia Romo has described in some detail, was "the preservation of the shape and health of Bahian traditions." The office sought to promote Bahian popular culture, too, both within Bahia as "education" and as an attraction for national and international cultural tourists. The Office of Culture and Promotion worked in schools, promoted conferences and lectures, sponsored art exhibitions, and trained journalists. It published an illustrated journal titled *Bahia tradicional e moderna* (Traditional and Modern Bahia) and collaborated with the Touring Clube do Brasil (Touring Club of Brazil) to disseminate its promotional agenda.[8] In the second issue of *Bahia tradicional e moderna* (July 1939), a one-page article, "Bahia Invites You," extolled the attractions of a city that was "day by day becoming a tourist center of universal fame." It noted especially the city's combination of colonial architecture, "modern comforts," and religious festivals. Four photographs accompanied the "invitation": a *roda* of capoeira, Baianas washing the patio of Bonfim Church, the procession of Bonfim, and the maritime procession of Our Lord of the Navigators.[9]

Just how much of this came to fruition or how effective it was will probably remain unknown. What is clear is that the Estado Novo state in Bahia was pushing an agenda of greater acceptance and inclusion of popular and African-Bahian cultural practices. One proposed art exhibition that was intended to present "the most varied aspects of the life of the people" included objects from Candomblé *terreiros* that eventually found space in the permanent collection of the State Museum of Bahia (Museu do Estado da Bahia).[10] The museum itself (founded in 1918) was undergoing an ambitious renewal under Landulfo and Isaías Alves and the museum's new director, José Valladares, who was in charge from 1939 to 1959. Valladares had worked with Gilberto Freyre on the First African Brazilian Congress in Recife in 1934. Almost immediately upon taking up the post he began to revise the mission of the museum to educate visitors about Bahian history and regional identity, play a larger role in Bahia's intellectual circles, and initiate direct contact with the public.[11] Not much is known of the early efforts of Valladares in adding to or reorganizing the collection, but one North American visitor to the museum in the very early 1940s reported the inclusion among its artifacts of the West African–influenced dress and jewelry associated with African-Brazilian women of Candomblé. As Romo points out, this inclusion of Bahia's African heritage alongside Indigenous and Portuguese contributions to the collection fit nicely within the emerging Freyrian discourse on Brazilian national identity as a synthesis of the biology and cultures of Native Brazilians, Africans, and Portuguese. Shaping Bahian identity to include and emphasize elements of African-Bahian culture (even if only as museum pieces) was a way of showing that "Bahian culture was Brazilian culture."[12]

Under Valladares, the State Museum of Bahia also undertook a publication series that sought to further the Estado Novo elite's cultural agenda. The first publication, by Bahian folklorist João da Silva Campos, came out in 1941 and was titled *Procissões tradicionais da Bahia* (Traditional Processions of Bahia).[13] Campos wrote nearly 250 pages covering thirty distinct processions, including several of those analyzed in this chapter and many that were extinct by the 1930s. Significantly, as Romo has pointed out, throughout Campos emphasized the contributions of "the humble classes, blacks and mulattos, freedmen and slaves, artisans, day-laborers, and others" over those of the orthodox Catholic Church.[14] Two years later, still during the Estado Novo, the museum published *Pesquisas etnológicas na Bahia* (*Ethnological Research in Bahia*) by Melville Herskovits, whose work in 1941 and 1942 on Candomblé, acculturation, and African survivals was favored and in small ways was facilitated by the Landulfo Alves government.[15] José Valladares wrote an introduction for the publication that unsurprisingly emphasized the importance of the African-Brazilian experience in Brazil and particularly in Bahia. In 1948 the museum published Edison Carneiro's *Candomblés da Bahia*, an extensive ethnographic treatment of the historical and current state of the African-Bahian religion in Salvador that was written by a well-known advocate of African-Bahian culture in Brazil.[16] Valladares and government institutions continued to play an important role alongside Bahian politicians and public intellectuals in embracing African-Bahian cultural traditions.

Meanwhile, local political elites and civilian notables who supported the regime increased their presence and involvement in the festivals. The mayor of Salvador typically attended a number of festivals annually. The mayor's office provided essential logistical and promotional support that was well publicized and symbolically significant, marking state government as a leading patron of the festivals. Such support suggests the extent to which the dominant political class acknowledged the importance of the festivals as an opportunity to play a greater role in controlling the forms and meanings of the festivals and controlling their contributions to the forms and meanings of *baianidade*. Consequently, the Estado Novo was an important phase in the consolidation of the political relationship between the dominant class—particularly its politicians and media-driven public discourse—and Salvador's popular festive culture. The increasing involvement of the modern state clearly included an acceptance—sometimes explicit, sometimes tacit, and typically qualified, but an acceptance nonetheless—of African-Bahian cultural practices as central to notions of *baianidade*.

The most obvious illustration of these points occurred in the context of the Festival of Bonfim. Interventors Alves and Pinto Aleixo, like their predecessor Juracy Magalhães, were honorary members of the Brotherhood of Bonfim and frequently attended the washing ceremonies. In 1938, for instance, José Luis Barreiros of the organizing committee for the washing ceremony sent a letter to the local newspapers listing fifty-five honorary presidents of the Lay Brotherhood of Bonfim. The list was a partial "who's who" of political elites in Salvador, including the interim interventor, Colonel Fernandes Dantas. Publicizing the oligarchic gravitas behind the reinstatement of the washing ritual was a clever move at a time when opposition to the washing within the Catholic Church was still influential.[17]

Significant political support for the washing continued throughout the Estado Novo. After 1939, Estado Novo officials, including Interventor Landulfo Alves, set a precedent of formally receiving the Baianas as they arrived at the Church of Nosso Senhor do Bonfim, although frequently their wives served as their ambassadors instead. At this point in the ritual, newspaper accounts typically mention the role played by the local political elite and/or their wives, who ceremonially "threw the first barrels of water on the floor of the high altar and applied the first broom strokes," while the majority of those present set about washing or applauding the washing of the front steps and the courtyard of the church.[18] In 1945, a number of Bahia's political and military elite participated in the washing ceremonies to commemorate the anticipated ending of hostilities in Europe. Interventor Pinto Aleixo, Admiral Lemos Bastos, and General Cândido Caldas each attended the washing ceremony, as did the secretaries of public security, education, and health. Throughout the dictatorship, the mayor's office provided the necessary logistical support, which went some way toward sustaining the ritual in the face of continual ecclesiastical censure. The mayor was typically chosen as the official patron. The wives of the topmost political figures of the Estado Novo regime continued to act as official patrons, again making it difficult for the opposition within the Catholic Church to come out against the washing without complicating their relationship with the political regime in power.[19]

Political elite attitudes toward ceremonies such as the Washing of Bonfim fit the wider corporativist social vision of the Estado Novo. They also fit a populist (or protopopulist) streak within Estado Novo political practices. Vargas and his advisors used propaganda and civic ceremonies to create a paternalistic bond between the dictator and working-class Brazilians, a relationship that became increasingly populist leading up to 1945.[20] Reflections of corporativism and touches of populism can also be noted among Vargas's appointed interventors in Bahia since 1930. The importance of the Senhor do Bonfim as Bahia's unofficial patron saint made the Festival of Bonfim especially useful as a public venue in this regard. It provided an opportunity for politicians to embrace a symbolic discourse of social harmony, a moment when "rich and poor," people of "various social classes" and "all colors," were united in their dedication to the saint. Moreover, as Robert Smith notes, in Latin America, the local patron saint implies a direct relationship between community members and the largesse of the saint that was not "mediated by officeholders, either religious or secular."[21] Starting in 1939, Estado Novo politicians and their wives stood at the entrance to the church: the iconographic representations of Our Lord of the Good End in the chapel were behind them and the people in the courtyard were below them. They were symbolically appropriating some of the special power, goodwill, and legitimacy bestowed by the saint, strengthening their social positions through the spectacle of religious commemoration. Ordep Serra is surely right that ritual washings destructure hierarchy and shift some initiative from institutional elites to humble practitioners. The Estado Novo political hierarchy was obviously keen to harness or associate itself with some of that initiative.[22]

The Washing of Bonfim was of course as much a ritual act of Candomblé worship of the *orixá* Oxalá as it was a popular Catholic practice, and this was part of its attraction for the political elite of the Estado Novo. Around 1940, newspapers began celebrating the fact that this festival also brought together the Candomblé community and those who considered themselves strictly Catholic. Although we do not know the interventors' positions on Candomblé in this period, we do know that the level of official persecution of Candomblé dropped off considerably after 1930.[23] By the late 1930s, Candomblé festivities were allowed to take place in Salvador, but the use of drums still required some sort of special dispensation from the police. In 1939, Getúlio Vargas's federal government rather famously issued a decree that prohibited states and municipalities from "establishing, subsidizing, or obstructing the exercise of religious cults."[24] According to oral history within the Candomblé community, the larger temples of Candomblé in Salvador interpreted this decree as protecting their legal right to drum, although in practice the police had final say for many more years. The requirement that *terreiros* obtain police permission to hold ceremonies was not lifted until 1976, although exceptions were made. For example, from 1940 to 1943, when Interventor Pinto Aleixo was still the commander of the Bahian Regional Command, he interceded on behalf of the Gantois *terreiro* so it could use drums.[25] The Estado Novo consolidated the important transition away from the 1920s practice of persecuting Candomblé toward a greater, but not unequivocal, acceptance of the legal right of adherents to practice their rituals, as long as they played by a certain number of rules.

Other festivals reveal how Estado Novo administrators used festive culture to foster social cohesion and political legitimacy. The Festival of Our Lord of the Navigators grew in importance as a populist venue for local politicians, despite concerns in the press that the festival was less "animated" each year. The Herskovitses estimated that "several thousand people" attended the festival in the lower city on New Year's Day in 1942, which does not sound like a festival in obvious decline.[26] In support of the Herskovitses' estimate, newspaper reporting for the 1930s to the 1950s shows a marked growth in attendees at the festival at both ends of the saint's journey.[27] By the early 1950s, newspapers were dedicating most of the front page to the celebrations, and the festival organizers had introduced a second procession in Boa Viagem that passed down the major avenues of the Peninsula de Itapagipe. The increasing popularity of the Festival of Our Lord of the Navigators made it attractive to Estado Novo politicians. After 1938, the newspapers mention the regular presence of the mayor and other high-ranking officials at the opening ceremony in the lower city. Typically these government figures would make speeches and unfurl the Bahian and Brazilian flags. In 1939, the mayor's office donated a Brazilian flag to fly in the bow of the *galeota* that transported the image of Our Lord of the Navigators. This became a new tradition, fusing local and regional celebrations with national identity. The speeches embraced the standard motifs of optimism and best wishes for the New Year for all Bahians and emphasized social unity and class, racial, and cultural harmony and cohesion, implicitly including the practice of Candomblé. During the rest of the year the flag would repose on the high altar in the Church of Our Lady of Conceição da Praia.[28] Through these appearances the Estado Novo regime expropriated some of the popular legitimacy of the festivals and in turn lent an element of significance and sanction and even incentive to the day's events. For instance, a reporter from the *Diário de Notícias* interviewed an older man who was "eating jaca fruit he had bought from a street vendor." This man was in favor of Vargas's interventor, General Renato Pinto Aleixo, because he was "for the people." The man knew this because, among other things, he had seen him in public places, including at the procession of Nossa Senhora da Conceição da Praia.[29]

Both the Washing of Bonfim and the Festival of Conceição da Praia provided venues for the Estado Novo to further demonstrate state paternalism, publicize its social vision, and to nominally present itself as the patron of Bahia's working class. It was under the Alves regime that we see the playing out of a populist turn in the inclusion of workers—qua workers—in the procession to the Church of Nosso Senhor do Bonfim. The press did not make too much of this emphasis on workers, nor do we know for certain if it was at the behest of the government. However, the presence of a category of "workers" cohered with the Estado Novo's emphasis on "representatives of class" taking a visible place in the corporativist social hierarchy.[30] In 1939, for the Festival of Conceição da Praia, Isaías Alves, the state minister for education and health, sponsored an organ concert on the evening of 8 December. The Bahian Department of the Press and Propaganda (Departamento Estadual de Imprensa e Propaganda) also sponsored a novena in 1944. (Novenas were the institutionalized prayers given in the church over the nine days leading up to and including the festival day of the saint.) Several other important figures in the city's commercial trade did the same. Furthermore, in keeping with the Estado Novo emphasis on drawing workers into official and unofficial social institutions and structures of the state, the official novenas of the first of December in 1944 were given over to the laboring class, for the "Night of the Workers." Not to be outdone, the Conceição Factory pursued its own policy of public relations and industrial paternalism by sponsoring the novenas on the seventh of December at the Church of Mares, near where the factory was located.[31]

Broadcasting the novenas of Bonfim was an effective way for the Estado Novo regime to draw Salvadorans and Bahians living beyond the capital into the process of regional and ultimately national integration. From the early 1940s, the mayor's Office of Propaganda and Culture (Diretoria de Cultura e Divulgação) organized and subsidized the broadcasts. Soon they would be broadcast nationally, a step in the process of making the Senhor do Bonfim a national icon, which included the saint's role as *padroeiro* (patron saint) of Brazil's expeditionary forces.[32] The Festival of Senhor do Bonfim contributed to these shifts, as an important factor in Salvador's (increasingly African-Bahian) self-identity and in how this identity was represented to the rest of Brazil. The importance of the regional and (after 1942) national broadcasts of the novenas of Bonfim should not be underestimated in this integrative process, by which African Bahians achieved a growing cultural presence in representations of Bahianness and Bahians achieved a growing presence in the cultural integration of the nation. It probably mattered that the novenas were central to orthodox Catholic practice and distinct from the washing ritual itself, but most of Salvador, and indeed most of Brazil, was increasingly aware that in Bahia, the Senhor do Bonfim was cherished by the large Candomblé community as the *orixá* Oxalá.

As if to emphasize the extent of the integration of Bahia's popular syncretic culture in post–Estado Novo Brazil, Adhemar Barros, the governor-elect of São Paulo, flew to Bahia in 1947 to "repay a promise" to the Senhor do Bonfim for his help in getting him elected. Presumably this was as much for Paulista domestic consumption as it was good Catholic practice. It provides some evidence of the extent and appeal of the Senhor do Bonfim as part of the image of Bahia.[33] Further evidence of the association of the Senhor do Bonfim with African-Bahian working-class culture comes from the number of sambas that reference the saint, some of which were written in Bahia but most of which emanated from the southeast region of the country. In the late 1920s, these references to Bahian spirituality were either neutral or associated solely with Catholicism. By the 1940s, songs such as "E não sou baiano" ("I Am Not Bahian") by Waldemar Ressurreição and "Já voltei da Bahia" ("I Just Got Back from Bahia") by Henrique Almeida and Estanislau Silva established much more explicit associations between the Senhor do Bonfim and Candomblé, although they did not mention the Washing of Bonfim.[34]

When the Estado Novo dictatorship ended in 1945, Bahia embraced democracy with the fervor of the rest of the nation. Part of this was attributable to the excitement of having participated in World War II on the winning side with the major western democracies. This boded well for Brazil's future, and Bahians had their own contributions to make to this transition. In the words of Cláudio Tavares, Salvador's popular festivals were a "veritable lesson in democracy" as so many of the key features were "created by the people themselves" and the saints did not play favorites—being poor and African Bahian did not hinder a person's ability to honor a saint during a popular festival and receive the saint's blessing in return.[35]

Brazil's transition to democracy intensified Bahians' hope that they would be able to take control of their affairs back from the federal government, or at least play a much bigger role in influencing the local agenda. Consequently, regional identification also intensified. As Otávio Mangabeira, Bahia's newly elected governor, took power in 1947, the press published constant predictions that the years 1948 and 1949 would witness a flourish of *baianidade* under this "Bahian [statesman] of universal fame, [who will be] directing our destinies by popular and secret ballot."[36] The entire city was asked to celebrate the fact that Salvador was taking control of its dignity and its fate after fifteen years of centralizing federal intrusion in some areas and unwarranted neglect in others. On top of all this, the four-hundred-year anniversary of the city's founding in 1549 meant the entire year of 1949 was one of the most intensely self-congratulatory moments in Bahian history. Much of the fanfare and year-long commemoration celebrated official history and the contributions of Bahia's dominant class to the history of Brazil.[37] Governor Mangabeira and Mayor Wanderley Pinho (a historian and high-ranking figure in the elite Geographic and Historic Institute of Bahia) made efforts to incorporate the city's popular festivals into the centennial celebrations. This was the principal way the governor and the mayor could ensure that all Bahians felt included in the festivities.[38] In fact, additional processions were added to the ritual calendar, such as the procession to the Church of Nosso Senhor do Bonfim on the final Friday of 1949 to give thanks to the Senhor do Bonfim for "the last four hundred years in the life of Bahia." All Bahians, "with no distinction between social class, rich and poor, great and small" gathered "in unity" to "honor all Brazil."[39]

In early January 1948, Mangabeira made an unofficial pledge to subsidize all the popular festivals for the year and was said to have given in-
structions to the mayor that his office was "to do everything possible to
assist the local neighborhood commissions in organizing the traditional
Bahian festivals."[40] The article that announced this pledge emphasized that
the government could not possibly fail to support the city's popular festivals now that Bahia had been successfully reintegrated into the fold of
democracy with the rest of Brazil. Part of Mangabeira's motivation for this
action was the emerging emphasis on Salvador's potential as a tourist destination, of which the governor was well aware and which his government
had made a priority.[41] The following year *A Tarde* reported that the "governor took the initiative . . . in contributing to the success of all the popular
festivals," uniting the city's ritual traditions with the 400th anniversary of
the founding of the city. The popular festivals were still to be organized
through the mayor's office, but under the aegis of a special committee, the
Central Office of Centennial Celebrations.[42] Throughout the year, the festivals included additional formal moments dedicated to marking the city's
history. For instance, during the Festival of Conceição da Praia in 1949, the
Portuguese residents of Bahia presented the Church of Nossa Senhora da
Conceição da Praia with an image of the recently canonized saint João do
Brito (1647–1693), a seventeenth-century Portuguese Jesuit who lived for a
while in Salvador before dying a martyr's death in India.[43]

Mangabeira's actions during the other festivals illustrate how far Bahian
political culture had shifted into a populist register under Vargas. Mangabeira "walked among the crowds" during even the biggest, most potentially
problematic festivals. He did so even though he was a traditional oligarch
who began his political career during Brazil's First Republic, a time of great
distance between the governing and the governed. He did so as much "in
the central areas as the poor and distant neighborhoods."[44] Mangabeira was
not a populist, but he made a point of being accessible and appearing toler-
ant. He was confident in his ability to reach out to people and build a consensus about the direction Bahia should take in a democratic age—within
limits, of course. Mangabeira never doubted that the dominant class had a
right to its power, but he also believed that elites should use that power to
govern benevolently. As former state senator Josephat Marinho suggested,
Mangabeira believed in a "reasonable democracy," one that would solve
the problems of poverty and improve the circumstances of the proletariat,
but slowly, as befitted what Mangabeira repeatedly called Brazil's "fragile

democracy." In the governor's view, the circumstances of the late 1940s did not yet permit the political Left or the people themselves to have much actual power. For Mangabeira, the popular festivals were an opportunity to get across his paternalistic message of a tutelary "Christian democracy" and Bahian unity across society.[45]

The intensification of the involvement of Bahian politicians in the popular festivals during the Vargas era reflected a number of local and national factors. Local pressure from below (as discussed in chapter 3) and the revival of the festivals created the opportunity for the Estado Novo leadership to try to manipulate the meanings of festivals. Administrative figures such as José Valladares and Isaías Alves used the apparatus of the state during this period to reshape Bahian identity to include explicitly African-Bahian cultural practices. Political elites after Magalhães inserted themselves in the festivals in ways that encouraged the inclusion of African-Bahian culture, doing so through a combination of ideas that drew upon traditional notions of Catholic hierarchy, corporativism, paternalism, and strands of populism. After 1945, Mangabeira and successive mayors of Salvador continued to embrace and sanction the African-Bahian aspects of popular festive culture. In this they were supported by the city's journalists, to which we now turn, who foregrounded African-Bahian practices within the popular festivals.

Journalists Recalibrate *Baianidade*

While politicians in the period 1930 to 1954 engaged with Salvador's festivities in a way that revealed their (still-qualified) acceptance of African-Bahian culture, the newspapers underwent an even more dramatic reversal of their position on black Bahian culture. A few examples of positive newspaper coverage of African-Bahian aspects of the festivals can be found prior to the Estado Novo, but these were exceptions that appeared in the context of voluminous and vitriolic criticism aimed at the Candomblé community for its "uncivilized" ritual behavior and "barbarism." However, from 1936, journalists, editors, and contributors built on the efforts of Edison Carneiro's articles for *Estado da Bahia* and quite probably on the success of the Second Afro-Brazilian Congress in 1937 to engage in a qualified celebration of black Bahian cultural practices by expanding their coverage of them and attaching positive meanings to them. By the end of the dictatorship in 1945, this kind of representation had become standard practice in all the daily secular newspapers (though not in the Catholic press).

This discursive recalibration of regional identity made sense to editors and journalists on a number of levels. As the Estado Novo emphasized popular culture as a repository of Brazilianness, factions within Bahia's dominant class were adopting similar positions at the local level, affirming Bahia's popular traditions as central to Bahianness. One example is a linguistic shift that took place between 1930 and 1950. In the mid-1930s, journalists typically referred to "the many stalls of food" at African-Bahian festivals, but by the 1940s, it was common for newspapers to use the term "Bahian food." This was part of a wider movement from generalized and even vague reporting to a virtual advertisement of Bahianness that was part of the news media's efforts to make Bahian festivals nationally relevant. By the 1940s, festivals amounted to a "show" for the rest of Brazil as well as an attraction for the hoped-for and increasing number of foreign tourists.

The festivals, prior to 1945, were also situated within the ideology of Estado Novo corporativism. The newspapers characterized the public rituals as moments of social cohesion and a leveling of class differences. During the festivals, the newspapers reported, a moment of "human solidarity" and even "equality of the races" was achieved.[46] Reflecting the reigning political orthodoxy in a dictatorship was clever tactics. Moreover, the emphasis on regional identity was clearly a local version of what was occurring at the national level during the Estado Novo, and it occurred locally for similar reasons. After the end of the dictatorship in 1945, the festivals were cast as "democratic" celebrations of Bahianness.

Perhaps less cynically, certain editors and journalists may have been keen to stimulate the growth of the festivals and to improve the status of the city's African-Bahian practices out of respect for cultural diversity and an adherence to the progressive liberal values that many of the city's journalists embraced.[47] This was particularly so after 1945, when the number of Bahia's major newspapers dropped to three, and two of these—the *Estado da Bahia* and *Diário de Notícias*—were owned by Assis Chateaubriand and edited by Odorico Tavares. The editorial line of both newspapers was sympathetic toward Bahian popular culture, reflecting the beliefs of Chateaubriand and Tavares in the value of popular culture to Brazilian national identity and its cultural formation. Moreover, because those who operated newspapers were at least partially concerned with making money, this editorial line presumably helped sell newspapers. This indicates that the acceptance of African-Bahian culture, within limits, was increasingly widespread among Bahian newspaper readers and suggests that perhaps African-derived culture was a component of a Bahianness that readers wanted to be a part of.

However one weighs these varied motivations, it is evident that from the mid-1930s the press began to use the festivals as opportunities to formulate and disseminate a public discourse of inclusive Bahianness that overtly included the city's African-Bahian heritage. The press functions as a window onto how the festivals contributed to the larger process of the acceptance and celebration of Salvador's African heritage. The newspapers also are a principal source for tracking the efforts of the dominant class to control the meanings of the festivals; they emphasized and encouraged certain aspects of the festivals for their readership in particular ways, contributing to the ongoing struggle over social memory, self-definition, and self-identity in Salvador.

The groundbreaking moment of the journalistic acceptance of Salvador's African heritage took place in May 1936, when the *Estado da Bahia* published the articles organized by Edison Carneiro. The newspaper followed this up less than a year later with positive coverage of the Second Afro-Brazilian Congress in Salvador in January 1937. During the next festival cycle (1936–37), festival reporting began to include mention of African-Bahian culture on a regular basis. The stanzas of the following poem, which appeared in *O Imparcial* in early 1937, incorporated African-Bahian cultural practices into a celebrated Bahianness associated with the Festival of Boa Viagem and Our Lord of the Navigators. The lines capture a number of the principal characteristics that were being woven into the emerging discourse of Bahian regional identity starting in the mid-1930s:

Festival so Bahian
Traditional
Picturesque.
But why is it that we no longer know the Festival of Boa Viagem?

———

Samba
Capoeira
Live music
Games of chance
Caruru, efó, vatapá, abará, [African-Bahian cuisine] etc. . . .
The Festival of N. S. da Boa Viagem and Bom Jesus dos Navegantes.[48]

The author is expressing concern that the current festival is different, less popular or animated ("we no longer know the Festival") than how he or she imagines it to have been, a common nostalgic refrain in the mid-1930s. The association of African-Bahian culture with the festival could not be clearer. Several weeks later, a journalist reporting on the merriment during the Festival of Bonfim and Ribeira Monday celebrated the associations between the festivals and the "samba, capoeira, [and] dancing." These examples were among the first to make these explicit associations in such a positive fashion.[49]

In addition to the efforts of Edison Carneiro, this shift toward explicit mention of African-Bahian culture clearly owed something to the early novels of Jorge Amado, which had begun to popularize Salvador's popular cultural practices. Jorge Amado's *Jubiabá* (1935), in particular, a novel about an old Candomblé priest of African descent, was a voyeuristic tour de force of what would become Salvadoran set pieces, populated by members of the city's bohemian and African-Bahian subcultures. In 1940 such portrayals inspired one journalist, who was looking for local color to add to his description of the informal festivities in the squares. He focused attention on the names market sellers gave to their food stalls. He described these as "picturesque, some linked to the survivals of Black religious practice (*religiões negras*), such as The Two Twins, The Little Bahiana, Janaína Lives Forever, Queen of the Sea, etc., which recall titles of Jorge Amado novels."[50]

Amado followed up *Jubiabá* with *Mar Morto* (1936), set among the lives of Salvador's fishermen, who were often involved in Candomblé culture. Following this, he published *Capitães da Areia* (1937), about street children and dominant-class misapprehensions of popular culture. By 1938 he had relocated to Brazil's southeast, and three years later, he went into exile. By 1940, Amado was only twenty-eight, but his work had been translated and published across Europe and the Soviet Union. His impact in Salvador was considerable. Although his class analysis was very much out of favor during the Estado Novo dictatorship, he did more than any other artist or intellectual to show African-Bahian working-class culture in a way that fused these practices with the very idea of Bahia. Moreover, Amado's national and international popularity illustrated how Bahia's associations with African-Bahian culture could be beneficial to and perhaps even profitable for the region, as there was clearly an audience beyond Bahia that was already receptive to such associations.

While the press handled the same or similar themes as Jorge Amado did, they avoided explicit class analysis or any hints of class or racial tension. Journalists worked to make it more palatable for elites to accept African-Bahian culture. In the reference to the names of food stalls in the article mentioned above, the names (and the beliefs of the practitioners) were rendered less threatening by the suggestions that they were merely "survivals [or remnants] of Black religious practice" and that black religious practices were on the wane and would disappear eventually. Moreover, there is a pedagogic tone to this sort of reporting in the late 1930s and early 1940s. Newspapers took on the role of educating their dominant-class readers about how these practices constituted folkways that were unique to Bahia.

This notion of African-Bahian culture as "folklore" emerged strongly in newspaper reporting around 1940. The impetus for this notion lay in the trend that began in the 1920s in government, artistic, and intellectual circles in Rio de Janeiro and São Paulo toward preserving what was seen as distinctly Brazilian, practices that were thought to be disappearing due to modernizing reforms. This trend was both academic and artistic. Public intellectuals such as Amadeu Amaral and Mario de Andrade participated, as did the São Paulo Municipal Department of Culture. Other figures who contributed include Arthur Ramos in São Paulo, Basílio Magalhães in Rio de Janeiro, and Luís da Câmara Cascudo and Gilberto Freyre in the northeast.[51] The trend was adopted by Brazil's national newspapers, regional media, and radio outlets and was often subsidized by Minister of Education and Health Gustavo Capanema.[52] Romo suggests that this emphasis on the folkloric in Bahia included a critique of the region's incomplete modernity. She cites arguments made in the 1930s and 1940s by Bahians that called attention to the irony that modernization was actually disrupting life in Salvador and not bringing the amenities that accompanied modernization elsewhere. Bahia was nevertheless losing what made it special. Thus the traditional, as opposed to the modern, qualities of Bahian culture were to be cherished against the slow crush of modernization. Tradition became synonymous with folklore, and vice versa.[53]

Given the national impact and regional influence of Jorge Amado and the emphasis in governmental and academic circles on popular culture or tradition, it is not surprising that after 1937 a number of specific features of Bahian working-class culture began to serve as symbols of the Bahian experience and icons of regional distinctiveness in the city's print media, particularly in the coverage of the popular festivals. Of particular salience was the embrace and elevation of the Baiana as a quintessential figure within the construction of *baianidade*. This is perhaps most clearly illustrated in the practice of interventors or their wives receiving the Baianas as they arrived at the Church of Nosso Senhor do Bonfim for the Washing of Bonfim. Museum director José Valladares's decision to include the jewelry and clothing of the Baianas in a collection that represented Bahia's regional heritage is another example. The mainstream newspapers such as the *Diário de Notícias* and the more conservative *A Tarde* noticeably increased their focus on the Baianas and their role within the washing ritual. In doing so they also emphasized the centrality of the ritual for Candomblé and the importance of the Candomblé community to the celebrations for Bahia's unofficial patron saint.[54] This was a sharp reversal of early-twentieth-century discourse on Baianas, their association with African-Brazilian religions, their occupation (selling food in the street), and even their dress. Then, the dominant class had been keen to modernize Salvador through urban renovations and regulatory efforts aimed at "civilizing" the social and cultural habits of the city's black demographic majority. Elites believed that the Baianas symbolized poverty, sexual promiscuity, and a lack of hygiene, in addition to their historical associations with slavery and Africa, both of which the press associated with "barbarism and backwardness."[55]

Among the newspapers, the democratic and popular *Diário da Bahia* was the leader in this reversal of the discourse on the Baiana and Candomblé in the context of the popular festivals. As early as 1937 it mentioned the deity Oxalá in association with the Senhor do Bonfim, but it did so in the context of an anecdote about the participation of an elderly woman, who went straight to the bar after the washing and drank a half glass of rum (*cachaça*), toasting Oxalá, who, the journalist pointed out, "is the same as Our Lord of the Good End, in the Nagô language." This was something of a distortion that passed off "Oxalá" as merely a Yoruban term for a Catholic entity.[56] Nevertheless, the precedent was set. Elsewhere in that year's reporting on the Washing of Bonfim the *Diário da Bahia* initiated another practice that was soon adopted by all the newspapers, that of including mention of *mães-de-santo*, *filhas-de-santo*, and even *ogans* (benefactors of *terreiros*) in a celebratory way. Previously, these terms were used only in lists of arrestees after police raids or in the context of discussions of black magic and barbarism.[57] But in 1941, the paper used "*mães-de-santo*" in place of the term "Baianas" in their headline. This editorial act directly linked the women to Candomblé in place of the more generalized and euphemistic "Baiana."[58] The articles in the *Diário da Bahia* were equally explicit in 1941 and 1942: Language such as "Oxalá, my father!" and "the Temple of Oxalá" was used in place of the term "Senhor do Bonfim."[59] In 1938, *O Imparcial* reported on the revival of the washing ritual as a showcase for the city's African-Brazilian traditions:

It [the washing] was yesterday, as it was in the old days. The water barrels, the decorated ox-carts, the negro women in their dresses with clay pots covered with craft paper [*papel de seda*] and modern vehicles [*caminhões*] bringing the water to wash the Church.

And the washing took place, as before, with samba, batuque and hymns for "Oxalá," as Old Africa doesn't miss a chance to appear.

Caring for their Orixás, the Candomblé initiates . . . went to wash the temple of "Oxalá [the Church of Nosso Senhor do Bonfim]."[60]

As the 1940s progressed, prizes were given by committees formed primarily of newspapermen for the best-turned-out Baiana and for the best-decorated car, the best-decorated cart, and the best-decorated mule.[61] By 1946 the Baianas were clearly the central attraction. They had been promoted in the order of the procession to first after the band, interestingly ahead of even the authorities.[62] From this point on, only rarely would an article on the Festival of Senhor do Bonfim run with photos that did not, somewhere, include an image of a Baiana. One of the photos was usually of a Baiana selling food.[63]

Newspaper editors in the early 1940s seemed to have also decided that mentioning the presence of Baianas in reports of the other major festivals was *de rigueur*. This was especially so of the festival of Conceição da Praia, the offering to Yemanjá during Rio Vermelho, and the post–washing ritual celebrations for Bonfim that extended from Thursday through the following Monday. In these cases reporters sometimes sought interviews with Baianas. In December 1940, for example, the *Diário de Notícias* carried a photo of its reporter eating in the street with Baianas and recorded their thoughts on the festival of Our Lady of Conceição da Praia, which largely focused on how much work they had to do to scrape together a living.[64] Candomblé was largely matriarchal. As the religion was increasingly accepted within reporting on the city's popular festivals, then the religious work of the Baianas—as spiritual leaders and accomplished individuals who actually ran their own churches—also came in for greater respect.

Part of the popular impetus for this journalistic embrace of the Baiana during the Estado Novo came from the national popularity of Carmen Miranda. Before her departure for the United States in 1940, Miranda, a personally endorsed favorite of dictator Getúlio Vargas, included in her popular repertoire a number of sambas from Brazilian radio and films that celebrated the Baiana and Bahia—"O que é que a Bahiana Tem?" ("What Is It that a Baiana's Got?," written by Dorival Caymmi) and "O Tabuleiro da Bahiana" ("The Food Tray of the Baiana," written by Ary Barroso). In 1933, as the municipal and federal governments in Rio de Janeiro began to shape and regulate carnival to suit its nation-building project, a rule was put in place that mandated that the processions of the samba schools in the Rio carnival had to include a section of women dressed as Baianas.[65] Of course, Carmen Miranda adopted her own version of the Baiana costume, initially when filming *Banana da Terra* in 1938. Miranda was not, however, the first to do so. By 1938, the Baiana costume was a familiar sight within the theatre world of Rio de Janeiro, where the first theatrical "Baiana" had appeared in 1892, and within Rio's culture of carnival fantasy, as a costume worn by young middle-class women in particular but also by men.[66]

In Salvador, too, the Baianas could be portrayed ironically. In 1944, young (presumably middle-class) women dressed as Baianas during the carnivalesque Festival of Rio Vermelho and performed a satirical washing of the Church of Rio Vermelho's patron saint, Our Lady of Sant'anna. As comedic targets and stock characters, Baianas had become signifiers of Bahia and African-Bahian society and culture. As newspapers deepened their discursive construction of Bahianness, they implicitly and explicitly traded on Miranda's popularization and Caymmi and Barroso's lyrical invocations of the Baiana as cultural referents. For instance, "the '*tabuleiro da Baiana*' overflowing with fruits" became a standard journalistic convention of festival reporting, beginning in 1940, when the *Diário da Bahia* playfully alluded to the creation of Carmen Miranda and Dorival Caymmi as a metaphor for the food available at the Festival of Conceição da Praia.[67]

Arguably a greater impetus for the resurrection of the Baiana came from the emphasis on Brazilian folklore and tradition in mainstream public discourse in Salvador just after the advent of the Estado Novo in 1937. This trend influenced politicians and journalists because it offered them opportunities to include popular culture and popular Bahians in their vision of a more inclusive regional identity. In January 1942, the conservative *A Tarde* published a piece in its Saturday edition on the clothing of Baianas accompanied by a photograph of a young Baiana impressively attired in her full regalia. The article was a lengthy and knowledgeable (and at times pedantic) discussion of the historical and social origins of various items of Baiana clothing and jewelry, although it was almost entirely devoid of explicit mention of the role of the Baiana as a woman typically deeply involved in the socioreligious world of Candomblé.[68]

Eighteen months later, in August 1943, *A Tarde* carried an editorial by Pedro Calmon, one of Bahia's most illustrious public intellectuals, that praised the Baiana "of old Brazil." The following month, *A Tarde* reprinted a piece on the Baiana that had been originally published in Rio de Janeiro by Pedro da Costa Rego, who was editorializing against the latest municipal regulations against street vending of food. He declared the Baiana a "rare species" of African-Brazilian culture because she had maintained her cultural (and racial) characteristics. Costa Rego went so far as to say that to "defend her" was "almost" the same as "preserving the national patrimony."[69] That same year, Pedro Calmon, representing the dominant Bahian position on the matter, argued of course that the Baiana *was* Brazilian national patrimony, emphasizing the presence of the Baiana over several centuries, not just on the streets but also in the national literature ("plebian muse of three centuries of poetry") and in the travel narratives of "admiring foreign visitors."[70] For Calmon, she was also a link back to Bahia's colonial economic heyday—Bahia (and Brazil's) glorious past—and rightly figured in a number of seventeenth-century European paintings created during the Dutch occupation of northeast Brazil. It mattered to Calmon and other shapers of Bahian public opinion that the arbiters of cultural tastes in Rio de Janeiro agreed that the Baiana was an important cultural treasure. It may have mattered more to them that the Baiana was present on the streets of the national capital in the first place, thus allowing Bahians to advance their claims to a central place in the nation's cultural heritage.

This would in part explain the obsession of the press with the debate in Rio de Janeiro over that city's municipal prohibitions against street vending. It is worth remembering at this point that Calmon's defense of the Baiana in 1943 was a reversal of the position of the dominant class earlier in the twentieth century, when elites from Bahia sought to remove the Baianas from public spaces as part of their "civilizing" and "modernizing" urban renewal projects.[71] It was easier for Calmon and his dominant-class readership to embrace the Baiana in the 1940s, in part due to the conviction that her type would disappear slowly anyway, a victim of the inexorable march of progress. This was a theme of both editorials in 1943 and provided some solace for those who might still find it difficult to accept Calmon's characterization of the Baiana as a symbol of regional pride.

This focus on the Baianas, even if it glossed over their attachment to African-Brazilian religious practices, made sense within the Estado Novo emphasis on creating a respectable working-class citizenry in Brazil. Of the available types within Salvador's working classes, the Baiana was one of the least threatening for a number of reasons.[72] Most important, she was publicly visible as a hard-working street vendor. In her private life she could be praised as the responsible head of a household (in the absence of a male head of household). If her affiliation with Candomblé could be overlooked, she could easily be embraced as a model member of Salvador's respectable working class. Such a (partial) characterization cohered with a longstanding desire of the dominant class to reform poor women and convert them into the guardians of dominant-class values regarding morality, hygiene, and the nuclear family.

Although the modernizing elite of the early 1920s in Bahia had not seen the Baiana as redeemable, elites under Vargas thought differently. For them, the expedient strategy was to co-opt popular culture instead of attempting to eradicate it. In this newer scenario, women were still useful for addressing modern anxieties, as emphasized by Susan Besse, and for disseminating standards of morality and social behavior, and the dominant-class meanings associated with being female still associated the Baiana with the domestic sphere and social reproduction.[73] The Baiana, according to a 1943 editorial published in Rio de Janeiro and reprinted in Salvador, was not "a sign of backwardness" but "represents in her manner the power of the woman who dedicates herself to work. She undertakes the domestic industry of making sweets, inspires dignity and respect." Occasionally this emphasis was even extended to the Baiana within the context of Candomblé. Also in 1943, the *Diário de Notícias* described those associated with the offering to Yemanjá as "a people profoundly good and hard-working."[74]

Closer scrutiny of how the Baiana was typically represented in the press reveals other conditions of her acceptance within the pantheon of Bahian iconography and illuminates the limited or qualified nature of that acceptance and that of African-Bahian culture. For instance, in a single editorial Calmon described the Baiana as "lovable" (*amaveis*), a "humble character" (*tipo humilde*), a "muse" (*musa*), and "much-loved by everyone" (*simpatia . . . de todos*). In the editorial in the Rio newspaper reprinted in Salvador she was described as "the nicely done up black woman" (*a negra limpinha*), "very humble, very sweet," (*muito humildes, muito amaveis*), and "courteous" (*tradição de cortesia*). Here was none of the old discourse of barbarism, of the dreaded "africanization of our civilization." Indeed, the Baiana here came to echo or overlap with a recent outpouring in Rio de Janeiro and São Paulo of official gratitude and elite nostalgia for the Mãe Preta, or African-Brazilian nursemaid. This outpouring was reaching its climax in the 1920s as Brazilian intellectuals and artists sought out positive narratives of Brazil's multiracial past that consolidated social hierarchy and contributed to national unity.[75] This representation of the Baiana—a symbol of blackness, symbolizing mutual respect between races and cultures, and at least suggestive of the possibilities of platonic interracial intimacy—fit within the reigning emphasis on social unity that pleased the Estado Novo ideologues in Bahia. It also would have pleased the traditional Bahian elite, who, as Paulo Santos Silva has shown, were thoroughly preoccupied after 1930 in writing out most references to cultural (including religious), racial, and class differences within the wider Bahian/Brazilian body politic in favor of social harmony.[76] Clearly, the actual lived realities and personal subjectivities of the Baianas were all but written out of these representations. Nevertheless, it must have been something of a relief to be favorably rather than unfavorably caricatured.

Another recurring symbol of regionalism that grew in visibility after 1937 was the African-Bahian foodstuffs sold by the Baianas (and other street vendors). Food was mentioned in newspaper coverage of the festivals several times in the late 1920s, but the real emphasis began in the middle 1930s.[77] Much was made of these culinary traditions, and journalists offered thick descriptions of "the absolute dominance [at the festivals] of *vatapá*, of *caruru, abará, acarajé* and of *efó*," and of "*moquecas*."[78] These were some of the things that Carmen Miranda had already informed Brazilians that "the Baiana's got." Journalists chose to personalize how Baianas contributed to Bahianness through food, making much of a particular Baiana or *barraqueiro* (owner of a food stall) as their choice, or better, the choice of the people, even the "leader among her contemporaries" in the arts of Bahian cuisine.[79] They also conveyed the timelessness of the "tradition." The street venders were said to succeed one another "as mothers give way to daughters, and daughters to granddaughters, while the food itself remained magically constant." (The food did not in fact remain constant. The portions got smaller and the vendors altered the proportions of palm oil, chili, and black-eyed peas in their fritters as a way of coping with the high cost of living.)[80] Interestingly, traditional Portuguese dishes were equally popular at the festivals (such as *mocotó* and *sarapatel*), but these were never used in journalistic constructions of *baianidade*.

This emphasis on African-Bahian foods (rather than on the foods that were part of mainstream cuisine) set Bahia apart from its neighbors in northeastern Brazil. A 1939 article in the *Estado da Bahia* highlights the extent of this fusing of regional identity and African-Bahian culinary traditions: The headline proudly proclaimed that the menu at a society party in Rio de Janeiro was to include "3,000 *acarajés* made in Bahia," suggesting that an authentic black-eyed pea fritter (the recipe for which was no great secret in Rio de Janeiro) could only come from Bahia.[81] Local modernist poet Godofredo Filho's poem *Eva*, published in 1942 in the illustrated weekly *O Cruzeiro*, contributed to this regional iconography. The poem was an homage to the Baiana Eva, who was "black through and through" (*uma preta de verdade*) and whose culinary prowess ("her *vatapá* shone brighter than the Milky Way") drew on the secrets of Candomblé and Africa.[82] When President Dutra visited Bahia in 1948, he made a point of publicly eating *acarajé* as part of what the U.S. consul in Salvador called the "*rotina Bahiana*" or "Bahian routine" for visiting politicians.[83]

The media reappraisal of African-Bahian culture is evident in the coverage of ritual celebrations for Iansã during the festivities for Santa Barbara on the fourth of December or coverage of celebrations in the *terreiros* and in private homes to celebrate the holy day of Cosmas and Damian (Cosme and Damião in Portuguese), patron saints of twins and triplets and children more generally, on the twenty-seventh of September. In the early 1940s these festivities, which were private but were typically open to the local community, were suddenly deemed newsworthy. Prior to this, these saints' days received meager attention and no mention of their importance to temples of Candomblé. Also, in 1943, *A Tarde* took pains to clarify the association of Santa Barbara with Janaína (another name for Yemanjá) in the context of her importance to fishermen.[84] The article went on to briefly stress Janaína's importance to all of Salvador, given her role in bringing success to the fishermen and hence providing the city with meat at a time when beef was in very short supply due to World War II.

Pausing to focus on the Candomblé ritual offering to Yemanjá during the days set aside for the Festival of Rio Vermelho, however, allows for a better appreciation of the recalibration of *baianidade* in the press, not least because this offering to Yemanjá was entirely devoid of associations with Catholicism. Newspapers did not begin to mention this waterborne rite in honor of the Goddess of the Sea until the early 1940s.[85] Overall more an act of Candomblé-related worship than even the Washing of Bonfim, the procession probably dates to 1925, originating in the initiative of local fisherman from up the Atlantic coast in the neighborhood of Rio Vermelho (which was then on the outskirts of Salvador). The procession was incorporated into the Festival of Rio Vermelho, which consisted of several weeks of Catholic ritual and processions and informal and increasingly carnivalesque celebrations in honor of the neighborhood and its patron saint, Nossa Senhora de Sant'anna. These Catholic and carnivalesque activities were what the newspapers had preferred to relate to their readership before 1940. After that year, this uneven reporting was rebalanced. The shift was quite pronounced in 1944 in the *Diário da Bahia*, which carried one article on the processional aspects of the Festival of Rio Vermelho and a few days later a second article on the offering to Yemanjá. About this time, other newspapers began to cover the offering to Yemanjá, including it in their series of reports on the festivities of Rio Vermelho but also occasionally devoting an entire article to the waterborne event.[86] As Rio Vermelho became a suburb of the city, its integration into the pantheon of Salvador's festivals was rather seamless. As its population grew, its principal festival did too, bringing in more and more celebrants from beyond the old municipal boundaries and lasting for a number of weeks. The reporting grew, too. Even accounting for all this demographic growth, it is still clear that the space given over to the public Candomblé ritual offering grew in both absolute and relative terms.

The content of the 1944 report in the *Diário da Bahia* on the offering to Yemanjá is worth a closer look. The article began with the lyrics of Caymmi's 1939 song "Queen of the Sea" ("Rainha do Mar"): "My mermaid's a beautiful girl / on the waves of the sea she inhabits." The song is a lyrical paean to Bahian folklore as much as it is to Yemanjá. The article went on to discuss many of the core elements of *baianidade*. It detailed the participation of the Baianas, who were representatives of "the glory days" and were "faithful to traditions" (and indeed carried in their clothing and jewelry "an orgy of memories"). The Baianas brought the offering to the vessel that would transport it to Yemanjá, just as they carried the water to the Washing of Bonfim. But this public ritual was not limited to the "humble people." Many others who were normally "indifferent to these sorts of things" contributed to the general offering, emphasizing the degree to which Candomblé was a part of wider Bahian culture and was not to be understood as limited to African Bahians. The festival brought together "Black and White. Rich and poor. All the social classes." The African-Bahian cuisine and the *tabuleiro* were of course mentioned, as was the special strain of samba identified with Bahia, the *samba de roda*, which the participants played and sang upon their return to shore from the successful offering to the Orixá. The newspaper also noted the visit of French sociologist, Roger Bastide, a professor at the University of São Paulo, who was researching African-Brazilian themes and "taking detailed and appreciative notes on what he was witnessing." Clearly Bastide's presence gave African-Bahian culture the imprimatur of national and international scholarly legitimacy.[87]

From 1945 to 1954, the Bahian print media continued to be at the center of the profusion of images and discourses that were redefining Bahianness. What stands out in the press coverage of the popular festivals, compared with earlier coverage, is that each of the festivals, as described, had come to play a particular role and made a particular contribution to what amounted to a composite representation of African-Bahian inclusiveness. By 1954, the visual imagery and discursive construction of the Festival of Bonfim and its washing ritual emphasized the syncretic nature of the festival. The press highlighted the importance of the Baianas during the Washing of Bonfim, but at the same time journalists mentioned the association of the ritual with Oxalá.[88] The relationship between Oxalá and the Senhor do Bonfim, as one newspaper put it, was one of "clasped hands" (*mãos dadas*).[89] This implied that Oxalá and the Senhor do Bonfim together constituted the unofficial patron saint of Bahia.

Journalists also moved from the occasionally personalized but usually generic "Baiana" and began to make particular individuals from the Candomblé community into icons. One of the first of these was the Baiana Maria de São Pedro, the "best cook of African-Bahian cuisine," who had a restaurant in the commercial district where Bahian writers, such as Jorge Amado and Odorico Tavares, took distinguished visitors from the world of arts and letters for lunch and photo opportunities.[90]

Additionally, the festivities related to Segunda-Feira Gorda da Ribeira (or Ribeira Monday) had very little to do with Candomblé, but in the decade after 1945 this mini-carnival became firmly associated with samba and *batucadas* and, increasingly, capoeira. For the entire day and evening of the festival, the Ribeira neighborhood was the site of a semiformalized carnival parade of decorated cars. The rest of the available public space was occupied by celebrants on foot and impromptu bands that played sambas and *batucadas*. In their coverage of the event, journalists increased their focus on impromptu samba gatherings, which "could form at any moment."[91] From 1948 the newspapers often carried photos of the circles of bodies that created the ring within which the music and the dancing took place.[92] The *batucadas* were as important to Ribeira as they were to carnival, and their presence at Ribeira was an important test of how animated carnival would be later that year. When the *batucadas* arrived to participate in the festivities at Ribeira, they "came to dominate everyone" with their "hot and languid rhythm."[93] If the *batucadas* and sambas and other related carnival practices did not quite fill a reporter's need for popular iconography, he would also include a mention of the young men who were organizing to play capoeira.[94] The main festival associated with capoeira was that of Conceição da Praia. This is the one journalists focused on when they spoke of how capoeira was an element of Bahianness. The simple explanation for

this lies in the fact that the events took place near the docks and the Mercado Modelo, where young men habitually practiced their capoeira at other
times of the year.

The offering to Yemanjá, that took place on February second, grew in
importance within the pre-carnival Festival of Rio Vermelho. Although the
press was rarely silent on the ritual offering, which began in the mid-1920s,
after World War II the newspapers isolated and celebrated the event as
a preeminent moment of folkloric Bahianness and popular religious expression.[95] Importantly, the elements that made up the festival were all the
result of the initiative of local fishermen (for whom Yemanjá was a patron
saint), other "people of modest means" (*populares*), and the Candomblé
community. This included the preparations on the docks, the ceremony
with its drumming, the many dozens of sailboats that accompanied the
maritime procession transporting the gifts to the appropriate spot on the
water for the offering, and the festivities afterward and their circles of
samba and capoeira. There was no financial support from either the commission of the Festival of Rio Vermelho or the municipal government for
these activities.[96]

Festivities for the twin Catholic saints Cosme and Damião were not announced annually in certain newspapers until after World War II. These
two were important within Candomblé ritual as well. In fact, they were
perhaps more important for Candomblé than they were for Catholic worship in Salvador. Announcing these festivities was tantamount to publicizing them on behalf of Candomblé, and indeed the articles mentioned that
many *terreiros* in the neighborhoods would be celebrating that evening.
There was little to no mention of parallel events related to the Catholic
Church. The popular and Candomblé practice of hosting a *caruru* (a term
that translates both as "okra" and the event at which it was served) also
crept into the press coverage of Salvador's public Candomblé ritual traditions for Cosme and Damião.[97] This may have been interesting to the press
corps in late September, during a lengthy lull over the final few months of
winter before the summer festival cycle started up again in early December.
Each festival the press covered made a different but complementary contribution to a composite representation of Bahianness.

Capoeira

Capoeira, like the Baiana, became a feature of festival reporting during the Vargas era. This occurred in particular after the legitimization and effective legalization of the practice in 1937 under Juracy Magalhães. At least this was the case for capoeira in its more modern, neutered form as popular recreation or physical fitness training (rather than a street tough's preferred method of violent assault). This reappraisal in the context of the popular festivals was especially pronounced with regard to the Festival of Conceição da Praia, the patron saint of stevedores. Many stevedores made a point of being at the festival and also contributed a disproportionate number of practitioners of capoeira throughout the year in the lower city. Their participation during the festival was a nearly seamless extension of their working lives; as mentioned above, the Church of Our Lady of Conceição da Praia and the festival itself were adjacent to the docks and were part of the spiritual as well as physical backdrop of the stevedores' working lives. In 1940, the *Diário da Bahia* dedicated a section of its report to "The Capoeira." The article described all of the participants: the ring of players in one corner of the festival square, the musical instruments, the hand clapping and singing of the other capoeiristas, and the crowd of onlookers appreciating the skills on display. But the article also maintained a small frisson of illegality or delinquency, pointing out that the space was in one of the most hidden corners of the festivities and that a policeman kept an alert eye on the participants in case things should get out of hand, in which case the participants would end up "making the short trip to the nearby police station."[98]

In 1940, when a Brazilian film company based in the southeast began to shoot footage for the cinematic adaptation of Amado's novel *Mar Morto*, which was set in Bahia, they went to Salvador. One scene they were keen to shoot was the opening shot of a game of capoeira on the beach. Amado himself pointed out that this was important to shoot in Salvador for the sake of authenticity, as capoeira practiced in Salvador had its own special nuances. The actual music and songs for the capoeira scene, according to Amado, would come from recordings made by North American linguist Lorenzo Dow Turner and sociologist E. Franklin Frazier, who were both in Salvador that year as part of well-publicized research trips to study African-Bahian life. The crew also filmed a re-creation of a waterborne ritual offering to Yemanjá. Unfortunately, the film seems to never have been completed, but it is telling that the first Brazilian effort to record Bahia for the big screen opened with shots of capoeira and that the narrative climaxes against a backdrop of a festive offering to the African-Bahian Candomblé *orixá* Yemanjá.[99] Meanwhile, the discursive emphasis on capoeira during the festival of Conceição da Praia was spreading. Soon it was being mentioned elsewhere and at other times of the year. By the late 1940s capoeira had become a feature of lyrical reporting on the day of the offering to Yemanjá on 2 February and on the Festivals of Bonfim, Ribeira, Santa Barbara, and Our Lord of the Navigators.

Samba

As one would expect, samba grew in significance in media discourse on the popular festivals. The principal place for the samba was the informal festivities in the squares—during the Festivals of Santa Barbara, Conceição da Praia, Bonfim, Yemanjá, and Rio Vermelho. Of these, the day most associated with samba was the Monday following the festival of Bonfim. This day was known as Ribeira Monday. It was not named after a saint but after the locale where everyone congregated—the Ribeira (literally, "shoreline") that began only a few hundred meters from the Church of Nosso Senhor do Bonfim but extended for up to a kilometer. The sambas the press mentioned were largely extemporaneous. Individuals arrived with instruments, lyrics, rhythms, and movements in the expectation that there would be samba at some point. Performances were rarely organized and relied heavily on improvisation.[100]

In 1943, a reporter for *Diário da Bahia* interwove his narrative of coming upon such a performance during Ribeira Monday with the lyrics from a nationwide samba hit from 1942, "Até parece que eu sou da Bahia" ("It's as Though I Am from Bahia").[101] The hit, which was composed and sung by artists in Rio de Janeiro, made playful use of popular African-Bahian religious practices. The anonymous character in the samba, presumably male, fights with a wife or girlfriend, and fearing her revenge, he protects himself with symbols and rituals associated with Candomblé. The protection is so strong that the woman's magic is reflected back on her, and he winds up with luck, money, and love. His Candomblé *orixá* protects him so well that it's as though he "is from Bahia." As the reporter came upon the circle, two things happened that indicate that he was witnessing a strictly working-class activity. One of the sambistas refers to the reporter as "doctor," a standard honorary title for someone who is educated and/or in a position of power: "Open the circle people, the doctor wants to see some samba." Then, almost gratuitously, another sambista says, "We watch and we see important people appreciating this popular diversion." The passage drives home the tenor of the entire report, which is that there is a separation between the dominant-class reporter and his readers and those who truly participate in and provide the spectacle of the festival. It is a "popular" festival, after all: "A festival of poor people. A festival of people who struggle and suffer. A festival for those with pressures to relieve . . . an unconscious desire for a diversion that allows a little forgetting of the sadness of their daily lives." In short, it was a mini-carnival, and that is how the Festival of Ribeira was typically understood. But it was a mini-carnival comprised of features specific to Bahia, including the *samba de roda*.[102]

The journalist's reference to a hit from Brazil's recording industry is just one sample of the rich vein of samba lyrics that associated Bahia with African-Bahian culture. Composers and performers of samba and closely related musical forms featured Bahia and specifically African-Bahian culture in the lyrics of songs that played on radio stations in metropolitan centers across Brazil in the early twentieth century. Samba lyrics emanating from the recording industry in Rio de Janeiro eulogized African Bahians and African-Bahian culture and religiosity and portrayed Bahia as a Brazilian cultural treasure. This process climaxed in the 1930s and 1940s.

The story of samba's rise to preeminence in Brazil's pantheon of symbols of cultural nationalism is well known.[103] Modernist artists and intellectuals set out to reshape how the nation's residents viewed themselves as Brazilians. Regional folk culture was lauded as authentically Brazilian by influential figures such as Mario de Andrade or incorporated into the classical music compositions of Heitor Villa-Lobos. Jorge Amado's early literary portrayals of the city's working-class population emphasized the role music and lyrics, particularly samba, played in people's lives culturally, socially, and occasionally politically. He did so most emphatically in *Jubiabá* (1935). The line between fiction and reality in Amado's early social realist novels is difficult to draw, which was perhaps part of the attraction of his work. At the very least we can say that the popularity of *Jubiabá* intensified the association of Bahia with samba and African-Bahian culture. Other cultural leaders joined Amado in his positive assessment of samba. In 1936, Edison Carneiro wrote a piece for a Bahian newspaper championing the samba as an art form. He also wrote an academic monograph in 1937 that explored samba as both folklore and popular culture, emphasizing its historical links to African forms of musical expression.[104]

Moreover, thanks to the efforts of scholars Agnes Mariano and Reginald

Prandi, we can appreciate through an examination of samba lyrics the extent to which the music industry, which was based in the southeast, contributed to the process of associating "Bahia" with African-Bahian culture at the local and national levels.[105] This use and inclusion of African-Bahian culture as a marker of *baianidade* dates to the earliest years of the music business in Rio de Janeiro. In 1902, the first record in Brazil was composed by a Bahian called Xisto Bahia. The song was a *lundu* (a predecessor of the samba) called "Isto é bom" ("This Is Good").[106] That same year, Casa Edison, the first commercial Brazilian record label, was founded. Only two years later, Mário Pinheiro sang a song (a *choro*) titled "Caruru," which referred to the stewed okra dish that was preferred in Candomblé *terreiros* as *comida de santo* (holy food).[107] The song used a figurative meaning of *caruru* as a loud social gathering or public disagreement and went on to playfully yet critically call attention to distinctions of culture and class in Salvador among whites, *mulatas, pardas* (called *cabrinhas* in the lyrics), and blacks.

Pinheiro's association of food with Bahia, especially *comida de santo*, continued into the 1910s and 1920s, as did the association of Bahia with African-Bahian culture. Food was one of the principle means of this association, although it would be some time after 1930 before elites would bring themselves to actually eat the African-Bahian food themselves, according to one of the early chroniclers of the social meanings of Bahian cuisine.[108] Food was convenient for samba lyrics because it lent itself to sexual double entendres about the fictional Baiana (and often by extension all Bahian women of color). The "cooking" in these cases suggested sexual activity. The less-suggestive sambas also peppered their lyrics with references to women of African descent and used terms of endearment such as *iôiô* ("sweetheart," male) and *iâiâ* ("sweetheart," female) that were associated with African-Bahian social relationships. Even if the majority of playful references to Bahia's religions focused on Christianity, such as the 1926 *maxixe* by Sebastião Cirino and Antônio Lopes de Amorim titled "Cristo nasceu na Bahia" ("Christ Was Born in Bahia"), *feitiço* (a spell, drawing on African or Indigenous cosmologies) and Candomblé were sometimes mentioned as well. For instance, in 1929, José Barbosa da Silva's song "Carga de burro" ("The Donkey's Burden") wrote of a *breve* (small pouch of religious paraphernalia with powers of protection) he picked up in Bahia from "a temple of Candomblé."[109]

From 1929, however, songs that touched on or fully incorporated Bahia into their lyrics used imagery that embraced a more complex and assertive (admittedly caricatured) African-Bahian culture. Candomblé worship was mentioned more often, and the practices that Salvador's dominant class had found so troubling in the post-abolition period became part of wider popular musical culture. Sátiro de Melo's 1930 "Essa Nega é da Bahia" ("That Black Woman Is from Bahia") referenced the *figa de guiné*, the small protective amulet that often graces a necklace or bracelet or a household of a member of the Candomblé community.[110] Alcebíades Barcelos's 1932 "A Baiana de Nagô" ("The Baiana of Nagô Candomblé") even more explicitly associated Bahia with Candomblé.[111] By 1938, as no less a personage than Carmen Miranda would put it in her 1938 success "Na Bahia" ("In Bahia"), "In Bahia Blacks perform Candomblé night and day."[112] These songs, among many others, demonstrate how the recording industry in Rio de Janeiro took the lead in embracing Candomblé culture ahead of the dominant discourse in Salvador as it was expressed in the local press. As early as the early 1930s, the term *macumba* (Macumba being a variant of Candomblé in Rio de Janeiro) was used by the music industry to describe music of the *terreiros* and sold as a distinct category. In the Salvador of the early and middle 1930s, in contrast, practically the only place Bahians would hear a positive message relating to Candomblé was through sambas played live or on the radio. During the 1930s, musicians and songwriters of the samba industry based in the southeast began to use Candomblé more and more as a reference point for songs that explored, or exploited, Bahianness.

In the early 1930s, not many Bahians owned radios. Most Bahians, including members of the dominant class, would have heard these songs played by live bands. Samba in the early 1920s was a fad in the clubs and revues that were popular with the elite. It was also acceptable for young members of the elite and the middle class to participate in "samba in the streets" (*pagode nas ruas*) during the popular festivals such as Bonfim or Ribeira Monday, and such participation was *de rigueur* for the bohemian set.[113] Two trends from the 1920s seem to have merged around 1930, leading to a relative flowering of the popular music industry in Salvador that helped popularize samba. First, there was the rise of the jazz band, which played all genres of popular music, much of it from North America—the foxtrot, the Charleston, tangos, and boleros.[114] This was a pronounced shift from the largely classical repertoire of European chamber music, although there was a tradition of popular and religious European music, too. These bands also played in a wide range of venues, from the dives frequented by prostitutes to elite balls and dances. It is not clear precisely what these jazz bands were playing, but it is clear that samba was in the repertoire of even the most respected jazz bands, regardless of the venue. Even the bands of the police and the Fire Department, which for all intents and purposes were the "official" bands of the mayor's office, inasmuch as the mayor's office commissioned them for almost every popular festival, included sambas in their performances in the 1920s.

Second, in the late 1920s there was a marked rise in interest among urban Brazilians in regional (and national) popular music and Brazilian composers. Among the diverse popular musical traditions that were suddenly played on the radios or performed live—including religious songs, cânticos, canções regionais, and folk songs—were batuques and sambas, especially sambas of local composers who had high standing because of their achievements in other genres of music.[115] From this point on, the evidence is clear that samba was definitely on the rise, even though there was much more than just samba being played in Salvador. Even during carnival samba had to share with the carnival marches that were more popular with the dominant class. Still, most local newspapers began to embrace samba with articles that made the point that samba in Rio de Janeiro was increasingly popular. It was also noted that foreign visitors approved of samba, such as the Japanese painter Fanyita, who proclaimed "samba brasileiro" a fantastic thing and said that "Brazilians have the best carnival in the world."[116] Rio de Janeiro's sambas and carnivals had also begun to make a name for themselves in Europe and North America.[117] Contemporary author Berilo Neves said that "carnival has contributed more to make Brazil known internationally than our poets, our thinkers, and our men of arts and letters." He added, "It's irritating to say it, but it's true."[118] From 1932, samba was increasingly part of radio programming in Bahia, and after December, the number of sambas that aired that year would increase, leading up the climax of carnival in February or March. Carmen Miranda first came to Bahia in 1932, where she performed her hits, many of which were sambas.

Many songs from 1929 onward associate African Bahians and Bahia with samba. Moreover, when the lyrics overtly mention samba, they typically suggest that one can learn samba only from a woman of color in Bahia (whose heart can be won only with the help of the Senhor do Bonfim). The word batuque also enters the lyrics alongside "samba," particularly in the work of Ary Barroso, such as in his 1931 songs "Batuque," "Terra de Iâiâ," and "Bahia."[119] This is significant, as Bahian elites still associated batuque with longstanding popular percussive practices that represented African "primitivism" and the threat to "civilization" that African-Bahian popular culture posed. From the perspective of its practitioners, however, the *batuque* may have been a more "pure" form of samba. At any rate, thanks to Barroso we can appreciate that *batuque* had become fashionable slang for a percussive performance and that the word was firmly and positively associated with Bahia.

Barroso went on to write several hits for Carmen Miranda in the late 1930s that referenced Bahia, including the 1938 hit "Na Baixa dos Sapateiros" ("On Shoemaker's Lane"). Ary Barroso, who was born in Minas Gerais and was living in Rio de Janeiro, had traveled to Bahia as a jobbing pianist for the first time in 1929. When he returned to Rio on 2 December 1940, local councilman Luis Monteiro da Costa sponsored a law decreeing that particular date to be the "Day of Samba," paying homage to Barroso and to the explicit linkages between Bahia and samba. The Day of Samba would soon become a national holiday. Bing Crosby later covered "Na Baixa dos Sapateiros" in 1944 for Walt Disney's film *The Three Caballeros*. Although the Portuguese title simply means "On Shoemakers Lane," the song was renamed in the United States as simply "Baia" [*sic*]. This renaming projected Bahia's cultural association with African-Bahian culture internationally, similar to the way "The Girl from Ipanema" would popularize the Rio de Janeiro beachfront neighborhood of the same name two decades later. In June 1956, Ary Barroso returned to Bahia and received the key to the city of Salvador from the mayor and was feted by the state legislature for services rendered to "our region" (*nossa terra*). The commemorations frequently pointed to the success of "Na Baixa dos Sapateiros" in the United States and worldwide and the positive name recognition it brought to Bahia. The music of Barroso was "one of the greatest vehicles of publicity for Bahia abroad," reported one journalist covering the event. The mayor of Salvador presented Barroso with the Order of the Figa. The *figa*, as mentioned above, was a charmed amulet associated with Candomblé, "a symbol of good fortune and happiness."[120]

Also prominent during this early period is the association of Bahia with African-Bahian women and a style of moving that emphasized the hips, balance, and an alluring gracefulness. The 1929 *maxixe*-samba "Baianinha" ("Little Baiana"), written by Bahian-born composer performer and playwright João Cândido Ferreira in partnership with Oscar Mota, captures this clearly. The woman in the song, who is identified as African-Bahian by her attire, "Has a certain sway / and undulant hips" (*Tem um certo requebrado / e um quadril ondulante*).[121] Ferreira, also known as de Chocolat, was already breaking ground for African Brazilians in theater; in 1926, he had founded the African-Brazilian Theater Review in Rio de

Janeiro. Another early example of this association of a particular movement style with Bahian women is in "Essa Nega é da Bahia" ("That Black Woman from Bahia"), in which Francisco Alves sang, "She really shakes her hips, My Goodness!" (*Ela mexe tanto as cadeiras, Meu Deus!*).[122]

Occasionally samba lyrics would drift more explicitly into racial politics, such as the *maxixe* by de Chocolat and Ary Barroso called "Nega também é gente" ("Black Women Are People Too"), which fit the emerging discourse of the 1930s that praised the contribution of Brazilians of African descent, in this case that of the African-Brazilian nanny who, as the samba lyrics put it, "comforted Brazil" (*ninou o Brasil*) and "suffered in silence" (*padeceu docemente*).[123] Perhaps the most illustrative samba lyrics that associated Bahia with African-Bahian culture and addressed the social position of African Bahians came from the pen of nationally known Bahian composer José de Assis Valente in "Etc." (1933), which was sung by Carmen Miranda, among others.[124] The lyrics asserted that while Bahia was "the land of the poet / Land of the man with the advanced degree, and etcetera" (*Bahia terra do poeta / Terra de doutor e "etecetra"* [*sic*]), working-class African Bahians who embraced samba and Candomblé "also have value" (*Eu tenho também o meu valor*).

The homage to African-Bahian culture and its association with Bahia in song lyrics should not really surprise us. Bahia had its own percussive traditions and an autochthonous samba culture, which evolved in a complex relationship to events in Rio de Janeiro. For example, a number of the early pioneers of the samba genre in Brazil were Bahian migrants, and the temples of Candomblé these migrants set up provided institutional and cultural support for the development of the secular musical traditions that would coalesce in samba. The most famous example, of course, is that of the Bahian-born *mãe-de-santo* Tia Ciata (Hilária Batista de Almeida, 1884–1924), who was one of the principal figures who provided structure for the working-class African-Brazilian musical world centered on Rio de Janeiro's Praça Onze and environs, the milieu in which the first official samba was created in 1917. Not all Bahia's cultural ambassadors were African Bahian, however. Antônio Lopes de Amorim (aka, The Duke), for instance, popularized the *maxixe* in France before World War I and was part of the music scene in Rio in the 1920s. Amorim was of decidedly European ancestry (and a dentist by trade). Nevertheless, the milieu in Rio de Janeiro from which samba emerged owed much to African-Bahian culture. Music written by migrants to the federal capital was often nostalgic about Salvador, and the links between the two cities were emotively recalled through the common motif of the lost love left in Salvador. It made sense, too, within the national emphasis on Brazil's African-Brazilian culture, that a site would emerge where that culture was emphasized, if only to free up the other cultural centers to emphasize culture not associated with Africa or Africa in Brazil. Of course, sometimes creativity runs dry and gives way to established tropes, even cultural inertia. As Hakon Mielche sardonically observed, "When a Brazilian composer wants words for his latest samba he asks his lyric writer to try once more to get the word 'Bahia' into the title and refrain."[125]

The early career of Bahian musician and composer Dorival Caymmi is instructive, as he would play an important role in establishing African-Bahian working-class culture as central to Bahianness. The importance of his role stemmed in part from his position in the music industry in Rio de Janeiro. In the mid-1930s, Caymmi emerged in Salvador as a promising young radio talent, especially after broadcaster Gilberto Martins offered him his own radio show in 1935. Martins had come to Salvador from Rio de Janeiro and had introduced live programming to Bahian radio. Caymmi's talents made him and his band, Três e Meio, household names in Salvador. The genre of music he was most associated with at this point was *canção-praieira* (songs about oceangoing fishermen), but Caymmi soon left Bahia for Rio de Janeiro, in 1938. Within two years he had risen to national prominence largely on the success of two songs, both of which were sambas that played an important role in fusing African-Bahian cultural practices with Bahian regional identity within Bahia and beyond.[126]

The two songs were "Que é que a Bahiana tem?" ("What Is It that a Baiana's Got?") and "A Preta do Acarajé" ("The Black Vendor of Acarajé").[127] "Que é que a Bahiana tem?" was rich with Bahian imagery. In fact, both songs (and several other hits Caymmi wrote over the next few years) were evocations of African-Bahian cultural distinctiveness—the clothes, the jewelry, the sensuality, and the cuisine of the Baiana and the relationship of Bahia to samba, Candomblé, and popular festivals. Three of Caymmi's songs mentioned the importance of Bonfim to working-class Bahians.

Although Caymmi was not the first to incorporate such images and practices into his artistic production, his contribution is particularly significant for two reasons. First, the extent of his influence meant that his songs had a major impact on how much of Brazil came to think about Bahia and in turn how Bahians thought about themselves. The fact that Caymmi's audience was national in scope was largely due to the film *Banana da Terra* (1939), in which "Que é que a Bahiana tem?" and "A Preta do Acarajé" featured, both sung by Carmen Miranda, the most popular performer in Brazil that year.

The film used actual scenes from Bahia as well as stage sets to construct a lyrical visual vocabulary of Bahia. For Bahians it was a matter of pride that a "native son" was at the center of this nationwide representation of Bahianness. The fact that Caymmi was from Bahia also enhanced the "authenticity" of the sambas and their lyrics and sentiments.

Second, the timing of Caymmi's biggest hits, from 1938 to 1943, was significant, as his songs were both a validation and an extension of the reappraisal of African-Bahian culture in Salvador. In late 1941, Caymmi returned briefly to Bahia to what was in effect a hero's welcome. Caymmi, who one journalist noted was "much loved by the people of this ancient city of Salvador," was invited by the municipal government to perform at Lapinha Square on the eve of the Festival of the Three Kings, on 5 January 1942, and his performance was a centerpiece of the celebrations. The performance was broadcast on the radio, and the newspaper *A Tarde* pointed out that Caymmi was adored for his "conservation of our traditions and Bahian art forms." We do not know what songs he chose to perform that night, but *A Tarde* described them as "genuinely Bahian," and it is very likely that he sang many of his sambas.[128] Caymmi's appearance brought together several of the more salient facets of Bahia's emerging regional identity: One of Brazil's most noted composers of sambas based on Bahian themes, flush from numerous successes while working in Rio de Janeiro's entertainment industry, was back in Bahia to perform carnival hits on a night that was traditionally one of Salvador's most religiously inspired (based on the arrival of the Three Wise Men before the baby Jesus), all sponsored by the local authorities. January 1942 must have been a busy month for Caymmi in Salvador, as he was also listed as a member of the Organizing Committee of the Washing of Bonfim for that year, alongside public servants, Candomblé figure Miguel Santana, and representatives from nearly every major newspaper and magazine in Salvador.[129]

Caymmi's visit to Bahia in 1941 and 1942 created a media sensation, but the pattern of associating Bahia with African-Bahian culture through the words of sambas and similar genres was already gaining momentum in the early 1930s. This trend climaxed in the 1930s and 1940s with the work of Caymmi, Carmen Miranda, and numerous other composers and producers such as Ary Barroso and Assis Valente. Their achievement was to prominently fuse the association of Bahia with African-Bahian culture—through lyrics and through the rise to prominence of samba—and to do so not just for Bahia but also for the Brazilian nation.

The Limits to Acceptance

A brief look at the limits of the inclusion of African-Bahian working-class culture allows for a keener appreciation of the degree to which the reformulation of Bahian regional identity was controlled by the dominant class. Throughout the newspapers' construction of the meanings of the city's popular festivals, journalists consistently employed the distinction between the sacred and the profane in their descriptions and reports on the public festivals. This conceptualization was quite useful in bringing Candomblé explicitly into the popular festivals—on the profane side. Because the binary was hierarchical to begin with, it was a perfect construction for incorporating Candomblé in a way that would not unduly threaten the primacy of the Catholic Church. When the Candomblé rituals were described in a way that emphasized their sacred nature, as they occasionally were, they were usually described as fetishistic (as a *religiosa fetichista*).[130] The binary of the sacred/profane was mapped onto the binary of European/African.

Also telling is the fact that journalists typically constructed African-Bahian practices at the festivals as a part of a larger event that remained the purview of the dominant class. So, for example, the Washing of Bonfim, with its popular Catholicism and its ritual obligations to Oxalá, was ideologically incorporated into the same ritual field as the other predominantly dominant-class aspects of the Festival of Senhor do Bonfim. The same was true of the newspaper coverage of the other public festivals. Capoeira and Candomblé ritual were constructed as part of the larger, officially Catholic festival of, for instance, Our Lady of the Immaculate Conception. Even the Festival of Yemanjá, which was entirely of the working class and Candomblé community, was typically constructed as part of the Festival of Rio Vermelho. The tourist literature funded by the municipal government and the guides authored by prominent Bahians, and especially those written by the more conservative authors, also ensured that the Catholic churches and colonial buildings and monuments remained more highly ranked in Salvador's cultural hierarchy.[131]

The limits to inclusion reveal themselves in other ways. The newspapers selectively chose how much to include of the Candomblé-related aspects of the popular festivals, and by the 1940s journalists were choosing almost exactly the same material each year. For instance, from the Herskovitses' field notes, it is clear that the waterborne processions in honor of Yemanjá, the offerings and dances and rituals as well as the sambas and *batucadas*, were not merely appendages to the Festival of Conceição da Praia but were central to the overall meanings of the festival for many in Salvador's working class. In fact, it is tempting to see the Festival of Conceição da Praia in 1942 as two festivals—the events that comprised the officially sanctioned festival, which took place under the aegis of the Catholic Church, and the events intimately related to Candomblé and firmly grounded in the cultural life of Salvador's working classes. The fact that newspapers chose not to publicize these latter aspects of the festivals for their middle- to upper-class readers reveals their role in a delicate discursive balancing act. After 1930, it was acceptable and even desirable to report on popular religious practices, but this discursive inclusion had to occur in a way that did not give too much weight or importance to African-Bahian cultural practices, and certainly in a way that did not elevate African-Bahian religious practices to parity with those of the Catholic Church. This may have been especially true of the Festival of Conceição da Praia, whose Catholic novenas were very traditional and very well attended by important political and economic elites.

We can see limits in the realm of performance as well. The festivals often ritualized and reinforced racial, class, and cultural difference, separation, and hierarchy. In doing so they flew in the face of the rhetoric of racial democracy and *mestiçagem* that gained currency in the Vargas era. The Washing of Bonfim provides an illustration of this "performance of difference." A most prominent feature of the newspapers' constructions of this festival was as an event that united all Bahians in a "complete religious synthesis,"[132] in which discrimination against color or class was absent.[133] There was some truth to this, in that most of Bahia's social groupings were represented and were even exhorted to attend by the organizers of the festival. For example, the pro-integralist newspaper *O Imparcial* explicitly called on the city's "religious and class organizations" to participate.[134] Within the Estado Novo vision of a harmonious corporativist social body, this was a laudable achievement. Following Victor Turner's insights that a sense of "communitas" was a typical outcome during local saint's days, it is likely that because the Senhor do Bonfim was the "patron saint" of Salvador, many festival-goers felt a kinship and a community spirit that was absent at other times of the year.[135] As the Estado Novo's corporativist grip on Brazil's nationalist rhetoric gave way to visions of freely functioning liberal democratic institutions, the festival gathering was no longer discussed as an exercise in "social harmony"; instead, it became a shining example of "our democracy." After 1945, as Brazil nominally embraced open elections, newspapers continued to claim to find much that was "democratic" and inclusive in the freer mingling experienced during the Festival of Senhor do Bonfim. Much was also made of the fact that the Senhor do Bonfim was the patron saint of the Allied nations that fought on the side of democracy in World War II.[136] In 1944, a "V" sign was hung alongside the cross in the Church of Nosso Senhor do Bonfim, and several musical groups showed up in "imaginative" military costumes as part of their performances during the festival.[137]

A closer reading of the Festival of Bonfim, however, reveals the extent to which popular festival practices were segregated by race and class. Observers of the Washing of Bonfim, such as Stephen Zweig in 1941, commented on the distinction between the raucous atmosphere of the spacious church courtyard, which was "given over to all the thousands who gather here . . . between the evening and the morning masses," and the "small lodging houses" around the courtyard that were "rented by the well-to-do families."[138] Historically, the devotees of the Bonfim festival were largely families on extended summer holidays (veranistas) who could afford to relocate to the quiet of Itapagipe Peninsula during the hottest months of the year. These families were the backbone of the Church's constituency and contributed much of the impetus for the festivals. The Festival of Senhor do Bonfim should not be considered a "middle-class affair," however. The fact remains that the festivities were also attended by the entire city. After his visit in 1936, Donald Pierson went as far as to describe certain popular festivals, including that of Bonfim on Saturday and Ribeira Monday as "largely dominated by the lower classes." The more "elevated classes participated only in their automobiles" driving back and forth, or "watching from the windows and doors of their houses."[139]

As Pierson suggested, class and, by extension, race made a difference in how Bahians experienced and participated in the celebrations. Take, for instance, the events of Ribeira Monday. Having a car was an obvious difference in how attendees experienced the event. Some revelers rented a taxi, or carro-de-praça, to drive them around, but the cost was often twice the rate set by the police and was beyond the means of most members of the working class. As the festivities settled into their evening pattern, another distinction became clear: Some revelers had invitations to the social clubs or had connections with the veranistas, but most did not. Many families left the peninsula between 6:00 p.m. and 8:00 p.m., while after 8:00 p.m. others attended private gatherings in homes or private dances in the clubs.[140] Those who were less well connected continued to celebrate in the streets. In fact, for the most dedicated young men, the festivities continued beyond the time when they could get home via public transportation. Those who worked on the docks and in the warehouses of the lower city often found that the most effective solution was to make their way to the Mercado Modelo and catch a few hours of sleep on the pavement before the workday began on Tuesday. Similar performances of difference can be seen in most other of the major popular festivals.[141]

Significantly, these divisions were also hierarchized. As Linda Curcio-Nagy has shown, publicly celebrated religious festivals perform powerful integrative functions, but they also serve to mark or reinforce social division.[142] Hierarchical distinctions of color and class were all the more forceful for their publicly ritualized enactment in festival such as the one for the Senhor do Bonfim.[143] From the very outset of the procession the participants divided themselves by criteria that were specific to their group or class. One of the most conspicuous distinctions was that while some rode in cars to the peninsula, others went by mule-driven carts, and most walked. While the adorned mules no doubt could be seen (in contrast to the automobiles) as representing a link with the past, especially by journalists who were keen to emphasize the "traditional" aspects of the festival, the reality was that most Salvadorans simply had no access to cars. A fuller modernity and a more equitable distribution of wealth had not yet been realized in Salvador.[144]

A festival can take many shapes over the course of its life and can be read on many different levels and from many different perspectives. Yet it is important to acknowledge the point that Salvador's festivals reinforced a hierarchized distinction between the culture associated with Bahia's dominant class and that associated with the masses in a number of ways. With regard to the festivals, this was done both discursively, through the written word, and through the actual performance of the festivals.

Conclusion

Partly in response to subaltern pressure, partly on their own initiative, and partly in keeping with national shifts in Brazil, politicians and journalists in Salvador reenacted and rewrote the discourse on African-Bahian culture in relation to the city's principal popular festivals. During the Estado

Novo, local political and economic elites made efforts to associate themselves with the festivals to further their political agendas, including being present at the both sacred (Catholic) and profane (popular Catholic and Candomblé) elements of the ritual of the Washing of Bonfim. The actions of Vargas's interventors during the 1930s and 1940s solidified a tradition of populist engagement with Salvador's festivals and institutionalized government support for African-Bahian culture as expressed at the popular festivals that would continue into the twenty-first century. After the Estado Novo ended in 1945, Bahia's first elected governor in over a decade, Otávio Mangabeira, an old-school oligarch who had not been previously known for political populism, played a role in the consolidation of this new relationship. Mangabeira's appearances at the popular festivals supported the wider dominant-class acceptance of African-Bahian culture. Moreover, the mayor's office under José Wanderley Pinho continued to incentivize the festivals and spread their reach to the city's expanding population. Although Governor Regis Pacheco (1951–55) showed perhaps less interest in the festivals than any politician since 1931, he still appeared at the Washing of Bonfim. Mayors Osvaldo Gordilho and Aristóteles Góes increased the municipal subsidies for the festivals. At the same time, journalists and editors between 1930 and 1954 undertook a reappraisal of the representation of African-Bahian practices, creating a new discourse of cultural inclusivity by embracing Salvador's popular festive culture and African-Bahian practices and including them in a construction of Bahian regional identity.

Politicians, their appointees, even members of the military and economic elite and editors and journalists took control of the meanings of African-Bahian practices to construct a new notion of what "Bahia" actually meant. Salvador's popular festivals played a key role in this process. The festivals provided the practitioners of *cultura negra* with a public, ritualized forum. There were limits to this reappraisal, however, and the discourse of inclusion never raised African-Bahian practices to the same level as their Catholic, western, or European counterparts. The Catholic framework for the festivals was presented as "sacred," while the festivities and practice related to Candomblé were considered "profane." Meanwhile, conservative actors within the Catholic Church remained staunchly opposed to the legitimization of Candomblé expression at the festivals, and their own press, such as *Catholic Week* (*Semana Cathólica*), reflected these positions quite forcefully. Within Salvador's dominant class, the inclusion of African-Bahian cultural practices was not uniformly embraced. Conservative voices pushed back and insisted on limits to this inclusion. The next chapter examines how carnival, the city's biggest public festival, provided African Bahians, politicians, and the press with another important set of public rituals that contributed to redefining Bahianness as in large part a celebration of African-Bahian culture.

5

Carnival of the People

Batucadas and *Afoxés*

In 1942, Salvadoran poet, journalist, and magazine editor Áureo Contreiras wrote a piece for the conservative daily *A Tarde* titled "The Value of the Cordões and Batucadas to Carnival." In his article, which was reprinted the following year in the *Diário de Notícias*, he argued that the small clubs from the poorer neighborhoods (the *pequenos clubes*), including the African-Bahian *batucadas* (small percussion-based carnival groups), were the "truest aspects of the festivities" and the "authentic core of the carnivalesque soul."[1] In making his case, Contreiras appealed to the nationalist discourse coming into vogue in the 1940s that Brazil was a mixture of Indians, Africans, and Portuguese—"the three sad races"—whose "shouts and songs" filled the streets during carnival. The *cordões* and *batucadas,* popular carnival institutions that paraded during the three days of carnival, were born in reaction to both the joys and the bitterness of everyday popular life. "Real carnival," Contreiras was saying, was carnival as practiced by the working classes. Contreiras also singled out these groups' use of the *pandeiro, cuíca,* and *reco-reco*[2] "and all the barbarous instruments evocative of the old slave quarters and of the Candomblé *terreiros*" as links to a bittersweet Bahian past that was nevertheless central to Brazil's formation. Contreiras's praise illustrates the larger discursive shift toward celebrating working-class African-Bahian contributions to carnival as the truest, most authentic component of this Bahian festive institution.

Contreiras's appeal reveals a number of things. It emphasizes the presence of African-Bahian agency in pushing *cultura negra*—the *batucadas,* in particular—to the forefront of Bahian carnival. In a manner similar to that described in the above discussion of the popular festivals, African Bahians took advantage of the transformative power of carnival to push for and receive greater cultural and symbolic relevance within the city's carnival and beyond. Carnival's ludic (playful, transgressive) nature holds a capacity for individuals or groups to transcend, expand, or magnify themselves and their social condition in public spaces.[3] The *batucadas* institutionalized and ritualized the presence of working-class African-Bahian musical practices and sociability. The *afoxés*, groups whose carnival participation was deeply influenced by the culture and cosmology of the *terreiros*, were perhaps an even more forceful (re)assertion of the right to coexist of Salvador's long-marginalized and persecuted African-Bahian religious institutions, subcultures, and values. These assertions deepened the process by which African-Bahian practices were incorporated into notions of regional identity and Bahianness, as Bahian carnival came to the fore as another venue of cultural political mediation and the creation of a common cultural framework for political negotiation and disputation. Finally, Contreiras's appeal also reveals the relevance of the Vargas-era project of creating a national Brazilian identity and how that project gave impetus to the contributions of journalists, authors, and public intellectuals, among others, to the ideological reappraisal of the place of African-Bahian culture in Bahia.

The reappraisal of African-Bahian contributions to carnival, part of the focus of this chapter, was largely carried out in the articles and editorials written by members of the Association of Carnival Chroniclers such as Contreiras. This association of reporters, which included one or two from each of the city's major newspapers, spent the greater part of January and February and sometimes March organizing and encouraging participation in the various dances, dress rehearsals (*ensaios*), and ceremonies leading up to carnival. The Association of Carnival Chroniclers assumed responsibility for publicizing carnival, mobilizing participation, and generally livening up the festivities. Their newspapers were a primary source of awards and prizes during carnival alongside those from the mayor's office, thus wielding a degree of fiscal leverage to influence carnival performance. The Carnival Chroniclers were also the principal commentators on the events of the three days of carnival and thus actively participated in constructing the meanings of the festivity for the city. Their efforts played a fundamental role in shaping the structure of carnival, how people and groups participated (or did not participate), and the dominant interpretations of carnival.

The standard historiographic narrative on Bahian carnival barely recognizes the period from 1930 to 1954. The story typically begins in the 1880s, when the largely white "official carnival," with its grand parades, emerged alongside a "popular carnival" made up of a wide variety of smaller associations, including associations organized by African Bahians.[4] From this point the narrative jumps to 1949 and the founding of the *afoxé* Filhos de Gandhy and the creation in 1951 of the *trio elétrico* (electric trio), which was initially three musicians with amplified music atop a vehicle.[5] Both were significant innovations. Filhos de Gandhy, now several thousand strong, creates one of the most striking visual images of today's Bahian carnival. The *trio elétrico*, greatly updated technologically to be much bigger and much louder, provides contemporary carnival with its official structure and much of its commercial attraction.

Nevertheless, changes in Bahian carnival during the years from 1930 to 1954 were particularly significant for Bahian regional identity and cultural politics. From its earliest days in the 1880s to the late 1930s, Bahian carnival centered on the official parades organized by the city's elite, the centerpiece of which was the three *grandes clubes* (big clubs): Cruz Vermelha (Red Cross), Inocentes em Progresso (Innocents Progressing), and Fantoches da Euterpe (Marionettes of Euterpe, the Greek muse of music, song, and dance). After 1930, however, the elite clubs fell into a prolonged period of financial disarray that mirrored Salvador's relative economic decline, which lasted into the 1950s. "Popular carnival" and the small clubs filled the vacuum, creating new meanings of carnival in Bahia. From the late 1930s to the early 1950s, African-Bahian carnival associations, especially the *batucadas,* increased their public presence during the three days of celebrations. The *batucadas* played sambas that had been created in the recording industry, but they also wrote and performed their own music and lyrics and thus were a public manifestation of a sort of raw, uncommercialized, African Bahianness. The 1940s became the "Era of the Batucadas." Their rise was demographic, but their popularity and favorable coverage in the press also increased. Furthermore, during the late 1940s the *afoxés* experienced a revival that gave them an opportunity to add their own contributions to the reshaping of Bahian regional identity.

After 1950, the elite clubs regained their financial footing and some of their former prominence, but they did not recover their previous level of dominance over the form, content, or meanings of carnival. For over a decade Salvador's carnival had favored the festive practices of working-class African Bahians as the central symbolic markers of Salvadoran carnival identity. The importance of samba and *batucadas* during carnival and the reanimation of the *afoxés* in the late 1940s had established a permanent and powerful cultural association between African-Bahianness and carnival in the dominant discourse. The demise of the elite clubs and the rise of the small clubs shifted how working-class Bahians experienced carnival away from a passive act (of appreciating the floats and their symbolic reinforcement of social hierarchy) toward their active participation.

Over the same period, moreover, carnival in Salvador spread and became more democratic and working class as the number of smaller clubs, including the *batucadas*, increased in the city's working-class neighborhoods. This demographic shift distinguished Salvador's participatory street carnival from Rio de Janeiro's more centralized spectacle. At the same time, from the 1930s, working-class Salvadorans spread popular carnival festivity beyond its traditional demarcation, invading the ritual space of the other major popular festivals and thus widening the presence of elements of African-Bahian culture such as samba and the *batucadas* beyond the spatial and temporal confines of the carnival calendar.[6] This chapter will discuss how carnival in Bahia changed after 1930 and how these changes contributed to the reshaping of the meanings of African-Bahian culture. Carnival was not, however, an egalitarian moment free of its historical-structural context. Carnival provided not only avenues of racial and class resistance against the dominant culture but also mechanisms by which the dominant class could co-opt and circumscribe subaltern initiatives and/or reinforce the status quo.[7] The chapter ends with an assessment of how carnival continued to reinforce Salvador's hierarchies of race and class.

Carnival in Salvador

The early precursor to carnival in Salvador and elsewhere in Brazil was the *entrudo*. Imported from Portugal, *entrudo* was characterized by street battles and coquettish play between women and men of all social classes involving water bombs and flour. Although slaves and servants worked hard to prepare festive meals, do extra laundry, and equip their masters with water and supplies, they along with free blacks found time to participate. Theoretically the *entrudo* was banned as early as 1853, largely on the grounds of being incompatible with "civilization." In practice, however, the practical jokes and rowdy behavior continued into the 1880s, even after the Bahian police "definitively banned" it in 1878. The Bahian press continued to note, and despair of, such behavior until 1901, especially when the elite were not involved, attacking it as "barbarous" and "uncivilized."[8]

The emergence of organized processions in the 1880s marked the beginnings of Salvador's modern street carnival, which elites envisioned as a more ordered and family-friendly event than the popular and promiscuous *entrudo*. In 1884 an elite carnival institution, the Cruz Vermelha Club, was the first to parade through the main streets of the city. This inspired other young men of elite families, and the following year a second carnival club, Fantoches da Euterpe, paraded in the streets. Soon after that, "dissidents" from Cruz Vermelha founded Inocentes em Progresso. All three *grandes clubes* were dominated by and catered to the interest of the elite and Salvador's small middle class. Their size and prestige dominated Salvador's official carnival throughout the First Republic. They constructed massive allegorical floats that passed through the center of town. Politicians associated themselves with the *grandes clubes*, and the municipal government subsidized them. The newspapers' extended carnival coverage prior to the 1930s focused on their preparations and performances. Not surprisingly, their activities drew heavily on European carnival customs for inspiration, particularly those of Venetian carnival, and this period is often referred to as the era of Carnaval Veneziano. The elite clubs held confetti battles and masked balls for their members on Friday and Saturday nights in the theaters of São João and Politeama, underlining the distinctions between themselves and "popular carnival."

The centerpiece of this period was the official carnival procession on the Sunday before Shrove Tuesday. The members of the three big clubs dressed up in costumes and paraded along a circuit with huge and complex *carros alegóricos*, or floats, that were decorated in keeping with the themes for that year. The crowds along the route threw rose petals, confetti, and streamers, applauding their favorites. The clubs imported most of the materials for their floats and costumes from France, Italy, and England. Even during the years when the elite clubs did not turn out (for financial or other reasons), they were, for most journalists, the "European" and therefore the civilized and modern ideal by which all lesser carnival associations were judged.

Many smaller clubs also participated in carnival during this period. Initially, most of these were middle class, with names such as Gentlemen of Malta, Sons of Venice, or Sons of Pluto. But we should hesitate before accepting Olga Von Simson's assertion of the early twentieth century as the era of "bourgeois carnival," as opposed to "popular carnival."[9] As early as the late 1890s, popular carnival institutions were in evidence in Salvador. Kim Butler has found "dozens" of "African" clubs after 1896, with names such as the African Knights, African Vagrants, African Hunters, Grandsons of Africa, Defenders of Africa, the African Embassy, and African Merrymakers. Many of these were the carnivalesque manifestations of Salvador's centuries-long traditions of African-Bahian *batuques*, festive, religious, or merely sociable gatherings around percussion, song, and dance. These were soon to be increasingly referred to in the sources, and at first mostly pejoratively, as *batucadas*. Others were simply *blocos* (literally "blocks," or coordinated groups of merrymakers), while at least a few were the first wave of *afoxés*.[10]

This evidence of so many small "Africanized" associations has led Vieira Filho to conclude that after 1904, while official carnival in Salvador may have been dominated by the bourgeoisie, carnival that took place outside the official circuit was very significantly working class, especially in African-Bahian working-class neighborhoods.[11] Once the *entrudo* faded away, along with the pranksterism and incivility that characterized it, the elite turned their anxieties and criticisms to "Africanized" cultural activities in public space.[12] Local authorities banned all Afro-centric clubs from carnival from 1905 to 1914.[13] Clearly, the decades prior to 1930 were a period when the Bahian elite, especially in the early 1910s, still felt very vulnerable to the possibility that post-abolition Salvador was becoming more "African" and less "European," as they understood these terms. The most salient social polarity in Salvadoran carnival, then, was a struggle over whether European or African-Creole norms would define Bahian culture.[14]

After the ban was lifted following carnival season in 1914, Afrocentric carnival clubs returned and grew in number during the 1920s. Even before 1914, the city's daily newspapers began to call attention to the largely African-Brazilian practice of samba music performance and dance within Salvador's carnival. Elites, too, were more accepting of samba. The *corta jaca* (a form of samba) and the *maxixe* (a precursor of samba) had been incorporated in the carnival program of elite processions and dances in Salvador as early as 1899, and by 1915, samba was appearing alongside opera overtures and other pieces of "erudite music" during concerts or revues. Then, in 1917, a national record label released what would become known as the first commercialized samba, the song "Pelo Telefone" ("On the Telephone").[15] Journalists reported the following year that carnival was given over to explicit engagement with the samba: African Bahians wrote, performed, and danced sambas for and during carnival. Later, in the 1920s, the reporting on sambas performed in the streets and plazas (although not in the official processions) was reasonably positive, albeit slightly patronizing. Samba, it seems, was an African-Bahian cultural practice that the dominant class could accept, especially during carnival.[16] Yet it would be more than a decade before the public discourse in Bahia enshrined samba within Bahian carnival and established the resoundingly positive associations between the city's largest, most public cultural event and the region's African-Bahian cultural heritage.

By the 1930s carnival in Salvador had settled into a general pattern. The festivities began on Sunday and ended on Tuesday night. The climactic main parade was typically held on Tuesday evening. The "dramatic and luxuriant" corteges of the elite clubs were the principal attraction, often peopled with "the most beautiful and distinctive feminine visions of our [high] society."[17] The principal allegorical characters on these floats were most often represented by light-skinned Bahians, while the lesser roles in the parades (but rarely on the actual floats), were filled by people of both European and African ancestry. In years when the elite clubs did not parade or contributed in a diminished fashion, there was still an official carnival dominated by dominant-class institutions such as the Athletic Association or the Bahian Tennis Association. Onlookers in the crowds demonstrated their enthusiasm and allegiances by shouting out the names of the elite clubs as they passed by.[18] Families set up chairs and even sofas along the main route so the older, younger, and better off could sit and watch the floats, a practice one scholar has characterized as an extension of the elites' reception rooms (*salas de visita*).[19] Originally floats were pulled by horse or donkey, but later motorized vehicles did the pulling. Lesser parades, some with allegorical floats and decorated cars, some with musicians aboard, toured up and down the procession route for much of each day on carnival Sunday and Monday.

The official route, where transit was strictly regulated and the crowds were well policed, was along the Rua Chile and, later in the period, along the Avenida Sete de Setembro. These routes were where the principal crowds gathered, arriving in fantasy dress and masks from early morning, often in same-sex groups. Costumes varied widely, although certain genres or types were very popular, even emblematic—the doctor, the baby with pacifier, the street urchin, the pregnant woman, and animals of all types. Characterizations of Brazilian folk types also made their appearance, such as the *caipira*, or country bumpkin; the *caboclo*, or Brazilian Indian (who was typically portrayed as having both indigenous and Portuguese ancestry); and the *vaqueiro*, or cowboy, of the interior of Bahia. Also represented were archetypes inspired by history and by Hollywood, such as North American cowboys and "Indians," Roman legionnaires, pirates, and the Pierrots and Harlequins of European carnivals past. The masks were playful, but perhaps they also contributed a maliciousness and licentiousness that was more suggestive than anything else, as Salvador was still intimate enough that even masks did not guarantee anonymity. As Edison Carneiro put it, the answer to the ritual entreaty "Can you guess who I am?" ("*Você me conhece?*") in Salvador was easily "Yes."[20] Ether in stylized canisters, or *lança-perfume*, contributed to the gaiety when it was sprayed on a handkerchief or on someone's costume below the nose, but it was burning agony when it was sprayed purposely in someone's eyes.[21] Moving through the crowds, roving associations of revelers in *blocos*, *cordões*, *batucadas*, and *afoxés* complicated the picture all along the routes and the outlying areas. Masks were prohibited after 6:00 p.m., although for several years during the war they were prohibited during the day as well. By the time the day's procession had finished, revelers had already begun congregating in bars, members' clubs, or the homes of friends or relatives, or they had returned home. Most everyone was off the streets by midnight.[22]

Beyond the Rua Chile the excitement spread farther, spilling in one direction along the Avenida Sete de Setembro and in the other direction into the plaza known as the Terreiro de Jesus and adjacent neighborhoods. The municipal government provided lighting and ornamentation along the length of the official parade route from the Terreiro de Jesus to Campo Grande at the end of Avenida Sete de Setembro. Local businessmen, especially those who ran hotels, bar, cafes, and shops, also contributed. Embracing the adage "Greater animation, greater profits" ("*Maior animação, maiores lucros*"), local business owners decorated the streets off the main parade route with streamers, flags, and lighting, even erecting stages for live music and getting involved in carnival play themselves. The same preparations occurred to lesser degrees in many of Salvador's outlying neighborhoods, often attracting significant local participation, leading to the formation of very local carnival traditions. Here, away from the "official" carnival, the celebration relied on the contributions of small neighborhood carnival clubs.

These small clubs—known as *blocos*, *cordões*, *batucadas*, and *afoxés*—were the central institutions and mainstays of popular carnival from 1930 to 1954. There was some imprecision, or at least overlap, in the usage of the four terms for the small clubs, even within the same newspapers or between members of the same association. In addition, clubs sometimes switched from one type to another. In general, however, all small clubs had an elected or self-appointed leadership (*diretoria*) and each had their own musicians, flag bearer (*porta estandarte*), and general members, called *sócios*.

The *blocos* and *cordões* were composed mainly of individuals from the middle class or from the poor and working classes. (The *batucadas* and *afoxés* will be described in detail below.) The main distinction between the *blocos* and *cordões* was that the *cordões* used a mobile cordon to keep control of their members as they paraded through large crowds and to keep out potential troublemakers. Partly for this reason the *cordões* tended to be smaller than the *blocos*. The size of the *blocos* and *cordões* at the beginning of the period averaged between twenty-five and seventy-five members, but by the end of the period some *blocos* had more than four hundred participants. Other than size, there was very little in practice that separated the *blocos* and the *cordões* from one another. They both grew out of nineteenth-century processional organizations known as *ranchos* and *ternos,* which sang, played music, and carried standards and were mostly associated with the Festival of the Three Kings. They both used a variety of wind and percussion instruments and played and sang a range of appropriate and inappropriate carnival songs. They specialized in the *marchas* (military marches rhythmically adapted for carnival) the radio and the record industry popularized from the early 1900s. The lyrics of this genre were festive and were often satirical, suggestive, and even raucous. Each year the *blocos* and *cordões* chose a theme that governed their choice of costume, songs, and behavior. Their masquerades fit their names. For instance, the Merchants of Baghdad wore baggy silk trousers and sash belts, open-necked silk shirts (if they wore any shirts at all), curly toed slippers, and hoop earrings and pendant necklaces, not to mention big, shiny turbans.[23]

Blocos and *cordões* could be either predominantly middle-class or working-class associations, and generally they were associated with a given profession or place of business. The *bloco* Vai Levando (Take It Away), for instance, was founded in the 1940s by dock workers. In photographs from 1946, this crew wears relaxed uniforms (flower-printed shirts) and is almost entirely African Bahian. Although *blocos* and *cordões* of the middle class could be quite racially mixed, it is striking that the majority of newspaper photographs showed mostly or entirely white or mostly or entirely black and mixed-race small carnival clubs.

The *blocos* and *cordões* were sexually mixed. Some smaller clubs seemed to be mostly women, as their names would indicate—Crioulas Farristas (Festive Creole Women), for instance. Indications from the sources suggest these were not men masquerading as women, although this was common—it was carnival, after all. The *bloco* Garotos do Morro (Kids from the

Hill) from Liberdade was presided over by Hilda Santos.[24] Also memorable from 1943 was the number of female (and male) carnival-goers dressed as U.S. soldiers, complete with the caps. Many women embraced the new fashion that year of a "uniform" that consisted of a blouse and short pants.[25] Yet even when the members of the small clubs were mostly women, the leaders were mostly male. Women members typically held only the position of flag bearer. The directors were generally responsible for deciding what days (or mornings or afternoons) the groups paraded through the streets, where they went, what competitions they entered, and what music they played. When not parading or competing, the members were free to celebrate carnival in their own ways.

Both the region's overall economic performance after 1930 and the war meant that participation in the smaller clubs waxed and waned. Establishing an accurate trajectory of individual clubs over the entire period is probably not possible, but the prevailing trend after 1930 was toward more new *blocos* and *cordões* that brought more people into organized ritual festivity. The first mention of public subsidies for the small clubs comes in the early 1940s, although newspaper-sponsored competitions that offered cash prizes date to the mid-1930s.[26] Thus although the elite clubs were the focus of official carnival in the early twentieth century, the small clubs played a role in the festivities and were poised to emerge as more relevant. Starting in the mid-1930s, the small clubs—the *blocos*, the *cordões*, and especially the *batucadas*—began to rival and eventually surpass the elite corteges as the centerpiece of Bahian carnival.

The Power and Demise of the Elite Clubs

In the early 1930s, politicians and the press gravitated to the power of the big clubs—Cruz Vermelha, Inocentes em Progresso, and Fantoches da Euterpe—and thus enhanced their aura. A central inspiration was the possibility that Salvador could to some degree repeat the success that Rio de Janeiro was having identifying itself nationally and internationally with its carnival. In the case of Rio de Janeiro, this was happening through the institutionalization of its "samba schools" (large working-class, neighborhood-based organizations) within its carnival format.[27] Bahia's dominant class, however, clearly preferred the big clubs as the centerpiece of the festivities, and the dominant narrative in the press in the days leading up to carnival focused on whether or not the clubs would participate, who their queens would be, what would happen at their events, and what the themes of their allegorical floats would be. Bahian elites, especially young adult children of political and economic leaders, continued to associate themselves entirely with the three elite clubs after 1930, as did the Estado Novo political regime.[28] This is somewhat surprising, given Vargas's emphasis on co-opting the working-class samba schools into typical patron-client relationships with his government. Bahian newspapers occasionally reminded everyone of Vargas's interest in fostering carnival activities in the national capital, for example pointing out that media reports from Rio de Janeiro "inform that Getúlio Vargas has authorized the Mayor's Office of Rio to augment the contribution toward Rio's carnival clubs."[29]

In Bahia, however, Vargas's administrators must have felt that the elite clubs provided a suitable conduit for connecting with Salvadorans, taking advantage of the longstanding ties of loyalty between members of the working class and the elite clubs. Before 1930, the municipal government had often provided a baseline of financial support for the official carnival parade. In addition, municipal authorities had typically provided traffic control during the festivities, liaised with privately organized neighborhood commissions of local business owners, and provided illumination and decoration for the central area. From the early 1930s, the mayor's office also began to subsidize the appearance of the three big clubs, which symbolized the power of their elite members and legitimized their position at the top of Salvadoran society.[30] This of course made sense for a number of reasons, and the clubs were not shy about pointing this out in their annual requests to the mayor's office for the subsidies that by 1930 they had almost come to expect. The benefit, as one letter put it, of the prosperity of the clubs would be "reflected in the progress of the city, intensifying the movement of its commerce, its industry, and its arts" as well as providing a much-deserved "sound distraction" for the population of the city and state.[31] There is also some indication that in the years when the big three were to be involved in the parade, the mayor's office provided financial resources for the official main parade route along Rua Chile at the expense of the more popular and traditional festivities along the Baixa dos Sapateiros. The mayor's office dragged its feet so much that despite that thoroughfare's traditional claims to rival the Rua Chile, by 1940 the Baixa dos Sapateiros was no longer part of the official parade route.[32]

After the beginning of the Estado Novo in 1937, the new government's administrators also appreciated the political advantages of associating themselves with a successful carnival. They seemed to have increased their support for carnival over the years before World War II. They still focused,

however, on the elite clubs, as illustrated by the fact that in 1939 the interventor, the mayor, the head of the Secretariat of Public Security, and other
high-ranking Estado Novo administrators and ideologues held honorary
positions on the Board of Directors of the Cruz Vermelha carnival club.
This was not an elitist or exclusionary act as it may seem. The big clubs
had a lot of popular support, especially Cruz Vermelha.[33] Working-class
Bahians had strong ties of loyalty to one elite club or another that at times
spilled over into assaults, sometimes with knives.[34] According to occasional
police reports in the newspapers, these disputes between club affiliates were
invariably between artisans or workers. Often entire professions identified
with a club. Shoemakers, for example, supported Cruz Vermelha. These
allegiances decreased the distance between elites and the rest of Salvador
and reinforced the ties of patronage that structured Salvador's social hierarchy.[35] The mayors, beginning with Estado Novo appointee Neves da Rocha
(1938–42), associated themselves with the festivities by presiding over such
events as the ceremony to crown the carnival queen.[36]

In the 1930s newspapers and radio programs, whose contents were often mentioned in the press, strongly supported the idea that the three elite
clubs were central to Salvador's carnival. Coverage focused on the institutions and activities of these—their floats, their parades, their dances. The
themes these clubs chose included references to the classical world, Western Europe, Asia and the Middle East, and Brazilian current events. These
themes rarely spoke directly to working-class or African-Bahian culture
prior to late 1938, and North American sociologist Donald Pierson recorded that "of the 168 young ladies from Bahia's best families on the floats
in the carnival parade of 1936, all were whites except two, and these were
very light mulattoes."[37] The three elite clubs dominated the extended and
much-publicized process of voting for the carnival queen, as their candidates were the only ones who had any chance of winning. Tellingly, photographs of the candidates never revealed any unambiguous African ancestry,
and the occasional biographical detail almost always emphasized that the
candidates, and especially the winners, were from the wealthier classes.
The winner in 1939, for example, was Senhorita Maria Regina Gouveia,
who "belonged to a traditional Bahian family."[38] Even though coverage of
the activities of small clubs and working-class events often squeezed into
the column inches devoted to the big clubs, especially from the mid-1930s,
this initially only served to establish their marginal status within the media
discourse on carnival prior to 1940.

This marginal status was not to last, as 1937 was the final year (with one exception) that the three big clubs paraded with their own separate corteges. In 1938, only Cruz Vermelha, the largest of the three, managed to participate. The elite clubs still held dances and events, but a main parade was beyond them because of financial problems. The global depression had placed a great strain on Bahia's economic growth that weakened the big clubs' capacity to parade their traditional lavish floats. Indeed, their prestige had sunk so low that in 1939 the Municipal Department of Trees and Gardens threatened to prohibit the clubs from participating that year if they constructed floats that were big enough to damage the trees lining the parade route.[39] The Department of Trees and Gardens need not have worried. Despite the promises in 1941 of a carnival "blitzkrieg" by "the assault cars of the big clubs," World War II ended the era of the *grandes clubes*.[40] Even though Brazil remained neutral until August 1942, the war stifled the mood for street carnival. Public festivity on the scale of previous years did not seem appropriate. The war also prevented the big clubs from importing the luxuries they needed for their floats and costumes. The conflict in Europe meant lean times for Bahia's commercial oligarchy that lasted into the 1950s. Carnival in 1940 was "almost good," but only because the big clubs managed to combine their resources to create one allegorical float, which the press dutifully praised as indicative of Salvador's spirit of wartime cooperation and sacrifice.[41] This was as good as it got until the "carnival of Victory" celebrations in 1946. Carnival in 1943 was "very, very cold," and most partying occurred at the dances in the headquarters of the various clubs rather than in the streets.[42] The following year it was an "indisputable failure."[43] Street carnival was effectively canceled in 1945, and it was left to the small clubs to carry out carnival's "offensive against unhappiness."[44]

After the war, the three elite clubs struggled to resurrect their dominance of carnival. In 1948, the Conselho Deliberativo dos Préstitos Carnavalescos (Carnival Processions Advisory Council)—representing Cruzeiro da Vitória (formerly Cruz Vermelha, which had changed its name during the war to avoid confusion with the International Red Cross), Fantoches da Eutuerpe, and Inocentes em Progresso—beseeched Governor Otávio Mangabeira to financially support the three big clubs in their effort to "return to the streets of the city, as they did before the war."[45] The governor turned them down on the grounds that the state was facing its own challenges and could not possibly subsidize all three individual cortejes, especially given their price tag of over one million cruzeiros each.[46] The

governor nevertheless gave each club "only a small subsidy" (100,000 cruzeiros each), which was not far off the subsidy in 1939 but which meant that
the clubs managed only one combined cortege, although each club had its
own float and its own flag, trumpeters, band, and honor guard.[47] Governor
Mangabeira let it be known that he would provide the required funding the
following year, for the four hundredth anniversary of Salvador's founding,
whose "maximum splendor" was more and more openly intended to attract
domestic and international tourists.[48]

In 1949, Governor Mangabeira was at least partly true to his word, although in the end he was not as generous as the clubs had perhaps expected.
Mangabeira was keenly interested in returning the big clubs to Salvador's
carnival. This was unusual, as state sponsorship (as opposed to municipal
subsidy) was not common in Bahia during these years. During the carnival
of 1949, Mangabeira and his family attended the official opening dance of
the festivities at the Athletic Association of Bahia. This was atypical for the
aristocratic Mangabeira, who was not known for his embrace of cultural
populism. He also visited various points around the city where the informal street carnival was most intense. Finally, on the evening of the grand
parade, the governor and his family and their guests, who were all from the
local political and social elite, observed the main event, which included the
three big clubs, as it passed the governor's mansion, which was adjacent to
the official parade route.[49]

It was not lost on Mangabeira that the weakening of the three big clubs
and their inability to afford lavish independent corteges had become a
metaphor for the demise of Bahia's political and economic influence at the
national level. Newspaper editorials laid the blame for the demise of Salvador's carnival on Vargas and in particular on the political and economic
priorities of the Estado Novo. In 1947, the *Diário de Notícias* accused the
dictator of "restricting carnival's liberties" and terminating the revival of
Salvador's "golden age." The newspapers frequently made a link between
carnival glory and Bahian glory, "showing the rest of Brazil what the 'Good
Land' [*Boa Terra*, i.e., Bahia] was capable of realizing." Regionalists felt that
Governor Mangabeira should attempt to revive carnival. In the democratic
fervor that marked both the Allies' defeat of the Axis powers and the end
of the Estado Novo, the electoral success in 1947 of Mangabeira, Bahia's
most nationally important native son, over Vargas's preferred candidate
symbolized Bahia's rejection of the Estado Novo in favor of regionalism.
A revived carnival would underscore this emphasis, especially if it came
during the four hundredth anniversary of the founding of the city. There

was even talk of Mangabeira winning the presidency in 1950, though this did not come to pass; Mangabeira failed to win the nomination of his own national party.[50] Hopes for the revival of Salvador's big three clubs and hence the capital's carnival glory fizzled out, too, at least for the moment. Elite carnival revelers had to content themselves with their dances, their carnival queen contest, and their confetti battles. The money was simply not there. The municipal government gave nothing in 1949, although in 1950 Mangabeira released a small subsidy that enabled the three clubs to return to their practice of forming a single cortege with one small float for each club.[51]

From 1951, however, correspondence between the clubs and the mayor's office reveals that the Mayor's office reprised its former role of heavily subsidizing the three elite clubs.[52] This included occasional help from the state government as well, leading to a revival of the elite clubs' parades and of their central position in carnival and carnival discourse.[53] For fifteen years carnival in Salvador had ceased to be about dominant-class "artistry and luxuriousness" and was instead very much about the "*batucada* and animation."[54] Any loss of Bahian political prestige during the Vargas era was somewhat compensated for by Brazil's wider embrace of symbols of African-Brazilian popular culture, which Bahia had in abundance and with which the region was becoming inextricably associated.

The Rise of the *Batucadas*

The decline of the elite clubs created a vacuum, and the lesser carnival associations—the *pequenos clubes*, or "small clubs"—became much more central to Bahian carnival. Even before 1938 the size, number, and initiative of the smaller clubs were already altering the balance of carnival toward the popular. The *Diário de Notícias* began its first competition for small clubs that year, since they were "more animated this year than ever before."[55] In the 1940s, the number of small clubs tripled to well over one hundred, transforming carnival from an elite-centered festival to a popular event dominated almost entirely by the small clubs.

The increase in the number and geographical spread of the *batucadas* contributed to this popularization. In his introduction to Anísio Félix's *Filhos de Gandhi*, Bahian historian Cid Teixeira referred to the 1940s as the "Era of the Batucadas."[56] Judging from the carnival-related articles in the newspapers, this was no overstatement, but it was not something that could have been foreseen two decades earlier. Carnivalesque *batucadas*, to all intents and purposes, did not exist in Salvador prior to 1930. Instead, Salvador boasted numerous small *blocos* and *cordões* with Afrocentric references in their names, which, thanks to the initiative and agency of the city's working classes, proliferated during the 1920s, picking up where they had left off before the ban on Afrocentric clubs between 1905 and 1914. The reaction in the newspapers was largely positive, especially from 1930 to 1934, when the elite clubs did not parade. The newspapers embraced "popular carnival" and enthused about all the small clubs equally, including those closely associated with African-Bahian culture.[57] In addition to the small number of *batucadas* and *afoxés* that were active but mostly anonymous in the early 1930s, we find *blocos* and *cordões* with names like Os Africanos em Pândega (The Festive Africans), Guerreiros da África (Warriors of Africa), Filhos da África (Sons of Africa), Lordes Africanos (African Lords), Ideal Africano (African Ideal), and Gongo Africano (African Gong). One was named Pândegos de África (African Merrymakers), possibly in homage to one of the first Afrocentric clubs from the 1890s. In 1935, while much was made of the revival of the big clubs and their official parade, significant attention was also given to the semiofficial parade of the small clubs, of which there were over forty, including "musical groups, clubs, *grupos africanos* [African groups], *cordões*, and *batucadas*."[58]

The *batucadas* emerged in the early or mid-1930s. From 1935 the newspapers begin to use the term *batucadas* in addition to *blocos* and *cordões*. This was the first year in which this was done in any systematic way, marking a change not only in nomenclature but also in carnival practice. At this point the Afrocentric *blocos* and *cordões*—the *grupos africanos*—largely disappear from view in press coverage. By 1938, the group A Negra Africana em Folia (Black African Women Celebrating) was the only one vibrant enough to make it into the newspapers. Perhaps many of the Afrocentric clubs became *batucadas* or samba schools or stayed as *blocos* or *cordões* but changed their names to something befitting a trend away from the Afrocentric, most likely influenced by the example set in Rio de Janeiro. Guerreiros de África, for example, may have hypothetically become a samba school, taking the name Bambas da zona (Neighborhood Hotshots) or Malandros da Avenida (Hustlers of the Avenue).

Supporting this supposition, newspaper coverage in 1935 included a large influx of previously unlisted names of small clubs that included all genres, not just *batucadas*. The members of the Afrocentric clubs may have joined one of these other genres. Surely most did not retire from carnival. Unfortunately, newspaper reports are too vague for us to be certain, and oral history interviews are inconclusive. Perhaps this apparent decline of the Afrocentric *cordões* or *afoxés* may have been influenced, like so much associated with carnival, by changing trends or fashions. In addition, perhaps the need to assert an African heritage had decreased as acceptance of cultural traditions increased under Magalhães and Vargas. This need may have been fulfilled within the emerging *batucadas* and samba schools, which were embraced in the nation's capital. Finally, newspaper reporting tended to follow the latest novelties more closely than the older practices. Regardless of the reason, however, the earlier working-class, Afrocentric clubs—the outgrowth of community organization and ethnic identification in the post-abolition period—clearly provided a platform for the rise of the *batucadas* and *afoxés* of the 1930s and 1940s, which in turn must be understood as heavily indebted to an African and Creole cultural community that had its own institutions, particularly those associated with Candomblé, and made minimal concessions to the dominant culture, notwithstanding ties of patronage with members of the middle class, especially light-skinned *mulatos*.[59]

By 1937, nine different *batucada* carnival associations were mentioned in the carnival coverage, roughly a quarter of all the small clubs whose genre (*bloco, cordão,* etc.) could be verified. It is not clear what led to a small club being mentioned, although generally the bigger, more active clubs were included or those that sent some sort of notice to the newspapers. Nevertheless, an assessment of the coverage provides a general idea of the increase in participation of the *batucadas*. For instance, in 1948, twenty-one different *batucadas* or samba schools were mentioned, representing just over half of the verifiable total. While the number of small clubs grew rapidly from the late 1930s, the rate of increase of the *batucadas* outpaced that of the *blocos* and *cordões*. In 1951, twenty *batucadas* were mentioned, although after that, the number leveled off and then began to decline.[60] However, in 1951, forty *batucadas* participated in the "Parade of the Batucadas," so while there remains some imprecision in determining the absolute numbers and relative weight of the participation of *batucudas* in Bahian carnival, forty was significant.

The presence of the *batucadas* in Salvador's carnival after 1930 grew from the city's rich musical heritage. Salvador was steeped in local historical traditions of percussion bands and public performances. These included the eighteenth- and nineteenth-century *batuques*, a particular subset of rhythms and dances with origins in the context of New World African and African-Bahian culture from which the *batucadas* derived their name.[61]

Salvador also boasted carnival precedents such as the *afoxés* of the early twentieth century and the nineteenth-century *cucumbís* described by Nina Rodrigues, Arthur Ramos, and others.[62] Both institutions brought groups of Africans and African Bahians onto the streets during carnival. However, the contemporary impetus for Salvador's carnival *batucadas* came from Rio de Janeiro's samba schools in the 1920s and the popularization of the *repinique* or *tambor*, the portable percussion instrument that allowed the players much greater mobility. Important too was the rise of cultural nationalism in Brazil and the consequent interest in regional or national musical genres and local composers of all genres. This intellectual trend was taken up in Salvador with some alacrity in the late 1920s, and the African-Bahian samba, the *batuque*, and then the *batucada* were obvious beneficiaries. During the First Republic, any public form of the *batuque* or *batucada* was likely to be singled out for dominant-class criticism in Salvador, although during the early days of samba in the 1910s and 1920s the popularity of these genres at clubs and theatre reviews rose and fell.

Salvador's *batucadas*, also fittingly known as samba schools (*escolas de samba*), were most often entirely male affairs. They typically had between ten and twenty working-class African-Bahian members. Donald Pierson described them as comprising "invariably blacks or dark mulattoes."[63] The members were effectively a roving percussion band. The *batucadas* were typically based in neighborhoods, although any associative ties could bring together musicians and revelers from a variety of neighborhoods or occupations. The costumes or uniforms were the biggest expense for the members, but they were also a point of pride. Each individual was responsible for acquiring the fabric and hiring a seamstress or doing their own sewing.[64] As the name *batucada* implies, percussion and particularly samba rhythms were their forte. They marched in single-file lines and played the samba hits of the day, although the musical style of the *batucadas* meant a different sort of rendition of these songs than what was heard on the radio. In addition, many *batucadas* played songs of their own creation. The *batucadas*, or *sambas do morro* ("sambas from the hill," or working-class neighborhoods), as they were also known in Bahia, were much more raw and less melodic. This was the African-Bahian cultural practice closest to the musical traditions of the working classes of Salvador.[65]

Two examples of *batucadas* from 1948 illustrate their general characteristics. Malandros em Folia (Hustlers Celebrating) was from the working-class district of Roça do Lobo in Tororó, and Samba School Malandros do Amor (Hustlers of Love) was from the working-class district of Alto

Figure 5.1. A carnival *batucada* in the streets of Salvador, late 1940s. Photo by Pierre Verger. By permission of the Fundação Pierre Verger. © Fundação Pierre Verger

das Pombas. The descriptive information comes from the unofficial daily of Bahia's Communist Party, *O Momento*. During its short legal life span (1945–47) in the immediate postwar climate of democratic openness, the Communist Party used its newspaper to celebrate African-Bahian culture as part of a broader emphasis on working-class life. The newspaper continued to publish, albeit sporadically, after Brazilian communists were proscribed from running for elections in 1948. Not surprisingly, *O Momento* reported more frequently on the African-Bahian *batucadas* than on *blocos* or *cordões*. This testifies to the relevance of the *batucadas* to poor and working-class Salvadorans. Malandros em Folia consisted of about ten men, seven women dancers known as *pastoras*, and three girls filling roles as two flag bearers and a mascot. Their principal leader was Otávio Neves de Jesus, nicknamed Dunga, a corporal in the police force (*cabo de polícia*) and, according to the newspaper, a hotshot (*craque*) on one of the local soccer teams, Botafogo. The group wrote their own sambas, which they played during their formal dry run (*ensaio*) through the neighborhood, bringing the neighbors to their doorways to watch. It also attracted a reporter for *O Momento*, who published the samba lyrics:

> *Nosso samba não pode parar*
> *Se alguém vier nos desacatar*
> *Damos couro até o sol raiar*
> *Com Bia na cuíca*
> *Bento no surdo e Balance*
> *Neves fazendo a marcação*
> *A turma todo dá couro*
> *Para alegrar os corações*

> Our samba can't be stopped
> If someone insults us
> We'll deliver the goods till the sun comes up
> With Bia on the *cuíca*
> Bento on the *surdo* drum and Balance
> Neves keeping time
> The band as one gives their all
> To spread happiness to everyone

At this point, each of the principal players sang their own piece. Bia, for example, who played the *cuíca*, sang first:

> *Fala cuíca malvada*
> *Fala cuíca*
> *No lugar que tem cuíca*
> *Tamborim não vale nada*

> Speak, wicked *cuíca*
> Speak *cuíca*
> Wherever there's a *cuíca*
> Tamborim[66] ain't worth nothing

Then Balance sang:

> *Crave o punhal no meu peito*
> *Tire sangue e lave a mão*

O relógio marca a hora
Da nossa separação.

Stick the knife in my chest
Draw blood and wipe the hand
The clock marks the hour
Of our separation.

Finally, Dunga sang lyrics recalling the name of the group:

Tenho direito de ser malandro
Mas não de ser um santo
Nossa Senhora lhe cubra
Com seu divino manto.

I have the right to be a *malandro*
But not to be a saint
Our Lady cover you
With her divine mantle.[67]

Two things stand out here. The first is the reference to the *malandro* (hustler), whose typical behaviors included skipping work, vagabondage, street fighting, womanizing, living by one's wits, or being otherwise "socially irresponsible." The reference to the hustler's lifestyle (*malandragem*) reminds us that the sambas the *batucadas* played during carnival were often edgier than those played over the radio (especially after 1938) or sambas whose lyrics were printed in the papers in the "For you to sing" columns. The popular sambas of the *batucadas* also represented a certain degree of rebellious assertiveness in their glorification of working-class male values that were associated with samba's socioeconomic context, values that were not necessarily shared or appreciated by the dominant class. Also notable in the lyrics cited above is a pleasure in performance and an assertive self-confidence and playful competitiveness that was one of the chief characteristics of Salvador's popular carnival during the Vargas era. These characteristics of mid-twentieth-century working men's culture in Salvador were manifested in song, dance, checkers, gambling, storytelling, chasing women, capoeira, football, and many other activities.[68]

A second notable feature of the lyrics was the frequency with which the groups improvised the words they sang.[69] There were often also back-and-forth dynamics between two singers. The extemporaneous and flexible nature of the samba genre meant the lyrics could be shaped to suit the circumstances, as when Malandros do Amor sought to flatter a reporter from *O Momento*:

> *Você não está conhecendo*
> *O reporter de* O Momento
> *É quem anda lutando*
> *Pra nos dar melhoramentos.*
> *Indicando o povo a se politizar.*

> You don't yet know
> The reporter from *O Momento*
> It's he who is fighting
> To bring us better lives
> Leading the people to become politically active.[70]

The reporter may have prompted these lyrics. Even so, the samba vocalists clearly had the skill to construct lyrics ex tempore or the journalist's artifice would not have had the desired effect. It should also be noted that the lyricists of the *batucadas* and other popular carnival associations seemed happy to participate in playful give-and-take with the newspaper reporter, although the reporter is more an observer than participant. The lyrics of this samba school clearly promoted the working class and the Communist Party, but this obviously must be appreciated within the context of the exchange with *O Momento*, the party's newspaper.

Vargas's Estado Novo administrators in Bahia seemed to acknowledge the importance of these small clubs and increased their subsidies by offering a variety of cash prizes to the victors in the numerous competitions of small clubs. This allowed a few of the clubs to more than recoup their licensing fees, assuming they paid them. There is no indication, however, that the subsidies favored the *batucadas* over the *blocos* or *cordões*.[71] Certainly municipal subsidy did not work as it did in Rio de Janeiro under the early Vargas regimes, where the samba schools were targeted and the subsidies were used to institutionalize the clubs and encourage them to support Vargas's cultural initiatives, such as by invoking patriotic themes. The nature of carnival in Salvador meant that controlling the political messages of the small clubs would have been too complicated and costly, and the returns would have been uncertain. Vargas's administrators in Salvador, when given the choice, seemed more disposed to align themselves with the elite clubs or the presentation of the carnival Queens. Even in the years in the 1940s when the big clubs did not participate in carnival, there is no evidence that politicians sought to associate themselves with particular small clubs or genre of clubs. This would have been an extreme degree of populism (in the Bahian context) that went well beyond where the Estado Novo interventors in Bahia or their immediate successors were willing to go.[72]

Governor Otávio Mangabeira (1947–51), who was democratically elected, also preferred to associate with the elite clubs or meet with (and, by 1951, pose with) the annual carnival queen.[73] However, he was more willing than his predecessors to associate his office with the small clubs. For example, in 1949, Mangabeira "traversed the sections of the city where popular street carnival takes place, confirming the animation of the people."[74] In 1951, perhaps partly in response to his acknowledgment of popular carnival, forty-six small clubs participated in a carnival warm-up parade that was an act of homage to the outgoing governor. Parade participants waved white hankies as they paused outside the governor's mansion to salute him.[75] Mangabeira's successor, Regis Pacheco, never seemed particularly interested in Salvador's festivals or popular culture. The mayor during Mangabeira's term, however, José Wanderley Pinho (1947–51), and particularly his successors, mayors Osvaldo Veloso Gordilho (1951–54) and Aristóteles Góes (1954–55), were very supportive of carnival while in office. They attended many social events related to carnival and walked the streets during carnival itself. The first consistent annual municipal subsidy for the small clubs began under Mayor Gordilho in the early 1950s: The mayor's office handed out cash prizes to every small club that competed on the main stages it had set up in the center of town.[76] These changes indicate a greater populism and attention to popular carnival, including specifically African-Bahian cultural practices, on the part of Bahian politicians.

Somewhat ironically, it was the elite clubs during the Estado Novo that partially presaged the new emphasis on African-Bahian culture within carnival. The carnival of 1940 was proclaimed the "Carnival of the Bahianas," and the elite clubs, "inspired by Carmen Miranda's success," asked women to come to their dances dressed as Baianas. Smaller clubs also held dances with the Baiana theme, and even local business owners operating during carnival were exhorted to dress as Baianas.[77] Granted, much of this association of carnival with African-Bahian women was done through parody (indeed, even parody of parody, given the tongue-in-cheek nature of Carmen Miranda's early use of the Baiana costume). In addition, the previous year, 1939, one of the corteges of the elite club Fantoches addressed the contributions of Mãe Preta, or the black nursemaid, to Brazilian civilization. One newspaper, to its credit, did not duck the central issue but pointed out that the nursemaid symbolized a servility based on race that had no place in the "current moment, radiant of democracy and equality."[78] Nevertheless, carnival's association with African-Bahian culture was becoming axiomatic, as the discursive meaning of Bahian carnival tipped in favor of African-Bahian culture.

This is not to say that the elite contributions to carnival fell out of favor with journalists. Even after the demise of the elite clubs, newspapers continued to publicize and cover elite dances and related carnival events. Local illustrated magazines such as *Festa*, which catered to the dominant class and promoted the developmentalist concerns of the Vargas regime, viewed carnival from the perspective of the elite clubs and strictly within the confines of events along Rua Chile during the Estado Novo.[79] But in the mainstream press from the late 1930s, the *batucadas* were central to the discursive construction of Salvador's carnival. Even during years when the *blocos* and *cordões* received more press coverage than the *batucadas*, journalist wrote of the *batucada* as the most authentic representation of the meaning and symbolic nature of Salvador's carnival.

On several occasions, newspapers suggested that the *batucadas* were the most numerous of the small clubs.[80] During this transitional period, radio stations brought samba schools and *batucadas* into their studios during the weeks leading up to carnival. Radio programs that featured the samba school Primeiro Nós (Us First) in 1937 and the *batucada* Bambas da Zona in 1939 illustrate the growing stature of small clubs as media personalities in their own right. In 1937 and 1938, the local musical and carnival group Deixa Falar ("Let them Speak," named after the first samba school in Rio de Janeiro) rode a wave of popularity. Part of their popularity may have stemmed from the fact that their African-Bahian president, Ponciano Nonato de Carvalho, was a member of the middle class (newspapers referred to him as a successful businessman [*negociante bemquisto*]) who perhaps understood how best to liaise with representatives in the media and the music industry.[81]

Not surprisingly, numerous sambas and *batucadas* (*batucada* was also the name of a subgenre of samba) focused on the theme that samba and the *batucada* carnival clubs were essential to both Bahianness and carnival. Most of these were creations of the recording industry centered in Rio de Janeiro, such as Vicente Paiva's 1940 song "Bahia, oi . . . Bahia!" ("Bahia, oh Bahia!"). The lyrics proclaimed, "After hearing the samba / that comes from

Bahia / sung by the Baiana / who swings like nobody. / . . . Who wouldn't want to be Bahian too?" Another Paiva song, his "Exaltação à Bahia" ("Exaltation of Bahia") of 1943, argued that "Where Bahia is truly itself / is in the *batuque* and the samba."[82] Most local sambas whose lyrics were reproduced in the newspapers, however, focused on the themes of carnival romance, female betrayal, and the hustler or social problems such as poverty rather than the themes of African-Bahian cuisine or Candomblé. A 1953 series that featured six local compositions (marchas and sambas) made no mention of African-Bahian culture.[83] But local radio composer and performer Batatinha did compose at least three sambas in the 1950s that referred to African-Bahian culture: "Iaiá no Samba," "Vatapa," and "Samba e Capoeira." The latter samba explicitly incorporated aspects of the musical style that accompanied capoeira.[84]

Perhaps most convincingly, however, a locally composed and quite rough *samba-batuque* from 1952, "Bahia Is the Good Land," illustrates that the practice of including African-Bahian culture in samba/*batucada* compositions was firmly rooted in the performative milieu of Salvadorans. The song includes lyrical passages that express aggression and competition. For instance, the lines "Bahia is the Good Land / Isn't jealous of anyone," and "Bahia has fought wars / But will never be defeated," illustrate the assertive combativeness of the *batucada* genre in Salvador. Moreover, the *batucada* picks up the theme of Bahia as the mother of Brazil: "If she [Bahia] is the mother of Brazil / It's important to say so." It also expressed the notion of racial democracy, which was gaining currency in Brazil. This point is exemplified in the insistence that Bahia "loves all its children," including "whites" and "blondes." *Batucadas* made the point that Bahia had its own culture, using the tropes that associated Bahia with *cultura negra*—the "Baiana" who "dances *batuque*," who "mixes the *caruru*"—and the likelihood that Candomblé beckons whomever falls romantically for a Bahian.[85]

The importance of the *batucadas* to Bahianness was a common theme in the more playful articles or pieces journalists wrote. For instance, two poems published in *A Tarde* in the late 1940s, written by Sílvio Valente (aka, Pepino Longo, or Long Cucumber), expressed the notion that the *batucada* was the musical reference point at the core of popular revelry. In lines from the poem "Evoé," Sílvio Valente remarked on the way that the "beguiling *batucadas* / Make a boring *morena* / Fall into a trance and samba."[86] Valente was underlining the importance of the African-Bahian *batucadas* to carnival (and indirectly to the African Bahians playing the *batucadas*), which enlivened the *morena*'s "boring" personality or approach to life. The mention of the trance, a feature of Candomblé worship, deepened the association of carnival with African-Bahian culture.

Valente also played on not-so-subtle racial and cultural stereotypes of the period, although he did so in a way that celebrated the cultural contribution of African Bahians. The poet distinguished between three categories—the blonde, the *morena* (a brunette of predominantly European descent), and the *mulata*—in the following lines: "Long live the blonde and the *mulata* / In sandals and slip-ons / And the *morena* who is my love!"[87] The lines "We don't make distinctions / Like the 'united' nations" alluded to the supposed lack of racial discrimination in Brazil, which made moments like carnival possible in the first place.[88] We see the same sentiments in a second poem by Valente, "Carnaval," from the same period, which argues that the universal musical power to excite of the "passing of the *batucadas*" created equality of revelry among "the fraternizing classes" and allowed "whites, black, mulattos" to "feel as brothers to one another." The *batucada* was also "the soul of the nocturnal race" (presumably meaning African Bahians) that was central to carnival. Finally, the poem said, through their performances the *batucadas* lent their African-Bahian soul to carnival in such a way as to transform it into a transcendent moment of racial equality in the tropics: "Blondes, *morenas*, *mulatas*, / In sandals and slip-ons, / Samba-ing in their hearts!"[89]

Valente was not the only journalist to situate Bahia's *batucadas* and carnival within the discourse of Brazil's fabled racial democracy and national identity. Intellectuals in the southeast "lauded the samba as Brazil's own most authentic native music" and portrayed Rio de Janeiro's samba schools as the fusion of the three races.[90] Bahian journalists and writers, particularly after 1940, situated their interpretations of Bahia's carnival experience within this framework of Brazil as a product of racial and cultural mixing and saw the various races "fraternizing" during carnival as evidence that racism did not exist in Brazil. The popularity of this shift is partly explained by the war, which allowed for and encouraged a more inclusive patriotic discourse of togetherness. According to this reporting, carnival was a time when "equality of race and color becomes reality for 72 hours" and "no one is concerned about who one's neighbor is, what the color of their skin is, or whether they are of respectable social position. Everyone finds themselves equal."[91]

In the hands of working-class Salvadorans, the *batucada* genre also lent itself to moments of cultural and racial affirmation. Noteworthy in this regard was a *bloco* called Preto Não é Mais Lacaio (The Black Man Is No Longer a Lackey). The group's 350 or so workers from the neighborhood of Liberdade took their name from the lyrics of the samba "Salve a Princesa" ("God Save the Princess [Isabel]"): "The Black man is no longer a lackey / The Black man no longer has a master / . . . Today the Black man can be a doctor/congressman and senator."[92] This is one of the more interesting aspects of the myth of racial democracy. Neither the *bloco* members nor the communist newspaper reporter who covered the story of the *bloco* likely believed that racial discrimination was nonexistent in Brazil. But the ideology of racial democracy gave people of color a rhetorical platform from which to criticize existing discrimination and inequality.[93]

By the early 1950s the media focus on the importance of the *batucadas* in Salvadoran carnival had begun to diminish, and the elite clubs and then the *trio elétrico* attracted the most attention. Yet the *batucadas* were still presented as a central feature of carnival in the growing working-class suburbs of the city. For instance, the *Estado da Bahia* paid homage to the Liberdade neighborhood, with its "great concentration of *batucadas, cordões* and *ranchos*," because its inhabitants knew "how to play the *batucada* (*batucar*)" and for "singing samba, for singing marchas."[94] Meanwhile, carnival in the Uruguai neighborhood opened with "clarions" that gave way to the "rhythmic cadence" and "primitive rhythms" of the *batucadas*, which unleashed the "almost primitive animation" of the festivities and the "natural enthusiasm of our poor" in these neighborhoods.[95]

The waning of focus on the small clubs and *batucadas* in particular was partly made up for in other areas of the print media such as editorials, especially in the culture and literature supplements that became the arbiters of cultural taste in Brazil after World War II. For instance, in 1949, modernist intellectual and journalist Cláudio Tavares contributed an article to the *Estado da Bahia* that was an extended treatment of the *rodas de samba* in Bahia, accompanied by photos by French photojournalist Pierre Verger. The article, "Rodas de Samba," was a republication of a piece originally published that year in the illustrated Brazilian monthly *A Cigarra*. Tavares discussed the origins and history of samba as well as its different characteristics and importance to African Bahians and to Bahia more widely.[96] In 1951, Tavares and other members of the media served as judges for the "parade of the *batucadas*," contributing to the continuing journalistic support for this popular element of Bahian carnival.[97]

A 1953 editorial in the *Diário de Notícias* lamented the recent municipal sanitation codes that threatened to remove the vending of food, and hence the Baiana, from the streets of Salvador. The author associated vague notions of African-Bahianness (or "blackness") with carnival, reminding readers that "the whites followed the footsteps of people of color," even going so far as to embrace the practice of African-Bahian religions.[98] Finally, in 1954, a full-page spread of carnival-related material that included history, discussion, and poetry, referred positively to African-Bahian culture in two poems about carnival. One, Laurindo de Brito's "Carnaval," needs to be read carefully. The phrases "negro carnival of death" and "macabre sambas of the worms" appear in the context of de Brito's poetic exaltation of an overly hallucinogenic, eroticized, and anarchic world turned upside down. Milton Costa Lima's poem was much more literal in its embrace of the contributions of popular festivity to Bahian carnival, namely dancing to sambas and to the primordial drums of the *batucadas*.[99]

In the early 1950s, other aspects of the performance of carnival and of carnival discourse contributed to a consolidation of the importance of African-Bahian culture in the context of carnival. In 1952, the main stage in the center of town was in the form of a Baiana's giant *tabuleiro*, the tray from which she hawked her wares. The *tabuleiro*/stage sat before a giant model of a Baiana that was ten meters tall from her midriff to the top of her headgear, and it was on this stage that the *batucadas* and *cordões* competed in the city's government-sponsored competition for the small clubs. It is not insignificant that this stage was set up and paid for by the mayor's office.[100]

Another example clearly associated Candomblé elements with carnival. In 1953, the Filhos de Liberdade, a short-lived carnival club that was much smaller than the big three, entered a float in the official parade that recreated a *terreiro*, complete with a *pai-de-santo* and *filhas-de-santo*. This was most likely the only such representation by any carnival club, at least after 1930. By contrast, another newer, also smaller club, Democrata, recreated Snow White and the Seven Dwarves. Fantoches had several floats with Viking mythology predominant, and Cruz Vermelho's emphasis was on aristocratic early modern Europe.[101] Finally, in 1949 there was a "popular competition" for a "Black carnival queen" that ran concurrently with the usual carnival queen competition, which was dominated by women of European descent. This shift toward greater inclusion of women of African descent in the competitions for carnival queen, which apparently only happened once, suggests a tentative trend toward broadening the range of conventions of beauty within the dominant discourse.[102]

The Era of the Batucadas began to close in the early 1950s, although the *batucadas* remained a popular feature of Bahian carnival well into the

1960s.[103] The closing was due to several factors. First, the elite carnival clubs got back on their feet. When a journalist for the *Estado da Bahia* wrote in 1952 that "the participation of the big clubs was entirely down to the government," he was not exaggerating. Mayor Oswaldo Gordilho's financial largesse was essential, and that it was forthcoming reveals how important he felt the big clubs were to carnival.[104] There were even a few additional dominant-class clubs to contend with: Club Democrata was founded in 1946, and the Spanish Club was making a real effort, as were two smaller clubs based in the otherwise working-class neighborhood of Liberdade— the Sons of Liberdade and the Gentlemen of Liberdade. The Yacht Club, the Tennis Club, and the Bahian Athletic Association—all of which were associated with the well-to-do or those who were aspiring to be so—had also begun to contribute dances and allegorical floats.

The *batucadas* suffered because of a few other important shifts in carnival participation. The arrival of the *trio elétrico* drew focus away from the *batucadas*. It is also possible, as one interviewee stressed, that in the 1950s the *batucadas* priced themselves out of existence as their members wanted or felt the need to dress in increasingly expensive clothing.[105] Additional *cordões* replaced the waning *batucadas*. They were cheaper, bigger, and provided more freedom of action because they didn't have to parade in a single file or even keep a rhythm. Two other carnival trends mostly in the 1960s— the *blocos de índios*, or groups dressed as Apaches, Sioux, Tupi-Guarani, and so forth, and the newer versions of samba schools (which were still very unlike those in Rio de Janeiro)—emerged in the same neighborhoods and drew from the same demographic as the *batucadas*.[106]

During the period 1938–52, when the presence of the *batucadas* at carnivals was at its height, they did not make a seismic change in carnival. Carnival was too complex and multifaceted. The aspects of carnival that were not specifically identified with African-Bahian culture still received most of the carnival coverage. Yet the *batucadas* did much to advance African-Bahian agency and performance and played a significant role in the discursive transformation of Bahian regional identity. During the 1930s, carnival in Salvador shifted to an emphasis on small clubs. This deepened with the rise of the *batucadas*. As a consequence, Salvador became more deeply associated with African-Bahian culture, and the percussive *batucadas*, once marginalized, were celebrated for defining the true soul of Bahian carnival. Even the odd media critique of carnival from the more conservative wings of the dominant class no longer referred negatively to anything that could be interpreted as African-Bahian culture. Instead, carnival criticism was restricted to its sexual license, its affront to family honor and to morality more generally, its materialism, or its inappropriateness in the context of Bahia's urban social crises.[107] The high point of the *batucadas*' existence, the 1940s, occurred in the midst of the transformation of Bahian regional identity and made a central contribution to the shifting dynamics of Bahian cultural politics in the Vargas era.

The *Afoxés*

In addition to the *batucadas* there was another markedly African-Bahian genre of carnival association known as *afoxés*. Whereas the *batucadas* drew a significant part of their impetus from the example of Rio de Janeiro, the *afoxés* were entirely a local phenomenon. As extensions of Salvador's institutions of Candomblé—they were often referred to as "Candomblé of the street"—they were certainly the most distinctive of Salvador's small clubs. Unlike the *batucadas*, the *afoxés* often used mobile cordons to set themselves apart from the rest of the carnival multitude. They kept very close to their cultural roots, principally honoring their African and African-Bahian religious heritage. Rather than playing and dancing to carnival music, the *afoxés* used the same or similar instruments, rhythms, and songs as those used in the *terreiros*. They also incorporated ritual language and ceremonies from Candomblé practice into their performances. The history and practice of the *afoxés* during the Vargas era provides ample evidence of the Candomblé community's insistent performative agency. The *afoxé* was effectively a public affirmation of Candomblé in a carnival context. By the early 1950s, the *afoxés* had revived as institutions, most notably with the founding of Filhos de Gandhy (Sons of Gandhi) in 1949, and the participants in the *afoxés* quite consciously made use of carnival festivity to expand the boundaries of what was culturally acceptable in Salvador.

The two best-known *afoxés* of the late nineteenth century were the rather exceptional Embaixada Africana (African Embassy), which was founded in 1895, and Pândegos da África (African Merrymakers), founded in 1896.[108] These clubs mirrored the structure of Fantoches and Cruz Vermelha, but whereas the elite clubs chose themes from Greco-Roman mythology, the exclusively African-Bahian clubs used explicitly Afrocentric themes, for example the glories of African civilizations, such as those of Egypt, Ethiopia, and West Africa. These clubs were accepted by the white minority that dominated carnival in those years, possibly, as Kim Butler has suggested, because of their novelty factor or because the elite saw the clubs as an improvement on *entrudo*. Other Afrocentric groups were not accepted.[109] The even smaller groups, those other "Africans" who "caused all sorts of confusion," were mercilessly criticized for their drumming and rowdy "un-civilized" behavior, which elites saw as degrading to Bahia. These would have been the *batuques*, which the persecution campaign targeted most fiercely, or any smaller *afoxés* that did not mimic the structure of Fantoches and Cruz Vermelha. The *batuques* and smaller *afoxés* were the main targets of the ban on Afrocentric carnival clubs from 1905 to 1914.[110]

After the ban (and perhaps clandestinely during it), several impor-tant *afoxés* were active in Salvador, including the Filhos d'Oxum (Sons of Oxum), Filhas de Oxun (Daughters of Oxun), Filhos de Obá (Sons of Obá), and Lordes Africanos (African Lords), all of which were mostly ignored by the press or received negative publicity.[111] In the early 1930s, a number of these remained active or returned to activity once the climate of repression against Candomblé subsided. Starting in 1930, the judgmental attitude of newspapers shifted, and reporters included a number of *afoxés* alongside the other small clubs in the coverage of events leading up to carnival in the early to mid-1930s. These included Ijexá, Pai Burukô (Father Burukô), Congo d'África (Congo of Africa), Otum Obá d'África (Otum Oba of Af-rica), Filhos de Obá, Filhos de Congo (Sons of the Congo), and Príncipe da África (African Prince). Despite these relatively novel inclusions, for the next decade or so it is difficult to know the extent of the *afoxés'* par-ticipation after 1930 or to track trends over the period, largely due to some slippage of nomenclature in the sources between the use of the term *afoxé* and the more general and inclusive *cordão* or even "club."[112] It may be that the early 1930s was a high point for *afoxé* participation, which then trails off after 1935 and then revives in the late 1940s. Perhaps the overall dip in carnival activity around World War II encouraged the *afoxés* to focus on their local neighborhoods, in which case it is unlikely that they would have been covered in the press. It is possible, too, that the leading members of the traditional older *afoxés* were dying off and no one was in line to replace them. This was the case with Congo d'África, which had been in existence for several decades when its founder and principal organizer Rodrigo died in 1945 (although in this case his son took over almost immediately, but succession was not always so seamless). The revival of the *afoxés* in the late 1940s coincided with the creation of the carnival group Filhos de Gandhy in 1949, founded by a group of dock workers and stevedores as an *afoxé*.

The use of Candomblé songs, instrumentation, rhythms, and ritual set the *afoxés* apart from the *batucadas* and other small clubs. The *agogo* (a bell that one strikes) and the mobile *atabaque* drums played central roles in the *afoxé*, and there was much samba, too. In the process of honoring their African and African-Bahian religious heritage within the wider festivity of carnival, specific instruments mattered greatly in this sophisticated percussive culture, as the precision of a variety of musical aspects was deeply enmeshed with individuals' relationships with the spiritual realm. It was not only a question of what type of drum to use, for instance, but also how its size and construction would affect its tone. The *afoxés* relied on a specific rhythm, that of Ijexá. The songs they sang honored the *orixás* and were a mix of African (particularly Yoruban) and Portuguese, but they were not the "powerful" songs that were sung in the *terreiros*. They were instead songs that would not give offense to the *orixás* or the ancestors because they were played in public.[113]

The performative roles in the older established *afoxés* included a king and queen, who were chosen in certain cases from the best dancers and singers. This indicates the importance of such talents not just during carnival but also within the ritual of the *terreiros*. Subordinate to the king and queen, but still prestigious, were positions within the honor guard. The individuals who filled all of these performative roles dressed in elaborate costumes. Many *caboclo afoxés* (those from *terreiros* that centered on gods, rituals, and powers that purportedly stemmed from native Brazilian ethnoreligious traditions) chose to honor their *caboclo*, or Indian protector, by representing him in the *afoxé*. The best dancer was chosen for this honor, wearing a costume that featured many feathers. If not the best dancer, the group might include a *feiticeiro* (someone who works with magic) who was responsible for carrying a figurative representation of an *orixá* or a *caboclo* or the *balotin*, an icon with spiritual or magical powers.

As with the other non-elite clubs, the majority of the officers in the few *afoxés* for which there is documentation were men. The principal singers and dancers were both women and men, although the musicians were all men. The role of the women was typically as Baianas, but of course within Candomblé, which was significantly matriarchal, being a Baiana was hardly a subordinate position if the woman was an initiate of long standing. The women also probably played important roles in organizing or overseeing the outreach activities of the *afoxés*.[114]

During carnival appearances there were various rituals to be completed, especially at the outset, such as the *padê*, the important initial ritual offering of *farofa* (manioc flour), a small vessel of water (*quartinha da água*), and most likely Brazilian rum to Exú, the intermediary between humans and the *orixás* who was associated with crossroads. This was an important *orixá* to appease.[115] There were also rites to protect the *afoxé* from the malign intentions of their competitors—"the troubles typical of the festivities of Rei Momo." These might include a "ritual animal sacrifice . . . by someone from another carnival *bloco*, done out of jealously or simple devilishness."[116]

Bahian writer Deoscóredes dos Santos has left testimony of his role in establishing an *afoxé* in the period 1935 to 1942 that illustrates not only the cultural richness of the *afoxés* but also their integration into the fabric of the working-class community.[117] Santos's *afoxé*, the Troça do Pai Burukô (Merry Band of Pai Burukô), first emerged in 1935 in the context of the important Candomblé *terreiro* Opô Afonjá when the young Santos and a few boyhood friends received permission to roam about the local neighborhood requesting small donations for their carnival costumes. In 1942, now grown to young men, Santos and his friends brought together thirty *sócios*, or members, to participate more widely in carnival that year. They named their *afoxé* for an object that was of spiritual significance to them in childhood (an old tree stump in the shape of a human) that was baptized Pai Burukô. Each of the members of the Troça do Pai Burukô paid 30$000 at the outset and 10$000 per month.[118] Practice runs began three months before carnival, on Sunday mornings. The *ensaio geral*, or final run-through, took place on the last Sunday before carnival weekend. All of the members, their relatives and friends, and members of fellow carnival associations came out for this rehearsal. Finally, on carnival Sunday, the members gathered early in the morning. The president used a whistle to convey his commands, among the first of which was to get everyone together for a drink of *cachaça*, or Brazilian rum. After everyone's responsibilities were outlined and the ritual animal sacrifice was made, the crew worked themselves up into a frenzy of song and set out into the surrounding neighborhoods.

The young men went to the houses of those they knew, often responding to invitations made long in advance, and found that this took up much more time than they had intended. At each visit they were expected to eat, dance, and "comply with all the formalities demanded of that type of festivity." At the end of each stop they extricated themselves from the host's insistent hospitality, only to begin the process again at the next house. The socializing was so intense that the *afoxé* remained on the go all three days of carnival from nine in the morning until six at night and until nine on Tuesday. By the end they were so exhausted they could not make the long walk home; many of them spent the night in the center of town collapsed in the house of a *filha-de-santo* of the *terreiro*. This particular *afoxé* was popular in the community, as evidenced by the sack of presents they received and the sack of invitations for the following year. The fact that the group's celebrations seemed to have been quite localized suggests the important social links between the *afoxé* and the immediate social environment.

The group recognized that some social responsibilities were incumbent and at least made an attempt to meet them. Carnival at this very local level, as represented to us by a middle-aged man looking back on his younger days, was about relationships between people who knew one another from the routines of everyday life and from their involvement in Candomblé. Carnival was also about reinforcing those relationships through spiritual, financial, and other types of communal exchanges. Santos makes another interesting point: He wrote that the initial stages of the merrymaking made the locals of São Gonçalo do Retiro, where the *terreiro* was based, "crazy with happiness and excitement, as they had never imagined that these lads, *abusados* (roguish, pesky, meddlesome), and *traquinas* (mischievous, wild, restless) as they were, could conceive and organize such festivities as those before them."[119] Successful organization and participation within a carnival *afoxé* seems to have been a way for working-class individuals to accrue status within the wider working-class, African-Bahian community.

The *afoxé* was clearly an opportunity for the Candomblé community to celebrate carnival in their own way, and carnival was for some individuals an opportunity to show their worth in a city whose stagnant economy and racial discrimination limited other socioeconomic avenues for doing so. Thus, although carnival did not explicitly threaten the social order, it provided an opportunity for this subordinate group to publicly assert their own cultural values. As Pai Burukô was not covered in newspapers in the 1940s (it was mentioned after 1950), it is legitimate to assume that other smaller *afoxés* for which we do not have a print source also formed and stuck close to their neighborhood roots, reinforcing social connections between the *terreiros* and their wider communities. There were, after all, over one hundred *terreiros* in operation in the 1940s.[120]

Also noteworthy within Santos's account is the dynamic on display between working-class carnival associations such as *afoxés* and the local government's administration of the festivities. The group needed a license to participate, and elected directors (president, secretary, etc.) were a requirement for a license, presumably so the police would have the name of someone they could hold responsible. There were certain other (unfortunately unspecified) bureaucratic regulations to be followed. Yet there did not seem to be any official opposition or discouragement in 1942 to the creation of another *afoxé*. Moreover, the young men of the *afoxé* did not seem particularly interested in and felt they had the luxury of ignoring whatever protocols were expected of them by the authorities. The consequences were nothing more than that they did not receive their gift from the mayor's office: "To receive this, it was necessary to fulfill many *protocolos* (forms to fill out), and the fellas, with their cheeky ideas and blood on the boil were not prepared to adhere to such regulations."[121]

Santos's *afoxé* seems to have been a bit ahead of the curve in 1942. Usually the founding of the group Filhos de Gandhy in 1949 is cited as the beginning of the mid-twentieth-century revival of the *afoxés*. That year a small group of stevedores founded a *bloco*, calling themselves the Sons of Gandhi, after the man whose passive resistance and assassination in 1948 was much in the news the previous year. The stevedores had also been inspired by a recent viewing of the film *Gunga Din* (1939), a Hollywood feature set in nineteenth-century India. Although contradictions within the oral history testimonies collected by Anísio Félix obscure the early years, it seems clear that after forming principally as a *bloco* or *cordão*, some members of the group began to introduce songs, instruments, and ceremonies from Candomblé. This was understandable, as many stevedores were part of the Candomblé community.

According to one of the founders, Djalma Conceição, at this point in the association's evolution a few ranking members went before the state tourist board, which was in charge of officially registering small clubs for the competitions, and suggested that the Sons of Gandhi be classified as an *afoxé* for the competitions on account of their instruments, which could not successfully compete with the largely percussion instruments of the others in the *bloco* category. The significance of this is that probably in the early 1950s (exact dates are difficult to determine), the *afoxés* were recognized by the tourism department of the municipal government, to the point that they had their own official category. In none of the newspapers up to that point was there a separate category for *afoxés* in carnival competitions. In fact, in 1948 the only *afoxé* to participate in the competition *O Momento* sponsored was given a special award. So it may be the combination of the insistence of the Candomblé community, the increased acceptance of African-Bahian culture, and the increased emphasis on tourism in the early 1950s that brought the *afoxé* firmly into the official carnival fold. The emergence of Filhos de Gandhy can perhaps be said to reflect these shifts.

Certainly the actual configuration of Filhos de Gandhy as an *afoxé* played a role in consolidating these dynamics. Filhos de Gandhy was not an explicit extension of a Candomblé *terreiro*. Its members were dock workers first and foremost who chose to incorporate some of the central characteristics of an *afoxé*, in particular the rituals and rhythms and songs and their colors, which were taken from Candomblé cosmology—white for Oxalá and blue for Ogum. Yet they also incorporated elements that were clearly not of the *terreiro*: embracing a personality from India, for instance, and the elephant, which was sacred to Hindus but not the *terreiros* (even though the elephant is one of the animals that represents Oxalá). Similar in a way to the adjustments Mestre Bimba made to the teaching and practice of capoeira, which made it more palatable to the dominant class, and also echoing the changes that occurred with the Washing of Bonfim that struck a compromise between the Catholic Church and the Candomblé community, the recombining of elements of the *terreiros* may have contributed to their acceptance and their celebrated popularity. In turn, Filhos de Gandhy seems to have enhanced the popularity and acceptance of the more traditional *afoxés* as well, which were each associated with a specific *terreiro*.[122] For example, in 1953, the minister of public security, Colonel Laurindo Regis, who oversaw the military police and the Civil Guard, sponsored a carnival event that prominently featured the *afoxé* Congo d'África. The event was also sponsored by a local councilman, Osório Villas Boas.[123] Certainly Filhos de Gandhy influenced the emergence of the *afoxé* phenomenon in Rio de Janeiro. In 1951, another Filhos de Gandhy was formed in Rio de Janeiro. The founders had participated in the original Filhos de Gandhy and in several of the more traditional *afoxés* in Salvador. The founding of Filhos de Gandhy had a greater impact in Salvador, however, clearly, striking a chord in bringing together people of African descent around an explicit embrace of African-Bahian culture.[124]

As it had done with the *batucadas*, the print media reversed its early-twentieth-century position on the *afoxés* and other "African groups" (*grupos africanos*) around and especially after 1930. Indeed, attention and even celebration of the *afoxés* reached a high point in the period 1937 to 1942. For example, in 1938, the *afoxé* Otum Obá da África headed the festivities during an advance carnival gathering in Rio Vermelho, "bringing the latest news from the Congo amidst the sound of *atabaques* (Candomblé drums)."[125] While the *afoxés* never rivaled the role of the *batucadas* at carnival, they had a place in the dominant discourse on African-Bahian culture, carnival, and the resignification of Bahianness in the 1930s and 1940s. After

1948, this discourse on the *afoxés* intensified briefly as they were officially institutionalized as part of Bahian carnival discourse. This flurry of print discourse accompanied and contributed to the revival of the *afoxé* after 1948. From this point on, there was a category for "*afoxés*" in the carnival competition for small clubs that was separate from the categories of *bloco*, *cordão*, and *batucada*. In the carnival coverage the most commonly mentioned *afoxé* was Filhos de Gandhy, which *Estado da Bahia* said in 1955 "deserve[s] a place of particular eminence within carnival." The second most mentioned was Congo d'África, although Pai do Burukô garnered frequent attention, too.[126]

The distinctive African-Bahian characteristics of the *afoxés* drew the attention of Salvador's second wave of modernists and writers after 1945. These middle-class progressive intellectuals in turn drew attention to the *afoxés* in two forums that pressed harder for recognition of African-Bahian culture than the mainstream dailies typically did. These were the communist party newspaper *O Momento*, and the national illustrated weekly *O Cruzeiro*. Darwin Brandão, a poet and keen folklorist, especially in the field of African-Bahian cuisine, and also a coeditor and frequent contributor to the Salvadoran modernist literary journal *Caderno da Bahia*, praised the *afoxé* in 1948 in *O Momento* as the distinguishing feature of Bahia's carnival and one of the region's principal contributions to Brazilian carnival.[127] His article, a lengthy discussion of the role of the *afoxé* in Candomblé, was part of a series *O Momento* ran that highlighted working-class carnival associations and included descriptions of several *afoxés*, some of which received no mention in the other daily newspapers.

Brandão's article described an *ensaio*, or carnival warm-up procession, and a party of the *afoxé* Congo d'África, which had "a huge following" within its neighborhood. The big attraction that night was the "hard samba" accompanied by the sounds of the *atabaque* drums and a few moments of "jaw dropping" individual performances—by Reginaldo Costa, for example, who seemed to have "springs in his legs." Costa did a few "capoeira leaps" as the music accelerated into the "Dance of the Agabi," which, according to Brandão "symbolized the struggle of the slave against the land owner, the slave master," or so he was told. This was just the kind of race consciousness and ritualized class struggle that a Communist newspaper could appreciate. It is significant, as Brandão pointed out, that the afoxé leadership chose the performance of the Agabi "especially for our report."

The degree to which figures within the Candomblé community tailored their performative practices to suit the wider political or social circumstances is impressive.

An article by another minor intellectual figure in Bahia, Cláudio Tavares, also highlighted the reemergence of the *afoxé* as a symbol of the particularity of Salvador's carnival. Tavares contributed the sensationally titled article "Afoxé, Barbaric Rhythm of Bahia" to the May 1948 issue of the Rio de Janeiro–based national magazine *O Cruzeiro*.[128] The article was a close, almost "thick" description of the same *afoxé*, Congo d'África. It discussed aspects of cosmology and phases of ritual and included song lyrics and descriptions of the group's costumes and dances. Accompanying the article were twenty-two photographs of different aspects of the *afoxé* by Pierre Verger. The article put the cultural practices of Congo d'África in the context of Africa's "totemic" contributions to Salvadoran carnival, via slavery and African-Bahian religion, and the cultural mixing of the three races, Brazilian Indian, European, and African. Carnival itself in Salvador, as Tavares marveled, was "filled up" by African Bahians, who were "the powerful propulsive force that moved Bahian carnival."[129]

The recovery of the *afoxés* from the late 1940s (or their rediscovery by the press) and their contributions to carnival were later relatively marginalized in the carnival coverage by the same factors that diminished the popularity of the *batucadas*—the reemergence of the big clubs after 1950 and the invention of the *trio elétrico*. Nevertheless, the *afoxés* played an important role in reshaping the discourse of Bahian regional identity in the 1930s and especially the late 1940s and early 1950s. African-Bahian insistence on taking to the streets during carnival as public expressions of Candomblé gave the festival in Bahia a unique identity. Certain members of Salvador's intelligentsia such as Darwin Brandão and Cláudio Tavares (and Edison Carneiro before them) recognized this as a valuable cultural resource. The popularity and excitement the Filhos de Gandhy generated helped cement a place for the *afoxés* within the official structure of carnival. *Afoxés* continued to feature in carnival in Salvador and experienced another revival of stunning proportions in the 1970s. In the 1940s and 1950s, however, the *afoxés* illustrated African-Bahian agency and the extent of *cultura negra* within carnival, further contributing to the degree to which Bahia was becoming associated with African-Bahian culture.

The Popularization of Carnival and the "Carnivalization" of the Festival Calendar

During the same years when the *batucadas* and other small clubs became the central features of carnival, two other changes were under way. The first was a demographic and geographic widening of carnival that contributed considerably to its popularization. The second was a "carnival creep," a spreading of carnival songs, institutions, and play to the city's other popular festivals that had a secularizing and popularizing effect. Both changes intensified and extended the city's association with African-Bahian culture. As changes in carnival practice and discourse such as the increased celebration and inclusion of the *batucadas* and *afoxés* extended the boundaries of the acceptability of African-Bahian cultural practices during the rest of the year, the extension and popularization of carnival magnified this influence, stretching the everyday boundaries of the acceptable to include more African-Bahian practices.[130]

The demographic shifts after 1940 were largely due to the city's dramatic population increase over the same time period. Salvador's population grew from 290,000 in 1940 to 415,000 by 1950. This increase was largely the consequence of in-migration rather than natural increase, so there were many more adults available to participate in carnival by 1954 than there had been twenty-four years earlier. After the three elite clubs made their comeback in the early 1950s, they had to contend with many more small clubs, many of which were locally based and provided carnival entertainment in neighborhoods that were some distance from the central attractions.[131] Even though other elite carnival institutions emerged—the Athletic Association and the dances at the Yacht Club, for instance—they had to compete with an almost exponential increase in the number of small clubs over the 1940s and 1950s. Not only were there more *batucadas* on the streets, but the number of *blocos* and *cordões* increased as well. The *blocos* were also bigger in size. Before 1940, few *blocos* numbered more than one hundred members, but the founding of the *bloco* Vai Levando (Take It Away) initiated the modern phenomenon of the "big *bloco*," which included two hundred to four hundred participants. This trend toward the big *bloco* was consolidated during World War II by Brazilian sailors from the battleship *Minas Gerais*, stationed in Salvador, who paraded as the Filhos do Mar (Sons of the Sea). Theirs was the biggest *bloco* to march in Bahia up to that point, and they led the way for other big *blocos* such as Filhos do Fogo (Sons of the Fire) and Filhos do Porto (Sons of the Port).

As the city grew to accommodate its increasing population, carnival spread geographically. The central, built-up commercial areas around the Terreiro de Jesus and the Rua Chile remained the official location for the biggest celebrations in the period 1930 to 1954. Beyond these central areas local shopkeepers combined forces, formed committees, and organized competitions, and local neighborhoods came to play larger roles as crucibles of carnival festivity. Even semirural residential neighborhoods took on a greater demographic and commercial density and infrastructure and began to host their own local carnival celebrations. During the 1930s, the main popular loci for carnival celebrations were the traditional areas of the Terreiro de Jesus, the Pelourinho, Maciel de Baixo, and along the street Baixa dos Sapateiros, in the center of town, as well as Santo Antonio, and the Calçada neighborhood in the district of Liberdade. By 1955, carnival *gritos*, or start-up parties, were being celebrated throughout the city in most working- and middle-class neighborhoods.

The *gritos* and celebrations in neighborhoods that were distant from the city center, such as São Caetano, Cidade Nova, Engenho Velho, Plataforma, Largo do Tanque, and Massaranduba, were announced in the daily newspapers during this period. Neighborhood notables would organize carnival clubs by drawing upon friends, relatives, and institutional networks of the local social club, the football club, or a Candomblé *terreiro*. For instance, clubs in outlying districts such as the Pirajá Athletic Club in Brotas held several carnival dances each season, usually for members and their guests. The clientele were local, and the institutions functioned to create associative ties in the neighborhoods and foster local identities. The clubs provided a structure for pooling scarce resources as well as a venue (by setting up public stages, lights, ornamentation, and so on) for shows and events that marked the public ritual life of the community. Just as the clubs were important institutions in the context of locally specific carnival-related events, carnival and the other major popular festivals were the most important times of the year for the clubs. This was when they could justify their existence to their members and garner financial reserves (through cover charges and the sale of food and drinks). Social and recreational clubs also provided an annual incentive for neighborhood musical groups to compete for prizes in the local festivities.[132]

Local clubs contributed greatly to the competitive nature of Salvadoran carnival. Throughout the period under study, newspapers encouraged rivalries between neighborhoods, and citywide carnival competitions meant that local pride as well as money was at stake. Newspapers may have overstated the rivalries, but other sources confirm their existence and suggest that they frequently occurred. During carnival in 1941 three members of the Guarda Civil were injured while breaking up an altercation between two *cordões* on Portas do Carmo Street in the city center. Three days earlier, also in the city center, two men were arrested and three were detained for "instigating a conflict between two carnival *blocos*." The weapons of choice were the sticks used to beat the *tambor* drums. Rivalries such as those between the neighborhoods of Uruguay and Massaranduba or between small clubs sometimes spilled over into violent conflicts that still color local carnival lore.[133]

The most well attended local neighborhoods were those that had established commercial shops with energetic proprietors, attractive prizes, and an annual tradition of successful festivity. The *grito* in the neighborhood of Uruguay was perhaps the most successful in this regard. A *grito*, literally a "cry" or "shout," was an organized public carnival warm-up that figuratively announced the (not necessarily immediate) arrival of carnival. The Uruguay *grito* drew on the generous financial support of the bottling company and distributor Fratelli Vita and other wealthy benefactors. Hence the Uruguay *grito* offered some of the biggest prizes to the small clubs that showed up, and this was the main incentive for participation. The Uruguay carnival's popularity may also have stemmed from the fact that it was a working-class neighborhood and the many popular *batucadas* felt comfortable there (rather than in the more solidly middle-class neighborhoods such as Tororó).[134] Such areas drew the attention of the mayor's office, which provided illumination only to the busiest locales or those that catered to the middle and upper classes (presumably in part because they were most able to petition successfully for support).[135] Up-and-coming areas lobbied for their own illumination, sometimes successfully, but the mayor's office was unable to increase its subsidies as quickly as carnival was growing.

In 1952, at least twelve local commissions sent requests to the government for funds several weeks before the carnival. Other groups may have requested assistance as carnival drew closer.[136] It is not clear what precisely motivated the mayor's office to support the spread of carnival foci into outlying neighborhoods. It may have been media pressure, a populist impulse, an attempt to insinuate a semblance of government influence into a process that was already well under way, or simply a belief that the grander the festivities, the greater the benefits for the city's businesses.[137] Whatever led the mayor's office to take notice, it is clear that the growth of popular carnival was keeping pace or even outpacing that of the official and extensively regulated cortege of elite clubs. Because carnival in outlying working-class areas was exclusively the domain of the small clubs, including the *batuca-das* and *afoxés*, the growth of carnival enhanced the importance of African-Bahian practices in the context of the wider carnival experience and the association of carnival with African-Bahian culture.

A second general carnival phenomenon contributed to the spread of the acceptance of African-Bahian culture and its increasing association with Salvador's public festival culture and *baianidade*. Carnival festivity during the Vargas era extended beyond the limits of its calendar and invaded the ritual festive space of the city's other popular religious festivals such as Bonfim or the Festival of the Three Kings. Bahians, especially young men and women, were importing carnival music, behaviors, and institutions such as the small clubs into the ritual space of the other festivals. They were no doubt encouraged by the spread of radio and the commercialization of Brazil's recording industry, which disseminated carnival music earlier and earlier in the cycle of festivities leading up to carnival. A consequence was the increasing secularization and further democratization of these other festivals. Events whose character had previously been defined by a balance between specific religious themes and appropriate festive activities, including specifically religious musical traditions on the one hand and profane revelry on the other, increasingly took on aspects of carnival in their structure as well as their content.[138] This intrusion of the carnivalesque tipped the balance away from the elements most closely associated with the dominant class (for example, the Catholic mass inside the churches).[139] As carnival included the percussive rhythms of the African-Bahian *batucadas*, the popular festivals became even more associated with African-Bahian culture after 1930. Through this process, the dominant class, firmly associated with high Catholicism, ceded some of its influence over the narrative and meaning of popular festivity in Salvador.

The traditional dominant-class elements of religious festivals lost ground to elements associated with Salvadoran carnival. The informal celebrations following the Festival of Our Lord of the Bonfim on Ribeira Monday provide one example. Ribeira Monday had been something of a carnival "warm-up" since the beginnings of Bahian carnival in the 1880s.[140] But the carnival associations shared the festival with groups of young men and women and boys and girls, called *ternos* and *ranchos*, who used Ribeira Monday to reprise their musical performances during the Festival of the Three Kings (6 January) and the weekend of the Bonfim festivities. By the late 1930s, however, the emphasis of Ribeira Monday had shifted almost entirely to being the first outing of the warm-up cycle for carnival. Carnival was even infiltrating Thursday's religious procession to the Church of Bonfim leading up to the Washing of Bonfim.[141] By 1942, the more traditional police and fire department bands that had always accompanied the procession to the church had introduced drum rhythms and carnival *marchas*, giving the procession a more carnivalesque character than before.[142] A report in a 1946 newspaper described the procession as "a giant rolling party" with *cordões* singing the "hits" as they marched along, "accompanied by a veritable percussion orchestra," which included instruments such as "*pandeiros, cuícas, gangues* and *atabaques*," all of which were more appropriate for carnival songs than for religious music and ritual, or at least more appropriate for a *roda de samba* than for a religious procession.[143]

The Festival of the Three Kings is the most salient example of a religious festival that took on aspects of carnival. Since the 1920s traditionalists had been concerned about a partial carnivalization of the Festival of the Three Kings, and by the end of the 1930s the change was pronounced, led mainly by young working-class and middle-class Salvadorans. The new emphasis on carnival traditions during the religious festival took place mostly in the emerging neighborhoods in the city's suburbs such as Brotas and in older neighborhoods, such as Liberdade, that were still growing.[144] The *ranchos* and *ternos* and their informal parades and musical performances were central to the Festival of the Three Kings, and their numbers were growing for most of the period from 1930 to 1954. The scope of the festival was growing, too, spreading into new parts of the city. In 1940, the papers began to announce the times and dates of the rehearsal sessions (*ensaios*) of the *ternos* and *ranchos*. These *ensaios* had become performative events in their own right, probably because of word of mouth among the young people.[145] They were adopted directly from the carnival tradition of both Rio de Janeiro and Salvador. Late-night dances at the headquarters of the *ternos* and *ranchos* often followed the rehearsals, and this may have been an opportunity to bring the group a little extra cash for costumes and decorations, especially from the sales of drinks.[146]

These extended rehearsals contributed to a significant degree of the carnivalization of the Festival of the Three Kings, not least because their repertoire included more and more carnival songs. Newspaper evidence suggests that their popularity began to rise in the late 1930s, diminished during the war, and increased again after 1945. By the end of the 1930s, carnival *batucadas* and *marchas* had begun to replace the traditional songs of the *ranchos* and *ternos* as the principal entertainment during the festival, even at the height of the events on the evening of the fifth of January.[147] Even the odd *afoxé* showed up during the festival in the 1940s and 1950s.

The organizations that assumed responsibility in many of the neighborhoods for organizing the local commemorations of the Festival of the Three Kings were in fact previously established Commissions for the Promotion of Carnival Festivity (Comissões Promotoras dos Festejos de Carnaval). With this sort of institutional overlap, it is perhaps not surprising that the carnivalization of the Festival of the Three Kings took place during the Vargas era.[148] Moreover, even the elite carnival clubs, which still held private commemorative functions for the Three Kings, had begun to treat these commemorations as part of the carnival cycle. Indeed, these functions of these clubs for the festival came to mark the beginning of carnival season. This change was reflected in radio broadcasts. In 1947, on the eve of the Day of the Three Kings, Radio Sociedade da Bahia broadcast a program dedicated to carnival music instead of the traditional religious *cânticos* (children's songs) associated with Epiphany in Salvador. These changes provoked a strong reaction from both folklorists and Catholics, who wished to preserve the "original aspects" (*notas originais*) of the Festival of the Three King.[149] For many, this meant protecting the sacredness of the festivals from secular popularization. But there was little that could be done to stop the shift, which was given impetus by wider trends toward secularization, the music industry, and possibly youthful, rebellious initiative. The Festival of the Three Kings faded in popularity after a final, government-sponsored revival for the quarto centennial celebrations in 1949, perhaps as a consequence of its inability to fully distinguish itself from the wider carnival cycle.[150]

None of this is to say that young people only wanted to dance to the latest carnival music. There were many who probably wished to preserve the original aspects of the festivals, and many young men and women and boys and girls still contributed to the more "traditional" activities. But by the 1950s the carnivalesque profane had clearly become an extensive and popular feature of several of Salvador's larger popular religious festivals.[151] Carnival had even begun to intrude on New Year's Eve celebrations and in the many social clubs dotted around Salvador. The *Estado da Bahia* excitedly reported that many of the evening's dance festivities were now "considered Gritos de Carnaval," and the article appended lyrics from a popular carnival samba-*batucada* for 1951. That same year the elite carnival club Fantoches brought in a samba school from Rio to welcome the New Year.[152]

Clearly, during the 1940s and 1950s, the balance shifted from older religions and musical traditions that were not especially identified as elements of African-Bahian culture (although African-Bahians certainly participated in them) toward more sambas and *batucadas* that were associated with African-Bahian culture.

The Limitations of Carnival

As with the other popular festivals, the discursive and performative inclusion of elements of African-Bahian culture in Bahian carnival traditions was done in a way that would contain it within clearly defined limitations and hierarchies. Perhaps somewhat surprisingly given carnival's reputation for disregarding social morality and convention, carnival festivity in Salvador was separated by class and race to a marked degree. It is instructive here to quote at length a passage from Donald Pierson's study of race relations in Salvador. Pierson wrote of carnival in 1936 that "proceeding, during, and following the parade [of the three *grandes clubes*], Negro *batucadas* and *cordões* pass through the milling crowds. The *batucadas* are usually composed of fifteen to twenty young men, invariably blacks or dark mulattoes. . . . A *cordão* consists of fifty or sixty people of both sexes and all ages, invariably blacks and dark mulattoes." In one such *cordão* of 43 participants (although from the wider description this was almost certainly an *afoxé*), "24 were blacks, 19 were dark mulattoes, and none were whites." In a survey of "9 *batucadas*, of a total of 157 young men, 113, or 72 per cent, were blacks; 40, or 25.5 per cent, were mulattoes, all dark except one (who, although light of skin, had kinky hair); 3 were *cafusos* [of Brazilian-Indian and African descent], and only 1 was white."[153]

Oral history interviewee José Ferreira also confirmed that "when Fantoches da Euterpe paraded there were no blacks, one didn't see a single African-Bahian."[154] In fact, even when the floats of the elite clubs depicted a scene from African-Bahian culture, the participants were whites in blackface. In 1955, the main float of the elite carnival club Cruzeiro da Vitória was a modest homage to the abolition of slavery. Twelve "young ladies from the cream of our society" (*senhorinhas da nossa melhor sociedade*) dressed as Baianas. Their faces were blackened and broken shackles hung from their wrists. Behind them rode the carnival queen, in this case dressed as Princess Isabel, the royal who signed the emancipation decree in 1888. It is hard to say how this was meant to be interpreted. The report described it as depicting "the drama of slavery," but clearly it can be easily read as the "slaves'" celebration of the moment of their emancipation by a white princess (and of a white carnival queen).[155]

Pierson acknowledged exceptions to the racial, cultural, and class divisions in Salvador's carnival but points out that in even informal circumstances people of different "races" only barely intermingled. He had this to say about the crowds of carnival onlookers: "In the milling, dancing, singing crowd one ordinarily sees whites with whites, blacks and dark mulattoes with blacks and dark mulattoes, the exceptions being that a white occasionally accompanies a group of dark mulattoes and blacks, while brancos da Bahia and light mulattoes are often to be seen with whites."[156]

Pierson's descriptions of the *afoxés* and *batucadas* also explicitly present a dramatic visual conflation of "race" and cultural practice. As such, what stands out is not just the historical fact that the *afoxés* and *batucadas* were comprised exclusively of Bahians of marked African ancestry. Such practices must have been strongly coded racially. Bahians were not so simplistic as to assume that everyone of marked African ancestry played in a *batucada*; but they would have agreed that *batucadas* were strictly comprised of individuals of marked African ancestry. Pierson's study problematized the correlation between cultural forms and the phenotypic characteristics of their practitioners, but this was a correlation that Bahians to large degree took for granted. Consequently, as journalists and others incorporated the *batucadas* into constructions of *baianidade*, they incorporated African Bahians into these constructions as well. Almost without exception, well into the 1950s the *blocos* in newspaper photographs were comprised either of Bahians of overwhelmingly European ancestry (some were of mixed-race ancestry with light skin) or they were overwhelmingly African-Brazilian (with some of mixed-race ancestry but with dark skin). The *batucadas* and *afoxés* in the photographs were always entirely African Brazilian. The photographs Pierre Verger took of *blocos* and *cordões* in the late 1940s and 1950s also show marked degrees of racial homogeneity in Salvador's small carnival clubs.[157] In photographs of the *bloco* of eighty rowers from Santa Cruz Sporting Club in Salvador in the 1940s, all of the members are light skinned. This was typical of the dominant-class or elite sporting clubs, "who did not want people with dark skin," as several informants affirmed.[158]

Despite the potential of popular festivity and performance to undermine the structures that governed the daily lives of the poor and working class in Salvador, the festivals in the city largely reinforced and legitimated socioeconomic hierarchies. Performance during carnival did both. It is true that some areas of carnival experience were integrated. Certain small clubs, for instance, were mixed, and in some public areas participants or onlookers were mixed. Photos of Bahian carnival by Pierre Verger in the late 1950s, for instance, show people of all physical types in areas next to the official parade route, such as the Praça da Sé.[159] Yet obvious differences in social status were operationalized during carnival. The rich participated in very different ways than the working class or the poor, which meant that the experiences of most whites and the vast majority of blacks diverged significantly. The grand corteges of the elite clubs, for instance, were clear symbols of class and racial superiority, and although the working class could claim an allegiance to one club or the other, their relationship to the clubs during carnival was primarily as spectators. The dominant class's confetti battles and costume balls were, for the most part, closed to the bulk of society and the majority of African Bahians. As oral history interviewee Antônia Conceição put it, when it came to accepting people of African descent into elite institutions, the dominant class was "very demanding." It was possible for a black person or family to be present for events at the Athletic Association of Bahia, for instance, but only if they had a college degree (*formatura*), "something [that was] very unusual."[160]

Elite events reinforced the social order and were structured as the symbolic pinnacle of Salvadoran carnival. Despite the relative decline of the elite clubs and the popularization of carnival, the elite managed to present a much-abridged annual version of their former parades and could convince themselves that they were still the centerpiece of the festivities. The costumes and masks of the revelers in the streets were also markers of status. The better versions were imported from Europe or were made from imported materials, perhaps of satin, and could be quite complex. In contrast, the poor might cut holes in the peel of a breadfruit or a pillow cover. Poor youths often chose their worst clothes and went as street urchins, perhaps to prove that they were not in fact street urchins.[161] This was part of the wider phenomenon of the "dirty *blocos*" (*blocos de sujos*) in both Rio de Janeiro and Salvador. This group was comprised of workers and domestic servants who, in the words of Rubem Braga, organized almost by chance in almost every neighborhood, darkened their faces with charcoal, dressed in the messiest clothes they could find, and perhaps carried an inside-out umbrella, all part of a "self-caricature" of their own urban poverty.[162]

Although African-Bahian cultural practices were increasingly accepted as an essential element of Salvador's carnival, the ludic nature of carnival could be used by the dominant class to reinforce hierarchy. For instance, Donald Pierson noted how in 1936, "in a spirit of levity common to the Carnival season, one will occasionally see a group of whites and light mulattoes burlesquing the *cordão* [in this case an entirely African-Bahian *afoxé*]. Encompassed by a rope, they pass through the crowd, singing, dancing, and beating their palms. In one of these *blocos*, as they are called, 16 of the participants were whites and 12 were mulattoes, all light except one. There were no blacks." Moreover, there continued to be places and times where samba and particularly more rudimentary *batucadas* were not permitted.

An article in *O Imparcial* suggests that even in 1937, the Rua Chile, the principal location of formal carnival and the main procession route for the big clubs, was not an entirely egalitarian space. That year, the police broke up a *roda de samba* there. *O Imparcial* neither defended nor criticized the sambistas. The tone was of detached regret that "*samba é pro terreiro*" ("samba is for the *terreiro*"), meaning that the Terreiro de Jesus, the principal square barely three blocks away from the Rua Chile, was the right place for such practices because it was understood to be where working-class African Bahians celebrated carnival. It did not seem to matter that the musicians the police disturbed were the locally famous group Três e Meio, who were at the time making an impression on local radio audiences in Salvador. Newspaper reports, in the 1930s especially, reinforce the point that the Terreiro de Jesus was the epicenter of popular and African-Bahian carnival practice. That was "the meeting point of the *batucadas* and the *afoxés*" during Salvador's festivities, which extended through the poor and working-class neighborhoods adjacent to the Rua Chile and along the Baixa dos Sapateiros, but not along the official parade route itself, or at least not without provoking some degree of class and racial tension.[163]

Interviewees underline this point that the Terreiro de Jesus, and other locales such as the Largo da Piedade, were understood as the "appropriate" place for African-Bahian and working-class cultural practices. Moreover, dominant-class whites rarely went to the Terreiro. According to José Ferreira, African Bahians consciously restricted their movements. It was a question of certain behaviors and certain people belonging in certain places and not belonging in others.[164] After carnival in 1935, a number of *batucadas* continued to practice for the Micareta, which was a brief reprise of carnival on the weekend of or just after Easter Sunday. *A Tarde* carried a criticism of this practice, arguing that carnival was over and the Micareta was a long way off and it was not the time to be drumming in public. These "*batuques*" were disturbing the peace, and the use of *batuques* (which is in quotes in the original), seems in this case to have been a reminder of the African origins of the practice. This is one example of how the language reporters and editors chose reinforced cultural hierarchy. *Batucadas* needed to stay in their rightful time and place.[165]

Finally, the rise of samba as a regional and national symbol had its critics. In 1937, professor emeritus Luís Pinto de Carvalho of Bahia's Medical School lambasted regional and national elites, including President Getúlio Vargas, for celebrating popular musical forms such as samba. Pinto de Carvalho insisted that the only proper material for musical education, general artistic development, and even social well-being, was classical music.[166] How many Bahians agreed with this position cannot be known, but his statement at the very least represents a strand of dominant-class discourse on samba. Echoing Pinto de Carvalho's sentiments in 1937, historian Pedro Calmon, who was director of the Law Faculty of Bahia, criticized samba as an inappropriate musical genre for representing Brazil internationally. He was specifically targeting Carmen Miranda and her "vulgar and degrading" performances abroad, although his criticism was also directed at associating Brazil with "Guinea blacks or Hottentots in striped shirts."[167] As these comments suggest, the association of Bahian carnival with African-Bahian practices was accompanied by a degree of criticism that limited and controlled the meanings of African-Bahian culture as they were assimilated into notions of Bahianness.

Conclusion

The key development in Bahian carnival from 1930 to 1954 was that the "artistry and luxuriousness" of the elite clubs gave way to the "*batucada* and animation" of Salvador's samba schools. The region's stagnant economy and World War II undermined the elite clubs' financial base and the willingness of the mayor's office to subsidize them, curtailing their ability to parade individual corteges and maintain their place as the centerpiece of the city's carnival celebrations. Throughout the 1930s and especially after the war, Salvador's African-Bahian poor and working classes formed more and more *batucadas* for the three-day pre-Lenten festivity. In this they were encouraged by the success of samba in Rio de Janeiro, the commercial success of the genre, and its elevation as a manifestation of Brazilianness and Brazilian racially inclusive national identity. Bahian journalists, too, were influenced by the rise of samba to national prominence and began to construct Salvador's *batucadas*, which performed sambas publicly, as positive contributions to the city's carnival. In addition, one of the conventions of samba, as performed in the radio studios in Bahia and the southeast of Brazil, was the frequent use of themes and imagery that invoked African-Bahian cultural practices, which began to stand in as the principal signifiers of Bahian identity in Brazilian urban popular music. *Afoxés* also played important roles during carnival and extended the presence of the *terreiro* into the secular festivities.[168] The *afoxé* Filhos de Gandhy, founded in 1949, became ambassadors of the institution as a distinctive cultural marker of Salvadoran carnival. The phenomena of the *batucadas* and the *afoxé* reinforced the general trend in Bahia after 1930 whereby journalists, academics, intellectuals, and public figures began to write and speak of African-Bahian cultural forms as positive contributions to and a central element of Bahian regional identity.

That African-Bahian practices did not become the principal (or even the only) defining feature of Salvador's carnival, as was the case with the samba schools in Rio de Janeiro, was due to several factors. While local political bosses in Rio de Janeiro recognized the political usefulness of the samba schools, Salvador's elites did not perceive a politically expedient need to institutionalize the diverse and small carnival associations around the city. Instead, the municipal government focused its energies and financial support on the three big clubs and was central to their revival in the early 1950s. Nevertheless, it supported popular carnival and the smaller clubs in smaller ways, not only in the downtown area but also in numerous outlying "hot spots." Some politicians also used carnival as an opportunity to enter African-Bahian space in a public and official capacity. For example, Mayor Aristóteles Góes (1954–55) made a point of attending both elite events and African-Bahian events during carnival. The *batucadas* and *afoxés* certainly benefited from this public show of support. This was known at the time as "the officialization of carnival," as both elite groups and African-Bahian groups became dependent on or were at least strongly influenced by government largesse.[169]

The Era of the Batucadas drew to a close in early 1950s. Much of this was due to the emergence in 1951 of the *trio elétrico*, which provided a spirited alternative to the *batucadas*. In 1950, two Bahian musicians, Adolfo Nascimento and Osmar Macedo, known affectionately as Dodô and Osmar, introduced the *dupla elétrico* (electric double) to Salvador's carnival. They played electric guitars atop a Ford pickup truck as the vehicle moved along the carnival circuit. But the duo did not remain a duo for long. The following year a third musician, Temístocles Aragão, joined the two pioneers and the *trio elétrico* was born.[170] The innovation quickly became popular. Fratelli Vita, a bottling conglomerate with a long history of sponsoring carnival, began sponsoring the trio of musicians, which appeared at carnival *gritos* in 1953 and 1954.[171] And in 1955, a second, "official" *trio elétrico* was organized by the mayor's office, which no doubt hoped to reap some of the benefits of the popularity the phenomenon generated.[172] The *trios elétricos* posed problems for the *batucadas* and even for the centrality of samba to Bahian carnival. The *trios* initially played a different type of music, called *frevo*, that was popular during carnival in another northeast city in Brazil, Recife.

Nevertheless, the period from the late 1930s to the early 1950s saw a rise in popularity of the *batucada* carnival associations of the poor and working-class neighborhoods that coincided with the demise of the grand corteges of the elite clubs. This combination facilitated the celebration, largely by journalists, of the place of the African-Bahian *batucada* in carnival. Carnival, of course, was arguably Salvador's most important popular festival in the configuration of Bahia's regional identity. As Nathalie Zemon Davis argued long ago, although dramatic changes in the social order are rare, carnival is powerful because over time the festival extends the boundaries of what is acceptable. What is initially an inversion, or perhaps merely an exception, becomes increasingly normative.[173] The dynamics of the Era of the Batucadas, particularly from 1938 to 1952, contributed to the consolidation of African-Bahian musical practices—such as the *batucada*, the samba, and, to lesser extent, the Candomblé-related *afoxés*—as central elements of Bahian regional identity during the Vargas era. Even after 1954 the *batucadas* did not disappear entirely. They and a number of *afoxés* continued to provide a bridge of ethnic identification and cultural agency between the Afrocentric clubs of the late nineteenth and early twentieth centuries, on the one hand, and the *afoxés* and *blocos afros* of the late twentieth and twenty-first centuries. Both played important roles in the reformulation of *baianidade* from 1930 to 1954 as African-Bahian cultural practices, and African Bahians were celebrated as "the powerful propulsive force that moved Bahian carnival."[174]

Finally, during these years the demographic and geographic spread of popular carnival and the carnivalization of several other popular religious festivals also deepened Bahia's association with African-Bahian practices. These practices shifted the balance in the festivals away from the religious representatives of the dominant class and toward the African-Bahian celebrants in the street. Carnival in Bahia between 1930 and 1954 was very much a carnival of the people. While carnival and carnival discourse transformed during the Era of the Batucadas, an important process was occurring more widely in Salvador. This was the consolidation of an explicit, self-conscious project carried out by key figures in Salvador's political and cultural elite that identified the inclusion and celebration of African-Bahian practices as central to Bahian regional identity. It is to this act of consolidation of a recreated Bahian identity that we now turn.

6

The Project of Regional Identity Formation

Culture, Politics, and Tourism

In 1952, the archbishop of Salvador, Dom Augusto Álvaro da Silva, lifted another ban on the Washing of Bonfim ritual. This one had lasted for three years. The lifting of the prohibition was emblematic of the wider process of the acceptance and inclusion of African-Bahian cultural practices since 1930.[1] When the ritual was performed on the morning of 15 January 1953, the mayor of Salvador was present to signal his support for the African-Bahian practice, and the governor of the state was present when the procession to the church began. Journalists were in place, ready to gather data for reports on the syncretic practice. In addition, folklorist Antônio Monteiro and the largely middle-class members of the Permanent Commission for the Symbolic Washing of Bonfim had played significant roles in pressuring the archbishop to lift the ban.

By 1953 it is possible to distinguish a much clearer project of regional identity formation, especially among members of the dominant class. Part of the motivation for this was the desire to pursue Bahia's potential for tourism. In keeping with this desire, the newspaper reports on the Washing of Bonfim in both 1953 and 1954 mentioned the presence of tourists. One of the accompanying photographs in 1953 captured what had very recently become a standard image of the festival—tourists participating alongside Baianas. Indeed, since the mid-1940s the emerging practice of photojournalism had contributed a new layer—this time of visual power—to the project of establishing and disseminating the relevance of African-Bahian culture to Bahian regional identity. In the hands of photographer Pierre Verger, photojournalism began to overlap with the academic practice of visual anthropology as a medium for associating Bahia with its African-Bahian heritage.

Verger was in Africa in 1953 and 1954 and missed the ritual Washing of Bonfim in those years, but one of his collaborators, Odorico Tavares, was present at the Church of Bonfim for the washing in 1954. Tavares positioned himself at the center of the dominant-class effort to create and disseminate a regional identity on the basis of including African-Bahian culture. Tavares was a modernist poet and journalist and the director of operations for two of Salvador's three major newspapers and a radio station. He embodied the convergence of the press, modernists, folklorists, photography, the emerging influence of Brazil's illustrated weekly magazines, the surge in Bahian promotional literature, local government, samba musicians, the literary elite, the fine arts, and, finally, the tourist industry. Odorico Tavares was born and raised in Pernambuco and therefore was an outsider, but by the early 1950s he was active in an influential network of people who were channeling the city's formal and informal ritual practices into a hegemonic discourse that reshaped the meanings of Salvador's modern twentieth-century regional identity. The carrying out of the Washing of Bonfim in 1953 and 1954 in honor of the Senhor do Bonfim and his Candomblé alter ego Oxalá—probably the principal public ritual expression of Bahianness—lent significant performative power to the consolidation of the reworking of Bahian regional identity. This chapter explores the important efforts of several key cultural and political actors during the years immediately following World War II, as aspects of African-Bahian agency and performance combined with the return of electoral politics, tourism, and the deepening importance of modernism to consolidate the notion of Bahia as inclusive of its African-Bahian traditions.[2]

The Candomblé Community, Antônio Monteiro, and Pierre Verger

The Candomblé community and its allies continued to make efforts toward influencing the reappraisal of African-Bahian practices after 1945, just as they had for most of the twentieth century through their insistent and enthusiastic participation in the city's public festivals. Key to the influence of the African-Bahian community was its ability to build alliances with important members of the dominant class. This is most clear, for example, in the community's efforts leading to the revival of the Washing of Bonfim. The Union of Afro-Brazilian Temples of Candomblé (União das Seitas Afro-Brasileiras), which was formed in 1937 to organize leaders within the Candomblé community to defend their right of religious practice, was replaced in 1946 by the Bahian Federation of African-Brazilian Worship

(Federação Baiana do Culto Afro-Brasileiro). Informally headquartered at the *terreiro* Casa Branca, the Federação continued to play a role in defending African-Bahian religious practices against its detractors while also encouraging members of its community to participate in public festivals.[3] Important leaders within the Candomblé community such as Miguel Santana, a ranking *ogan* of the *terreiro* Opô Afonjá who had assumed the presidency of the Bonfim festival's organizing committee in 1939 and 1940, and João da Gomeia, continued to encourage the community to participate in the washing ritual. Even during years when the Church insisted there would be no washing, Baianas showed up to perform a truncated version of their obligation to Oxalá. Odorico Tavares reported for *O Cruzeiro* that in 1948 the gates around the patio were closed to shut out those who wanted to perform the washing, but a number of those present jumped the gates and washed the patio anyway. Tavares did not report how many were members of the Candomblé community. That the gates were at least five feet high surely put off most of those of a certain age or the women wearing the Baiana's ceremonial clothing, but this incident reveals a degree of popular initiative. Typically, however, those who arrived during years of the prohibition were ushered away by the police, as they were in 1951.[4]

We also have a glimpse of the efforts of the Candomblé community to influence the construction of the historical memory of the Washing of Bonfim. In 1953, the *Diário de Notícias* carried a brief announcement of a Candomblé ritual celebration in front of the house of Miguel Santa [*sic*, presumably Santana] in honor of the "ancestors" who had "initiated" the "symbolic washing." This was likely Santana's way of keeping alive the memory of the contributions of Mãe Aninha and other *mães-de-santo* and *filhas-de-santo* to originating and perpetuating the ritual and was illustrative of the proactive work of the Candomblé community to maintain its status and influence in the city's public festivities.[5] This reflects a wider trend after 1945 in which leading figures within the Candomblé community took leading roles in legitimating their cultural practices using the conventions of the dominant culture, especially scholarship.[6] This process intensified after 1954, but Mestre Didi, for instance, published a Yoruba dictionary as early as 1946. It would not be long before members of the Candomblé community would support Yoruba language courses offered by the Center for Afro-Oriental Studies (CEAO), which was founded in 1959 as part of the Federal University of Bahia.[7]

The principal player in the consolidation of the Washing of Bonfim after World War II, however, was Antônio Monteiro (b. 1918). In the 1940s,

Monteiro was a keen folklorist, an amateur historian, and most likely an *ogan* of a *terreiro*. When the Herskovitses began their research on Candomblé ceremony in November 1941, Monteiro was by chance one of their first contacts and informants within the community. Frances Herskovits met him at the first Candomblé she attended and noted that he "seemed to know his way about, sang the Nagô songs, and said he worked at the Nina Rodriguez [*sic*] Institute [then part of Bahia's Medical School.]" During this period, Monteiro was very well informed about Candomblé practice in Salvador and served as First Secretary for the Union of Afro-Brazilian Temples of Candomblé.[8] By the early 1950s Monteiro was an active member of the Bahian Sub-Commission for Folklore. The press referred to him as "professor," for instance, in March 1951, when he gave a talk at the commission's meetings about the Candomblé ceremony of the Waters of Oxalá. During this time he made several newspaper contributions a year on African-Bahian religious practices that demonstrate his extensive understanding of Candomblé cosmology and liturgy.[9] In 1951, Monteiro also played a key role in the organization of the Bahian Center for Black Studies (Centro de Estudos Afro-Brasileiros) and served as its first Secretary General. He contributed a talk to the center's first lecture series.[10]

Monteiro built on the work of the Organizing Committee of the Washing of Bonfim from the early 1940s in efforts to promote the Washing of Bonfim. He created (most likely in 1949) the Permanent Commission for the Symbolic Washing of Bonfim, which he headed and which included "intellectuals, parliamentarians and journalists." The objective of this commission was to coordinate the efforts of politicians, the press, and the Candomblé hierarchy to convince the Catholic Church to lift the ban on the washing of the church.[11] During the period the ban was in place, between 1949 and 1951, the commission worked with the Devotion of Bonfim, a religious brotherhood that consisted of important figures in Bahian society, to have the ban lifted and the gates to the church open to the crowds. As part of these efforts, in 1952, while the ban was still in place, the commission helped organize an unofficial washing that took place "to the sound of *batucadas*" on a section of the steps leading up to the gates, where part of the washing typically occurred.[12]

Eventually this combined pressure brought results, and the ban was lifted. Monteiro's Permanent Commission for the Symbolic Washing of Bonfim was central to the Church's decision to open the gates and allow restricted access to the inside of the church building. In an interview some time after the fact, Monteiro elaborated on his tactics: "I sent a dispatch to all the authorities: governor of the state, mayor, regional commander, all the command, head of police, head of the fire department, head of the police department band . . . to say that their wives would be the *madrinhas* (godmothers, but also the sponsors or even the chaperones) of the Baianas and to present awards to those who were best turned out. . . . And the wives showed up with their presents . . . [as did] more than one hundred thousand people." Monteiro also vaguely mentioned that he approached a relative in the Church about the ban, suggesting that he had some sort of inside connection that may have made a difference.[13]

Once the ban was lifted, the commission under Monteiro consolidated the importance of the washing ritual in a number of ways. Monteiro met each year with the mayor and the governor and encouraged them to attend, which they did. He liaised with the Bahian Sub-Commission for Folklore, of which he was a member, as were a number of intellectuals from traditional elite families. The folklore commission held its meetings at the Geographic and Historical Institute of Bahia, an elite cultural institution that preserved the region's official history. Monteiro and the press emphasized the idea of tradition, and the prizes that were to be given out by the *madrinhas* were an effort to attract "the Baianas to appear with greater authenticity."[14] As was to be expected, the press corps was enthusiastically in favor of lifting the ban and endorsed the work of the commission. They injected drama into the process by exaggerating the degree to which the ban threatened a "venerable" and "most Bahian of traditions" and portrayed the Catholic Church as high-handed and insensitive, determined to succeed in "wiping it out."[15] In 1954, the press carried numerous photos of Mayor Aristóteles Góes and Governor Regis Pacheco at the head of the procession. There were also photos of Mayor Góes at the washing itself, holding a broom, standing next to several dignified-looking Baianas. Photographers also took care to include at least one image of a female member of the elite participating in the ritual.[16] Finally, to "maintain the splendor of the washing," the Permanent Commission for the Symbolic Washing of Bonfim and the Bahian Sub-Commission for Folklore appealed "to the business sectors and private individuals to donate items of some value (but not money) to present to the participants in the procession leading up to the washing." Some businessmen provided flowers for the Baianas to carry to the church and to present to the Senhor do Bonfim and Oxalá. Finally, the permanent commission arranged to include a press car in the procession, presumably to ensure the most favorable coverage of the event.[17]

However, the Catholic Church had only partially relented, and the proponents of the washing did not have it all their own way. The Church allowed what the press referred to as a "symbolic washing." "Symbolic" in this case meant that only hand-picked elite men and (especially) women were to wash the inside of the church, alongside a certain number of representative Baianas. In 1953, the Church iterated its position quite forcefully in a letter sent to the newspapers, reminding everyone that the ecclesiastical ban of the washing was still in force. The ban, as they put it, was to protect the church from "any profaning or demonstration of African-Bahian religious practice [fetichismo]." Such actions were described as "an assault on the beacons of our civilized and Christian city."[18] This makes it clear that the prohibition was not about the generic act of washing the church, a practice that was not unique to Salvador. What the Church sought to ban were the rituals associated with Oxalá and Candomblé, the most explicit of which was the practice whereby women fell into traces while being "ridden" or possessed by their Candomblé orixá.[19] In fact, the masses had been prevented from entering the church during the washings of 1937–48, but after 1953 the limits on the behavior of the masses of African Bahians were more clearly established and strictly enforced. The larger group of practitioners of Candomblé could not enter the church. In addition, the Permanent Commission for the Symbolic Washing of Bonfim sided with the Catholic Church about what was referred to as the "moralization" of the ritual celebrations. This meant minimizing the excess with which some Bahians typically celebrated, including drinking to the point of drunkenness or singing "indecorous" songs. These conditions, plus with the inclusion of ranking politicians and society ladies and the involvement of local businesses, were part of the compromises necessary to convince the ecclesiastical hierarchy to agree to allow the washing ritual to take place within the confines of the Church.

Even so, the restoration of the ritual was not an immediate success. One editorial in 1953 criticized the small number of participants. Another article reported that the tradition was reviving only "little by little," even though the overall tone of the article was optimistic. However, in 1954 and 1955, again after concerted efforts by the Permanent Commission for the Symbolic Washing of Bonfim, the ceremony was "regaining its former splendor." The public reception of the reinstated washing ritual continued to improve, and in 1964 Monteiro and the commission handed their roles to organs of the state responsible for tourism. After that point, the mayor's office liaised directly with the terreiros and the Candomblé community in the lead-up to the Washing of Bonfim.[20]

Monteiro was not the only folklorist, writer, or scholar after World War II to push for greater recognition of the sophistication, vitality, and importance of African-Bahian practices. In 1946, several newspapers reported that (mostly unidentified) scholars from outside Bahia had come to witness the Festival of Senhor do Bonfim. The establishment in 1947 of the Brazilian National Commission for Folklore also stimulated the interest of local amateurs and professional scholars in Bahian folklore. The Bahian Sub-Commission for Folklore, founded in 1948 and headed by Antonio Vianna, met monthly in the late 1940s and early 1950s. In February 1950, the Bahian Sub-Commission was treated to a talk by Antônio Monteiro on the Bonfim festival cycle.[21] Vianna's own *Casos e coisas* came out during this period, as did the work of his daughter, Hildegardes Vianna, who put together a guide to Bahian cooking in the early 1950s. She was perhaps stimulated by the success in 1948 of folklorist Darwin Brandão's own study of Bahian cuisine, *A Cozinha Bahiana*.[22]

The Bahian Sub-Commission for Folklore contributed to the spate of serious and critically well-received publications on African-Bahian topics in the postwar period, many of which were subsidized by the Bahian government. The authors of these studies seemed to agree with the sentiments of Renato Almeida, who argued in 1949 at the very conservative and traditional First Bahian History Conference that "folkloric phenomena" (*fenômenos folclóricos*) as objects of serious scholarship were central to understanding "the formation of Bahian society," including, significantly, even the formation of the "highest social classes."[23] According to Vilhena, during the period 1948–52 the Bahian Sub-Commission for Folklore commissioned more articles than São Paulo did (twenty-eight compared to twenty-seven), and twice as many as the states that commissioned the third and fourth highest number of articles (Rio Grande do Sul and Ceará, both of which commissioned fourteen).[24] This fertile context for folklore studies in Bahia both reflected and contributed to the elevation of the importance of African-Bahian culture and its contributions to Bahianness.

Folklore meant much more in Bahia than just African-Bahian culture, and the longstanding preferences among the scholarly folklorists in Salvador for rural rather than urban folk life meant that African-Bahian culture was just one of many subgenres of Bahian folklore. Nevertheless, figures such as Antônio Monteiro and Cláudio Tavares continued to push African-Bahian culture toward the center of folklore studies in Bahia as well as nationally.[25] The successive Brazilian National Congresses of Folklore, which took place in Rio de Janeiro in 1951 and in Curitiba in 1953, kept folklore studies in the newspapers during this period. Papers on African-Bahian culture by both Monterio (on ethnobotany of the *terreiros*) and Tavares (on capoeira and the *afoxés*) were chosen by the Bahian Sub-Commission for Folklore for presentation at the First Brazilian National Congress of Folklore in 1951.[26] In 1952, Bahian governor Regis Pacheco signed an accord with the Brazilian and Bahian folklore commissions that promised logistical and financial support from the state for folklore studies in Bahia, while the Bahian commission was hopeful that funds from the mayor's office would be forthcoming to send delegations to the national congress in Curitiba in 1953.[27]

As Monteiro and the Candomblé community cooperated to reestablish the Washing of Bonfim as part of the Festival of Bonfim, another important cultural figure of the period, Mestre Pastinha (Vicente Ferreira Pastinha, 1889–1981) sought to celebrate the African origins of Bahian culture in the realm of capoeira. Mestre Pastinha was the most influential of a small number of figures in codifying and publicizing a style of capoeira that emphasized its roots in African culture. This more Afrocentric version was known as capoeira *angola* and was purposely contrasted with the capoeira *regional* style Mestre Bimba pioneered (discussed in chapter 3). Bimba had incorporated kicks and moves from other martial arts into *capoeira regional*, which left him open to accusations that he had "whitened" capoeira.[28] But by the postwar years, both styles had become relatively institutionalized. The training was formalized, the masters taught in academies rather than in the streets and squares, the academies were registered with the appropriate authorities and were attended by middle-class students, and each academy had links to the state via contacts with the police, the military, sports education, and tourism.

In 1949 (after several earlier efforts), Pastinha succeeded in establishing his academy, the Centro Esportivo de Capoeira Angola, in a soap factory where he worked as a watchman. The original statutes declared that the "genuine 'Angola' . . . has been passed on to us by the primitive Africans that disembarked here [in Salvador]."[29] Pastinha's emphasis on the African roots of his style was celebrated and reinforced in the writings of figures such as Jorge Amado and Edison Carneiro, and the capoeira of both Bimba and Pastinha were important means of establishing African-Bahian culture within Bahian regional identity. In 1955, with official support, Pastinha was able to move his academy from the soap factory to a more central address, and the academy slowly became one of the most well known within the history of the sport. Both Jorge Amado and (purportedly) President Getúlio

Vargas during these years referred to capoeira as "our only truly national sport."[30]

The efforts of the Candomblé community to work with dominant-class allies or bring in outsiders who could further their ethnopolitical agendas continued in the period after 1945. For instance, the community supported São Paulo–based French sociologist Roger Bastide during his visits, which began in 1944. These visits led to numerous publications on Candomblé that depicted it as a microcosm of Africa.[31] One of the most influential contributors in this regard, however, was Pierre Verger. Verger had worked around the world in the 1930s as a photojournalist for several prestigious agencies, and his work had been published in a number of illustrated magazines in Europe, the United States, and Brazil. In 1946 Verger, at age forty-four, returned to Brazil to live. He moved to Salvador and made it his base for the next fifty years.[32] Fascinated with Bahia and especially with its very visual, very public, and very vibrant African-Bahian culture, Verger fixed his camera on the city's African-Bahian population. Recalling this period later in his life, he remarked, perhaps jokingly, that during these first few months he scarcely realized that white people lived in Bahia.[33] He rarely turned his lenses on a light-skinned person. He eventually took over thirteen thousand photos of Brazil, many of these in Bahia.

It was not long before Verger was drawn to Candomblé, recognizing it as the key institution within African-Bahian cultural life. Verger's intellectual relationship with local culture began to move beyond his initial interest in it as merely a photographic subject. In 1948 he was initiated into a *terreiro*, Opô Afonjá, and began a long, deep study of the connections between African-Bahian and West African religions. Verger frequently traveled between northeast Brazil and West Africa, taking photographs, interviewing, and studying (but rarely practicing) the religion of the *orixás*. Part of his travel at this early stage was funded by the French Institute on Black Africa (IFAN), which not only supported Verger but also gave his subject matter the stamp of scholarly legitimacy.

In 1953, while he was in Benin, Verger was brought further into the religious life of West Africa when he was initiated as a *babalaô*, a priest or diviner of Ifá within the Yoruba religion. At this point he took the name Fatumbí. He began doing less commercial photography so he could spend time on deeper ethnographic studies of Yoruban religion and its New World offshoots, including pioneering work in visual anthropology, but he also studied ethnobotany and researched the cultural and economic connections between West Africa and Salvador, Cuba, Haiti, Surinam, and

French Guyana. In 1954, Verger published an early collection of photographs titled *Dieux d'Afrique* (*Gods of Africa*), which documented what he saw as the ethnoreligious and ritual continuities between West Africa and Bahia. The book used both photography and text to establish analogies between African-Brazilian culture (especially in Bahia) and Yoruba culture in West Africa. After 1954, Verger frequently moved between Salvador, Benin, and Nigeria, and he eventually spent seventeen years of his life in West Africa. He also earned a doctorate in history from the Sorbonne, worked on museum collections in Salvador, and contributed to films and videos on Yoruban religious culture. In addition, he took a position as professor at the Federal University of Bahia as well as other visiting posts at the University of Ifé, Nigeria.[34]

However, it is Verger's early contributions to deepening the association of Bahia with African-Bahian culture that is the focus here. Verger's first means of influence was through his photojournalism, a practice that was just gaining ground in Brazil. Even before he settled in Bahia, Verger had been an early practitioner of the art.[35] From 1946 to 1951 he contributed fifty-two separate sets of themed photos to *O Cruzeiro* and *A Cigarra*, the first a Brazilian illustrated weekly on the model of North America's *Life Magazine* and the second an illustrated monthly. Both magazines were part of Assis Chateaubriand's media empire. Twenty-five of the fifty-two sets of photographs were on the culture and people of Salvador (totaling 373 published photos), roughly half of which were accompanied by written text from Odorico Tavares, a fellow outsider who had arrived from Pernambuco four years earlier to run Chateaubriand's two newspapers.[36]

The topics covered a variety of elements of culture that were increasingly considered typical of Bahia and *baianidade* including waterborne commerce, dock workers, popular poets, laundresses, and several of the city's popular festivals. In Verger's hands, these aspects of culture possessed dignity, grace, and even grandeur. Verger's photographs for *O Cruzeiro* and the text that accompanied them (by several authors) also depicted a wide spectrum of African-Bahian culture—capoeira, cuisine, *afoxés*, and the Baiana. For *A Cigarra*, he contributed photos on samba and a set of graphic photos of Candomblé initiation rites that were almost certainly some of the first for a general audience that treated the religion respectfully, albeit a little sensationally. The text that accompanied the Candomblé photos was written by Roger Bastide. In 1951, Tavares and Verger contributed a piece to *O Cruzeiro* titled "The Decline and Death of the Washing of Bonfim," which both lamented and attacked the Catholic Church's ban on the Washing of

Bonfim. This criticism reached a national audience. Tavares, who wrote the text, and Verger blamed the Church for the deterioration of the entire four-day Festival of Bonfim and offered quotes from two Baianas. Each was "teary-eyed" and stunned by the attacks on their cultural practices. For them (and presumably for Verger and Tavares), there was nothing wrong with dancing samba or singing. It was a way of expressing one's happiness and gratitude toward the saints and *orixás*.[37]

Three of Verger's contributions for *O Cruzeiro* and *A Cigarra* that focused on aspects of African-Bahian culture—capoeira, the *afoxés*, and samba—were accompanied by text written by the brother of Odorico Tavares, Cláudio Tavares, a left-leaning modernist poet. Angela Lühning suggests that the Tavares brothers influenced the choice of subject matter as much or more so than Verger himself, who was just becoming acclimated to Salvador and learning the Portuguese language. However, the choices fell well within the sphere of what had attracted Verger's professional eye previously in his career.[38] Each of the three articles included over twenty photographs of Bahians, mainly African Bahians, participating in an *afoxé* or performing or about to perform capoeira and samba. The message of the photographs and text was clear. These African-Bahian cultural forms were vibrant and complex. Verger's framing of Bahia as deeply bound to African-Bahian practices made an important contribution to how the middle class across Brazil, especially in the influential urban southeast (where the principal readership of *O Cruzeiro* and *A Cigarra* was located), came to understand a region that most would never visit.[39]

Verger arrived in Bahia after Edison Carneiro had moved to Rio de Janeiro and Jorge Amado was spending less and less time in Salvador. Arthur Ramos, the most influential of Brazilian scholars on African-Brazilian culture, had died in 1949. Despite these losses, Salvador still offered a vibrant climate for the study of folklore. Much of these studies echoed Gilberto Freyre's emphasis on the African origins of Brazilian *national* culture and contributed to discourses of *mestiçagem* and creolization. Verger's work contributed to this, too, but he went a step further. Verger was the most Afrocentric Bahian-based student (rather than practitioner) of African-Bahian culture and the figure whose emphasis was most clearly on Africa in the Diaspora, both historically and in the present. His photographic and written contributions brought a much greater focus on African-derived cultures in the new world, and he steadfastly refused to diminish or relegate the African components of "Bahianness" in favor of its European or Brazilian components. Even when Verger overstated the similarities between religious practices in Bahia and West Africa, what he produced increased awareness of Africa within Bahianness.

Pierre Verger came to see himself as "the messenger," the one whose movement between the continents allowed him to bring mid- to late-twentieth-century African religious culture back to Salvador to enrich the "Africanness" of Bahian culture.[40] Even before he wrote most of his scholarly work, the publication of which occurred after 1954, Verger influenced the scholarship of others, most notably Roger Bastide, who authored the piece on Candomblé for *A Cigarra* in 1949.[41] Verger also helped his friend and fellow countryman Gilbert Rouget in 1948. Rouget, an ethnomusicologist for the Musée de l'Homme in Paris, was sent by Claude Lévi-Strauss to Salvador, and Verger made the necessary introductions within the Candomblé community. Verger took Rouget to the *terreiro* Opô Afonjá for the Festival of the Waters of Oxalá in the company of the U.S. consul to Bahia, who was presumably charged with supporting Rouget's mission. Typical of Verger's modesty, he reveals how moved he was by the beauty of the ceremony but does not say that he arrived with the U.S. consul or whether the members of Opô Afonjá were impressed with a visit from a representative of the United States. Perhaps by 1948 visits by international scholars had become somewhat commonplace at the *terreiro*. Finally, Verger also contributed logistically to UNESCO's studies on race relations in Brazil, for instance serving as Alfred Métraux's host and guide during a trip to Salvador and providing most of the photographs for Métraux's September 1952 compilation of articles on race relations in Brazil that was published in UNESCO's *Courier*.[42]

One of Verger's most important contributions was his enrichment of knowledge of the African origins of Candomblé within the *terreiros*. This was a contribution to the second phase of a trend that had been set in motion in the 1930s by Martiniano do Bonfim and Mãe Aninha and others that emphasized the Nagô-Ketu tradition, although Verger also developed relationships with *terreiros* of other traditions. One of the principal motivations for Verger's early work (indeed for most of his career) was his desire to "unify" Africa and its New World cultures through enhanced mutual comprehension across the diaspora.[43] In 1951, Verger told the priestess of one of Salvador's bigger *terreiros* that he planned to spend a year in West Africa studying the roots of New World religions. The priestess, Mãe Senhora (Maria Bibiana do Espírito Santo), soon initiated him into her Opô Afonjá *terreiro*. This process brought Verger into the workings of the *terreiro* and into the orbit of her influence. This turned out to be a very "shrewd move" on the part of Mãe Senhora (those were Verger's own words).[44] Mãe Senhora insisted that during his trip to Africa Verger would, as he later put it, "go to speak on behalf of Bahian Candomblé in Africa." As an initiate, Verger was more free to move in political-religious circles in Benin and Nigeria that might have been closed to a total outsider.

Verger had a less well-known relationship with another important Candomblé figure. Tia Massi (Maximiana Maria da Conceição) of the *terreiro* Casa Branca almost got to Verger before Mãe Senhora did, likely with the same intent. Tia Massi began the process of making Verger an *ogan* of Casa Branca, but the process was never finalized. Even after Verger had gravitated to Mãe Senhora's orbit of influence, Tia Massi maintained a close relationship with him. Verger reciprocated by returning from Africa in 1953 with an African parrot that Tia Massi had asked him to obtain. She insisted that the parrot was a gift from her personal *orixá*, Oxaguian, and characterized Verger as merely an instrument of Oxaguian's will.[45]

Verger was generous about sharing what he had learned about the practice of religion in West Africa. These exchanges were of course spiritually and materially enriching for Salvador's Candomblé community and Mãe Senhora in particular, as it increased the prestige of her temple and lineage. As Paulina Alberto points out, the timing was propitious for the Candomblé community, especially the temples in the Nagô-Ketu tradition, because World War II had severed the increasingly tenuous commercial links between Bahia and West Africa that many of the larger temples relied on to replenish their spiritual authority.[46] When Verger was in Nigeria and Benin in 1952, he met with several high-ranking political figures and religious leaders. They were very interested in what Verger had to tell them about Candomblé in Brazil, especially about Mãe Senhora, her African ancestry, and her *terreiro*. The king of the Yoruba nation in Nigeria gave Verger letters and a number of sacred objects to take back with him to Salvador to reinforce the power of the *orixá* Xangô at Opô Afonjá. He even allowed Verger to take photos of a royal priest. He also sent Mãe Senhora a letter that conferred on her the honorary title of Iyá Nassô, or Royal Priestess of Xangô. Verger conveyed all this to Mãe Senhora and Opô Afonjá in 1953 in a number of public ceremonies that were attended by representatives from throughout the Candomblé community. The ceremonies were well publicized in the local press, and newspapers as far away as Rio de Janeiro took up the story. The temple of Mãe Senhora went on to become a "splendorous 'court' of intellectuals, artists and politicians," all of whom embraced and popularized or in some way reinforced the presence of Africa in Bahia.[47]

Less than a year before this took place, Mãe Senhora had celebrated the fiftieth anniversary of her relationship with her *orixá* at the *terreiro*, and representatives from the Office of President of Brazil and the Ministry of Education had participated in the event. Clearly, Salvador's most influential *terreiros* continued to cultivate their relationships with offices and individuals with the power to improve their circumstances. Verger's interests; his connections with figures such as Jorge Amado, Odorico Tavares, and Métraux; and his access to Africa placed him in a unique position, and various leaders within the *terreiros* moved to take advantage of this. The consequence of this initiative was a deeper association of Bahia with African-Bahian Candomblé.

The State, Tourism, and the Arrival of Carybé

After 1930, Bahia's political elite used popular festivals as a means to establish political legitimacy, and their participation in the celebration of Bahia's traditions deepened the process of cultural inclusion in Salvador. But their desire to promote tourism to the region was an additional motivation for their embrace of the city's popular cultural traditions, including African-Bahian culture. The suitability of Salvador as a tourist destination was already evident to the city's inhabitants in the 1930s, as transatlantic and North American cruise ships stopped off at Salvador on the way to or from Rio de Janeiro. Salvador held a number of attractions, including its colonial residential and religious architecture, its public squares, its cobblestone streets, its location on a beautiful bay, and of course its cultural traditions. In the words of Mayor José Wanderley Pinho, these made the city "the greatest tourist attraction in Brazil and one of the most exquisite curiosities of the Americas."[48]

During these early years the tourists' time in the city was greatly limited. They may have visited the historical sites and shopped at the Mercado Modelo for "ceramic pieces, lacework panels . . . and a thousand other things that only foreigners would think interesting," but they slept and largely ate on board because the city had only the rudiments of an infrastructure for serving the needs of tourists. Sometimes visiting tour groups stayed only for a morning. The Bahian chapter of the Touring Club of Brazil, a principal protagonist in bringing visitors to Bahia, worked in the 1930s with both the mayor's office and the local press to improve the situation. In 1940 they brought "six dozen Brazilian tourists from the south" by boat who disembarked at 8:00 a.m. to tour some of the city's churches and have a lunch of Bahian cuisine at the Yacht Club. But they reboarded their ship and set sail at 1:00 p.m. If the mayor's office wanted to influence the visitors' impressions of the city it had to act quickly, so it sent representatives to the lunch armed with "statistical information." They also handed out "com- pendiums with information on Bahia, its churches, and its history."[49] Part of the impetus for these efforts came from a broader federal initiative and collaboration between Vargas's Department of Press and Propaganda, its state affiliates, and members of the Touring Club of Brazil.[50] It is not known what percentage of the municipal government's "statistical information" emphasized the city's African-Bahian traditions. Meanwhile, the press rev- eled in the adventurous spirit of "The Curious American," who "ate vatapá [and] learned capoeira" and pointed out that not all the passengers from the ocean liners stayed on the beaten path during their brief stopover. This meant that most did. However, the message was that this was something that could change to the benefit of the city. The relationship between the press and the Bahian affiliate of the Touring Club of Brazil was strength- ened by the presence of Oswaldo Valente, who sat on the board of directors of the Bahian affiliate and was also an editor at the *Diário de Notícias*.[51]

After 1945 Salvador's relationship with tourism began to intensify. Sev- eral of the larger oceangoing cruise liners began to call at Salvador on their way to Rio de Janeiro for carnival. Progress was slow, however. In January 1947, mayoral candidate José Wanderley Pinho spoke to the Rotary Club about his concerns that Salvador did not have a single hotel stylish enough to house the dignitaries who were expected for the city's 400th anniversary celebrations.[52] The big changes such as the creation of tourist boards, gov- ernment subsidies for the culture industry, and advertising campaigns to attract tourists would not come until the 1970s.[53] However, in the 1950s the city's potential as a tourist destination had become an important factor in Salvador's cultural politics, and government officials, businessmen, and es- pecially journalists had begun to promote tourism. In his opening address to the Bahian state legislature in 1949, Otávio Mangabeira emphasized that Bahia should encourage national and international tourism.[54] Initiatives included tax breaks for the hotel sector and a municipal "tourist tax" on hotel stays and outbound transportation in 1951 to fund further efforts to attract tourists.[55] In 1953, the Municipal Department of Tourism was formed against a backdrop of newspaper editorializing and government- sponsored publications about the city and its attractions for tourists. There was initially very little activity in the private sector to promote tourism.

Even the police department was on board with these initiatives. During the ban on the Washing of Bonfim in 1951, when anyone approaching the patio for the washing was at risk of arrest, the police pointedly escorted "two gorgeous Baianas, fat, magnificently well dressed, loaded down with jewelry and with attractive decorated vases of water on their heads" to the gates so they could throw water on the stairs. This was staged so as not to disappoint the tourists and photographers who had showed up for the Washing of Bonfim that year.[56]

These efforts quickly fused with the growing embrace of Salvador's popular culture and traditions after 1930. In the early 1950s flights between Rio and Salvador were available, as were transatlantic flights to the Bahian capital, further strengthening the notion that tourism in Bahia had a future. Significantly, the Society of Friends of the City was founded in early 1953, of which Otávio Mangabeira and an impressive number of other prominent Bahians were members. These included politicians, scions of traditional families, professors at the medical college, financiers, engineers, judges, prominent business leaders, artists, architects, and journalists (including Odorico Tavares). The goals of the society were "safeguard[ing] the historical, cultural and artistic patrimony of the city . . . promoting tourism . . . and fighting for the social well-being of the people." For the members of this society of prominent Bahians, an increase in cultural tourism was positively correlated with improved social conditions in Salvador.[57]

The centerpiece of the shift toward tourism was the use of public funds to build the famed modernist Hotel da Bahia. This took place from 1948 to 1952. The project was overseen by Diogenes Rebouças and Paulo Antunes Ribeiro.[58] The municipal government commissioned Genaro de Carvalho to produce two murals for its interior, including *Regional Festivals*, a two-hundred-square-meter, colorfully vibrant collage that included African-Bahian cultural themes. The inaugural celebrations included a presentation of "African-Bahian dances" for the distinguished guests, a number of them from out of state. The hotel's night club (*boate*) was called the Xangô Night Club, after the Candomblé *orixá*. The hotel was central to Bahians' early efforts to shape their image inside and outside the state. It was a focal point for tourists, national politicians, and foreign dignitaries and their entourages and hosted conferences, business expos, and exhibitions of modern art. On 9 February 1956, it hosted a pre-carnival "grand dance" called the Festival of the Red Rooster to commemorate the Year of Tourism in Bahia. This was a joint venture sponsored by private capital and the municipal Department of Tourism. It hosted three hundred "members of high society" for a week. The guests were flown up to Salvador in five planes from Rio de Janeiro, São Paulo, and Porto Alegre. The invitations were a pamphlet that listed the "complete tourist itinerary" of the city.[59]

Other efforts reveal the intersection of the growing interest in promoting tourism and African-Bahian culture. For instance, beginning in 1950 the municipal Department of Tourism began to contract capoeira masters such as Mestre Pastinha to perform in official capoeira shows for tourists.[60] In 1954, the department organized the lighting and ornamentation for the festivals, although this was not much of an improvement over its contribution in previous years.[61] In 1959, A Tarde announced that the Hotel da Bahia had partnered with the company Bahia Turismo to contribute to building a "huge terreiro of Candomblé," presumably as a tourist attraction.[62]

Carnival celebrations were increasingly assessed in the context of tourism. Editorials and occasional commentary pressured the municipal and state governments of the late 1930s and early 1940s to provide more financial support for carnival. Carnival, it was argued, would function as valuable publicity for the commerce of the city.[63] After World War II, A Tarde vigorously promoted the notion of city's tourist potential during carnival and lamented its lack of actual tourists, apart from those from the interior of the state. The newspaper would occasionally, somewhat wistfully, note how many North Americans had traveled to Rio de Janeiro to participate in its carnival. The lesser hotels in Salvador, such as Hotel Sul Americano (Sulacap), the Meridional, the Grande Hotel, and the Palace Hotel, were also keen to encourage the growth of carnival. These were all located on the Rua Chile, and their owners and managers contributed to the ornamentation of the streets and carnival competitions and encouraged government support for carnival activities. In the early 1950s, several municipal agencies were created to stimulate the expansion and professionalization of Salvador's tourist infrastructure. But for the most part, domestic and international tourism remained unimportant until well into the 1970s.[64] In a letter to the mayor's office requesting additional subsidies for the 1955 carnival presentation (floats, costumes, etc.), the president of Fantoches, Arlindo Gomes, warned that if his club was unable to put on an exhibition during carnival it would dissuade the "population of the interior of the state" from coming to the capital for carnival. The letter reveals how underdeveloped the tourist industry was at that time; Gomes did not even mention visitors from outside Bahia or beyond Brazil's borders.[65]

An important point to make about tourism in Salvador is that there was very little impetus from the private sector for the project of creating a regional identity. If there was, one would expect to have seen it during carnival. Yet while the larger commercial forces of consumption and advertising were under way after 1930 in a modernizing Brazil, they were very slow to influence carnival in Salvador during this period. Occasionally, sponsors such as the local branch of Phillips, the makers of radios and phonographs, would sponsor a confetti battle on the Rua Chile, as they did in 1938.[66] But apart from the nationwide growth of the radio and music industries, the growth of consumer culture and tourism in Brazil made only a minor impact on carnival in Salvador. As carnival approached, the shop windows in Salvador began to display carnival items such as masks, serpentines, confetti and the popular *lança perfume* (canisters of ether). Meanwhile, advertisements in the newspapers multiplied slowly. The first to employ the strategy of using carnival to sell merchandise began only in 1940, although very tentatively, which is not surprising as there were few consumer goods to choose from. During the war years and immediate postwar period, the disposable income of Salvadorans was limited. A woman might be enticed by carnival associated advertising to buy some sheet music or a man might buy a straw hat (*chapéu de palha*), a new sports shirt, a new tie, a new handkerchief, or new socks, but more extensive or regular purchases of consumer goods were not part of the celebrations.[67] In fact, the cars in carnival parades did not carry product advertising until 1941. The Águia Central Bakery and Jacaré Liquors were two of the first companies to pioneer this method of reaching consumers.[68] Not until the 1950s did radio shows that promoted the latest songs for the following year's carnival begin to included advertising. For example, in 1950, Biodental Toothpaste (Elixir Dentifrício) sponsored a program of carnival music.[69]

Clearly, if Bahian carnival did not attract advertising and private investment, the other popular festivals stood even a lesser chance of doing so. If the city was going to trade on cultural tourism, the incentive to do so would have to come from the city or from state government. This realization encouraged the public subsidy needed to construct the Hotel da Bahia in the early 1950s. Nevertheless, despite the new importance of the idea of attracting tourists to Bahian, it would be several decades before infrastructure, government subsidies, and actual tourists would come together to make cultural tourism a significant factor in the relationship between cultural practitioners, the state, and the private sector.

In the early 1950s, the Bahian government sponsored a yearlong fellowship for the Argentine artist Carybé (Hector Julio Paride Bernabó), an act that had far-reaching consequences for the reframing

Figure 6.1. Baianas at the Washing of Bonfim, by Carybé. From Tavares, *Festa do Bonfim*. By permission of the Instituto Carybé.

of Bahian history and culture. Mangabeira's secretary of health and education, Anísio Teixeira, arranged the funds for Carybé to relocate to Bahia. Carybé was emerging as one of South America's most notable practitioners of "folkloric" art," primarily line drawings that captured popular culture and everyday life in ways that emphasized the vitality and dignity of individuals. His work even gave the impression that it had been produced by a member of the popular classes. Teixeira almost certainly brought Carybé to Bahia to use these skills to create a visual register of *baianidade*.[70] Even if that was not his intention, it was certainly the result.

Carybé's initial commission for the government was for one of five panels of the newly built "scholastic park," the Carneiro Ribeiro Educational Center. The resulting mural depicted a panorama of Salvador as seen from the Bay of All Saints. Over the next few decades Carybé fulfilled more commissions for murals on buildings (typically government, financial, or residential apartment buildings) than any of his contemporaries. His subject matter was typically an idealized historical episode or a visual expression of some aspect of Bahian popular culture, such as the play of capoeira in the apartment complex Residência Cintra Monteiro (1951). By the 1960s his work had evolved into what can best be described as a mélange of visual expressions of the cultural iconography of Bahianness, mixing *orixás* with fishermen, backlands cowboys, goods for agro-export, samba, sailboats, Brazilian Indians, and musical instruments.[71]

Part of Carybé's early work in Salvador was collected and published in the *Recôncavo Collection* (*Coleção Recôncavo*), a series of ten pamphlets printed in 1951 by the Livraria Turista Editora (the Tourist Bookshop Press with close links to the Bahian government). The pamphlets were primarily a vehicle for the illustrations Carybé had done on commission for the Bahian Museum of Art on specific popular themes such as the Festival of Bonfim and the Festival of Conceição da Praia (neither of which illustrated the inside of a Catholic church), and the Festival of Yemanjá. These illustrations also depicted capoeira, Candomblé, and other African-Bahian themes. The accompanying text in the pamphlets was written by members of Salvador's progressive middle class, including Odorico Tavares; emerging young writers Carlos Vasconcelos Maia (who from 1959 would oversee the State Department of Tourism), Wilson Rocha, José Pedreira, and Carlos Eduardo da Rocha; Pierre Verger; and Carybé himself (on capoeira and Candomblé). The initial print run was for fifteen hundred copies, and the works were republished in 1955, this time directly by the Bahian state government.

By that year Carybé had etched himself into Bahian lore as the "gringo," as Tavares would put it, who embraced Salvador's bohemian life and popular culture. In "A Festa do Bonfim de Mestre Carybé," Tavares introduced Carybé's designs for the pamphlet *The Festival of Bonfim* by developing a profile for Carybé that complemented the emerging image of Bahia as a lively, exotic, and somewhat hedonistic yet welcoming destination. Carybé,

Figure 6.2. Capoeira during the festival of Conceição de Praia, by Carybé. The two men on the left are playing the *berimbau*, the traditional instrument that accompanies the *roda de capoeira*. From Tavares, *Conceição da Praia*. By permission of the Instituto Carybé.

for example, was not at the Festival of Bonfim to fulfill the terms of his government art fellowship. Instead, he was there to "enjoy everything the festival had to offer," in short, "to enjoy life" as one only can in Bahia. He "participated in the rodas de samba, played along with the capoeiristas, ate vatapá or galinha de xim-xim [African-Bahian dishes] at the stall of Maria de São Pedro [the Baiana most noted for her cuisine]." He might be found at the Blue Angel Bar, a bohemian hotspot, "drinking whiskey." As an outsider, Carybé was a perfect point of reference to reinforce what was specifically Bahian about Bahia, not just for potential tourists but for Bahians themselves. Not only had this man traveled much of South America before deciding that Bahia was the place to settle (if not quite settle down), but he had chosen it because of the attractions of its popular culture. In the process, of course, Carybé, whose designs created perhaps the preeminent visual register of Salvador's African-Bahian working-class culture, ran the risk of becoming a caricature himself, his public persona blurring the line between reality and the fiction of a bohemian in a Jorge Amado novel.[72]

The Federal University of Bahia, particularly during the tenure of Edgard Santos, the rector in charge from 1946 to 1961, also influenced the recalibration of Bahian regional identity. As Risério points out in his history of the postwar avant-garde in Bahia, Santos's stewardship had a tremendous influence in Salvador. As rector, Santos encouraged the university to provide key institutional support that brought together the figures responsible for changing the intellectual climate in Salvador through their work in theatre, music, and the fine arts. His vision was to use the university as a modernizing influence on the city, to "put Bahia on the map of Brazil" through the convergence of cultural and economic revitalization. The university would provide support for the arts as well as the skilled workforce and technical expertise for that great engine of Bahian modernization, Petrobras and the petroleum industry from the 1950s.[73] Although Santos had little interest in popular culture, his support of modernist artists in the fields of music, theater, dance, and the fine arts facilitated their (occasional) inclusion of African-Bahian culture, which contributed to the consolidation of the association of Bahia with African-Bahian traditions in the late 1950s. His backing of the creation of the Bahian Museum of Modern Art was a prime example of this. Also influential, although a bit beyond our period, in 1958 Santos encouraged Portuguese intellectual George Agostinho da Silva to pursue the creation of CEAO, in which Pierre Verger and anthropologist Vivaldo Costa Lima had both agreed to participate. This was a significant step in the institutionalization of African-Bahian studies in Bahia.

These efforts by political and cultural figures made important contributions to the consolidation of a more inclusive Bahian regional identity after 1945. Politicians such as José Wanderley Pinho, Otávio Mangabeira, and Anísio Teixeira recognized the potential importance of tourism to Bahia. The building of the Hotel da Bahia and the art fellowship overseen by the Minister of Education and Health to attract Carybé created a tourist infrastructure and an artistic brand for Bahia, and both, especially the latter, were associated with African-Bahian culture. The increasing involvement of the state in supporting the festivals and aspects of African-Bahian culture set an important precedent that established long-lasting relationships between the state, politicians, the press, the practitioners of African-Bahian culture, and the tourist industry. These relationships matured after 1970 and continued to foster the association of Bahia with African-Bahian traditions into the twenty-first century.

The Press, Tourism, and Odorico Tavares

In the late 1940s, Bahia's newspapers increasingly promoted the importance of the city's festivals and African-Bahian culture for tourism. Especially after 1945, editors and journalists promoted tourism as part of their embrace of the importance of *cultura negra* to Bahian regional identity. For instance, overall coverage in most of the newspapers of the bigger festivals such as Bonfim or carnival had come to contain some mention of the presence of "outsiders," "tourists," or "foreign visitors." Mention of these generic figures sometimes included pictures or their names in the article. They were typically constructed as appreciative of the city's African-Bahian heritage, and were almost invariably a positive contribution to the events.

A key figure in this process was newspaper editor, journalist, and author Odorico Tavares. Tavares very explicitly linked African-Bahian culture and popular religious festivals with a potential tourist industry in Bahia. He reminded Bahians that Salvador (in particular) was a unique destination. Visits of internationally famous figures were newsworthy in and of themselves, but coverage of the activities of Pablo Neruda or Orson Welles in the city offered opportunities for journalists to be explicit about what Salvador had to offer. It was typically Tavares who played tour guide and host to these figures, and it was Tavares who made sure their visits received positive news coverage.

Journalists used actual and potential tourists to make a case for protecting and even expanding the popular, African-Bahian aspects of the city's festivals. From the first year of the revival of the Washing of Bonfim in 1937, the *Diário da Bahia* made the point that the *ogans* and *filhas-de-santo* brought an interesting and novel air to the festivities for the visitors "who were there in great number," although in the 1930s most "visitors" were from the interior of the state of Bahia.[74] As the Catholic Church moved to curtail the extent of the Washing of Bonfim in the late 1940s, the mainstream press raised the specter of disappointed tourists, or "outsiders," in its castigation of the Church.

In 1953, *Diário de Notícias* published a photograph of a tourist "insisting on" sweeping the steps of Bonfim Church alongside the Baianas. Her presence in the photograph catches the eye; her attire contrasts with the all-white costume of the Baiana next to her. Her smile is self-conscious and her pose is dainty as she half bends with one hand on a broom and the other hand clutching to her midriff what seems to be her handbag. Her clothes and hairstyle clearly mark her as upper middle class. The caption reads, "Even tourists insist on grabbing a broom to wash a little" ("*Os turistas fazem questão de pegar numa vassoura e lavar um pouquinho*"). It is not clear whether she is Brazilian or from abroad, but this ambiguity enhances the purpose of the photo—to show the attractiveness of the popular ritual to outsiders, regardless of the point of origin of visitors.[75] That same year, the press criticized the municipal government for its restrictions on street vending, which threatened to limit the public presence of Baiana food sellers, characterizing the restrictions as decimating traditions that attracted tourists to the city.[76]

One newspaper, *O Momento*, was interested in African-Bahian culture for explicitly political reasons. The editorial staff and the journalists at this unofficial organ of the state's Communist Party included modernists and liberal progressives.[77] The newspaper's overt embrace of African-Bahian culture was perhaps the clearest illustration that the city's middle-class intelligentsia supported the agenda of social inclusion and were committed to defending the way of life of the Bahian working class. Promoting workers' concerns and workers' lifestyles was also a way to win votes (when the Communist Party was briefly legal) and raise consciousness.[78]

No discussion of the changing public discourse on African-Bahian culture from 1945 to 1954 would be complete without assessing the numerous influential contributions of Odorico Tavares, a central figure in the city's media and art scene. Tavares's rise to a position of prominence within the cultural life of the city began with his arrival in Salvador in 1942 at the behest of media mogul Assis Chateaubriand. Tavares eventually took over as director of Chateaubriand's two Salvadoran newspapers, the *Estado da Bahia* and the *Diário de Notícias*, as well as Chateaubriand's newly acquired local radio station PRA-4. Tavares's interests were a good fit with the progressive politics of the city's professionals and artists; as a young journalist in his home state of Pernambuco, Tavares had courted intimidation and even physical harm for his criticisms of dictator Getúlio Vargas. For Chateaubriand, transferring Tavares and his family to Salvador seemed the sensible thing to do. He made an almost immediate impact in his new home city, where he would spend the rest of his life. Under Tavares's directorship, both the *Estado da Bahia* and the *Diário de Notícias* continued to celebrate and foreground African-Bahian culture, situating it alongside middle-class and highbrow discussions, critiques, and reviews of literature, film, and scholarship. Tavares himself edited the cultural supplement for the *Diário de Notícias*, to which he also contributed.

During the late 1940s and early 1950s, his newspapers republished the texts of numerous *O Cruzeiro* articles on African-Bahian culture in Salvador, many of which he had written. They also reproduced some of Verger's photos that accompanied these articles. Included in this series were extended discussions of capoeira, of samba, of the dress of the Baianas, of the twin saints Cosme and Damião, and of several popular festivals. For instance, Tavares wrote on Salvador's cult of Yemanjá and its offerings, stressing the festive context of the *batucadas* and anonymous local sambas and "songs of Africa full of the most profound mysticism." Tavares linked the rituals to the African past and to the ways that many working-class Bahians made their living on the water. Tavares did not know much about Bahia when he came to Salvador, and he devoted himself to the study of these phenomena. His articles cited historical and scholarly sources, as well as those from within the Candomblé community.[79] His newspapers also republished the texts from the ten-part government primer on Salvador, the *Coleção Recôncavo*, each part of which focused on an aspect of the city's history and heritage, including text from the pamphlet on the *orixás* written by Pierre Verger. Among Tavares's three contributions to the pamphlets in the collection were one each on the Festival of Conceição da Praia and the Festival of Bonfim. Both celebrated the festivals' inclusive nature as Bahians from all walks of life came together in celebration, and he foregrounded African-Bahian culture—African-Bahian food, capoeira, and samba—as showpieces of the events. The combination of capoeira and samba allowed Tavares to celebrate African-Bahian cultural performance as "quasi-magical, graceful and light."[80] This was a far cry from the dominant-class criticism of the 1920s.

His brother, Cláudio Tavares, wrote a text on samba that was published in one of Odorico Tavares's newspapers. Odorico also published Cláudio's 1948 articles on capoeira and *afoxés*.[81] These writings on Bahian popular culture, when taken together, make it clear that Odorico Tavares was one of the city's most important publicists and disseminators of the idea that Bahia was indelibly linked to African-Bahian culture. An important transition in thinking about African-Bahian culture had taken place. For Tavares, and for Pierre Verger as well, African-Bahian culture was not simply a holdover from the past that would most likely disappear with the process of modernization. Instead, African-Bahian culture was now constructed as a vibrant element in Salvador's ongoing sociocultural formation.

Tavares participated in the Washing of Bonfim in 1954. He appeared in a photo taken (by his newspaper) during the event, alongside the mayor of Salvador, three Baianas, two children, and a society lady. This was illustrative of Tavares's modus operandi. He was not shy about using his own presence (magnified through skillful use of his media) as evidence of the value of the African-Bahian events he was associating with. When samba writer Ary Barroso visited Bahia in 1956, it was Tavares who organized a festival in his honor. He did so on the very street for which Barroso's 1938 hit samba "Na Baixa dos Sapateiros" ("On Shoemakers Lane") was titled, the Baixa dos Sapateiros.[82]

Tavares was influential not just because of his role in the media, but also because of his relationships with important figures in Salvador such as Jorge Amado, State Museum of Bahia director José Valladares, Minister of Education Anísio Teixeira, and Fernando Góis, vice president of the Bank of Bahia. He also possessed the perfect set of skills and interests for postwar Bahia. So seamless was his relationship with the changes in Bahian culture and Bahian cultural identity during this period that it is hard to determine the line between his influence on particular events and his ability to insert himself in the midst of changes that were already under way. Tavares did more than simply bring together the power of the press, popular culture, tourism, art, and politics. He personified the fusion of these cultural resources. As an art collector, for instance, he brought together European masters, national or local artists whose subject matter had little to do with African-Bahian popular culture (such as Carlos Bastos), and artists whose subject matter did include African-Bahian practices, such as Carybé. In the 1950s he purchased the work of African-Bahian artists to add to his collection and provide impetus to their careers.

Tavares was thus a key figure in the expanding network that linked the press, practitioners of African-Bahian culture and especially the Candomblé community, public intellectuals, the plastic arts, the tourist industry and the government. Perhaps as an outsider he could act relatively freely, like Juracy Magalhães, Roger Bastide, or Pierre Verger. He was not part of already established patron-client relationships. Instead, he owed his place in Salvador to Assis Chateaubriand, arguably a more powerful figure in national politics than any single Bahian in the 1950s. His newspapers certainly backed him, ranking him in 1949 among the great and the good as one of Bahia's "most outstanding and influential individuals" ("*de maior destaque e influência*"). Moreover, it wasn't only his press. In 1961, the municipal legislature awarded Tavares the honorific title of "Citizen of Bahia" in a formal ceremony that recognized his important contributions to Bahia over the preceding nineteen years. The printed version of Tavares's acceptance speech, *Discurso de um cidadão* (A Citizen's Speech), included a preface by Jorge Amado and designs by Carybé.[83]

Odorico Tavares's influence over the content of the radio station he directed is more difficult to gauge. Alessandra Cruz suggests that in 1943 the programming changed to include entire shows dedicated to samba, featuring local artists such as Riachão and Batatinha.[84] It is not clear just how much of an innovation this was, as samba had frequently been worked into radio programming in Salvador from the mid-1930s, especially during the months leading up to carnival. Dorival Caymmi and his band Três e Meio had performed regularly on all three of Bahia's radio stations in the mid-1930s, and these performances most likely included samba. In 1939, Radio Sociedade began to seriously promote local Bahian music, including samba.[85] But Caymmi's relocation to Rio de Janeiro in 1938 had created a vacuum in Salvador for composers and performers of popular music, and Tavares's radio station enthusiastically filled the gap by increasing the air time dedicated to samba and samba-related music. This shift in programming in the early 1940s nurtured local production and made a generation of Bahian sambistas—Riachão, Batatinha, Tião Motorista, Nelson Silvério, Walmir Lima, Panela, and Garrafão, to name but a few—into household names locally. In an earlier era, musicians like these men would have either left for Rio de Janeiro or would have been known only to those familiar with the local music scene.[86]

Tavares hired Antônio Maria to be the artistic director of Radio Sociedade, perhaps to oversee and consolidate this shift toward a greater concentration on local talent. Like Tavares, Maria was originally from Recife. He had already worked for Chateaubriand in Fortaleza before he moved to Salvador in 1944. A few years later he moved to Rio de Janeiro. Despite the brevity of his time in Salvador, it is Maria who is generally credited with "discovering" Bahia's most identifiable local samba "stars," Batatinha and Riachão. Both became local celebrities who embodied Bahia's association with Samba. Although Riachão was already something of a public figure in samba circles in Salvador by the early 1940s, Batatinha was working as a low-level employee in the office of one of Tavares's newspapers when Maria suggested that he perform on the radio.

Tavares's newspapers were not the only print media that included discussion of African-Bahian culture after 1945. Although the arts and literature section of *A Tarde* was the most high brow of the city's newspapers, it published extended pieces by civil servant, author, and folklorist Herundino Leal. Examples include his 1954 piece about the Festival of Yemanjá, his 1955 article that praised the contributions of "Africans in Brazil," or his 1956 article about capoeira. He wrote many other articles about the popular festivals.[87] Another key contributor to the *A Tarde* cultural supplement was Heron de Alencar, the editor of the paper. De Alencar worked briefly as a medical school professor, retired young, and dedicated himself to journalism and cultural criticism in Bahia from 1947 to 1952, before leaving for the Sorbonne. As editor of the literary supplement, de Alencar used *A Tarde* to support a group of young modernist writers who wrote for him and for their own journal, *Caderno da Bahia*.[88] These writers (who were mostly from the northeast of Brazil beyond Salvador) were central to Bahia's second phase of literary modernism, and from 1948 to 1951 they put out six issues of *Caderno*. The editors of the journal sought to "renovate" Bahian literature by turning to the region's popular traditions, including its African-Bahian heritage.[89] The journal's content covered music, film, and the arts, and many of the contributing editors were artists who were the top local practitioners in their fields. The journal also published original poems, stories, and essays.

These culture producers were not African-Bahian, and it is clear that they found it difficult to include working-class voices in their journal. Nevertheless, a number of them at least asked important questions. Examples include Walter de Silveira's inquiry into whether black poetry existed in Brazil. (His answer, a critique of the Brazilian education system, was that it did not.) Meanwhile, the editors chose topics intended to integrate African-Bahian culture into a wider, Bahian cultural and intellectual framework. The journal published articles by Edison Carneiro (on the census of 1940) and Roger Bastide (on Candomblé herbs), both of which criticized discrimination against African Bahians and African-Bahian culture. Other articles by folklorists, anthropologists, and ethnographers demonstrated that African-Bahian culture was a worthy object of study. The influence of the journal in this regard is difficult to determine. However, Carla de Santana suggests that this group's position on African-Bahian culture and the place of African Bahians in Brazilian society grew out of the positions established at the Second Afro-Brazilian Congress in Salvador in 1937.[90] Moreover, according to Karina Nascimento, this group provided important foundations for the acceptance of modernist influences on literature and art in Bahia after 1945, including the modernists' embrace of African-Bahian culture and art.[91]

In addition to the newspapers, the radio, and relatively short-lived arts and culture journals such as *Caderno da Bahia*, other publications broadened the dissemination and impact of Bahia's more inclusive regional identity. Tavares's work for *O Cruzeiro* was compiled in a publication titled *Bahia—imagens da terra e do povo* (1951). The third edition of this book, which was published in 1961, was so well received in São Paulo that it won first prize at the First Bienal do Livro for Best Book in the category "Miscellaneous" (*Avulso*).[92] Tavares's work was only one of a significant number of what have been referred to as *guias da Bahia* (Bahia guidebooks), which were printed partly for the tourist trade in Bahia. They were also the consequence of local intellectuals' pride in the local history and culture of the state. These were in effect guides to *baianidade*, written by both native and resident Bahians as conscious contributions to shaping the discourse on Bahia.

The publications of these *guias* began in earnest in 1946 and continued through the 1950s. Most of them foregrounded the contribution of African-Bahian culture to making Bahia distinct. These were different from the scholarly work of the handful of social scientists who had called attention to Afro-Bahian culture in the 1930s and 1940s. It should be emphasized, too, that this work after World War II was funded largely by Bahian governmental bodies, with later editions published by commercial presses, underlining the point that the messages of these publications were part of a government agenda to celebrate and encourage Bahian regionalism. In the cases in which journalists authored the texts, their work typically also appeared in the dailies, which most likely compensated them for it. Clearly in this literature the textual representations of African-Bahian practices is indicative of the degree to which Salvador's dominant classes—or at least the opinion shapers among them, that is, the journalists, authors, intellectuals and even politicians—had come to not just include but also embrace African-Bahian practices within their ideological construction of Bahianness.

In 1945, novelist Jorge Amado wrote one of the first guides "to the streets and mysteries of the city of Salvador," *Bahia de Todos os Santos*, which included sections on the contributions of African-Bahian culture to the city of Bahia and to the condition of being Bahian.[93] Two years later, musician Dorival Caymmi wrote *Cancioneiro da Bahia*, a volume of Bahian "lore" that his own compositions had in part already publicized. Caymmi juxtaposed pages of musical notations with writings on aspects of Bahian popular culture that had inspired him. For example, he noted that the term *balangandans,* which referred to the charms that hung from necklaces and bracelets of the Baianas, was not part of contemporary usage when he employed it in the song "Que é que a Bahiana tem?" ("What Is It that a Baiana's Got?"). He explained with some pride that he had revived the term from "days gone by." His use of *balangandans* in the song's lyrics not only reintroduced the word but also led to something of a fashion craze. In 1953, middle-class and elite Salvadoran women began to wear the jewelry associated with African-Bahian women as a fashion statement and status symbol. Caymmi's book was illustrated with the type of pseudo–art naïf line drawings that were becoming the visual signature associated with African-Bahian popular culture, and by extension with Bahia, thanks to the illustrators of several of Jorge Amado's very early editions and the work of the artist Carybé after 1950. The year the book came out Caymmi returned to Bahia, a trip that was the subject of yet another piece by Odorico Tavares for *O Cruzeiro,* "Caymmi in Bahia," with photographs by Pierre Verger.[94]

The success of Amado's and Caymmi's books was possibly the impetus for a spate of generalist, often picturesque works on Bahian history and culture. The next round of *guias da Bahia* included the following works: Afrânio Peixoto's 1945 compendium *Breviário da Bahia*; Eduardo Tourinho's *Alma e corpo da Bahia* (1950); the above-mentioned collection of Carybé's illustrations for the *Coleção Recôncavo* (1951, 1955); Odorico Tavares's *Bahia; imagens da terra e do povo* (1951), illustrated by Carybé; José Valladares's *Bêabá da Bahia* (1951), for which the Bahian Ministry of Health and Education flew in renowned painter Carlos Thiré to do the illustrations; and Herman Lima's *Roteiro da Bahia* (1953).[95] Each of these authors focused at one point or another on the Washing of Bonfim, portraying it as a popular expression of Bahianness because it brought together what they perceived as two distinct worlds, that of Catholicism and that of Candomblé, making the ritual a preeminent symbol of inclusive Bahian regional identity. (Caymmi had also used the symbolic resonance of Bonfim to great effect in his lyrics.) Stefan Zweig's account of the washing ritual (reproduced in part in chapter 3) formed the bulk of and, more important, the justification for Afrânio Peixoto's own account in *Breviário da*

Bahia.[96] The authority of Zweig and the approving (indeed marveling) tone of his account were important to Peixoto, one of Bahia's more distinguished men of letters and public intellectuals. The approval of cultured Europeans (Zweig was a very well-known author and playwright at the time) was still a factor in convincing elite Bahians to accept the legitimacy of popular Bahian culture, much as how the interest of Frenchman Blaise Cendrars had encouraged Brazilian modernists in Rio to embrace popular culture in the 1920s.[97] Not surprisingly, Peixoto's position was somewhat more patronizing. He told his Bahian readership, "Do not laugh, do not condemn, simply comprehend," and he asked them to respect the beliefs of "our Negroes."[98]

Herman Lima also mentioned Zweig's account in *Roteiro da Bahia*, but the importance of *Roteiro* lies in its rhetorical efforts to integrate Bahia into the larger Brazilian elite imaginary. Lima was born and raised in the Brazilian state of Ceará and was a former student of Afrânio Peixoto. While he was living and working in Rio de Janeiro, Lima effectively argued for Bahia as the *mãe* (mother) of Brazil, not just because of its history of providing the nation with great statesmen and diplomats (for being, in Joaquim Nabuco's famous nineteenth-century phrase, later popularized by Gilberto Freyre and José Lins, the "Virginia of Brazil") but also because Bahia was the birthplace of "oppressed Brazilians" and many of their inimitable ways. In doing so, Lima almost unnoticeably merged Freyre's rural sugar plantation with Salvador's popular neighborhoods.[99] Importantly, this picturesque piece on Salvador, with a chapter on the celebrations of Bonfim, was published in the scholarly *Cadernos* [sic] *de Cultura*, between issues containing a critical study of "Variations on the Short Story," an essay titled "Three Phases of the Modernist Movement," and a translation of Rimbaud's *Une saison en enfer*. As these examples demonstrate, from 1945 to 1954, an extraordinary array of talent converged to promote the idea of Bahia as the guardian of African-Brazilian traditions within Brazil. Popular festivals, especially the Festival of Senhor do Bonfim and its washing ritual, played a central role in this process.

Odorico Tavares was also centrally involved in the emergence of Salvador as one of Brazil's leading centers for the visual and dramatic arts. Tavares, who was himself a modernist poet and an avid art collector, greatly facilitated the modernist movement in Salvador after World War II in the plastic arts. Modernism in the arts flowered decidedly later in Bahia than in Brazil's southeast, where the movement emerged in the 1910s and 1920s. Nevertheless, modernism in Bahia democratically embraced working-class and popular culture and rejected the politics and aesthetics associated with the traditional Brazilian oligarchy, as had its precursor in the south. In Salvador, these emphases encouraged the celebration of African-Bahian culture, and modernists in Bahia incorporated African-Bahian themes into public artistic renditions of Bahianness.

Tavares's social position in the media and his involvement in the arts in Salvador led him to initiate or involve himself in most of the principal campaigns in the city that touched on the culture industry, especially as it related to tourism. A number of these campaigns led to the creation of important museums and theaters over the course of the 1950s and into the 1960s. Tavares also established himself near the center of the soon-to-be-thriving modern art scene in Bahia, not least through his own personal patronage of the arts. In this process of "incentivizing culture," Tavares built on the previous efforts of the central figures of the first wave of modernism, Jorge Amado in particular.[100] Amado himself gave impetus to this second wave in 1944; he played an important role in the organization (alongside Paulista modernist Manoel Martins) of the first modern art exhibit in Bahia, which showed work from Salvador's few modernists alongside modernists working in the nation's southeast as well as internationally. In his roles as newspaper editor, art collector, influence peddler, and ambassador for Bahianness, Tavares mediated between the art world and the state government under Mangabeira, which began to promote modern art as "synonymous with modernity, freedom and democracy."[101] The U.S. embassy and the Rockefeller Foundation also promoted modern art in Brazil, including Bahia, as part of a broader cultural mission to consolidate Brazil's allegiance to the United States after World War II.[102] Important Bahian commentators began drawing parallels between Western "civilization" and a vibrant modern art scene in Bahia, often using Tavares's media outlets to do so.[103]

Not everyone was pleased, however. The reaction of the traditional establishment included criticisms in the Catholic Church weekly *Semana Cathólica* that denounced the modernists' "Satanic palette."[104] Despite such hostility, a number of local young artists embraced the inspiration of African-Bahian culture in their work. Artists such as Mário Cravo Júnior, Genaro de Carvalho, Carlos Bastos, and Rubem Valentim drew on aspects of the cosmology, symbolism, and aesthetics associated with Candomblé. Mário Cravo Júnior's sculpture of the Candomblé deity Exú was applauded by the Bahian artistic establishment in 1951. His piece won second prize at the III Bahian Salon of the Fine Arts.[105] Other artists also drew on the popular motifs of Bahia and depictions of African-Bahian life as they saw it, such as the early primitive artist Willys (Thales de Araújo Porto), José de Dome, and João Alves, although none can be said to have relied on or been closely associated with depictions of African-Bahian culture. Each worked in relative obscurity until they were brought into the increasingly professional fold of artistic production in Salvador after 1945. For example, the work of Willys and João Alves was included in the 1957 exhibit "Artists from Bahia" at the Modern Art Museum in São Paulo.[106]

In the late 1940s and early 1950s, José Valladares, the director of the State Museum of Bahia and a prolific art critic and event organizer, and Anísio Teixeira, Mangabeira's minister of education and health, put together a series of Bahian Salons of the Fine Arts (Salão Bahiano de Belas Artes), in part to provide a venue for this local production. They invited national figures to compete for prizes in an effort to locate Bahian art within the broader national and international context of modern art. The first was held in 1949 at the Hotel da Bahia, before its construction was even completed. Successive Bahian Salon exhibitions occurred almost every year through the 1950s.[107] Tavares's two dailies, of course, were principal tools for publicizing the events to a Bahian elite that was hesitant to embrace the genre of modern art. José Valladares himself was a frequent contributor to the cultural supplements in Tavares's newspapers.[108]

Tavares was also central to the development of two local venues for showing modernist artwork in Salvador, the bohemian bar/café called Anjo Azul (Blue Angel) and the Galeria Oxumarê (named after a rather mysterious Candomblé orixá associated with color, movement, and financial success as well as transformation and transgression). The Anjo Azul, which was founded by designer and antiquarian José Pedreiro, was known for its intellectual and/or bohemian clientele and was favored as a venue for social events related to the art scene. It hosted such events as a cocktail party honoring the success of the first Bahian Salon Exhibition of 1949 and a 1950 art auction to benefit the literary magazine *Caderno da Bahia*. The Anjo Azul also showcased local artists by putting individual pieces on permanent display and hosting temporary exhibits, such as the one by Carybé in 1950. It was even something of a bookstore.[109] The Galeria Oxumarê, which was founded in 1950 by writers and artists Carlos Eduardo da Rocha, Zitelman de Oliva, José Martins Catharino, and Manoel Cintra Monteiro, was one of the city's first commercial art galleries. The space belonged to the Tavares-led Diários Associados in Bahia, which leased it to the gallery.[110] It was one of the city's most significant art venues during the 1950s. It mounted exhibits of work by Willys (1953), Rubem Valentim (1954), and Portinari (1954) and played an important role in making it possible for artists in Salvador to make a living from their talent.

Because modern art was associated with Bahia's longing for modern civilization, the movement helped redefine Bahian (and Brazilian) civilization in a way that included the region's African-Bahian culture. As both Risério and Sansi-Roca emphasize, this artistic movement was not a simple expropriation of popular culture, although there was certainly an element of this. The Candomblé community maintained its ties with these local modern artists, some of whom were *ogans* of the more powerful temples, such as the painter Rubem Valentim, who was affiliated with Opô Afonjá. Most of these newly emerging cultural producers could be seen at the *terreiros* during important festivities alongside Pierre Verger, Carybé, or Odorico Tavares himself.[111] In fact, over the course of the 1950s a few individuals who had been brought up within the Candomblé community or were part of Salvador's African-Bahian working poor, such as woodcarvers Hélio de Oliveira and Agnaldo dos Santos and the painter Rafael, were integrated into the modern art movement in Bahia, which by 1960 was institutionalized within the School of Fine Arts at the Federal University of Bahia. In an article for *O Cruzeiro,* Tavares publicized the work of Rafael ("the best primitive painter in Bahia"), whose paintings centered on the origins and associated qualities of the *orixás* of Candomblé. In the context of the emerging primitive art scene and art market in Brazil, Tavares found in Rafael a perfect combination of the untrained primitive painter who was also working class, African Bahian, and deeply associated with African-Bahian traditions.[112]

Conclusion

Between 1945 and 1954, Salvador was as intellectually and cultural vibrant as it had been in decades, and the foundations were in place for the even livelier cultural changes of the second half of the twentieth century. In the ten years after World War II, government officials, media representatives, and artists focused attention on the idea that African-Bahian culture was a defining feature of Bahian regional identity. One can see this convergence in the work of figures such as Antônio Monteiro, Pierre Verger, Carybé, and Odorico Tavares. Monteiro the folklorist and Verger the photographer and scholar steeped themselves intellectually in the cultural world of the Candomblé community and negotiated access to information within the terreiros. The larger *terreiros* allied themselves with these figures if they felt such cooperation would enhance their own prestige and their leverage with the dominant class. Monteiro and Verger represented the Candomblé community in ways that emphasized the legitimacy of its cultural practices and its links to Africa. The work of Carybé, which was partially sponsored by the Bahian state, quickly became the most popular artistic visual register of African-Bahian working-class culture, while Tavares took advantage of his position vis-à-vis the media and culture industries to foster the concept of African-Bahian cultural inclusion in Salvador. The work of Verger, Carybé, and Tavares was at least partly produced and certainly disseminated with the intent of developing Salvador as a tourist destination, and their vision of a culturally inclusive Bahia was circulated through both local and national print media. Odorico Tavares's efforts in particular helped draw African-Bahian culture into the local modernist movement, which was the most dynamic, far reaching, and progressive intellectual shift in twentieth-century Bahia.[113] Associating African-Bahian culture with the energy, authority, and influence of the modernist movement enhanced its acceptability and added momentum to the recodification of its practices.

Conclusion and Epilogue

Cultural Politics in Bahia

By the middle of the 1950s, the formulation of Bahian regional identity that continues to characterize Bahia was in place. This process began somewhat tentatively in the 1930s as a number of political and intellectual trends merged with initiative from the working classes. Juracy Magalhães, Vargas's appointed interventor, created an atmosphere that was propitious for the development of a definition of Bahian identity that included African Bahians and their culture. He acknowledged the legitimacy of popular culture in a way that encouraged Bahians to begin to move away from the aggressive repression of African-Bahian culture that had marked the 1920s. Even more significantly, writers such as Jorge Amado and scholars such as Edison Carneiro argued that African-Bahian culture was unique to Bahia and had made contributions to the nation. As such, it was worthy of at least the patronage of the dominant class, if not its respect. In 1936, Carneiro contributed to the publication of a series of articles on Bahian institutions in *Estado da Bahia* that included capoeira, samba, and Candomblé. From this moment the local press began to portray aspects of *cultura negra* in a more positive light. Meanwhile, and most significantly, African-Bahian cultural leaders played important roles in asserting the right to practice, and implicitly to oversee the production and development of what they saw as their culture. This coming together of trends, agendas, and historical actors solidified the notion that Bahia was "Brazil's Black Rome." Bahia, once identified as the preserve of elite statesmen, orators, and poets, became increasingly identified with African-Bahian spirituality and culture. This would provide a framework for Salvador's cultural politics for the rest of the twentieth century.

Salvador's major popular festivals made key contributions to this reshaping of Bahian regional identity. The Festival of Senhor do Bonfim, the Festival of Conceição da Praia, the Festival of Senhor dos Navegantes, Ribeira Monday, the Festival of Yemanjá, and Bahian carnival provided forums within which African Bahians asserted the legitimacy of "black culture." During these festivals, African Bahians brought in public performative markers of their culture, such as the rituals associated with Candomblé, the practice of capoeira, *rodas de samba*, the *batucadas*, the presence of the Baiana, and African-Bahian culinary traditions. The dominant-class media and a small number of public intellectuals began a celebratory and inclusive discourse on these practices beginning in the mid-1930s. During the Vargas era (1930–54) political and economic elites moved to support the festivals, in some cases reviving them, in other cases supporting their expansion. The motives of the elites were likely a desire to use the festivals to encourage political and social cohesion and to establish them as central elements of Bahian regional identity.

Coinciding roughly with the end of the Estado Novo in 1945, a more conscious dominant-class project of consolidating and reformulating Bahian regional identity emerged. The African-Bahian community continued to assert its right to perform and practice its culture, supported by key figures within the city's artistic and cultural community. Individuals such as Antônio Monteiro, Pierre Verger, Carybé, and Odorico Tavares celebrated the cultural inclusion of African Bahians not only as a way of supporting the legitimacy of their cultural practices but also as an opportunity to re-create Bahia's regional identity. This celebration took many artistic and literary forms, ranging from scholarship on folklore, line drawings, photography, murals, and woodcarvings to novels, travel and tourist literature, local newspapers, and national illustrated weeklies. Local government bodies dedicated a portion of their slim budgets to supporting the festivals and popular carnival. In the late 1940s, municipal officials set up a stage in the center of town in the form of a Baiana's giant *tabuleiro*, revealing their interest in participating in the redefinition of an inclusive Bahian regional identity. Municipal officials also subsidized the performance of native son Dorival Caymmi on one of his rare trips back to Salvador from Rio de Janeiro, where his work as a lyricist and performer had catalyzed the association of Bahia with African-Bahian working-class culture.

By the mid-1950s, the notion that African-Bahian culture was a principal marker of regional identity was powerfully entrenched. This coincides with the end of the Vargas era in 1954, but not because of Vargas's suicide and the end of his time in power. Rather, the date of 1954 aligns with the standard periodization of Bahian historiography that sees the mid-1950s as the beginning of a fundamental restructuring of Salvador's economy and society. The founding of the national oil company Petrobras in 1953 would be increasingly transformative for Bahia, as Salvador's immediate hinterland became Brazil's single significant domestic source of oil for the next three decades. In 1956, the Paulo Afonso hydroelectric facility significantly increased the energy available for consumption in Salvador, while the federal Superintendency for the Development of Brazil's Northeast (Superintendência do Desenvolvimento do Nordeste, or SUDENE) channeled unparalleled public investment into the northeast. In the 1950s, interstate BR-324 was begun in order to link the northeast to the industrial production of the southeast. Finally, the development in the 1960s of a state-led petrochemical industry intensified the region's capitalist modes of production, leading to the growth of an industrial working class and a growing middle class made up of specialists, technocrats, and bureaucrats, many of whom were of African descent.[1] These transformations have been called Salvador's "industrial revolution," and although the connotations of that phrase overstate the changes after 1954, most scholars accept that the decade of the 1950s was a socioeconomic watershed in the twentieth-century history of Bahia.[2]

The founding of Petrobras and the election of Antônio Balbino to the governorship (1955–59) symbolized a shift in the thinking of Bahian elites. With the discovery of oil, a number of powerful figures led by banker and businessman Clemente Mariani felt it propitious and finally possible to pursue industrial-based economic development rather than relying so heavily on agro-exports and an embrace of the region's colonial history and popular traditions. Balbino created an economic planning commission that sought to stimulate industrial growth based on import substitution and redirecting agro-export profits into local industry, thus changing a centuries-old pattern of regional planning based on agro-export. In 1959, Juracy Magalhães, who had supported Balbino's candidacy and had briefly served as president of Petrobras in 1954, succeeded Balbino as the governor, and the focus of the dominant class moved squarely to economic development.[3] Beginning in the mid-1950s, Bahia's *cultura negra* and its traditions combined and competed with modernization to be based on *ouro negro*— "black gold."[4]

A number of cultural changes, too, mark the mid-1950s as something of a watershed. The invention in 1951 of the *trio elétrico*, a moving vehicle fitted to amplify live music, eventually reshaped carnival, initially reviving the media focus on the "official" carnival of organized processions, which had been eclipsed since the 1940s. As the number of *trio elétricos* increased from the mid-1950s, they blurred the divide between popular carnival and elite and middle-class carnival.[5] Agnes Mariano points to the installation of a TV transmitter in Bahia in 1960 as the end of an era when the idea of Bahia was conveyed largely through musical imagery and lyrics. Television created the environment for the formulation of a new set of (primarily visual) "symbolic references for Bahians."[6]

Although the specifics of Bahian regional identity formation after 1930 were particular to Bahia, scholars have addressed similar processes in other states and/or regions in Brazil. The general pattern that has emerged in recent work on São Paulo, Rio de Janeiro, Rio Grande do Sul, and Pernambuco, for instance, is one in which regional elites sought to negotiate favorable cultural terms for their region's inclusion in the broader process of the nation's identity formation. To do so, they emphasized what was unique to their state or region. In each of these instances local elites made choices based on what they thought would work best in the context of their relationships with subordinate groups, working within the confines of the process of national identity formation emanating from the federal government and the cultural industries in Rio de Janeiro.[7]

The most problematic aspects of this process of national identity formation, more often than not, related to the subject of race. Trends gaining momentum at the intellectual core of Brazil's national identity after 1922 acknowledged the mixed-race background and argued that therein lay the key to Brazilian distinctiveness. Thus, regional elites debated and made important choices about how much of the notion of racial inclusion to accept in their constructions of regional identity. The idea of the importance of popular or working-class culture to Brazilianness accompanied the notion of racial inclusivity. Again, regional elites had important choices to make. In the case of São Paulo, elites chose to construct the region around its "explicitly racist" *bandeirante* past.[8] In Pernambuco, after 1930, political elites rejected the notion of racial mixing and constructed the *homem do Nordeste* (the man from the northeast) as "a strong, capable, educable, and cooperative white worker and citizen."[9] Oliven points out that in the southernmost state, Rio Grande do Sul, the representative figure of regional identity—the *gaúcho*, or Brazilian cowboy—was socially constructed over the latter half of the twentieth century in such a way as to erase the role of African-Brazilian labor in the history of the region and even the very presence of African Brazilians (as well as Brazilian Indians and even German and Italian immigrants). However, black Brazilians were symbolically important to carnival in Porto Alegre, the capital city, although carnival played much less of a role in constructions of regional identity in Rio Grande do Sul than it did (and does) in Bahia.[10]

Compared with these regional examples, it seems that it was in Bahia that the idea of racial and especially cultural inclusivity was taken the furthest, at least discursively. This distinction is largely explained by the convergence of several factors addressed in this study. The first was the combined agency of working-class African Bahians and the Candomblé community in Salvador and their dominant-class allies. The second was the fact that a centerpiece of cultural inclusion in Rio de Janeiro, at both the regional and national levels, was African-Brazilian culture, particularly samba and its contribution to carnival but also certain cultural attributes of Brazilians that came from Africa. For example, according to Gilberto Freyre himself, these African contributions were notable in Bahia—in the Bahians' "communicative nature," "grace," "spontaneity," and "contagious smile."[11] Finally, and significantly, as this study shows, the number and symbolic power of Salvador's major popular festivals provided an essential ingredient. They provided performative ritual symbols of regional identity that were deeply fused with the social and cultural world of Salvador's African-Bahian working-class population. The religious festivals played key roles within the cultural politics leading to the reformulation of Bahian regional identity, and reveal the important influence on this process of African Bahians and their dominant-class allies between 1930 and 1954. The contributions of ordinary Bahians to this reformulation is similar to recent findings in other regions of Brazil in which ordinary people played more influential roles in regional politics than previously recognized. In Bahia, however, the path of influence lay much more squarely within the realm of culture.[12]

Scholars working on the twentieth-century history of the African diaspora have traced similar processes and situated these processes within the cultural-political context at both the national and regional level. A central preoccupation of this scholarship is to account for the historical circumstances leading to the elevation of cultural practices associated with working class, Afro-Latin populations to the level of defining features of national identity.[13] In the context of populations almost exclusively of people of African descent, such as in Jamaica or Guyana, the focus is on the processes through which "blackness" is constructed and struggled over within discourses that come to define the nation. Most explore their findings through an application of the notion of hegemony and emphasize the contested nature of the cultural politics at work within processes of nation state and national identity formation.[14]

In Bahia, the formation of a culturally inclusive discourse of Bahian regional identity was at times a strongly contested process. Individuals and institutions with less accepting or alternative interpretations of African-Bahian culture and African Bahians pushed back against the celebration of samba, capoeira, and Candomblé. The Catholic press consistently criticized the Candomblé elements of the city's popular festivals. The archbishop of Salvador himself stepped in to enforce prohibitions on the Washing of Bonfim twice between 1930 and 1954 because of its relationship with *fetichismo*. Occasional opinion pieces in the press questioned the appropriateness of the use of capoeira and samba as markers of regional and national identity. The festivals and carnival provide illustrations of the limited nature of the cultural inclusion of African-Bahian culture and the compromises that accompanied it. Most strikingly, the actors responsible for the revival of the ritual Washing of Bonfim in both 1937 and 1953 were forced to accept compromises and a "moralization" of the event in order to convince the Catholic Church to repeal or overlook its ban. The inside of the church remained the purview of the *gente de destaque*, the dominant-class families of Bahia.

Even with the compromises in place, positions that were critical of Candomblé, "moralized" or not, continued to be voiced in conservative newspapers such as the *Semana Cathólica*, which in 1953 was still lobbying against the Washing of Bonfim for being "saturated with *fetichismo*" and "an assault on the basic tenements of Christian civilization."[15] In 1950, the archbishop of Salvador, Augusto Álvaro da Silva, referred to Candomblé as "stupid" and "corrupting."[16] It is telling that the *terreiros* continued to be bound by legal restrictions and were subject to potential, and occasionally real, persecution until 1976. During the Era of the Batucadas, from the late 1930s to the early 1950s, newspaper coverage continued to focus on the elite clubs and middle-class carnival groups, suggesting that if the elite clubs had not fallen on hard times, the *batucadas* would have remained much more marginal to the discourse on carnival in Salvador. Public intellectual Pedro Calmon and others who resented the elevation of samba to a national symbol criticized it often. The Baiana was unable to slip into the pantheon of Bahianness unchallenged. In 1953 and 1954, hygiene campaigns of the local government targeted the Baianas who sold food in the street and put in place a number of restrictions. Thus even the Baiana felt the pressure to quite literally clean up her act.[17]

Salvador's cultural-ideological glass ceiling also made its presence felt in the arena of discourse. The act of including the culture of the subordinate group did not in fact raise that group's culture to a position equivalent to that of the dominant group. Although African-Bahian cultural practices were celebrated, they were not celebrated as equal with the practices associated with the dominant class. Alongside the "ideological inclusion" of African Bahian practices, the process of establishing differential values to the cultural components of Bahianness could be considered an "ideological ranking." In Salvador, the dominant class, not surprisingly, still defined its own culture as the most advanced, civilized, and rational. They associated this culture with "whiteness." In 1954, Brazilian public intellectual Abdias do Nascimento critiqued this phenomenon when he asked rhetorically, "Why should we [Brazilians] erect whiteness as the only measure of value, as the true ideal of life and the supreme template of beauty?"[18]

There is direct evidence that this hierarchical valuing was at work in Bahia. Anadelia Romo calls attention to a survey carried out by Bahian sociologist Thales de Azevedo in 1955 that questioned a small sample of mostly dominant-class students about the characteristics that they associated with African Bahians (pretos). The study found that the students did not associate a single positive characteristic with African Bahians. The top six associations were, in order of frequency, superstitious, unintelligent, submissive, sad, untrustworthy, and lazy. The association of "blackness" with "superstitious" clearly indicates not just a racial judgment but also a clear cultural prejudice. No doubt the power of this association drew on prejudices against Candomblé, which was frequently chastised (when not outright lambasted) in the Catholic press as the worst sort of superstition. The obvious contrast for the respondents would have been the association of "whiteness" with logic and reason. Thus even though a process was under way that was redefining Candomblé as a tradition that contributed to regional identity, for Europhile elites, it was clearly not equivalent to "European" culture and its (supposed) associated practices and traits.[19] The progressive middle-class allies of the African-Bahian working class also critiqued certain aspects of African-Bahian culture. One of the subtexts of Jorge Amado's early literary work was that African Bahians needed to become more class conscious, to organize to better resist their exploitation, while Edison Carneiro was strongly wedded to the idea that the rougher edges of African-Bahian culture needed to be reformed for the "uplift" of all African Bahians. Influential education reformers in the 1940s and 1950s, such as Isaías Alves and Anísio Teixeira, embraced policies that were critical of African-Bahian culture as holding back progress, reflecting their position that "whiteness was still an ideal."[20] This is not to say, however, that only the dominant class appreciated or strove for the qualities its members associated with "whiteness." Mestre Pastinha, for instance, wanted to use his capoeira instruction to teach the value of self-control and further the formal education of his pupils. However, he was clearly expanding the associations of these qualities by aligning them with *cultura negra*.[21]

On the discursive level, Salvadoran festivals were conceived of as structured by a binary of sacred and profane that dated back to medieval Christianity, in which the "sacred" related to the aspects of the festival directly linked to Catholicism and the "profane" described the associated public festivity. Candomblé was situated within the "profane." Festivals were also typically constructed as Catholic events that remained the purview of the dominant class, while their African-Bahian aspects were situated as lesser, almost dependent features. When the elite club's participation in carnival was minimal (during dips in their economic resources, for instance), journalists' reminiscences about the golden era of elite clubs were commonplace, reminding everyone of the rightful order of things that someday might be restored. Reproducing the ideological ranking of the sacred and the profane, government-produced literature aimed at visitors or tourists stressed the Catholic churches and colonial buildings as the dominant features of Salvador's official history.

Despite the rhetoric of racial democracy and *mestiçagem* (racial and cultural mixing) that was gaining favor, particularly in the mid-1940s, the festivals were often performative arenas that ritualized and reinforced racial, class, and cultural difference, separation, and hierarchy. The Washing of Bonfim played a role in dominant-class discourse as an event that united all Bahians in a "complete religious synthesis" in which discrimination against color or class was absent.[22] Yet foreign observers such as Stephan Zweig and Donald Pierson noted the relative separation between the festive culture of the working classes and that of the dominant class. Carnival embodied the same apparent contradiction. The publication of Gilberto Freyre's *Casa grande e senzala* in 1933 provided an intellectual framework in which Bahian journalists and writers could situate Bahian carnival within ideas about racial harmony in Brazil that would crystallize in the concept of a "racial democracy." Nevertheless, carnival lent itself to quite significant degrees of class and racial separation.

This political and cultural give-and-take, this struggle and negotiation over the extent to which African-Bahian culture would or should be included, is captured well by Mallon and Roseberry's conceptualization of hegemony. Applying the concept of hegemony—as "a problematic, contested, political process"—to Bahian cultural politics after 1930 helps us to more clearly appreciate the important political role of cultural practice and discourse and to identify the political work of the reformulation of Bahian regional identity. The concept helps us understand the political importance of "the words, images, symbols, forms, organizations, institutions and movements used by subordinate populations to talk about, understand, confront, accommodate or resist their domination."[23] The choices and actions of the historical actors detailed in this study, who included Mãe Aninha and Juracy Magalhães, Edison Carneiro and Otávio Mangabeira, Mestre Pastinha and Odorico Tavares, and hundreds if not thousands of anonymous Bahians, contributed—sometimes consciously, often incidentally—to shaping a significant "common material and meaningful framework" through which power and domination came to be negotiated in Salvador.[24]

I do not find, however, that this led to a hegemonic outcome, in Mallon's conceptualization of that term. Even so, it is probably not too much to suggest that a "thin" hegemonic outcome—resigned acceptance rather than active consent[25]—came to characterize class relations and cultural politics in Salvador. The "common framework" was viable enough to channel the process of contestation and struggle between the dominant and subordinate classes, so that the dominant class did not come to rely on simple force or coercion (which is always bound up with consent to some degree) and the subordinate class did not resort to outright rebellion (or flight). Yet it is very difficult to measure this or establish causality in Bahia during the Vargas era. There is also the fact that the Candomblé community cannot be seen as a like-for-like stand-in for the Salvadoran working class. Factors related to class rather than culture (inasmuch as these can be analytically separated) also played important roles in the ways that, and the degrees to which, subordinate-class Bahians related to and accepted (or did not accept) dominant-class rule and the prevailing socioeconomic structure.

Other scholars have explored how cultural inclusion has abetted particular political outcomes and agendas in Brazil. Most typically, this story begins with the emergence of the notion that Brazil was a twentieth-century racial democracy. The role or function of this notion, which is strongly allied to the powerful idea of *mestiço* nationalism, rose to the level of official discourse and official history from the 1930s, at which point these notions worked to diffuse racial tensions in urban Brazil.[26] Roger Bastide, writing about São Paulo in 1955, was one of the first to make the point that the "ideal of [racial] democracy . . . limits the dangers of open conflict" that might arise out of tensions over race and class.[27] In Bahia, as early as 1 October 1932, *A Tarde* reprinted an article from Rio de Janeiro by journalist travel writer and author Berilo Neves that praised race relations in Brazil and articulated a number of the fundamentals of the nation's supposed racial democracy (although no one was yet using this exact terminology). These included the points that in Brazil many whites also had African ancestry, just too far back to notice; that people of African descent in Brazil had made great contributions to the nation (mostly as slaves); that a person of color in Brazil who had success or merit would be treated as well as his white peers; and that in the United States the racial dynamics were much worse and much more fixed.[28] This shift toward portraying Brazil as a racial democracy and a mixed-race nation in the 1930s helped create a propitious environment and discursive space for the cultural inclusion of African-Bahian traditions within Bahia's regional identity. Following Góis Dantas and others, I see Bahia's process of cultural inclusion as the primary way that racial democracy played out in Bahia, although I emphasize cultural mixing rather than racial mixing or racial harmony.[29]

Epilogue

Although the discovery and development of Bahia's oil reserves in the mid-1950s spurred political and economic elites to embrace a program of state-directed economic modernization based on developing industrial capacity, the cross-class alliance between leaders in the Candomblé community and members of the city's cultural and intellectual elite remained relatively strong after 1954. Jorge Amado, Pierre Verger, Carybé, and Odorico Tavares continued to champion African-Bahian culture as central to notions of Bahianness, while Candomblé figures such as Mãe Senhora and Mãe Menininha continued to liaise with both the state and the dominant-class cultural elite. Institutions of the Bahian state also continued to play a role, in particular through the figure of Edgard Santos, the rector of the Federal University of Bahia (1946–61), whose support for the arts in Salvador indirectly but powerfully catalyzed the relationship between African-Bahian culture and the city's intellectual and cultural avant-garde. Then, in 1958, Governor Juracy Magalhães invited architect and designer Lina Bo Bardi to Salvador to oversee the Bahian Museum of Modern Art, a decision that stimulated the relationship between modern artists and Bahian popular culture for many years.[30] In 1959, the Center for Afro-Oriental Studies was founded by Portuguese philosopher George Agostinho da Silva. The center was dedicated to the study of African and Asian cultures and provided the institutional support for a series of cultural and educational exchanges between Bahia and West Africa that continued into the 1970s. Meanwhile, a generation of Bahian academics emerged with specializations in African-Bahian culture and personal and professional links to the world of Candomblé. Their trips to Africa were reciprocated—most significantly by Senegalese president Leopold Senghor in 1962. Members of the Candomblé community took advantage of available educational and cultural opportunities to move in Salvador's much more secular intellectual circles. In the process, they made CEAO into an institutional beachhead that continued the push for the legitimacy of African-Bahian culture.[31] The federal state, too, became involved, supporting the association of Bahia with its African heritage for its diplomatic efforts to attract newly independent African nations as trading partners.[32] Thus the cross-class alliance of the 1930–54 period continued into the 1960s to mold a common material and meaningful framework around the notion that African-Bahian culture was of fundamental importance to Bahian regional identity.

In the 1960s and especially the 1970s, several factors converged to shift the context within which this process occurred, a shift that in fact intensified the relevance of this common framework. The foremost feature of Bahian politics over the final third of the twentieth century was the figure of Antônio Carlos Magalhães. Bahians typically use the term *carlismo* (after Carlos, his second name, and a name that resonated with an Iberian monarchist movement also called *carlismo*) to characterize Magalhães's statewide personalist political machine, which was rooted in extensive patron-client relationships and significant control of the media. Magalhães dominated Salvador's process of conservative economic modernization for most of the 1970s, 1980s, and 1990s. Economically, the creation of an industrial pole at Aratu (Centro Industrial de Aratu) in the late 1960s and another at Camaçari (Polo Petroquímico de Camaçari) in the mid-1970s stimulated Bahia's industrialization, and the African-Bahian middle class grew substantially as African Bahians found jobs in industrial, commercial, and public sectors. The promise of social mobility for African Bahians appeared to be going some way toward being fulfilled. Bacelar suggests, however, that in fact this social ascension meant that African Bahians became aware of new barriers of racial discrimination in the modern, capitalist workplace.[33]

In 1974, in the midst of these transformations, the first *bloco afro*, Ilê Aiyê, was founded. The *blocos afros* were carnival clubs that built on the traditions of the *batucadas* and *afoxés*, supplanting the *blocos de índios* of the 1960s (in which men dressed as North American or Brazilian Indians for carnival). The *blocos afros* consciously embraced an African-Bahian aesthetic and celebrated Bahia's African heritage. Risério describes this process as a "reafricanization" of Bahian festive culture, particularly of carnival. The effect of the *blocos* on carnival was monumental. Throughout the 1980s, between sixty thousand and one hundred thousand Bahians, mostly young and overwhelmingly African Bahian, participated in *blocos afros* during carnival in Salvador every year.[34] Vovô, a co-founder of Ilê Aiyê, notes that the political influence of the *bloco* occurred predominantly in the cultural arena: "Our most important message is the festival, the spectacle. . . . Through carnival we . . . have managed to change a lot of things around here."[35] Not unrelated perhaps was the fact that in 1976, the *terreiros* were freed from the requirement of appealing to the police for a license to drum, a reform put in law under Governor Roberto Santos, responding to "pressure [from] Bahia's artistic-intellectual community."[36] Meanwhile, the *bloco afro* Olodum went on to gain international recognition when it appeared with Paul Simon on his 1990 album *Rhythm of the Saints* and subsequently appeared in a Michael Jackson video in 1995. Although there had often been an international component to the tradition of African-Bahian cultural producers forming alliances with the dominant class—for example, with Melville Herskovits, Roger Bastide, and Pierre Verger—these years marked an extraordinary phase of that dynamic.

Risério characterizes the emergence of the *blocos afros* as a consummation of the process begun with the politics of identity that was evident within the *afoxés* of Bahian carnival of the late nineteenth century.[37] My work emphasizes the role of the *afoxés*, *batucadas*, and other aspects of African-Bahian culture in the popular festivals of the 1930s, 1940s, and 1950s.[38] However, an important new dynamic began in the 1970s in Bahia's cultural politics that drew upon the growing influence of the Black Power and "soul" movements in the United States.[39] This black consciousness movement was institutionalized in Brazil's Movimento Negro Unificado (Unified Black Movement), which in Bahia eventually allied itself with cultural institutions such as the *blocos afros* to "generate political awareness,"[40] injecting an element of explicit racialization into Bahia's cultural politics, as illustrated by the fact that Ilê Aiyê restricted its membership to Brazilians of African descent.[41] The Black Power movement was especially powerful in Bahia's emerging black middle class. For example, both founders of Ilê Aiyê worked at Camaçarí and were members of the black middle class in Salvador.

The impact of the *blocos afros* was also felt in the tourist sector. From the mid-1970s the city's tourist infrastructure grew, as did the number of tourists visiting Bahia. In these early year, most tourists were from Rio de Janeiro and São Paulo. The number of foreign tourists, however, increased dramatically in the 1980s.[42] This accelerated growth was driven by Salvador's proximity to beaches, its historic city center, and its "folkloric" cultural heritage.[43] The expansion of carnival from three days to seven in 1981 further stimulated the tourist and culture industries in Salvador, as did the power of the *trio elétrico* to commercialize carnival and, in the early 1990s, the renovation of the historic center of Salvador, a UNESCO world heritage site. These changes occurred in a context of negotiated relationships between the political machine of Antônio Carlos Magalhães, international and nongovernmental organizations, private capital, and many of the institutions that supported African-Bahian culture, including the *blocos afros* and the Candomblé *terreiros*. The consequences of this convergence have been critically examined from a wide variety of disciplinary perspectives.[44] One of the most interesting and controversial aspects, however, is the fact that by the end of the 1990s, Magalhães could count on the support of Jorge Amado, Olodum, Ilê Aiyê, and the *afoxé* Filhos de Gandhy. The *blocos afros* may have compromised their original political independence, but some have argued that they did so in exchange for greater effectiveness in carrying out their social programs among poorer, disenfranchised populations in Salvador.[45] Despite the complexity of these interactions leading into the twenty-first century, one can still discern the outlines of the cultural-political framework that first emerged in the period 1930 to 1954. When assessing the current cultural politics around Bahian regional identity, this framework of African-Bahian cultural inclusion, created through discourse as well as through performative practices, continues to provide a major contribution to the ways that relations of power and consent between the dominant and subordinate classes are negotiated in Salvador. This looks to me to be the case for the foreseeable future.

Appendix

"A Bahia é terra boa," by Pedro Caldas[1]

"A Bahia é terra boa," by Pedro Caldas[1]	Translation
A Bahia é terra boa	Bahia is the Good Land
Não inveja a ninguém	Isn't jealous of anyone
Ama aos filhos que são seus	It loves its children
E os de fora que aqui vem	And those from far off who come
A Bahia é combatida	Bahia has fought wars
Mas vencida não será	But will never be defeated
Se ela é mãe do Brasil	If she is the mother of Brazil
Que importa se falar	It's important to say so
Diz alguém que na Bahia	Some say that in Bahia
Gente preta é só o que tem	All they have is black people
Mentira, tudo é inveja	It is a lie, just envy
Branco e loura há também	White and blondes it has too
A Bahia não faz caso	Bahia doesn't bother
De quem vive a lhe intrigar	With those who live to scheme
Se ela é mãe do Brasil	If she is the mother of Brazil
Que importa se falar	It's important to say so
Uma Baiana faz pirraça	Baiana can be spiteful
Faz batuque e faz lundu	She dances batuque and lundu
Faz carinhos sem igual	She is caring without equal
Ainda mexe o cururu	Even mixes the caruru
Com um baiano e uma baiana	With a Bahian and a Baiana
Ninguém queira se meter	Nobody will want to mess
Quem gostar de qualquer um	Whoever falls for either
Cairá no canjerê	Will wind up in the Candomblé

Note

1. *Estado da Bahia*, 13 February 1952.

Notes

Introduction

1. Alberto, "Para africano ver"; Dávila, *Hotel Trópico*, 55–59; Araujo, *Public Memory of Slavery*, 63–64. In 2006, when the Brazilian government organized the Second Conference of Intellectuals from Africa and the Diaspora, they chose Salvador to host the event. President Lula da Silva officially opened the conference. "Second Conference of Intellectuals from Africa and the Diaspora, Salvador de [sic] Bahia, Brazil, 12–14 July 2006," UNESCO document 175 EX/21, 1 September 2006, Unesdoc.unesco.org/images/0014/001469/146986e.pdf/. On the centrality and relevance of culture in Salvador, see Risério, *História da cidade da Bahia*, 584. Risério points out that the culture industries in the state currently generate more income than the tourist sector.

2. In *Negro no Brasil*, 7, Edison Carneiro and Aydano Ferraz credited Eugênia Anna dos Santos (Mãe Aninha) with popularizing the phrase "Roma Negra" as descriptive of Salvador and the central idea that went along with it: Bahia was the seat of the highest legitimate authority on African-Brazilian religious expression due to its recent close cultural links with West Africa. In *City of Women*, 17, Landes reported that "one prominent negro woman even called the city the 'Negro Rome.'" This woman was presumably Aninha, as Carneiro was one of Landes's principal informants. See also Lima, "Roma Negra," *Diário de Notícias*, 10 October 1960, in which Lima suggests that Aninha was "in the habit of calling Bahia" the Black Rome, although Lima implies this information came from a conversation Aninha had with North American researcher Donald Pierson. Pierson interviewed Aninha and put her forward as a vigorous defender of African-Bahian religious expression but does not mention her in connection with the phrase "Black Rome"; see *Negroes in Brazil*, 292–94. Interestingly, the notion of Bahia as the Black Rome was circulating in the francophone world in the 1920s, particularly among those interested in African culture, as suggested by Paul Morand's brief reference to Bahia as the "*Rome noire*" in his 1928 "Paris-Tombouctou" travel log, in Morand, *Oeuvres*, 20.

3. My use of "discourse" here owes much to cultural theorists. Discourse emphasizes the ways that spoken and written language—and the beliefs, values, categories, and common sense or understood experiences that lie within that language—emerge and exist as groupings of statements within a context of social relations and influence thinking and action that in turn affects those relations. See MacDonnel, *Theories of Discourse*, for a discussion of the development of scholarly uses of discourse.

4. Reis, "Tambores e temores," 142.

5. It is possible to find cultural politics in most scholarship on people of African descent in Bahia prior to 1889. A sampling of recent work that approaches such dynamics most explicitly includes Lara, "Significados cruzados"; Reis, "Tambores e temores"; Reis, *Slave Rebellion in Brazil*; Reis, *Death Is a Festival*; Reis, *Domingos Sodré*; Santos, "Divertimentos estrondosos"; Harding, *Refuge in Thunder*, chaps. 7 and 8; Reis and Silva, *Negociação e conflito*; Nishida, *Slavery and Identity*; and Graden, *Slavery to Freedom*.

6. *Bahia*, 17 March 1911, quoted in Bacelar, *Hierarquia das raças*, 50.

7. Butler, *Freedoms Given, Freedoms Won*, 175–89; Schwarcz, *Espetáculo das raças*, esp. 202–17; Borges, "Puffy, Ugly, Slothful, Inert"; and Borges, *Family in Bahia*. Romo's *Brazil's Living Museum*, chap. 1, provides an important reassessment of the complex positions of the medical profession on race and social reform. Some physicians questioned racial determinism more thoroughly than did the rest of Bahia's dominant class.

8. On the repression of Candomblé under Police Chief Pedro de Azevedo Gordilho, see Lühning, "Acabe com este santo."

9. Quoted in Vianna, *Festas de santos*, 19.

10. Ferreira Filho, "Desafricanizar as ruas"; Albuquerque, "Santos, Deuses e Heróis nas ruas," 103–6. On Bahian jurisprudence and African ancestry in the 1920s, see Faria, "Festa das Cadernetas." On the "*mulher de saião*," see Peixoto, *Breviário da Bahia*, quoted in Ferreira Filho, "Desafricanizar as ruas," 246n16.

11. Butler, *Freedoms Given, Freedoms Won*, 177–89; Fry, Carrara, and Martins-Costa, "Negros e brancos," 252–60.

12. On the early modernists, see Alves, *Arco e Flexa*; and Silva, *Âncoras de tradição*, 91–92.

13. A contributor to *A Tarde*, 24 August 1929, quoted in Butler, *Freedoms Given, Freedoms Won*, 188. See also Lühning, "Acabe com este santo," 204.

14. Butler, *Freedoms Given, Freedoms Won*, 180–81; Vieira Filho, "Africanização," 136–44.

15. Vianna, *A Bahia já foi assim*, 125–26.

16. Nina Rodrigues, *Animismo fetichista*, 49–50; Lühning, "Acabe com este santo," 197; interview with Pai-de-Santo Jubiabá in *Estado da Bahia*, 11 May 1936.

17. Fry, Carrara, and Martins-Costa, "Negros e brancos," 260–63.

18. Dantas, *Vovó nagô*, 145–240; Braga, *Na Gamela*, 37–123; Lühning, "Acabe com este santo"; Lima, "Candomblé da Bahia na década de trinta"; Butler, *Freedoms Given, Freedoms Won*, 203–9; "Afterward: Ginga Baiana," 166–67; Sansi-Roca, *Fetishes and Monuments*, 51–61; Castillo, *Entre a oralidade*, 116–44; Parés, "'Nagoization' Process"; Romo, *Brazil's Living Museum*, 61–85.

19. On the importance of modernists and modernism to the formation of Brazilian national identity and the work of state agencies in this process, see Williams, *Culture Wars in Brazil*; Martins, *Modernist Idea*; and Vianna, *Mystery of Samba*. See also Travassos, *Modernismo e música brasileira*; and Amaral, *Blaise Cendrars no Brasil*. On the early history of racial democracy, see Alberto, *Terms of Inclusion*, 5–20 and passim.

20. Dantas, *Vovó nagô*, 149–50; Alberto, *Terms of Inclusion*, 112–27; Lühning, "Acabe com este santo"; Lima, "Candomblé da Bahia na década de trinta"; Sansi-Roca, *Fetishes and Monuments*, 51–61; Castillo, *Entre a oralidade*, 120–25; Romo, *Brazil's Living Museum*, 10–12.

21. Silva, *Âncoras de tradição*, chap. 2; Borges, *Family in Bahia*, 30–40; Romo, *Brazil's Living Museum*, chap. 3.

22. Williams, *Culture Wars in Brazil*; Borges, "Recognition of Afro-Brazilian Symbols"; McCann, *Hello, Hello Brazil*, chap. 2; Soihet, *Subversão pelo riso*; Raphael, "Samba and Social Control"; Assunção, *Capoeira*, 141, 164–65.

23. On the delayed influence of modernism in Bahia, see Barbosa, "Descompasso."

24. *Diário de Notícias*, 10 and 13 January 1940. See Vianna, *Mystery of Samba*, on the influence of Freyre's work within the context of a wider reevaluation of Brazilian "native" culture.

25. *Diário de Notícias*, 15 January 1950.

26. Machado, "Prefácio," quoted in Ickes, "Salvador's Transformist Hegemony," 156. *Formação e evolução étnica da cidade de Salvador* was written to coincide with commemorations of the four hundredth anniversary of Salvador's founding in 1549.

27. Other regions of Brazil of course had just as much right to claim to be repositories of Brazilianness, but by different criteria. See for example, Oliven, *Tradition Matters*; and Blake, *Vigorous Core*. See also Weinstein, "Racializing Regional Difference."

28. Valladares, "Introduction," 11, quoted in Romo, *Brazil's Living Museum*, 185.

29. Kurtz, "Hegemony," 103.

30. Roseberry, "Hegemony and the Language of Contention," 358.

31. For critiques of these static understandings of hegemony, see Scott, *Weapons of the Weak*; Scott, *Domination and the Arts of Resistance*; and Sayer, "Everyday Forms of State Formation."

32. Laclau and Mouffe, *Hegemony and Socialist Strategy*; Comaroff and Comaroff, *Ethnography and the Historical Imagination*, 28–31. On the functionalism of Laclau and Mouffe and their proximity to the Comaroffs on the issues of discourse, see Kurtz, "Hegemony," 117–19, 122–25. See also Lears, "Concept of Cultural Hegemony," 589–93.

33. Roseberry, "Hegemony and the Language of Contention," 360; Mallon, *Peasant and Nation*, 6–7; Mallon, "Promise and Dilemma of Subaltern Studies"; Fox, *Gandhian Utopia*; Lears, "Concept of Cultural Hegemony."

34. Mallon, *Peasant and Nation*, 6–7.

35. The phrase "common material and meaningful framework" is Roseberry's ("Hegemony and the Language of Contention," 361), although he and Mallon ("Reflections on the Ruins," 70–71) overlap significantly in their conceptualizations, as he points out ("Hegemony," 363). On the fashioning of hegemony out of previous discourses, or "residual culture," see Williams, *Marxism and Literature*, 112. On the relevance of ideology in transforming discourse, see Comaroff and Comaroff, *Of Revelation and Revolution*, 21–30; and Mouffe, "Hegemony and Ideology." See also Vaughan, *Cultural Politics*, esp. 20–24, 157–62; and Wade, *Music, Race, and Nation*, 8–11.

36. Mallon, *Peasant and Nation*, 6–7.

37. Ibid.

38. Ibid., 7.

39. For an example of a convincing argument for a hegemonic outcome in relation to Brazilian notions of racial harmony or "racial democracy," see Hanchard, *Orpheus and Power*, especially chapter 3.

40. Two valuable contributions are Bacelar, "Frente Negra," which underlines the attraction of a race-based political party for Salvador's working class up until Vargas's elimination of political parties in 1937, and Souza, "Entre o religioso e o político," which emphasizes the impressive influence of the Church-run mutual-aid society for workers in Bahia, the conservative Círculo Operário. The UK Foreign Office and U.S. State Department had representatives in Bahia during the Vargas era whose records allow for a rudimentary assessment of the relationship between labor and the state in Salvador. The unofficial Communist daily *O Momento* (1946–48) is also useful. See also Magalhães, *Minhas Memórias*; and Carvalho, "Juracy Magalhães."

41. Although I can only say that the reformulation from 1930 to 1954 led to a formation of hegemony and not a hegemonic outcome, this does not, however, close the door on further studies of specific moments after 1930 that may turn out to be accurately characterizable as a hegemonic outcome, or the applicability of alternative interpretations of hegemonic outcomes that place greater weight on function than agency.

42. Mendoza, *Shaping Society*, 31. Important starting points on the structural salience and power of festival and ritual are Geertz, *Interpretation of Cultures*, especially chapter 15; and Turner, *Ritual Process* (on procession, ritual, and pilgrimage and his concepts of "*communitas*," the "liminal," and "liminoid"). Intervening contributions have enhanced and broadened the theoretical underpinnings of festival scholarship, especially for twentieth-century festivals. For a discussion of the theoretical genealogy of the "performative turn" and its contribution to the study of history, see Burke, "Performing History."

43. Bauman, "Performance and Honor," 133, quoted in Nájera-Ramírez, *Fiesta*, 5; and Guss, *Festive State*, 9. See also Falassi, *Time Out of Time*; Turner, *Celebration*; Bauman and Abrahams, *"And Other Neighborly Names"*; and Singer, *Traditional India*.

44. Matta, *Carnivals, Rogues, and Heroes*, 16. Matta extensively uses popular festivities and lesser rituals to generalize about the "nature" of being Brazilian.

45. For a discussion of capoeira as performance, ritual, and play, see Lewis, *Ring of Liberation*. For samba, see Leopoldi, *Escola de samba*; and Browning, *Samba*.

46. Drewal, "Dancing for Ogun"; Drewal, *Yoruba Ritual*.

47. Quoted in Dunn, "Black Rome and the Chocolate City," 850.

48. Mendoza, *Shaping Society*; Guss, *Festive State*; Nájera-Ramírez, *Fiesta*. See also Ramos, *Identity, Ritual and Power;* Couto, *Puxada*; Couto, *Tempo de festas*; Esteves, *Império do Divino*; Cunha, *Carnavais*; Cunha, *Ecos da folia*; Brandão, *Cultura na rua*; Soares, *Devotos da cor*; Burton, *Afro-Creole*; Nájera-Ramírez, Cantú, and Romero, *Dancing Across Borders;* Goldstein, *Spectacular City*; and Fabricant, "Performing Politics." In *South Italian Festivals*, Tak instructively combines history and anthropology in a study of ritual and socioeconomic change. The collection of essays in Beezley, Martin, and French, *Rituals of Rule*, gives an excellent sense of the flexibility and continuing importance of ritual and festivity in Mexico despite a changing historical context. Underlining the utility of festivity as a unit of analysis, Nájera-Ramírez points out that "it is difficult to identify even one ethnographic study of Mexico that ignores festival altogether"; Nájera-Ramírez, *Fiesta*, 9.

49. Wade, *Music, Race, and Nation*, 8–11.

50. Butler, *Freedoms Given, Freedoms Won*, 133. Sodré proposed that the play (*o jogo*) of subaltern African Brazilians was always central to efforts to resist the impositions of the dominant order; see Sodré, *Terreiro e cidade*, esp. 122–49. See also Burton, *Afro-Creole*; Riggio, *Carnival*.

51. Nájera-Ramírez, *Fiesta*, 92.

52. Pedro Calmon, "Sr. José Lins é a favor do samba," *Estado da Bahia*, 15 July 1937. See also McCann, *Hello, Hello Brazil*, 63–65.

53. For an important examination of this process in another context, see Williams, *Stains on My Name*.

54. Bahian scholarly literature also uses *branca-mestiço* (white and mixed race) to refer to the dominant class. *Afrodescendentes* (people of African descent) is increasingly used in Brazil in addition to or in place of *afro-mestiço*.

55. Baer, *Brazilian Economy*, 52.

Chapter 1. Salvador, Bahia, 1930–1954

1. On the discovery of petroleum and its intensification of Salvador's capitalist modes of production from the 1950s, see Jelin, "Formas de organização"; and Vianna, Souza, and Faria, *Bahia de todos os pobres*.

2. On Bahia's early-twentieth-century cacao boom, see Mahony, "Afro-Brazilians, Land Reform"; Mahony, "Past to Do Justice"; and Mahony, "Local and the Global."

3. Santos, *Centro da cidade do Salvador*, 67. The remaining 20 percent was mostly unprocessed cacao exported out of Ilhéus, the primary port of the cacao region, the majority of which was shipped directly to Salvador for processing.

4. Santos, *Centro da cidade do Salvador*, 76–81.

5. Amado, *Disparate Regional Development in Brazil*, 76; Santos, *Centro da cidade do Salvador*, chap. 2.

6. In 1942, regional oligarch "Colonel" Lins de Albuquerque threw a large party at a local club and called it the Festa do Ouriçuri to drum up excitement about the future of the commodity. British Consul Macrae to British Ambassador Sir Noel Charles, 18 December 1942, FO 128/406, Public Record Office, Kew (hereafter cited as PRO).

7. Santos, *Centro da cidade do Salvador*, chap. 2. For a summary of dependency theory literature as applied to regions, see Amado, *Disparate Regional Development in Brazil*, 4–20. Very little statistical work has been done to confirm or qualify the accuracy of dependency frameworks in explaining Bahia's particular situation.

8. For British Foreign Office observations on regional infrastructure and development, see FO 371/22724 and FO 371/21428, PRO; Marriot to Ambassador Sir Hugh Gurney, 26 July 1938, FO 371/21424, PRO; "Development of Foodstuffs Production in Brazil," FO 371/30360, PRO. See also U.S. Consul Robert Johnson to U.S. Ambassador Herschel Johnson, 11 April 1950, RG 84, Classified General Records, Salvador, Box 19, Subseries 570, National Archives and Records Administration, College Park, Maryland (hereafter cited as NARA II); and Goldsmith and Wilson, "Poverty and Distorted Industrialization," 440–41. For an argument that federal policies that favored industrialization during the Vargas era meant that the northeast subsidized the southeast, especially in the years 1948 to 1956, see Furtado, *Política de desenvolvimento*; and Love, "Furtado," 200.

9. Santos, *Centro da cidade do Salvador*, 76–81.

10. Bacelar, *Galegos*, 29; Pierson, *Negroes in Brazil*, 12–15; Smith, *Brazil*, cited in Levine, *Brazilian Legacies*, 28. On colonial social relationships and habits of mind in Bahia, see Schwarz, *Sugar Plantations*, 245–337; Freyre, *Masters and the Slaves*; Freyre, *Mansions and the Shanties Bahia e baianos*; Prado, *Colonial Background*, 313–439; and Holanda, *Raízes do Brasil*.

11. Borges, *Family in Bahia*, 30.

12. Borges, "Anos trinta e política"; Pandolfi, *Repensando*; Levine, *Vargas Regime*; Silva and Falcon, *Feixe e o prisma*; Skidmore, *Politics in Brazil*; Oliveira, Velloso, and Gomes, *Estado Novo*; Medeiros, *Ideologia Autoritária*. For an appraisal of the Vargas legacy for Brazilians, see Levine, *Father of the Poor?*

13. Williams, *Culture Wars in Brazil*; Borges, "Recognition of Afro-Brazilian Symbols"; McCann, *Hello, Hello Brazil*, chap. 2; Vianna, *Mystery of Samba*; Soihet, *Subversão pelo riso*; Raphael, "Samba and Social Control"; Cunha, "Sua alma em sua palma"; Garcia, "Canção popular"; Vieira, "Capoeiragem."

14. Ickes, "Salvador's Transformist Hegemony," chap. 2; Borges, *Family in Bahia*, 44.

15. Paiva, "Development of Brazilian Agriculture," 1096; Baer, *Brazilian Economy*, 35–38, 53–54.

16. Mariani, "Análise do problema econômico Baiano."

17. *Imparcial*, 11 August 1934.

18. Silva, *Âncoras de tradição*, 71.

19. British consular reports to Rio, FO 128/447 and FO 128/448, PRO.

20. Consul Kenneth Yearns to Ambassador Herschel Johnson, 1 December 1948, 1, RG 84, Classified General Records, Salvador, Confidential File Box 18 (1948), NARA II. On the strength of the Bahian contingent, see "Corrêa, Luiz Antonio Villas-bôas, Villas-bôas Correia (depoimento, 1997), Rio de Janeiro, CPDOC/ALERJ, Fundação Getúlio Vargas, 1998," 20–21, interview conducted by Américo Oscar Freire and Marieta de Moraes Ferreira, 10 September 1997, http://www.fgv.br/cpdoc/historal/arq/Entrevista588.pdf/.

21. The initial power struggle after 1945 between the UDN and the PSD was superseded in the early 1950s in Bahia by that between the UDN and the PTB.

22. The 1950 union election results indicate how well the more volatile elements elsewhere in Brazil were co-opted into the system in Bahia by the Bahian branch of the Ministry of Labor. The elections returned leadership slates completely acceptable to the ministry in nine out of ten unions, and the tenth slate, of the Moinho da Bahia, was not even "sufficiently communist" to worry its management. Consul Robert Johnson to Ambassador Herschel Johnson, 12 July 1950, RG 84, Classified General Records, Salvador, Box 19, Subseries 560, NARA II.

23. For British Foreign Office observations on petroleum development in Bahia, see the reports in FO 128/437, FO 128/444, and FO 371/90611, PRO. See also U.S. Consul Kenneth Yearns to U.S. Ambassador Herschel Johnson, 1 December 1948, RG 84, Classified General Records, Salvador, Box 18, NARA II.

24. For the oil industry, see RG 84, Classified General Records, Salvador, Box 67, Subseries 863.6, NARA II.

25. The *confisco cambial* was a way of generating revenue from agro-exports to subsidize industry. Profits in foreign currencies, particularly profits from the export of coffee, were taxed through the manipulation of market exchange rates.

26. Consul Kenneth Yearns to Department of State, 29 January 1948, RG 84, Box 66, Vol. 16, NARA II; Tosta Filho, *Secção B do volume II*. See also Guimarães, "Formação e a crise," 68–88; and Furtado, *Operação nordeste*, 42–47.

27. Romo, "Race and Reform," 243; *Programa de recuperação econômica da Bahia*. See also "Utopian Pauper," *Time*, 12 September 1960.

28. Salvador became Brazil's first diocese (in 1551) and first archdiocese (in 1676). The U.S. consul described the influence of the Catholic Church on social and political life in Salvador as "incalculably strong." Consul Robert Johnson to Ambassador Herschel Johnson, 11 April 1950, RG 84, Classified General Records, Salvador, Box 19, NARA II.

29. There was no census in 1930. IBGE, *Anuário Estatístico do Brasil*, 1973, 46.

30. Verger, *Fluxo e refluxo*.

31. Fryer, *Rhythms*, 10. The cultural genealogies of both samba and capoeira reveal the hand of mixed-race and white Brazilians as well. See Chasteen, "Pre-History of Samba"; and Sandroni, *Feitiço decente*.

32. Talmon-Chvaicer, *Hidden History*, 18.

33. Reis and Mamigonian, "Nagô and Mina," 94–96.

34. Butler, *Freedoms Given, Freedoms Won*, chap. 6.

35. Meade, *"Civilizing" Rio*.

36. Leite, "Bahia civiliza-se."

37. Romo, *Brazil's Living Museum*, 4–5.

38. Albuquerque, *Algazarra nas ruas*, 36; Ferreira Filho, "Desafricanizar as ruas"; Fraga Filho, *Encruzilhadas*. In 1952, Bahia's Associação Comercial sought the U.S. consulate's help in getting access to information for publication in a new weekly newspaper intended "to promote commercial progress." The two topics mentioned were "foreign capital and investment trends," and "history of immigration to the United States." Consul Robert Johnson to Counselor of Embassy for Public Affairs Herbert Cerwin, 14 August 1952, RG 84, Classified General Records, Salvador, Box 75, NARA II.

39. Matory, "English Professors of Brazil." French photojournalist Pierre Verger mentions a certain Hipólito dos Reis who once lived in his neighborhood, a former slave who had at one point returned to Lagos and subsequently had gone back to Salvador to set up a business importing "African products used in Candomblé." Quoted in Nóbrega and Echeverria, *Verger*, 190. This sort of cultural exchange probably ended in the 1930s.

40. The census of 1940 showed the racial composition of Salvador to be 35 percent white and 65 percent Afro-Brazilian (26 percent *preto*; 39 percent *outro*). These statistics probably underestimated the percentage of Salvador's Afro-descendents. IBGE, *Características demográficas*. The categories *pardo* and *cor não-declarada* (no color declared) were lumped together by the publishers of the census compilations on the assumption that these were persons of some African ancestry who would have been offended by a designation of nonwhite.

41. Santos, *Centro da cidade do Salvador*, 47. Unfortunately, sparse demographic data makes it difficult to appreciate who was arriving from where and what they did upon arriving, factors that may have influenced the nature and internal dynamics of working-class Salvador in the 1930s and 1940s.

42. On the backlands bosses, see Pang, *Bahia in the First Brazilian Republic*; Assis, "Questões," 43; and Barreiros, "Educação."

43. Santos, "Caixeiros da Bahia."

44. Borges, *Family in Bahia*, passim, esp. 40; Santos, *Centro da cidade do Salvador*, 46.

45. Borges, *Family in Bahia*, 30–31.

46. Santos, "Caixeiros da Bahia"; Bacelar, *Galegos*; Bacelar, *Negros e Espanhóis*.

47. Santos, "Caixeiros da Bahia."

48. Pierson, *Negroes in Brazil*, 22.

49. On the reality that mulattoes in Brazil more generally face as much discrimination as their darker-skinned counterparts, see Valle Silva, "High Cost of Not Being White"; Skidmore, *Black into White*; and Telles, *Race in Another America*.

50. Bacelar, "Frente negra." See also Azevedo, *Elites de cor*; and Guimarães, "Cor, classes e status."

51. In "Frente negra," 77, Bacelar points out how little we know of individuals such as Maxwel Porphirio de Assumpção. See also Alberto, *Terms of Inclusion*, 147.

52. Castro, *Miguel Santana*.

53. Castillo, *Entre a oralidade*, 118–99. In particular, see Martiniano do Bonfim's assertion that he "obeys the laws of the whites" (126). See also Clay, "Negro," 36–47, on João da Gomeia and Manuel Paim on "black" religion.

54. For excellent critical discussions of the essentialization of certain aspects of culture as embodiments of "race" within contemporary Bahian identity politics, see Pinho, *Mama Africa*; Selka, *Religion and the Politics of Ethnic Identity*, chap. 6.

55. Butler, *Freedoms Given, Freedoms Won*, 55, 194–96; Carneiro, *Candomblés da Bahia*; Landes, *City of Women*.

56. Carneiro, *Candomblés da Bahia*; Landes, *City of Women*.

57. Bacelar, "Frente negra"; Butler, *Freedoms Given, Freedoms Won*, 129–31. See also Hanchard, *Orpheus and Power*; and Davis, *Avoiding the Dark*, 182–92.

58. Female interviewees were less likely than males to self-identify as "workers," whether they were domestics, laundresses, food vendors, seamstresses, or factory workers. In these cases, the women's primary self-identification when speaking collectively was as a woman, wife, or mother or as a particular type of worker.

59. For anecdotal information on working-class income, see Melville J. and Frances S. Herskovits Field Notes, Salvador, Bahia, Book E, pp. 51–54, Series II, Melville J. and Frances S. Herskovits Papers, Schomburg Center for Research in Black Culture, New York Public Library, New York, New York (hereafter cited as HFN). In Santos, "Sobrevivências e tensões sociais," pt. 3, chaps. 1 and 2, the author suggests that during the First Republic workers in unions or associations looked down upon those whose employment was less certain, revealing one of the more salient divisions between working-class men in Salvador.

60. See for example, Luciano da Silva, interview by the author, Salvador, 10 November 1999; José da Silva, interview by the author, Salvador, 31 October 1999.

61. Santos, *Centro da cidade do Salvador*, 47. On the "casual and marginal nature" of much employment in Rio de Janeiro during the First Republic, analogous to Salvador during the Vargas era, see Meade, *"Civilizing" Rio*, chaps. 2 and 5; Chalhoub, *Trabalho, Lar e Botequim*.

62. Book E, 51–53, HFN.

63. Ibid.

64. The following discussion relies on information on occupation and gender in Book E, 31–54, HFN.

65. Book A, 2, HFN.

66. In 1938, Carneiro stated to Landes that a typical *mãe-de-santo* supported herself and her children with an average income of 100$000 per month, about the same as the

lower rung of public sector work or the income of an assistant to a tradesman. The fortunes of all the houses fluctuated, depending on, among other things, the number of *ogans* (patrons or supporters) and the seasonal intake of initiates. During less successful times, the smaller houses struggled. See Landes, *City of Women*, 40.

67. Men also earned in this way.

68. Book E, 54, HFN.

69. Book E, 39, 42, HFN.

70. In 1983, at the II Conferência Mundial da Tradição dos Orixá e Cultura, Mãe Stella de Oxossi and several other leading *mães-de-santo* insisted that Candomblé should be understood as a religion separate from Catholicism. Asserting that "Iansã is not Santa Barbara" ("*Iansã não é Santa Barbara*"), they effectively declared Candomblé divinities to be independent of any associations with the Catholic saints, syncretic or otherwise. This assertion has some importance for the historical understanding of the relationship between Candomblé and Catholicism. While I respect the conceptual and political work that such a statement does for the living, the degree to which historical actors conceived of the *orixás* as distinct from Catholic saints remains an open question. *Jornal da Bahia*, 29 July 1983.

71. Candomblé is commonly understood as a single religion, but in fact, as Giesler explores in detail, it is a highly diverse "set of variants" that share a Wittgensteinian family resemblance rather than a unified set of distinctive features. Giesler, "Conceptualizing Religion," x.

72. As Sansi-Roca points out, this echoed the equally contrived notions of Yoruban superiority from even earlier in the process of Portuguese colonization. Sansi-Roca, *Fetishes and Monuments*, 62n6.

73. As pointed out in Castillo, *Entre a oralidade*, 128. See also Parés, "Jeje," on the fact that Araketu did not lose as much prestige or attention as they might have because their Jeje-Nagô tradition was at least partly Nagô-Ketu and therefore benefited from the ascendency of Nagô-Ketu.

74. Dantas, *Vovó Nagô*. See also Prandi, *Candomblés de São Paulo*; Capone, *Quête de l'Afrique*; Matory, *Black Atlantic Religion*; and Parés, "Birth of the Yoruba Hegemony."

75. On the high number of abandoned children in 1933, "without bread and without shelter," see Guarda Civil, "Relatório: Escola Profíssional para Menores," Secretaria de Segurança Pública, Cx 16, Pc 01, Arquivo Público do Estado da Bahia, Seção Republicana (hereafter cited as APEB). See also Fraga Filho, *Mendigos, moleques e vadios*. On prostitution, see Santana, "Prostituição Feminina."

76. *7 anos que mudaram a Bahia*, 12–14.

77. Meat shortages during the war and the postwar period seemed to cause most public remonstration. Consul Macrae to Rio de Janeiro, November 1943, FO 128/423, PRO. On the history of Salvador's chronic food shortages prior to 1930, see Santos, "Sobrevivências e tensões sociais"; and Consul Macrae to Consular Department, 5 December 1941, FO 371/30364, PRO.

78. Neves, "Invasão em Salvador"; *7 anos que mudaram a Bahia*, 14.

79. Sampaio puts the illiteracy rate in Bahia (not Salvador) in 1920 at 75 percent; Sampaio, *Partidos*, 51–52.

80. IBGE, *Características demográficas*, 197.

81. Butler, *Freedoms Given, Freedoms Won*, 135; IBGE, *Características demográficas*, 202.

82. IBGE, *Caracteristícas demográficas*, 289, 295–96. According to the IBGE, in an international context this was considered a "very high" rate of mortality. Infant death in the first year was six times higher in Salvador than the United States, and infant death in the second year was sixteen times higher.

83. Ibid., 305.

Chapter 2. The Revitalization of African-Bahian Culture

1. *Tenente* literally means "lieutenant," but it was also the general name for any young army officer adhering to *tenentismo*, a movement that expressed disaffection with the oligarchic politics of the early twentieth century.

2. Magalhães, *Minhas Memórias Provisórias*, 73.

3. The Latin *mater* (mother), which has overtones of the classical world, was occasionally used in newspapers and magazines to emphasize the notion that Bahia was the birthplace of Brazil.

4. Gomes and Seigel, "Sabina's Oranges," 11, 22–24.

5. Magalhães, *Minhas Memórias Provisórias*, 69–108; Magalhães, *Defendendo o meu governo*; Pang, *Bahia in the First Brazilian Republic*, 195–201; Santos, "Prefácio"; Carvalho, "Juracy Magalhães."

6. Dantas, *Vovó Nagô*, 145–240; Braga, *Na gamela*, 37–123; Lühning, "Acabe com este santo"; Lima, "Candomblé da Bahia na década de 1930"; Butler, *Freedoms Given, Freedoms Won*, 203–9; "Afterword: Ginga Baiana," 166–67; Matory, *Black Atlantic Religion*, 117–69; Sansi-Roca, *Fetishes and Monuments*, 51–61; Castillo, *Entre a oralidade*, 116–44; Pares, "'Nagoization' Process"; Romo, *Brazil's Living Museum*, 61–85.

7. Wider scholarship on Magalhães's term in office (1931–36) has focused mostly on elite politics. See Pang, *Bahia in the First Brazilian Republic*, 195–201; Sampaio, *Poder e Representação*; and Carvalho, "Juracy Magalhães."

8. Pang, *Bahia in the First Brazilian Republic*, 198.

9. On the Ministry of Labor under Vargas, see Wolfe, " Faustian Bargain Not Made," 78–80. The telegrams are found throughout JM/Municípios cig, Pastas CCXV–CCXXX, and JM/Municípios d, Pasta XV, Centro de Pesquisa e Documentação de História Contemporânea do Brasil Fundação Getúlio Vargas, Rio de Janeiro (hereafter cited as CP-DOC). Of course there were elements of cynicism and expediency behind these telegrams, and not all workers were enamored with Juracy or Vargas.

10. The Moreira curriculum vita of sorts is document JM 30.12.20, CPDOC.

11. Magalhães, *Minhas Memórias Provisórias*, 80.

12. On "expanding the traditional social-welfare infrastructure" in Bahia, see Borges, *Family in Bahia*, 149; *Cartilha histórica da Bahia*, 32; and *Diário de Notícias*, 30 June 1937.

13. Carvalho, "Juracy Magalhães"; Silva, *Âncoras de tradição*, 70.

14. Lima and Oliveira, *Cartas*, 153.

15. Lühning, "Acabe com este santo," 199–202. Dantas, *Vovó Nagô*, 186, states the law dated to 1934. Lühning's earliest mention in the press suggesting the possibility of an official license or permission to hold a ceremony of Candomblé comes from *A Tarde* in May 1937, several months before Magalhães left office. Ruth Landes, *City of Women*, passim, refers to the licensing system from her time in Salvador in 1937 and 1938, and Herskovits and Herskovits, Book I, 27 and passim, HFN, refer to the licensing system as well as the often fractious relations between the police and the *terreiros* in 1941.

16. Lima, "Candomblé da Bahia na década de 1930," 40–41.

17. Lühning, "Acabe com este santo," 202.

18. Quote from Pierson, *Negroes in Brazil*, 271. See also Gomes, "Caminhando com Ruth Landes." On hopeful attitudes of elites in the 1920s and 1930s toward the "whitening" away of the country's "negro problem," see Skidmore, *Black into White*. Even the vehemently anti-Candomblé newspaper *Semana Cathólica* occasionally took the less aggressive line that with time the "fetish cults" would disappear. *Semana Cathólica*, 18 January 1942.

19. Butler, "Afterword," 165. See also Nishida, *Slavery and Identity*; Harding, *Refuge in Thunder*; Graden, *Slavery to Freedom*; Reis, *Domingos Sodré*; and Castillo and Parés, "Marcelina e seu mundo."

20. Lühning, "Acabe com este santo," 202. See also Book B, p. 29/Series II, HFN; Braga, *Na gamela*, 59–73.

21. Carneiro, *Candomblés da Bahia*, 39–40. Carneiro mentions that the much newer *terreiros* were setting up in "ordinary houses" along main roads in the slowly growing suburbs.

22. Lima, "Candomblé da Bahia na década de 1930," 2004; Matory, "English Professors of Brazil," 91–95; Pares, "'Nagoization' Process"; Castillo, *Entre a oralidade*, 103–44.

23. Carneiro, *Candomblés da Bahia*, esp. 50–53.

24. Romo, *Brazil's Living Museum*, chap. 4.

25. Castillo, *Entre a oralidade*, 128.

26. Dantas, *Vovó Nagô*; Capone, *Quête de l'Afrique*; Pares, "'Nagoization' Process."

27. Albuquerque, "Santos"; Kraay, "Cold as the Stone."

28. *Estado da Bahia*, 14 May 1936, quoted in Castillo, *Entre a oralidade*, 118.

29. Carneiro, *Religiões negras*, 121–22, quoted in Castillo, *Entre a oralidade*, 119.

30. Amado, "Professor Souza Carneiro," *A Tarde*, 20 June 1981, quoted in Oliveira, "Estudos africanistas," 25. Edison's older brother, Nelson, later represented Bahia as a federal deputy from 1947 to 1955.

31. Silva, "Edison Carneiro."

32. Borges, "Recognition of Afro-Brazilian Symbols," 59. Borges also suggested that the economic depression of the early 1930s and World War II encouraged Bahian elites to be more self-consciously "Brazilian." See Borges, *Family in Bahia*, 45.

33. Braga, *Na gamela*, 24.

34. Castillo, *Entre a oralidade*, 120–27. The articles were published over several months. See, for instance, *Estado da Bahia*, 11 May, 14 May, 21 May, 28 May, 9 June, 19 June, 2 July, 29 August, and 26 October 1936.

35. *A Tarde*, 12 December and 17 December 1936, cited in Lühning, "Acabe com este santo," 206.

36. Carneiro, *Religiões negras*; Carneiro *Negros Bantus*; Nina Rodrigues, *Os africanos*; Freyre, *Masters and the Slaves*; Ramos, *Folclore*. On the First Afro-Brazilian Congress, see Romo, *Brazil's Living Museum*, 53–61.

37. Castillo, *Entre a oralidade*, 118.

38. Amado was the first to do so, with the exception of the 1922 republication of Xavier Marques's very racist *Feiticeiro*. Oliveira, "Estudos africanistas," 25, relates briefly that Edison Carneiro's father, Antonio Joaquim de Souza Carneiro, also published two novels with principal African-Brazilian characters. Amado has written of being influenced by Souza

Carneiro, perhaps including Souza Carneiro's emphasis on African-Bahian characters and settings.

39. On the misreadings of Jorge Amado, see Viera, "Testimonial Fiction." See also Brower, Fitz, and Martinez-Vidal, *Jorge Amado*.

40. *Estado da Bahia*, 28 May 1936.

41. Carneiro, "Dona Anninha [*sic*]," *Estado da Bahia*, 25 January 1938.

42. Castillo, *Entre a oralidade*, 135–36, 143.

43. Pierson, *Negroes in Brazil*, 293, quoted in Lima, "Candomblé da Bahia na década de 1930," 216; Romo, *Brazil's Living Museum*, 84–85.

44. *Estado da Bahia*, 5 January 1938.

45. *Estado da Bahia*, 11 January 1936, quoted in Lima, "Candomblé da Bahia na década de 1930," 41–42.

46. Lima and Oliveira, *Cartas*, 153.

47. Mestre João Pequeno, personal communication, Salvador, 24 October 1999, 25–26; José Ferreira, interview by the author, Salvador, 11 November 1999, 107–9; Sodre, *Mestre Bimba*, 93–95.

48. Lewis, *Ring of Liberation*, 18–50.

49. Pires, "Movimentos," 51–52.

50. Assunção, *Capoeira*, 120–25.

51. Reis, *Pernas*, 100–109.

52. Querino, *Bahia de outrora*, 74–75.

53. Ângelo Decânio Filho, personal communication, Paripe, Bahia, January 1998; and Reis, "Mestre Bimba e Mestre Pastinha," which cites additional interviews with Mestre Bimba.

54. *A Tarde,* 26 October 1931.

55. Assunção has been unable to find evidence confirming whether the event was in 1936 or 1937; see Assunção, *Capoeira*, 238n65. Compare Talmon-Chvaicer, *Hidden History*, 122.

56. *A Tarde*, 1 July 1936.

57. Ibid.

58. Reis, *Pernas*, chap. 2; Rego, *Capoeira Angola*, 316–17, quoted in Reis, *Pernas*, 108–9; no author, *Ginástica nacional: Diário de Notícias*, 5 January 1940; Vieira, "Capoeiragem disciplinada." The director of the Physical Education Division is quoted in Reis, *Pernas*, 106.

59. Assunção, *Capoeira*, 138.

60. Reis, *Pernas*, 27–28; Assunção, *Capoeira*, 144–49.

61. Santos, "Mixed-Race Nation," 125; Reis, *Pernas*, chaps. 3 and 4.

62. Tavares and Verger, "Ciclo do Bonfim," 66. In its 24 January 1943 issue, *Semana Cathólica* suggested that the ban prohibited laypeople from washing the inside of the church, as do newspaper reports of early twentieth century; see Santana, *Alma e festa*, 204–5.

63. *Diário de Notícias*, 15 January 1937. In its 15 January 1937 issue, *Imparcial* reported that the tradition "had died" but "after many years" had revived that year. Complicating the possibility of establishing the chronology of the ban, the *Diário de Notícias* wrote of a fifteen-year ban from 1916 to 1931; see the 10 January 1940 issue.

64. For a sample of the vitriol during the Old Republic, see Guimarães, "Religião popular," 84–85. For its continuation beyond 1930, see *Semana Cathólica*, 3 January 1937 and 2 January, 15 January, and 22 January 1939. In 1937, the actual priest in charge of Bonfim spoke out against the washing; see "Não está certo," *Imparcial*, 13 January 1937.

65. Guimarães, "Religião popular," 85.

66. *Diário de Notícias*, 15 January 1953.

67. Serra, *Rumores de festa*, 72; Prandi, *Mitologia dos Orixás*, 519–22.

68. On the relationship between the Church and popular Catholicism in the context of the Old Republic (1889–1930), see Guimarães, "Religião popular," 68–88.

69. *Diário da Bahia*, 12 January and 14 January 1927; *A Tarde*, 13 January 1928 and 18 January 1929; Santana, *Alma e festa*, 212–13. What is not clear from year to year, however, is the degree to which the Candomblé community was involved and whether they gained admittance to the inside of the Church.

70. Livro de Atas da Devoção ao Senhor do Bonfim, de 1931 a 1977, Arquivo da Irmandade Devoção ao Senhor do Bonfim, Salvador; *Diário de Notícias*, 13 January 1938.

71. *Diário de Notícias*, 14 January 1934, quoted in Santana, *Alma e festa*, 212.

72. *Imparcial*, 15 January 1937; *Diário de Notícias*, 15 January 1937. None of the members of the Organizing Committee (who are listed in the newspaper) were mentioned in the Livro de Atas da Devoção ao Senhor do Bonfim. For an abbreviated listing of figures responsible for encouraging or organizing the washing, see *Diário de Notícias*, 13 January 1938; and *Imparcial*, 10 January 1937.

73. What we know of the workings of the lay brotherhood comes from newspapers from later in the period. For instance, the *Diário de Notícias*, 12 January 1944, makes it clear that businessmen of the commercial and financial district made contributions toward the washing and other Bonfim commemorations. The *Diário de Notícias*, 10 January 1940, suggests there was an early phase of revival from 1931 and especially 1932, led by José Barreiros and Edmundo Almeida. This is the only reference to this early revival among the sources I consulted.

74. See *Imparcial*, 13 and 15 January 1937; and *Diário de Notícias*, 15 January 1937.

75. *Diário da Bahia*, 15 January 1937.

76. *Imparcial*, 13 January 1937.

77. *Diário de Notícias*, 10 January 1940. This may not have happened every year before 1937.

78. *Diário de Notícias*, 10 January 1940.

79. She was living in Rio de Janeiro prior to 1935 and died in early 1938.

80. In 1939, *Semana Cathólica* was critical of those elites ("*distintas e piedosas senhoras da nossa sociedade*") who had agreed to support the efforts of Miguel Santana's organizing committee. *Semana Cathólica*, 15 January 1939. See also *Diário de Notícias*, 10 January 1940; and Santana, *Miguel Santana*, 40–41.

81. Monteiro interviewed by Guimarães in "Religião popular," 93.

82. *Semana Cathólica*, 15 January 1939.

83. The first Afro-Brazilian Congress was held in Recife in 1934 and had little to do with African-Bahian culture and very little impact on Bahian cultural politics.

84. Carneiro and Ferraz, "Prefácio," in *Negro no Brasil*; *Estado da Bahia*, 8, 9, 11, 12, 13, 14, 18, 19, and 21 January 1937. See also Oliveira, "Estudos Africanistas"; Dantas, *Vovó Nagô*,

esp. 182–216; Ickes, "Salvador's Transformist Hegemony," 17–18; Castillo, *Entre a oralidade*, 116–39; and Romo, *Brazil's Living Museum*, chap. 2.

85. Carneiro, "Congresso Afro-Brasileiro da Bahia," 99–100.

86. *Estado da Bahia*, 7 August 1936.

87. *A Tarde*, 17 December 1936, quoted in Lühning, "Acabe com este santo," 216.

88. The original name for this organization was the African Council. See Braga, *Na gamela*, 168–75.

89. On Arthur Ramos, see Cunha, "Sua alma em sua palma."

90. Dantas, *Vovó Nagô*; Sansi-Roca, *Fetishes and Monuments*, chaps. 2 and 3; Castillo, *Entre a oralidade*, 127 passim.

91. Carneiro and Ferraz, *Negro no Brasil*. Carneiro elaborates on his distinction between legitimate African-Brazilian practices and those that brought the entire religion into disrepute. See Carneiro, *Candomblés da Bahia*, 106–7.

92. Romo, *Brazil's Living Museum*, 66–85. See also Dantas, *Vovó Nagô*, 192–201.

Chapter 3. Performing Bahia

1. Although the press repeatedly lauded the Senhor do Bonfim as the people's choice for the patron saint of Salvador and especially Bahia, the official patron saint of Salvador, according to the Catholic Church, remained St. Francis Xavier. Bahia had no official patron saint until 1971 (when the pope declared it to be Our Lady of the Immaculate Conception), but these facts were largely overlooked in favor of the Senhor do Bonfim. For the terms of the debate between the custom of popular verdict versus the theological position, see *Diário de Notícias*, 12 January 1944; *Diário de Notícias*, 12 January 1945; and *Diário de Notícias*, 10 March 1953.

2. On the phenomenon of syncretism within the African Diaspora, see Apter, "Herskovits's Heritage." For how syncretism relates to cultural politics in Bahia, see Selka, *Religion and the Politics of Ethnic Identity*, 73–81.

3. Zweig, *Brazil*, 263–66. Bomfim is an alternative spelling of Bonfim. This passage appeared as an editorial in *A Tarde* (15 January 1942) six weeks before Zweig and his wife committed double suicide in Petrópolis. The only notable discrepancy between the English and Portuguese versions was that the English phrase "black spirits" was translated as *demônios loucos* (crazed demons).

4. The crucifixion of Christ is, of course, normally commemorated during Easter (Semana Santa). But according to Carvalho, annual April rains made the route from the city to the Church of Nosso Senhor do Bonfim nearly impassable. Consequently, in the late eighteenth century, the day commemorating the Senhor do Bonfim was moved to the second Sunday after Epiphany. See Carvalho, *Devoção*. On the early history of the church and the cult of the Senhor do Bonfim, see also Groetelaars, *Quem é o Senhor do Bonfim?*; Guimarães, "Religião popular"; Santana, *Alma e festa*; and *Diário de Notícias*, 10 January 1940, 12 January 1945.

5. Couto, "Lavagens." See also, for example, Reis, *Death Is a Festival*; Reis, *Domingos Sodré*; Harding, *Refuge in Thunder*; Nishida, *Slavery and Identity*; and Graden, *Slavery to Freedom*, 103–32.

6. Serra, *Rumores de festa*, 72; Prandi, *Mitologia*, 519–22.

7. *Diário de Notícias*, 7 January 1931.

8. *Diário de Notícias*, 5 January 1937 and 6 January 1939; *Imparcial*, 5 January 1937; Carneiro, *Folguedos tradicionais*, passim.

9. Campos, *Procissões*, 3.

10. Ibid., 132. Campos also called attention to something akin to a revival in the late 1930s for nearly all the larger festivals, but in more "modern" guises. See ibid., 129–255, passim (especially 132, 209, 243, 248, 255).

11. This second lifting is discussed in chapter 6.

12. Santos, *Centro da cidade do Salvador*, 47; Neves, "Invasão em Salvador."

13. *Diário de Notícias*, 4 January 1945.

14. *Diário de Notícias*, 7 January 1938. Deôdeto Porto, interview by the author, Salvador, 4 November 1999; Neves, "Invasão em Salvador."

15. On the sacred and the profane, see Eliade, *Sagrado*; Serra, *Rumores de festa*; and Heers, *Fêtes des fous*.

16. Serra provides some thick description of the events inside the church over the course of the festivals, especially in contrast to festivities beyond the church walls. See Serra, *Rumores de festa*, 58–62.

17. Mielche, *From Santos to Bahia*, 336–38.

18. *Diário da Bahia*, 18 January 1941.

19. *Diário de Notícias*, 10 January 1942. *Diário de Notícias*, 14 January 1944.

20. Book I, 12–13, HFN.

21. Book I, 12–17, HFN.

22. Book I, 16, HFN.

23. Book I, 5–12, HFN.

24. For descriptions of the festival during the 1930s and 1940s, see the history provided in *Estado da Bahia*, 4 December 1952. See also *A Tarde*, 4 December 1943; *Diário de Notícias*, 2 December 1942; and *Estado da Bahia*, 4 December 1947.

25. *Estado da Bahia*, 3 December 1951. For the samba, see also *Estado da Bahia*, 4 December 1947.

26. Lima, "Candomblé da Bahia na década de trinta," 39.

27. Carneiro, *Candomblés da Bahia*.

28. Frazier, "Negro Family in Bahia," 472.

29. Carneiro quoted in Landes, *City of Women*, 89.

30. Book I, 17, HFN.

31. The Herskovitses were informed they were witnessing an offering from Yemanjá to Oshun, a different *orixá*. Given the cosmological differences among *terreiros* and the cosmological overlap between the two *orixás*, this may have been the case for some *terreiros*. But it is more likely that the Herskovitses misunderstood or were misinformed.

32. Book I, 18, HFN.

33. The master fisherman was either an *ogan* (secular patron) for one of Salvador's temples of Candomblé or a *pai-de-santo*. The Herskovitses refer to him as both in different places in their field notes.

34. Book I, 18–20, HFN.

35. *Diário de Notícias*, 31 December 1945 and 3 January 1946.

36. Book III, 7, HFN.

37. Book III, 7, HFN. The "I" here could be either Melville or Frances, as they both contributed equally to their field notes. It is unclear who actually wrote a particular section.

38. Campos, *Procissões*, 134; Alberto, "Na Bahia"; Tavares, *Bahia*, 31; *Diário de Notícias*, 3 January 1945.

39. On the samba, capoeira, and African-Bahian food that would accompany the festivities in Boa Viagem, see *Imparcial*, 1 January 1937.

40. Book III, 7, HFN. See also *Diário de Notícias*, 3 January 1931.

41. Today the Festival of Rio Vermelho is practically synonymous with the Festival of Yemanjá, but during the Vargas era the Festival of Rio Vermelho went on for many days in honor of the neighborhood patron saint Nossa Senhora de Sant'Anna, and several days were dedicated to "announcing" the not-too-distant arrival of carnival. The day of the offering to Yemanjá fell during this wider festivity. For newspaper coverage, however, the two were not synonymous.

42. Book IV, 35, HFN.

43. Lody, *Eparrei, Bárbara*; Serra, *Rumores de festa*, 59–60.

44. Americo Lopes, interview by the author, Salvador, 11 November 1999.

45. Ibid.

46. José Ferreira, interview by the author, Salvador, 11 November 1999, 52.

47. Luciano da Silva, interview by the author, Salvador, 10 November 1999, 34.

48. Mielche, *From Santos to Bahia*, 335; *Diário de Notícias*, 6 December 1940.

49. Americo Lopes, interview by the author.

50. In the early 1940s, 80$000 was roughly $6.50. *Diário de Notícias*, 6 December 1940. For a comparison, the Herskovitses reported that in 1942 stalls in the established markets cost 2$000 per day (roughly $0.16), while open-air market stalls cost 1$500 per day (roughly $0.12). HFN, Book E, 54.

51. In the early 1940s, 11$600 was roughly $0.95. *Diário de Notícias*, 6 December 1940 and 19 January 1954.

52. José Ferreira, interview by the author, Salvador, 4 November 1999, 5.

53. For fascinating visual imagery of working life on the docks in the 1940s, including a *roda de capoeira* (probably at least partially staged, judging by the self-conscious behavior of the participants), see Santos, "Dia na rampa."

54. Cruz, "Samba na roda," chap. 3.

55. José Ferreira, interview by the author, Salvador, 4 November 1999, 5.

56. Mestre João Pequeno, personal communication, Salvador, 24 October 1999, 16–17.

57. José Ferreira, interview by the author, Salvador, 4 November 1999, 8–9; 11 November 1999, 111.

58. Franciso de Assis, personal communication with author, Salvador, 30 September 1999, 14–15, 17.

59. HFN; see also Landes, *City of Women*, 62–71.

60. Lühning, "Compositor Mozart Camargo Guarnieri em Salvador." On Dow Turner's informants, see Cunha, "Ponto de vista." The mother of the famous local *sambista* Riachão was a *filha-de-santo*. See Cruz, "Samba na roda," 69; and Prandi, *Segredos guardados*, chap. 8.

61. Tavares, "Rodas de samba na Bahia."

62. Antônia Conceição, interview by the author, Salvador, 2 November 1999, 14–20; Luciano da Silva, interview by the author, Salvador, 10 November 1999, 15; Luisa Santos, interview by the author, Salvador, 23 October 1999, 5, 24. For a samba in the African-Bahian

working-class community to celebrate a baptism, see *A Tarde*, 5 February 1934. The samba event made the newspapers because a shooting occurred.

63. Sodré, *Samba*; José Ferreira, interview by author, Salvador, 4 November 1999, 5, 7; Franciso de Assis, personal communication, Salvador, 30 September 1999, 8–10, 21–22; Hilda dos Santos, personal communication, Salvador, 25 October 1999, 2–4, 9; Ermita Cruz, interview by the author, Salvador, 23 October 1999, 5, 16.

64. Döring, "Samba de roda do Sembagota."

65. Americo Lopes, interview by the author, Salvador, 11 November 1999; *A Tarde*, 1 November 1932.

66. Cruz, "Samba na roda," 83–92.

67. "Feitiço de Mulatas," *A Tarde*, 4 February 1931.

68. *A Tarde*, 20 February 1935.

69. Döring, "Mundo Musical Popular," manuscript in possession of author; Cruz, "Samba na roda," 92–98.

70. Riachão, interview conducted by Jackson Paim, 21 March 2003, quoted in Cruz, "Samba na roda," 127.

Chapter 4. Rituals of Inclusion

1. Lima, "Candomblé da Bahia na década de trinta," 41–42. Moreover, tales of the reliance of elected politicians on the Candomblé cults—and their relationships with the various saints—to win political power were part of working-class lore. See Book B, 10, HFN; and Book I, 7–8, HFN. On the unequal treatment of larger and smaller terreiros, see Lühning, "Acabe com este santo," 201–2.

2. *A Tarde*, 24 November 1941, quoted in Lühning, "Acabe com este santo," 206–7, 217.

3. *A Tarde*; 22 April 1926, quoted in Campos, *Procissões*, 4; and Romo, "Race and Reform," 123.

4. *A Tarde* had the largest circulation in Bahia (average daily circulation of nineteen thousand in 1948) and was closely identified with the interests of the conservative traditional oligarchy. It was owned by Simões Filho, a conservative politician. *O Imparcial* belonged consecutively to several traditional political elites, all conservative, and in the middle to late 1930s the newspaper was sympathetic to integralism in Brazil. It ceased publication in the 1940s. *Diário de Notícias* (daily circulation of ten thousand) was also sympathetic to integralism in the mid-1930s, but it reversed this position in 1936 to support Magalhães. It was purchased by Assis Chateaubriand's media empire in 1942. Chateaubriand had already purchased *Estado da Bahia* in 1938 (daily circulation of eight thousand). Subsequently, both were generally center-left on social issues and center-right on politics and economics, supporting both Governor Mangabeira (1947–51) and President Vargas (1951–54). The *Diário da Bahia* was owned by Pedro Lago, a conservative politician, and was a center-right publication for much of the period, but in the years after World War II, when it hardly circulated, it was understood to be "leftist" by the American consulate in Bahia. During these years the *Diário da Bahia* was the most celebratory of the noncommunist newspapers of the "popular" aspects of the festivals. *O Momento*, the unofficial organ of the Communist Party in Bahia (which is archived at the Biblioteca Nacional in Rio de Janeiro), was in daily circulation from roughly 1945 to 1948, then less and less frequently until its dissolution in the mid-1950s. U.S. Consul Robert Johnson to U.S. Ambassador

Herschel Johnson, 5 January 1952, RG 84, Classified General Records, Salvador, Box 19, NARA II. Circulation figures from American Embassy to American Consulate, Foreign Service Operations Memorandum, Subject: "Press," 24 December 1948, RG 84, Brazil/Salvador/Consulate, Box 66, Vol. 16, NARA II. After 1945, a number of Communists worked for the three main dailies even when the editorial line of those newspapers was overtly anti-Communist.

5. Silva, *Âncoras de tradição*, 83–86; Carvalho and Tavares, *Apontamentos*.

6. Sampaio, "Governador," 117.

7. For an expanded assessment of Alves's and Pinto Aleixo's time in power, see Ickes, "Salvador's Transformist Hegemony," chap. 2.

8. No author, *Educação e saúde na Bahia*, as discussed in Romo, *Brazil's Living Museum*, 89–92. See also Ickes, "Salvador's Transformist Hegemony," 89–91; Alves, *Educação e brasilidade*; Alves, *Dever da juventude*; and Alves, *Missão nacional*.

9. *Bahia tradicional e moderna* (ano I, no. 2) July 1939, 45.

10. Romo, *Brazil's Living Museum*, 90.

11. Ibid., 93–97.

12. Ibid., 92–100.

13. Campos, *Procissões*.

14. Romo, *Brazil's Living Museum*, 100–102.

15. Herskovits, *Pesquisas Etnológicas*.

16. Carneiro, *Candomblés da Bahia*.

17. *Diário de Notícias*, 8 January 1938. See also *Diário de Notícias*, 10 January 1942. The Livro de Atas da Devoção ao Senhor do Bonfim, de 1931 a 1977 shows that for the years 1938 to 1944, in particular, the brotherhood averaged close to forty individuals, mostly political/administrative figures within the Estado Novo and a smattering of colonels, doctors, and engineers. The minute book is in the Arquivo da Irmandade Devoção ao Senhor do Bonfim, Salvador.

18. *Diário de Notícias*, 14 January 1944.

19. *Diário de Notícias*, 12 January 1945. According to Monteiro, the washing in 1943, too, was attended by Interventor Pinto Aleixo and top civilian and military personnel in a show of unity—"civic, religious, and popular"—in support of the Allied war effort, which Brazil had recently joined. See *A Tarde Suplemento*, 18 January 1969.

20. Williams, *Culture Wars*; Wolfe, "Father of the Poor," 88; Levine, *Father of the Poor?* 68–69, 81.

21. Smith, *Art of Festival*, 73.

22. Serra, *Rumores de festa*, 75.

23. Lima, "Candomblé da Bahia na década de 1930"; Lühning, "Acabe com este santo"; Braga, *Na gamela*.

24. Nóbrega and Echeverria, *Mãe Menininha*, 107n11.

25. Barbosa, "Federação," 70, quoted in Nóbrega and Echeverria, *Mãe Menininha*, 99–100. This was a separate occasion from the one related in the Herskovits anecdote at the beginning of the chapter.

26. Campos believed that the number of ships in the 1930s was less than there had traditionally been but put the number at 225 for 1938, up from his averages over the 1930s, which hovered around 150. See Campos, *Procissões*, 133.

27. Judging the accuracy of this contention is not straightforward: The first several pages of the year were missing from a significant number of the bound newspapers in the collections of the Biblioteca Central do Estado da Bahia and the Instituto Histórico e Geográfico da Bahia.

28. Campos, *Procissões*, 136.

29. *Diário de Notícias*, 17 February 1943.

30. *Diário de Notícias*, 14 January 1944.

31. *Diário de Notícias*, 6 December 1939; *Diário de Notícias*, 1 December 1944.

32. *A Tarde*, 9 January 1942; *Diário de Notícias*, 20 January 1946. The expeditionary forces were approximately twenty-five thousand Brazilian soldiers who fought alongside the Allies in Europe in 1944 and 1945.

33. *Diário de Notícias*, 2 February 1947.

34. Ressurreição, "E não sou baiano," original recording by Trio de Ouro, Odeon, 1945; Almeida and Silva, "Já voltei da Bahia," original recording by Odete Amaral, Odeon, 1942. See also Herivelto Martins and Humberto Porto, "Na Bahia," original recording by Trio de Ouro, Odeon, 1938; Raimundo Olavo, Norberto Martins, and Cláudio Luiz, "Mandei fazer um patuá," original recording by Roberto Silva, Star, 1948; Raimundo Olavo and J. Kleber, "Você foi fazer feitiço," original recording by Roberto Silva, Star, 1949.

35. Tavares, "Rodas de samba na Bahia."

36. *Diário de Notícias*, 16 January 1945.

37. *Estado da Bahia*, 28 March 1949.

38. *Estado da Bahia*, 29 December 1949. Tavares lamented the absence of any popular contribution to the specific centennial festivities. See Tavares, "Rodas de samba na Bahia." Within the wider commemorations, there was at least one reference to the contributions of slaves, nestled among the imagery of the grand parade of 29 March that included allegories of the ships that brought settlers to Salvador. One newspaper caption for a photograph of three African-Bahian women in nineteenth-century dress, presumably part of the parade that included reenactments, limited its acknowledgment of African and African-Brazilian labor in Brazil to praising the contributions of "faithful" wet nurses and domestic servants. *Estado da Bahia*, 30 March 1949.

39. *Estado da Bahia*, 30 March 1949.

40. *Estado da Bahia*, 3 January 1948.

41. Consul Kenneth Yearns to Ambassador Herschel Johnson, 18 April 1949, RG 84, Classified General Records, Salvador, Box 72, 1949, NARA II.

42. *A Tarde*, 28 February 1949; *Estado da Bahia*, 25 February 1949

43. *Estado da Bahia*, 28 December 1948.

44. Marinho, "Otávio Mangabeira," 137.

45. Mangabeira quoted in Marinho, "Otávio Mangabeira," 139. For Mangabeira's use of "fragile democracy" and "Christian democracy," see the report on Mangabeira's speech to open the new session of the state legislature in 1949 in Consul Kenneth Yearns to Ambassador Herschel Johnson, 18 April 1949, RG 84 Classified General Records, Salvador, Box 72, 1949, NARA II.

46. *Diário de Notícias*, 1 December 1944.

47. Each of the major dailies employed several journalists who were sympathetic to issues faced by Salvador's poor African-Bahian population, a number of whom later worked

for the Communist Party daily *O Momento* during its brief legal existence in 1946. See Falcão, *Partido*, 227–28.

48. *Imparcial*, 1 January 1937.

49. *Imparcial*, 17 January 1937.

50. *Diário de Notícias*, 6 December 1940.

51. Amaral, *Blaise Cendrars no Brasil*; Amaral, *Tradições populares*; Andrade, *Música de feitiçaria*; Travassos, *Modernismo e música brasileira*; Soares, *Mario de Andrade*; Magalhães and Campos, *Folcore no Brasil*; Cascudo, *Dicionário do folclore brasileiro*.

52. Vilhena, *Projeto e missão*, 80–94.

53. Romo, "Race and Reform," chap. 3.

54. *Diário de Notícias*, 10 January 1940; 14 and 16 January 1944; and 9 and 11 January 1945; *A Tarde*, 11 and 18 January 1946; *Estado da Bahia*, 14 January 1942.

55. Ferreira Filho, "Desafricanizar as ruas"; Leite, "Bahia civiliza-se."

56. *Diário da Bahia*, 15 January 1937.

57. See, among others, Braga, *Na gamela*; Dantas, *Vovó Nagô*; and Lühning, "Acabe com este santo." Perhaps most revealing in this context was the eventual use of *fetichismo* (fetishism) devoid of explicit negative connotations. See *Diário da Notícias*, 11 January 1946.

58. "Baiana" was a more neutral term in part because it had a socioeconomic referent as well, namely, women who sold foodstuffs on street corners, one of the principal ways that the women of Candomblé traditionally earned a living. A rare early reference in 1931 to a Baiana at the Festival of Senhor do Bonfim was explicitly made in the context of cooking and eating rather than in the context of Candomblé. See *Diário de Notícias*, 19 January 1931.

59. *Diário da Bahia*, 18 January 1941; *Diário da Bahia*, 16 January 1942.

60. *Imparcial*, 10 January 1938.

61. *Diário de Notícias*, 10 January 1940.

62. *Diário de Notícias*, 18 January 1946 and 24 January 1947.

63. *Diário de Notícias*, 8 December 1943. See also *Diário da Bahia*, 3 February 1944.

64. *Diário de Notícias*, 6 December 1940.

65. Rio de Janeiro had its own legacy of the Baiana. At the beginning of the nineteenth century, economic migrants from Bahia had begun moving to the national capital, a process that peaked in the early twentieth century. These former Bahians had rejuvenated their African-Brazilian cultural heritage over the past century as part of Rio's popular and working-class culture.

66. Castro, *Carmen*, 171–77; Gomes and Seigel, "Sabina's Oranges, 16–18. According to *Diário da Bahia*, even the *taboleiro* had national exposure prior to Carmen Miranda: "Those famous tabloeiros that had already made a triumphal entrance in Brazilian literature [of previous centuries]." See *Diário da Bahia*, 8 December 1942.

67. *Diário da Bahia*, 8 December 1940.

68. *A Tarde*, 31 January 1942.

69. *A Tarde*, 20 August 1943. Costa Rego's analogy was that "no one would dare deprive Paris of the curious little book stalls along the Seine just because there were sumptuous editorial houses along the boulevard."

70. *A Tarde*, 21 July 1943.

71. Ferreira Filho, "Desafricanizar as ruas."

72. *A Tarde* reproduced an article titled "Bahia City of Tenderness," by Paulista

Domingos Laurito, which praised the Candomblé community—and by extension the city of Salvador—for its gentle ways. *A Tarde*, 5 October 1940.

73. For these issues leading up to and during the early years of the Vargas era, especially in the southeast of Brazil, see Besse, *Restructuring Patriarchy*.

74. *A Tarde*, 20 August 1943; *Diário de Notícias*, 3 February 1943.

75. Gomes and Seigel, "Sabina's Oranges," 11, 22–24; Deiab, "Mãe-preta na literatura brasileira"; Alberto, *Terms of Inclusion*, 89–94.

76. Silva, *Âncoras de tradição*, especially chap. 11.

77. *Diário de Notícias* mentioned the "delicious plate of *caruru* and spicy *vatapá*" available during the festival, but to date I have found no other mention in the late 1920s or early 1930s. See *Diário de Notícias*, 19 January 1931. In its 18 November 1936 issue, *O Imparcial* commented only on "the food." Ferreira Filho points out that prior to 1930 the elite were very critical of selling food at the festivals and elsewhere because of their concerns about public hygiene and sanitation. Ferreira Filho, "Desafricanizar as ruas," 244.

78. Vianna, *Casos e coisas*, 19–20; *Diário da Bahia*, 8 December 1942. *Vatapá* is a puree of dried shrimp, peanuts, coconut milk, palm oil, and spices; *abará* are steamed black-eyed pea patties steamed in banana leaves; a *moqueca* is a seafood stew, often made in Bahia with palm oil and coconut milk.

79. *Diário da Bahia*, 8 December 1940.

80. Vianna, *Casos e coisas*, 19–20; *A Tarde*, 7 December 1940; *Diário de Notícias*, 6 December 1940; *Diário da Bahia*, 8 December 1940.

81. *Estado da Bahia*, 9 August 1939, quoted in Lühning, "Acabe com este santo," 206.

82. Godofredo Filho, "Eva." See also Tavares, "Cozinha Baiana," in *Bahia*, 129–40.

83. U.S. Consul to Rio de Janeiro, 1 December 1948, RG 84, Classified General Records, Salvador, Box 18, NARA II.

84. This seems to be a mistake on the part of *A Tarde*, as Santa Barbara was in fact generally associated with Iansã, not Yemanjá.

85. There were brief announcements in a few newspapers in 1928 but few to none after that until 1940. These early announcements may have been due to the novelty of the ceremony, which only dates to the mid-1920s.

86. *Diário de Notícias*, 3 February 1943; *A Tarde*, 2 February 1945.

87. *Diário da Bahia*, 3 February 1944.

88. *Diário de Notícias*, 6, 15, and 16 January 1954.

89. *Diário de Notícias*, 15 January 1953.

90. *Estado da Bahia*, 15 January 1951.

91. *Diário de Notícias*, 16 January 1945.

92. *Diário de Notícias*, 20 January 1948; *Estado da Bahia*, 17 January 1950.

93. *Estado da Bahia*, 18 January 1949.

94. *Diário de Notícias*, 6 January 1954.

95. *Diário de Notícias*, 1 February 1945; *Diário de Notícias*, 1 February and 2 February 1946; *Diário de Notícias*, 2 February, 1949; *Diário de Notícias*, 1 February 1953.

96. *Diário de Notícias*, 3 February 1953.

97. *Estado da Bahia*, 27 September 1948 and 27 September 1952; *Diário de Notícias*, 27 September 1953.

98. *Diário da Bahia*, 8 December 1940.

99. *Estado da Bahia*, 30 October 1940; *Diário de Notícias*, 6 November 1940.

100. Luciano da Silva, interview by the author, Salvador, 10 November 1999, 18, 19, 35.

101. Batista and Martins, "Até parece que eu sou da Bahia," original recording by Déo, Columbia, 1942.

102. *Diário da Bahia*, 19 January 1943.

103. Vianna, *Mystery of Samba*; McCann, *Hello, Hello Brazil*.

104. Carneiro, "Samba," *Estado da Bahia*, 2 July 1936; Carneiro, *Negros Bantus*.

105. The bulk of the following assessment of song lyrics comes from the material compiled in Mariano, "*Invenção da baianidade*," 223–54; Prandi, *Segredos guardados*, chap. 9; and "Letras de Música," on the Bahian government website Bahia! at http://www.bahia.com.br/node/6640/ (accessed 22 June 2012). See also "Gravações raras: No tempo dos 78 rpm (1902 a 1964)," http://musicachiado.webs.com/GravacoesRaras/500Raridadesem78rpm.htm/ (accessed 22 June 2012).

106. Bahia, "Isto é bom," original recording by Baiano, Casa Edison, 1902.

107. Author unknown, "Caruru," original recording by Mário Pinheiro.

108. Vianna, *Bahia já foi assim*, 125–26.

109. Cirino and Amorim, "Cristo nasceu na Bahia," original recording by Artur Castro, Odeon, 1926; Barbosa da Silva, "Carga de Burro," original recording by Mário Reis, Odeon, 1929. Barbosa da Silva was also known as Sinhô.

110. De Melo, "Essa Nega é da Bahia" original recording by Francisco Alves, Odeon, 1930.

111. Barcelos, "A Baiana de Nagô," original recording by Antônio Moreira de Silva, Odeon, 1932.

112. Herivelto Martins and Humberto Porto, "Na Bahia," original recording by Carmen Miranda and Trio de Ouro, Odeon, 1938.

113. *A Tarde*, 21 January 1924, cited in Döring, "Mundo musical popular," manuscript in possession of author.

114. Indeed, one letter writer to *A Tarde* blamed the "irritating dissonances of North America music" for rendering Brazilian youth incapable of "appreciating the beauties of a symphony." See *A Tarde*, 6 September 1932.

115. *A Tarde*, 26 November 1931 and 28 November 1931.

116. *A Tarde*, 9 December 1931.

117. *A Tarde*, 17 August 1932.

118. *Diário de Notícias,* 4 February 1932.

119. Barroso, "Batuque," original recording by Elisa Coelho, Victor, 1931; Barroso, "Terra de Iaia," original recording by Elisa Coelho, Victor, 1931; Barroso, "Bahia," original recording by Sílvio Caldas, Victor, 1931.

120. *Estado da Bahia*, 15 June, 18 June, and 22 June 1956.

121. Ferreira and Mota, "Baianinha," original recording by Laís Areda, Odeon, 1929.

122. De Melo, "Essa Nega é da Bahia."

123. Ferreira and Barroso, "Nega também é gente," original recording by Francisco Alves, Odeon, 1934.

124. Valente, "Etc.," original recording by Carmen Miranda, Victor, 1933.

125. Moura, *Tia Ciata*; Rio, *Religiões do Rio*; Lopes, *Negro*. See also Moura, "Mapa político; Mielche, *From Santos to Bahia*, 313, quoted in Romo, *Brazil's Living Museum*, 135; and Ickes, "Salvador's Transformist Hegemony," 228.

126. Risério, *Caymmi*; Caymmi, *Dorival Caymmi*, 77–105.

127. Caymmi, "Que é que a Bahiana tem?," original recording by Carmen Miranda and Dorival Caymmi, Odeon, 1939; Caymmi, "A Preta do Acarajé," original recording by Carmen Miranda and Dorival Caymmi, Odeon, 1939.

128. *A Tarde*, 6 January 1942.

129. *Diário de Notícias*, 6 January and 10 January 1942.

130. *Diário de Notícias*, 1 February 1946.

131. Prefeitura Municipal de Salvador, *Roteiro turístico*.

132. *Diário de Notícias*, 14 January, 1945.

133. *Diário de Notícias*, 15 January 1937, 20 January 1946, 15 January 1938, and 10 January 1940.

134. *Imparcial*, 15 January 1937.

135. See Turner, *Ritual Process*; and Turner and Turner, *Image and Pilgrimage*, especially 239.

136. *Diário de Notícias*, 16 January 1945, and 11 January and 18 January 1946.

137. *Diário de Notícias*, 16 Janeiro 1944.

138. Zweig, *Brazil*, 261–62.

139. Pierson, *Negroes in Brazil*, 366–67.

140. *Diário de Noticias*, 16 January 1940, 22 January 1946, and 16 January 1954.

141. For the Festival of the Three Kings, see Ickes, "Salvador's Transformist Hegemony," 219–21.

142. Curcio-Nagy, "From Native Icon."

143. On this point, Curcio-Nagy's "Giants and Gypsies" follows Leach's emphasis on the festival as structurally reinforcing. See Leach, *Culture and Communication*.

144. Pierson noted that during a popular festival in 1936 in which 116 cars drove past, whites occupied 77.6 percent of the cars, "mixed bloods" occupied 22.4 percent of the cars, and no cars were occupied by blacks. See Pierson, *Negroes in Brazil*, 183.

Chapter 5. Carnival of the People

1. *A Tarde*, 9 February 1942; *Diário de Notícias*, 8 March 1943.

2. A *cuíca* is a high-pitched, hand-held percussion instrument played by rubbing a thin stick that is stuck through the drum head. It is often said to mimic human speech. A *reco-reco* is also held by hand. The sound comes from scraping a stick across sideways ridges along a hollow tube.

3. Turner, *Anthropology of Performance*; Burton, *Afro-Creole*, chap. 4; Davis, *Society and Culture*, chaps. 4 and 5; Da Matta, *Carnivals*. Also, on the power of the ludic, see Schechner, "Carnival (Theory) After Bakhtin," 9–10.

4. Butler, *Freedoms Given, Freedoms Won,* 172–75; Fry, Carrara, and Martins-Costa, "Negros e brancos"; Ferreira Filho, "Desafricanizar as ruas."

5. Butler, "Afterword," 164–67; Góes, *50 anos do trio elétrico*, 36–40; Risério, *Carnaval Ijexá*, 16–18; Moura, "Carnaval como engenho," 172. On the *trio elétrico*, see also Metz, "Alegria." Guerreiro, "Trilhas do samba-reggae," is a notable exception.

6. Emphasizing the power of carnival beyond its official time and place, Piers Armstrong notes that for the early twenty-first century, "temporal and spatial boundaries between carnival and everyday culture are relatively open so that the two domains are less

polarized and their respective performative modes converge." See Armstrong, "Bahian Carnival," 449.

7. Matta employed the work of Victor Turner to update Bahktin's interpretation (in *Rabelais and His World*) of carnival as a moment of cathartic democracy and symbolic resistance to the repressive and exploitative structures that ordered daily life; see Matta, *Carnivals*. Queiroz disagreed, arguing that Matta ignored the hierarchy and power differentials that were still present during carnival and that the dominant bourgeois value system domesticated carnival for many years; see Queiroz, *Carnaval brasileiro*. Most scholars of carnival in Brazil mark out positions between these two poles. See Ortiz, *Consciência Fragmentada*, especially 13–27; Stam, "Carnival, Politics and Brazilian Culture"; Soihet, *Subverção pelo riso*; Cavalcanti, *Rito e o tempo*. See also Raphael, "Samba and Social Control; Tupy, *Carnavais de guerra*; Severiano, *Getúlio Vargas e música popular*; Matos, *Acertei no milhar*; and Cunha, *Ecos da folia*.

8. Butler, *Freedoms Given, Freedoms Won*, 172–75. See also Fry, Carrara, and Martins-Costa, "Negros e brancos"; and Ferreira Filho, "Desafricanizar as ruas."

9. Simson, "Espaço urbano." For Simson, "popular carnival" did not emerge in Rio de Janeiro and São Paulo until the 1920s.

10. Butler, *Freedoms Given, Freedoms Won*, 177. See also Fry, Carrara, and Martins-Costa, "Negros e brancos," 254–60.

11. Vieira Filho, "Africanização do carnaval de Salvador," 128–49.

12. Vianna, "Do entrudo ao carnaval," 285; Risério, "Carnaval," 92.

13. *Jornal A Bahia*, 16 February 1906; Fry, Carrara, and Martins-Costa, "Negros e brancos," 255–56.

14. Butler, *Freedoms Given, Freedoms Won*, 171, 187–88.

15. Donga and Mouro de Almeida, "Pelo telephone," original recording by Banda Odeon, Odeon, 1917. See Hertzman, "Surveillance and Difference," 233–36, for a discussion of the degree to which it is legitimate to refer to "Pelo Telefone" as a "samba."

16. Butler, *Freedoms Given, Freedoms Won*, 180–81; Vieira Filho, "Africanização do carnaval de Salvador," 136–44.

17. *Imparcial*, 13 January 1937.

18. Walkyrio Meyer and Delza Meyer, interview by the author, Salvador, 21 October 1999, 23–24.

19. Durval Lima Filho, interview by the author, Salvador, 26 October 1999, 25–26; *Diário de Notícias*, 16 February 1947; Moura, "Mapa político," n.p.

20. Edison Carneiro, "Caretas da Bahia," p. 133C, Arquivo Edison Carneiro, Texto 36, 211.2, Biblioteca Amadeu Amaral. Cunha elaborates on the contribution of anonymity to carnivalesque transgression in late-nineteenth-century Rio de Janeiro. See Cunha, *Ecos da folia*, 21–41.

21. José Ferreira, interview by the author, Salvador, 11 November 1999, 115–16.

22. José Ferreira, interviews by the author, Salvador, 4 November 1999, 44–45, and 11 November 1999, 69–70. On restrictions and censorship during carnival, see Cx 6456 Pc 03, 1906–43, Secretaria de Segurança Pública, APEB.

23. For photos, see *Estado da Bahia*, 17 February 1954; and Verger, *Retratos da Bahia*, 126–27.

24. *Momento*, 1 February 1948.

25. José Ferreira, interview by the author, Salvador, 4 November 1999, 45–46.

26. *Diário de Notícias*, 10 March 1943.

27. *Imparcial*, 29 January 1937.

28. During the 1930s, newspapers did not mention politicians or political positions with regard to carnival. This was likely the convention of carnival reporting at the time. However, sporadic correspondence in the Pasta Clubes Carnavalescos in Salvador's municipal archive (the Arquivo Histórico Municipal de Salvador) shows that the mayor's office subsidized the big clubs.

29. *Diário de Notícias*, 11 February 1939.

30. Newspaper articles throughout the period remarked on the waxing and waning of state and especially municipal support for the big clubs. The municipal budget for 1939, the only year available, indicated that in 1939, Cruz Vermelha and Fantoches da Euterpe received 30:000$00 contos de reis each ($1,500), while Inocentes em Progresso received 20:000$000 ($1,000), a not insignificant amount of money at the time. Livro de orçamento de 1939, Fundo Prefeitura Orçamento, Arquivo Histórico Municipal de Salvador (hereafter cited as AHMS).

31. Cornelio Daltro de Azevedo to the Mayor of Salvador, 6 July 1935, Pasta Clubes Carnavalescos, AHMS.

32. See, for example, *Diário de Notícias*, 11 February 1939. See also the possibly tongue-in-cheek report on the unenthusiastic response of the mayor to requests for support for the popular and predominantly African-Bahian carnival in the Plaza Terreiro de Jesus in *A Tarde*, 9 February 1933.

33. *Diário de Notícias*, 13 February 1939.

34. Pierson was in Salvador in 1936 and tells us simply that "the rivalries, especially between Cruz Vermelha and the Fantoshes [sic], are intense, the Inocentes em Progresso appearing to be rather generally admired." Pierson, *Negroes in Brazil*, 201.

35. *Diário de Notícias*, 6 February 1937.

36. *A Tarde*, 24 January 1942.

37. Pierson, *Negroes in Brazil*, 202–3.

38. *Diário de Notícias*, 3 March 1939. From the report in *Diário de Notícias* it would seem that "the delicacy of her features" was the deciding factor for Ms. Gouveia's election.

39. *Diário de Notícias*, 16 January 1939.

40. *Diário de Notícias*, 10 January 1941.

41. *Diário de Notícias*, 22 February 1941; *Diário de Notícias*, 3 February and 7 February 1940.

42. *Diário de Notícias*, 8 March 1943.

43. *Diário de Notícias*, 20 February 1944.

44. *A Tarde*, 1 February 1945; *Diário de Notícias*, 11 February 1945.

45. *Diário de Notícias*, 11 January 1948.

46. At the official exchange rate, one million cruzeiros was fifty-four thousand U.S. dollars.

47. Fundo Prefeitura Orçamento, Livro de orçamento de 1939, AHMS.

48. *A Tarde*, 10 January 1948.

49. *A Tarde*, 28 February 1948; *A Tarde*, 28 February 1949.

50. *Diário de Notícias*, 11 February 1947.

51. *Diário de Notícias*, 25 January 1950; *A Tarde*, 20 January 1951.

52. Caixa Clubes Carnavalescos e Esportivos, AHMS.

53. *A Tarde*, 7 February 1951; *Estado da Bahia*, 17 February 1955.

54. "Animation" in Portuguese referred to the excitement and enthusiasm ordinary Bahians brought to the festivities. The quote contrasting luxuriousness and *batucada* comes from an anonymous interviewee who was comparing Salvador with Rio de Janeiro in *Diário de Notícias*, 10 February 1937. See Queiroz, *Carnaval brasileiro*, 18, on similar distinctions that occurred during São Paulo's carnival.

55. *Diário de Notícias*, 10 January 1938.

56. Teixeira, "Prefácio."

57. Interesting to note that according to Soihet, prior to 1930 the press in Rio de Janeiro rarely mentioned the activities in the Praça Onze, which was the principal site for African-Carioca cultural expression during carnival. After 1930, however, this changed incrementally. See Soihet, *Subversão pelo riso*, 58.

58. For a sampling, see *A Tarde*, 2 February 1930; *A Tarde*, 4 February 1931; *A Tarde*, 25 February 1933; and *A Tarde*, 1 March 1935.

59. Butler, *Freedoms Given, Freedoms Won*, 184–85.

60. *A Tarde*, 20 January 1951.

61. For the *batuque* in post-abolition Salvador, see Fry, Carrara, and Martins-Costa, "Negros e brancos," 252–60.

62. Nina Rodrigues, *Os africanos*; Ramos, *Folclore negro no Brasil*; Mello Moraes, *Festas e tradições*, 76, 132.

63. Pierson, *Negroes in Brazil*, 201.

64. Luciano da Silva, interview by the author, Salvador, 10 November 1999, 30; Inail Alves, interview by the author, Salvador, 18 October 1999, 20.

65. Not long after the record labels began professionalizing samba compositions for a national market, the name *batucada* was given to a type of samba that featured an upbeat tempo and a greater emphasis on percussion.

66. A *tamborim* is a small, stick-beaten frame drum (not to be confused with the English-language tambourine).

67. *Momento*, 5 February 1948. Although the Communist Party in Brazil was effectively outlawed in 1947, *O Momento* continued to publish, albeit increasingly sporadically, until 1957.

68. José Ferreira, interviews by the author, Salvador, 4 November 1999 and 11 November 1999, passim; Luciano da Silva, interview by the author, Salvador, 10 November 1999, passim. Jorge Amado's social realism novels such as *Suor*, *Pais de Carnival*, and *Jubiabá* capture well Salvador's working-class competitive masculinity.

69. *A Tarde*, 17 January 1949.

70. *Momento*, 28 January 1948.

71. *Diário de Notícias*, 10 February 1941.

72. There were some attempts by the regimes in power between 1930 and 1954 to establish more formal political control over the carnival sphere. There were prohibitions on criticizing "the federal, state and municipal authorities"; military and religious associations and institutions; and even consular officers during wartime. There were also local efforts to "moralize" carnival behavior, especially those of the city's working classes, via

punitive restrictions on hard liquor, controls over gambling, and use of *lança perfume*, for instance. See the numerous *portarias* in Cx 6456 Pc 03, 1906–43, Secretaria de Segurança Pública, APEB. For additional information on carnival's relationship to the state outside the realm of cultural politics, see Ickes, "Salvador's Transformist Hegemony," chap. 5.

73. *A Tarde*, 16 January 1951.

74. *A Tarde*, 28 February 1949.

75. *A Tarde*, 31 January 1951; *A Tarde*, 12 January 1951.

76. *Estado da Bahia*, 23 February 1955; *Estado da Bahia*, 2 February 1952; *A Tarde*, 21 January 1953.

77. *Diário de Notícias*, 20 January 1940 and 3 February 1940.

78. *Diário de Notícias*, 18 February 1939.

79. *Festa* II, no. 6 (April 1941).

80. *Diário de Notícias*, 22 February 1939.

81. *Imparcial*, 23 January 1937.

82. Vicente Paiva and Augusto Mesquita, "Bahia, oi . . . Bahia!," original recording by Anjos do Inferno, Columbia, 1940; Vicente Paiva and Chianca de Garcia, "Exaltation of Bahia," original recording by Heleninha Costa, Columbia, 1942.

83. *Diário de Notícias*, 8 January, 19 January, 22 January, 23 January, and 25 January 1953. See also *Diário de Notícias*, 20 January 1940; and *Estado da Bahia*, 5 February 1947 and 14 January 1955. For additional examples of local sambas lyrics, see Cruz, "Samba na roda," chap. 4.

84. "Batatinha," *Enciclopédia nordeste*, http://www.onordeste.com/onordeste/enciclopedianordeste/index.php?titulo=Batata&ltr=b&id_perso=570/.

85. Pedro Caldas, "Bahia é terra boa," *Estado da Bahia*, 13 February 1952. See appendix for lyrics in Portuguese and English translation.

86. "A Batucada gostosa / Faz a morena tão prosa / Cair no santo e sambar," *A Tarde*, 9 February, 1948, quoted in Leal, *Pergunte ao seu avô*, 174–75.

87. *Vivam a loura e a mulata / De sandália de alpercata / E a morena que é meu bem!*

88. *Não façamos distinções / Como as "unidas" Nações.*

89. *A Tarde*, 28 February 1949, quoted in Leal, *Pergunte ao seu avô*, 176–79:

> *Ao passar das batucadas*
> *batendo forte o tambor,*
> *as classes fraternizadas*
> *se encontram no mesmo ardor.*
> *Nessa cadência soturna*
> *a alma da raça noturna*
> *eleva clamores vôos.*
> *E brancos, pretos, mulatos*
> *seguindo os passos exatos*
> *se sentem todos irmãos.*
> *Louras, morenas, mulatas,*
> *De sandália e alpercata,*
> *Sambando no coração!*

90. Raphael, "Samba Schools," 261; Queiroz, *Carnaval brasileiro*, 58–59. On racial democracy in Brazil, see, among others, Hanchard, *Orpheus and Power*; Guimarães, *Classes, raças, e democracia*, 137–46; Twine, *Racism in a Racial Democracy*; and Alberto, *Terms of Inclusion*.

91. Fry, Carrara, and Martins-Costa, "Negros e brancos," 235; *Diário de Notícias*, 4 and 13 February 1944. The year that racial democracy is most explicit in coverage of carnival is 1944, especially in *Diário de Notícias*, 4 February ("the festival annuls prejudice"), 13 February (carnival has at least the one virtue of "effecting an authentic equality of the races"), and February 20.

92. Francisco da Silva Fárrea Júnior and Luís Soberano, "Salve a Princesa," original recording by Trio de Ouro, Odeon, 1948. The Portuguese: *Preto não é mais lacaio / Preto não tem mais senhor. . . . / Hoje preto pode ser doutor / Deputado e senador.* The group was reported on in *O Momento*, 1 February 1948. There was also a *bloco* in Bahia called Preto não é Mais Lacaio in the late 1940s. It is worth noting a parallel phenomenon in late 1940s Rio de Janeiro, where the carnival club Unidos de Tijuca was expressing politicized African-Brazilian racial pride and alternative readings of the myth of racial democracy in its carnival costumes and allegorical floats. See Tupy, *Carnavais de guerra*, 112–13.

93. Alberto, *Terms of Inclusion*, 179; Fuente, *Nation for All*.

94. "Homenagem a Liberdade," *Estado da Bahia*, 28 January 1955.

95. *Diário de Notícias*, 9 January 1954. See also *A Tarde*, 19 February, 1954.

96. Tavares, "Rodas de Samba."

97. "Desfile de batucadas," *A Tarde*, 20 January 1951.

98. *Diário de Notícias*, 21 January 1953.

99. Lima, "Meu Carnaval da Bahia," *A Tarde*, 25 February 1954; De Brito, "Carnaval," *A Tarde*, 25 February 1954.

100. *Estado da Bahia*, 2 February and 27 February 1952. For a photograph that was published in the 27 February issue, literally dozens of Baianas posed in front of the giant tabuleiro/stage.

101. *A Tarde*, 16 February 1953.

102. *Estado da Bahia*, 11 February 1949; *A Tarde*, 3 February 1949.

103. Guerreiro, "Trilhas do samba-reggae," 120–22.

104. *Estado da Bahia*, 2 February 1952. See also the documents in the Caixa Clubes Carnavalescos e Esportivos, AHMS.

105. José Ferreira, interview by the author, Salvador, 11 November 1999, 112.

106. Guerreiro, "Trilhas do samba-reggae," 120–22; José Ferreira, interview by the author, Salvador, 11 November 1999, 111–12; Godi, "De índio a negro."

107. See, for example, *Diário de Notícias*, 3 February 1940.

108. There is some disagreement over the use of *afoxé* for the Embaixada Africana and Pândegos da África. The Embaixada Africana may more rightly be considered a carnival club than an *afoxé* despite the fact that it had linkages with members of the Candomblé community. Fry, Carrara, and Martins-Costa see Pândegos da África as an intermediary group "bringing into contact and communication distinct value systems"; see Fry, Carrara, and Martins-Costa, "Negros e brancos," 262. Risério suggests that the press temporarily accepted the two institutions as improvements on the "horrors" of carnival's predecessor, the Entrudo; see Risério, "Carnaval," 92. See also Carneiro, *Folguedos tradicionais*, 102; and Vieira Filho, "Africanização do carnaval de Salvador," 20–21, 115, 181–90.

109. Butler, *Freedoms Given, Freedoms Won*, 176–82.

110. Albuquerque, "Esperanças de Boaventuras," 220.

111. Carneiro, Félix, Nina Rodrigues, and Querino were the first to discuss the *afoxés* of the late nineteenth century. See Carneiro, *Folguedos tradicionais*, 102; Félix, *Filhos de Gandhi*; Nina Rodrigues, *Africanos*; and Manuel Querino, *Raça*. See also Butler, *Freedoms Given, Freedoms Won*, 175–85.

112. For instance, as early as 1931 the *Diário da Bahia* mentioned that "Ubá África" [*sic;* "Obá África"] was inviting its associates to an *ensaio*, or warmup, at the end of which would be a feast of the typical food of the Candomblé community—"vatapá, acarajé, abará"—suggesting that Ubá África was an *afoxé*. But the *Diário da Bahia* described them as a "carnival Club" (*club carnavalesco*). See *Diário da Bahia*, 13 February 1931. Meanwhile, the organizers of carnival in the largely African-Bahian working-class neighborhood of Maciel de Baixo offered a prize for the "best *cordão 'affoxé'* [*sic*]" in 1933. *A Tarde*, 25 February 1933.

113. Carneiro, *Sabedoria popular*, 111; see also Tavares and Verger, "Afoxé, ritmo bárbaro."

114. *Momento*, 4 February 1948. For the *afoxé* Congo d'África in the late 1940s, one director was a woman, but the other seven members of the *diretoria*—the director, secretary, treasurer, song director (*cobrador*), speaker (*orador*), band treasurer (*fiscal da charanga*), and band master (*contra-mestre*)—were all men.

115. Jaime Moreira de Pinho, interview by Félix, in *Filhos de Gandhi*; Pierson, *Negroes in Brazil*, 201.

116. Santos, *Axé Opô Afonjá*, 92.

117. Ibid., 90–95.

118. In 1942, 30 cruzeiros (30$000) was worth $2.50, and 10 cruzeiros (10$000) was worth just under $1.00.

119. Santos, *Axé Opô Afonjá*, 94.

120. Carneiro, *Candomblés da Bahia*, 20.

121. Santos, *Axé Opô Afonjá*, 95.

122. Félix, *Filhos de Gandhi*; Morales, "Afoxé filhos de Gandhi"; Djalma Conceição, interview by Félix, in *Filhos de Gandhi*.

123. *Diário de Notícias*, 18 January 1953.

124. Lody, *Afoxé*, 5–6.

125. *Diário da Bahia*, 22 Janurary 1938.

126. *Estado da Bahia*, 23 February 1955.

127. *Momento*, 4 February 1948.

128. Tavares and Verger, "Afoxé, ritmo bárbaro."

129. Ibid., 57.

130. Davis, *Society and Culture*, chaps. 4 and 5.

131. The number of small clubs was increasing throughout the 1930s, even before the definitive decline of the elite clubs, even though the well-established small clubs probably numbered less than forty. The war in Europe and its economic consequences decreased the number of small clubs on the streets. However, they rebounded during the 1940s.

132. On the social context of the working-class neighborhood clubs, see Amado, *Jubiabá*, 295–319; and *Diário de Notícias*, 4 and 6 January 1945.

133. Secretaria de Segurança Pública, Cx 21, Pc 1, Partes da Polícia 1941, APEB; José Ferreira, interview by the author, Salvador, 11 November 1999, 66–68; Deôdeto Porto, interview by the author, Salvador, 4 November 1999, 44–45.

134. José Ferreira, interview by the author, Salvador, 11 November 1999, 72–73.

135. See, among others, Walter Santos, secretary of the Commission of Carnival Festivity of the Rua do Uruguay to Wanderley Pinho, Mayor, 1 February 1950, in Caixa Clubes Carnavalescos e Esportivos, AHMS.

136. *Estado da Bahia*, 2 February 1952.

137. *Diário de Notícias*, 7 February 1947.

138. One must not lose sight of Campos's point that these festivals were originally founded by the exuberant masses and devotees of popular Catholicism and that their profane nature was always evident. See Campos, *Procissões*, passim.

139. I use "carnivalesque" here to generalize about the presence of small clubs and music typical of Bahian carnival rather than in the Bahktinian sense of the inversion of the social order. See Bahktin, *Rabelais and His World*. Some of this momentary inversion may have been present, however. Indeed, such momentary inversion may have played a role in the spread of carnival to the other popular religious festivals in the first place.

140. Santana, *Alma e festa*, 196–99.

141. *Diário de Notícias*, 19 January 1938.

142. *A Tarde*, 15 January 1942.

143. *Diário de Notícias*, 18 January 1946.

144. *Imparcial*, 1925, quoted in Hildegardes Vianna, "Noite de Reis," http://www.fundacaocultural.ba.gov.br/04/revista%20da%20bahia/Folguedos/noite.htm/. The June festivals of Saint John, Saint Anthony, and Saint Peter were also already partially devoted to traditional samba by the 1930s even though those festivals had their own musical traditions. *Batucadas* were popular there, too, by 1937 and 1938. These festivals, however, remain outside the scope of this study.

145. José Ferreira, interview by the author, Salvador, 11 November 1999, 113.

146. *Diário de Notícias*, 4 January 1939, 5 January 1940, and 2 January 1941.

147. *Imparcial*, 6 January 1937; *Diário de Notícias*, 6 January 1939; *A Tarde*, 4 January 1942.

148. *Diário de Notícias*, 4 and 6 January 1945 and 5 January 1950.

149. *Diário de Notícias*, 5 January 1944.

150. Vianna, "Noite de Reis." Couto observed a similar carnivalization in the 1970s in Ilhéus at the Festival of the Hauling of the Mast. See Couto, *Puxada do mastro*, 186–87.

151. *Imparcial*, 6 January 1937 and 4 January 1942; *Diário de Notícias*, 5 January 1944 and 5 January 1947.

152. *Estado da Bahia*, 30 December 1950.

153. Pierson, *Negroes in Brazil*, 201–2.

154. José Ferreira, interview by author, Salvador, 4 November 1999, 31. In 1949, a photograph of the fifteen members of the "Feminine Wing" of the elite club Inocentes em Progresso revealed only light complexions. *A Tarde*, 22 February 1949. Pierson has some excellent anecdotal passages on racial and racist assumptions among white Bahians in *Negroes in Brazil*, chaps. 1–8.

155. *Estado da Bahia*, 19 February 1955.

156. Pierson, *Negroes in Brazil*, 202.

157. Verger, *Retratos da Bahia*, 122–35. See photographs of the carnival group Mexican Embassy at http://www.pierreverger.org/.

158. Walkyrio Meyer and Delza Meyer, interview by the author, Salvador, 21 October 1999, 14–16.

159. Verger, *Retratos da Bahia*, 122–24.

160. Antônia Conceição, interview by the author, Salvador, 2 November 1999, 38.

161. Edison Carneiro, "Caretas da Bahia," p. 133A, Texto 36, 211.2, Arquivo Edison Carneiro, Biblioteca Amadeu Amaral.

162. *A Tarde*, 26 July 1937. For a newspaper editorial concerned with the "great number" forced to "beg for charity . . . [on] every corner" during carnival, disrupting the gaiety of the celebrations, see *Diário de Notícias*, 18 February 1947.

163. *Imparcial*, 11 February 1937; Leal, *Pergunte ao seu avô*, 205–6. Três e Meio was one of Dorival Caymmi's early bands.

164. Walkyrio Meyer and Delza Meyer, interview by the author, Salvador, 21 October 1999, 27–28; José Ferreira, interview by author, Salvador, 4 November 1999, 38–41.

165. *A Tarde*, 19 March 1935. For additional examples of samba at the "wrong" time or place and even a suggestion that samba affected worker productivity, see *A Tarde*, 18 May 1946 and 4 December 1947, quoted in Cruz, "Samba na roda," 43.

166. "Originalidades," *Imparcial*, 10 March 1937; "Opinões musicais," *Imparcial*, 17 March 1937, discussed in Cruz, "Samba na roda," 44–48.

167. Pedro Calmon, "Sr. José Lins é a favor do samba," *Estado da Bahia*, 15 July 1937. See also McCann, *Hello, Hello Brazil*, 63–65.

168. In extending their presence, the *afoxés* were playing the role described for them by Sodré, as "mytho-cultural patrimony" and as "poles of African-Brazilian ethnic identification." Sodré, *Terreiro e a cidade*, 62.

169. *Estado da Bahia*, 23 February 1955 and 27 February 1952.

170. Leal, *Pergunte ao seu avô*, 205–9; Góes, *50 anos do trio elétrico*, 40–51.

171. *Diário de Notícias*, 4 February 1954.

172. *A Tarde*, 7 February 1955.

173. Davis, *Society and Culture*, chaps. 4 and 5.

174. Tavares and Verger, "Afoxé, ritmo bárbaro," 57.

Chapter 6. The Project of Regional Identity Formation

1. The ban was lifted in 1952, but the Washing of Bonfim was canceled at the last minute that year because of a tragic bus accident that killed eighteen people in the Bonfim neighborhood days before the event.

2. Risério discusses some of the contributions in the 1950s of "the vanguard" of artists, musicians, scholars, and filmmakers and focuses on the creation of a distinct "cultural personality" in Salvador, while Sansi-Roca focuses primarily on the modernists who were working in the plastic arts and their relationship to and use of African-Bahian culture. See Risério, *Avant-garde na Bahia*; Sansi-Roca, *Fetishes and Monuments*.

3. Guimarães, "Religião popular," 93. In 1951, the Federação, under President Jorge Manoel da Rocha, publicly criticized the publishing of photographs of Candomblé initiation rituals in *Paris-Match*, and it later criticized a *mãe-de-santo* who had allowed access

to sacred rituals for a piece published in *O Cruzeiro*. Their intention was to protect the secrecy of the ritual and the public image of Candomblé. See Tacca, *Imagens do sagrado*.

4. Tavares and Verger, "Decadência e morte da lavagem," 76, 103. On the involvement of Miguel Santana, see *Diário de Notícias*, 10 January 1940. On the participation of João da Gomeia, see *Diário de Notícias*, 14 January 1944.

5. *Diário de Notícias*, 15 January 1953.

6. Sansi-Roca, *Fetishes and Monuments*, 57.

7. Santos, *Yorubá tal qual se fala*; Oliveira, "Agostinho de Silva," 130–31.

8. Book I, 9, 12–16, HFN.

9. *A Tarde*, 1 December 1955; *Estado da Bahia*, 27 March 1951. Monteiro was at one point the president of the Ebé Oxossi Civil Society of the Terreiro Gantois and had a leadership position in the Federation of African-Brazilian Cults of Candomblé, although it is not clear if he held these or similar positions in the early 1950s. Salvador's auxiliary bishop from 1951 was Antônio Mendonça Monteiro, a different person altogether.

10. *A Tarde*, 14 May and 9 July 1951.

11. *Diário de Notícias*, 16 January 1953 and 3 January 1954. For the composition of the commission in 1954, see *Estado da Bahia*, 12 January 1954. See also Monteiro, "Procissão folclórica."

12. *Estado da Bahia*, 9 January 1950 and 11 January 1951.

13. Interview with Monteiro conducted by Guimarães, in Guimarães, "Religião popular," 98.

14. Guimarães, "Religião popular," 98.

15. *Estado da Bahia*, 14 January 1953.

16. *Estado da Bahia*, 15 January 1954.

17. *Diário de Notícias*, 8 January and 11 January 1953.

18. *Diário de Notícias*, 14 January 1953.

19. *Estado da Bahia*, 16 January 1954.

20. *Diário de Notícias*, 16 January 1953; Guimarães, "Religião popular," 98.

21. *Estado da Bahia*, 13 February 1950.

22. Vianna, *Casos e coisas da Bahia*; Vianna, *Cozinha bahiana*; Brandão, *Cozinha bahiana*. Also published during this period were Lima, *Festa de Egun*, complete with *calorosos elogios* (enthusiastic praise) from Gustavo Barroso on the back flap; Querino, *Raça*; Carneiro, *Candomblés da Bahia*; Viana Filho, *Negro na Bahia*; and Valladares and Carybé, *Torça da bahiana*.

23. *Diário de Notícias*, 10 January 1950; Almeida, "Folclore na sociedade Baciana," 167–72.

24. For more on the regional and national importance of "folklore studies" in Brazil, see Vilhena, *Projeto e missão*. For the statistics see Vilhena, *Projeto e missão*, 302–3. Interestingly, from 1953 to 1963, the Comissão Bahiana commissioned only seven articles.

25. See Monteiro, "Propagadores da tradição" in the Rio de Janeiro daily *O Globo*.

26. *A Tarde*, 9 April 1951.

27. *Estado da Bahia*, 17 January 1952; *Diário da Bahia*, 26 July 1953. The National Congress of Folklore was held in Salvador in 1957.

28. Assunção shows these accusations to be wide of the mark and rather nonsensical. See Assunção, *Capoeira*, 144–46.

29. Ibid., 155.

30. Amado, *Bahia de todos os santos*, 210; Assunção, *Capoeira*, 141.

31. Sansi-Roca, *Fetishes and Monuments*, 54–55; Bastide, *Candomblé da Bahia*. See also Romo, *Brazil's Living Museum*, 148–49; and Capone, "Transatlantic Dialogue."

32. Verger told an interviewer that Jorge Amado's novel *Jubiabá* had inspired him to visit the city. Amado's novel about a Candomblé priest is set in and around the bar called the Lantern of the Drowned, the haunt of prostitutes, musicians, bohemians, and *malandros* (Brazilian street hustlers). Verger, *Depoimento à Corrupio Vídeo*, 1986, quoted in Nóbrega and Echeverria, *Verger*, 150.

33. Ibid., 158.

34. Lody and Baradel, *Olhar viajante de Pierre Fatumbí Verger*; Verger, Pivin, and Saint Léon, *Messager*.

35. Rolim, "Primeiras imagens," chap. 2.

36. Nóbrega and Echeverria, *Verger*, 458–61.

37. Tavares and Verger, "Decadência e morte da lavagem."

38. Rolim, "Primeiras imagens"; Lühning, *Pierre Verger*, 19–20.

39. Barbosa, "Imagens de Salvador."

40. Verger, *50 anos de fotografia*, 255–58. Verger's influence in enriching the "Africanness" of Bahia has been pointed out by Risério, *Avant-garde na Bahia*, 88–89, and long ago by Fry, "*Gallus africanus est*."

41. Verger and Bastide, *Verger/Bastide*; Sansi-Roca, *Fetishes and Monuments*, 53–57; Bastide, *Candomblé da Bahia*. See also Romo, *Brazil's Living Museum*, 148–49.

42. Verger, interview with Corrupio Video, 1986, quoted in Nóbrega and Echevarria, *Verger*, 178; Métraux to Herskovits, 29 January 1951, 323.1 "Race Questions," UNESCO Archive, Paris; Métraux, "Inquiry into Race Relations in Brazil."

43. According to Lühning, this perspective intensely irritated Melville Herskovits because to Herskovits, Verger's traveling back and forth remixed West African and Bahian religious culture and jeopardized what Herskovits saw as the "natural laboratory" of Salvador. Lühning, "Pierre Fabumbí Verger," 4.

44. Nóbrega and Echevarria, *Verger*, 179.

45. Pai-de-Santo Eduardo Ijexá also benefited from Verger's travels and his willingness to deliver correspondence between Eduardo Ijexá and the king of Ilesha. Nóbrega and Echevarria, *Verger*, 178, 204.

46. Alberto, *Terms of Inclusion*, 223.

47. Sansi-Roca, *Fetishes and Monuments*, 71. See also Alberto, *Terms of Inclusion*, 224–26.

48. Pinho, *Mensagem-Relatório*, 31.

49. See the August 1936 correspondence between the Bahian Section of the Touring Club of Brazil, the mayor's office, and Meridional Films in Caixa Clubes Carnavelesco e Esportivos, AHMS.

50. *Diário de Notícias*, 3 January 1940 and 31 March 1942; *Estado da Bahia*, 15 January 1952.

51. *Diário da Bahia*, 7 February 1941.

52. *Estado da Bahia*, 31 January 1947.

53. Queiroz, "Gestão pública e a competitividade," chap. 4.

54. Yearns to Johnson, 18 April 1949, RG 84, Classified General Records, Salvador, Box 72, 1949, NARA II.

55. Queiroz, "Gestão pública e a competitividade," 314.

56. Tavares and Verger, "Decadência e morte da lavagem."

57. In 1955, *Estado da Bahia* criticized the two previous mayors for not having done enough for the popular festivals, although they had focused on improving carnival. According to the daily, the attitude in the mayor's office toward tourism had changed for the better in 1955; it congratulated Mayor Hélio Machado for improving both Conceição da Praia and Senhor dos Navegantes for tourism. It did not specify what "improving" the festivals actually meant, but this usually indicated providing more resources for decoration, organization, policing, and subsidies for participants and live music. On the tourist tax and the Amigos of the City, see Queiroz, "Gestão pública e a competitividade," 319–20; and *Diário de Notícias*, 14 January 1953.

58. Two other "grand" hotels in Bahia were built with state funds and were inaugurated with great fanfare in the early 1950s. The Grande Hotel de Cipó, located to the north of Salvador (which was inaugurated by President Getúlio Vargas), and the Grande Hotel de Itaparica, which was located on the principal island in Salvador's Bay of All Saints. *A Tarde*, 11 January 1952.

59. *A Tarde*, 27 December 1955.

60. Moura, "Capoeira," quoted in Capoeira, *Capoeira*, 199.

61. *Estado da Bahia*, 16 February 1954.

62. *A Tarde*, 5 January 1959; Pasta Recortes, Fundação Pierre Verger (hereafter cited as FPV).

63. *Imparcial*, 29 January 1937; *Diário de Notícias*, 10 February and 5 March 1938.

64. *A Tarde*, 28 February 1949; Leal, *Pergunte ao seu avô*, 30.

65. Arlindo Gomes to the Mayor of Salvador, 17 February 1954, Caixa Clubes Carnavalescos e Esportivos, AHMS; Queiroz, "Evolução do sistema institucional público"; Queiroz, "Gestão pública e a competitividade," 299–337.

66. *Diário de Notícias*, 25 February 1938.

67. *Diário de Notícias*, 9 January 1948 and 31 January 1940.

68. Leal, *Pergunte ao seu avô*, 200.

69. *A Tarde*, 16 November 1950.

70. Solange Bernabó, personal communication with the author, Salvador, 28 May 2009.

71. Andrade et al. suggest this insight into the development of Carybé's work after the 1950s. Andrade, Andrade, and Freire, "Avant-Garde na Bahia."

72. Tavares, *Festa do Bonfim*.

73. Risério, *Avant-garde na Bahia*, 22, 39–40, 47.

74. *Diário da Bahia*, 15 January 1937.

75. *Diário de Notícias*, 16 January 1953.

76. *Diário de Notícias*, 21 January 1953.

77. In 1945, Jorge Amado was elected to the federal legislature on the Communist Party ticket. Indeed, many of the literati and most public intellectuals in Bahia were either active members of the Communist Party or at least sympathetic to a leftist progressive social agenda.

78. Many contributors to *O Momento* also contributed to the Communist Party's intellectual journal *Revista Seiva*, which was in circulation in 1950 and 1951. *Revista Seiva*

was much more theoretical and literary and rarely dealt directly with working-class life in Salvador.

79. See the bibliography for the numerous articles Odorico Tavares wrote for *O Cruzeiro* on Bahian society and culture.

80. Tavares, "Conceicão da Praia."

81. Tavares, "Rodas de samba na Bahia"; Tavares and Verger, "Capoeira"; Tavares and Verger, "Afoxé."

82. *Estado da Bahia*, 18 June 1956.

83. *Estado da Bahia*, 28 March 1949; Tavares, Amado, and Carybé, *Discurso de um cidadão*.

84. Cruz, "Samba na roda," 94. Gileno Amado was named as the president of Radio Sociedade, and Tavares was given the more important position of general director.

85. "História," Sociedade online, http://www.radiosociedadeam.com.br/portal/historia.aspx/ (accessed 28 June 2012). Radio Sociedade was under the artistic direction of Mestre Jatobá in 1939.

86. Cruz, "Samba na roda," 94–95.

87. *Diário de Notícias*, 2 February 1954; Leal, "Africanos no Brasil"; Leal, "Capoeira"; Leal, *Pergunte ao seu avô*, 187–88.

88. Nascimento, "Movimento *Caderno da Bahia*," 165.

89. Gomes, "Presença," 189. The first wave began with pioneering Bahian modernist poet Godofredo Filho, who published "Poema Candomblé" in *O Jornal* in 1927. Jorge Amado was the most popular writer of this literature.

90. Santana, "Caleidoscópio," 82–83.

91. Nascimento, "Movimento *Caderno da Bahia*," 94–96. See also Rocha, "Influências africanas nas artes da Bahia."

92. "Que é que a Bahia tem," *Correio Paulistano*, 15 September 1961. See also *A Tarde*, 17 December 1961, which carried mention of the award and a reprint of Tavares's essay, "Lagoa de Abaeté," including designs by Carybé.

93. Amado, *Bahia de todos os santos*. By 1973, this guide was in its twenty-fourth edition.

94. Caymmi, *Cancioneiro da Bahia*. For the *balangandans* as fashion statement, see *Diário de Notícias*, 21 January 1953.

95. Peixoto, *Breviário da Bahia*; Tourinho, *Alma e corpo da Bahia*; Tavares, *Bahia*; Valladares, *Bêabá da Bahia*; and Lima, *Roteiro da Bahia*. For the contributions of Carlos Thiré, see *Estado da Bahia*, 17 February 1950; and Lima, *Roteiro da Bahia*.

96. On Zweig, see Peixoto, *Breviário da Bahia*, 128–29. Zweig's account was repeated in several Bahian dailies in the early 1940s.

97. Amaral, *Blaise Cendrars no Brasil*.

98. Peixoto, *Breviário da Bahia*, 128–29.

99. Freyre himself contributed to this elision with a somewhat bizarre eulogy to the "aristocratic sudenese negro," which Freyre claimed was preferred by urban businessmen in Salvador and was of "special importance" to Brazilian democracy. See Freyre, "Prefácio," 15.

100. Rocha, "Odorico Tavares."

101. Sansi-Roca, *Fetishes and Monuments*, 127–28. See also Paraíso, "Entrevista Juarez Paraíso."

102. Scaldaferri, *Primórdios*; Sansi-Roca, *Fetishes and Monuments*, 127–34. The first art exhibit the U.S. embassy sponsored in Bahia was in 1944; it sponsored several more in the late 1940s.

103. See, for example, José Valladares, "Salão Baiano," 11 November 1951, Pacote Recortes Literários, FPV.

104. Bastos, *Carlos Bastos*, 40.

105. *Estado da Bahia*, 1 December 1951. Cravo Júnior also won third prize at the first Bienal Internacional de São Paulo in 1951.

106. Araujo, "Odorico Tavares," 20.

107. The Salon Baiano of 1954 showcased approximately ninety pieces of art; see Valladares, *Artes maiores e menores*, 159.

108. Valladares, *Dominicais*.

109. *Estado da Bahia*, 4 December 1949; Valladares, "Belas Artes na Bahia de hoje."

110. Ludwig, "Mudanças na vida cultural de Salvador," 15n13; Santana, "Odorico Tavares," 26.

111. Risério remarks that Carybé was such a frequent visitor to the workshop of Mário Cravo Júnior that he "could be considered part of the furniture." Risério, *Avant-garde na Bahia*, 79.

112. Tavares and Verger, "Rafael, o pintor."

113. Risério, *Avante-garde*.

Conclusion and Epilogue

1. On these transformations, see Oliveira, *Elo perdido*; Jelin, "Formas de organização"; and Vianna, Souza, and Faria, *Bahia de todos os pobres*.

2. Singer, "Economia urbana," quoted in Risério, *História da cidade da Bahia*, 518.

3. Guimarães, "Formação e a crise," 68–118; Borges, "Modernidade negociada," 20–24; Romo, "Race and Reform in Bahia," 243. Guimarães establishes the founding of Petrobras as central to this periodization; see Guimarães, *Sonho de classe*, 50–51.

4. For an example of how this combination was entering into the dominant discourse by the end of the Vargas era, in 1952 the director of publicity of the Flamengo Boating Club in Rio de Janeiro contacted the mayor's office in Salvador for help in putting together a charity event for blind children, to be held in the national capital. The minister of education was scheduled to attend and the event was to be filmed and televised. The theme of the event was "A Night in Bahia," and the centerpiece of the decoration was to be a mock *adro* of the Church of Bonfim measuring three meters by five meters. The director of publicity pointed out that he was Bahian and went on to request "some liters of our petroleum" to place in glass jars to sell. Antônio Fraga Mascarenhas to Sr. Prefeito da Cidade de Salvador, 21 May 1952, Caixa Clubes Carnavalescos e Esportivos, AHMS.

5. Queiroz, "Gestão pública e a competitividade." Serra has written on this with respect to the Festival of Bonfim; see Serra, *Rumores de festa*, 87–90.

6. Mariano, *Invenção da baianidade*, 23.

7. Weinstein, *For Social Peace in Brazil*; Vianna, *Mystery of Samba*; Soihet, *Subversão pelo riso*; Blake, *Vigorous Core of Our Nationality*; Oliven, *Tradition Matters*. For the ways that specific ethnic groups rather than regional elites engaged similar strategies, see Lesser, *Negotiating National Identity*.

8. Weinstein, "Racializing Regional Difference," 240.

9. Blake, *Vigorous Core of Our Nationality*, 221.

10. Oliven, *Tradition Matters*, 82–88; Wade, *Blackness and Race Mixture*; Applebaum has discussed the racialization of regional identities in Latin America; see Applebaum, *Muddied Waters*.

11. Dantas, *Vovó Nagô*, 150–65. Quotes from Freyre, *Casa grande e senzala*, in Dantas, *Vovó Nagô*, 158.

12. Kittleson, *Practice of Politics*; Woodard, *Place in Politics*.

13. See, for example, Moore, *Nationalizing Blackness*; Wade, *Music, Race and Nation*; Andrews, *Blackness in the White Nation*; Chasteen, *National Rhythms*. For analyses of more recent manifestations of similar cultural politics, see Hagedorn, *Divine Utterances*; and Brown, *Light Inside*. See also Paul Gilroy's widely influential *Black Atlantic*.

14. See, for example, Thomas, *Modern Blackness*; and Williams, *Stains on My Name*. See also Burton, *Afro-Creole*; and Waters, *Race, Class, and Political Symbols*.

15. *Semana Cathólica*, 11 January 1953. For further examples of negative representations of Candomblé in the 1950s, see also Santos, *Poder da cultura e a cultura no poder*, 55–63.

16. Silva, "Carta Pastoral," quoted in Guimarães, "Religião popular," 85.

17. *Estado da Bahia*, 6 February 1954.

18. Mouffe, "Hegemony and Ideology in Gramsci," 191–92; Nascimento, "Sociologia," quoted in Alberto, *Terms of Inclusion*, 219–20. See also Ortiz, *Consciência fragmentada*, 45–66; Williams, *Stains on My Name*, 31.

19. Azevedo, "Comportamento," 149, discussed in Romo, *Brazil's Living Museum*, 147.

20. Romo, *Brazil's Living Museum*, 150, 178–79.

21. Assunção, *Capoeira*, 157.

22. *Diário de Notícias*, 14 January, 1945.

23. Roseberry, "Hegemony and the Language of Contention," 358–61.

24. Ibid., 361.

25. Knight, "Weapons and Arches," 43n1.

26. Costa, *Brazilian Empire*, chap. 9; Hasenbalg, *Discriminação e desigualdades raciais*, 256; Raphael, "Samba and Social Control"; Fry, *Para inglês ver*; Hanchard, *Orpheus and Power*; Davis, *Avoiding the Dark*; Alberto, *Terms of Inclusion*. For Bahia, see Bacelar, *Hierarquia das raças*; Agier, *Anthropologie du carnaval*; and Risério, *Avant-garde na Bahia*. Santos examines how African-Bahian culture became a "trademark" for Bahia from the 1960s, supporting the notion of racial democracy in official foreign policy circles; see Santos, *Poder da cultura e a cultura no poder*. See also Alberto, *Terms of Inclusion*, Chapters 3, 5, and 6.

27. Bastide, "Manifestações de preconceito," 124, quoted in Santos, *Poder da cultura e a cultura no poder*, 13.

28. *A Tarde*, October 1, 1932. When the Frente Negra da Bahia was establishing itself, an announcement of its founding described it as "something new (*novidade*) for . . . men of color, for whom among us no distinction is made"; Azevedo, *Elites de cor*, 186, quoted in Bacelar, *Hierarquia das raças*, 153. The year that racial democracy is most explicit in coverage of carnival is 1944, especially in the *Diário de Notícias*: 4 February ("the festival during which prejudice disappears and equality between the races becomes a reality for 72 hours"); 13 February (carnival has at least the one virtue of "effecting a true equality of the races"); and 20 February (when the caption for a photo of soldiers called attention to the different racial groups represented).

29. Dantas, *Vovó Nagô*, 149–50; Alberto, *Terms of Inclusion*, 112–27; Lühning, "Acabe com este santo"; Lima, "Candomblé da Bahia na década de trinta"; Sansi-Roca, *Fetishes and Monuments*, 51–61; Castillo, *Entre a oralidade*, 120–25; Romo, *Brazil's Living Museum*, 10–12.

30. Risério, *Avant-garde en Bahia*, 60–61, 111–21.

31. Bacelar, *Hierarquia das raças*, 131–35.

32. Alberto, "Para africano ver"; Dávila, *Hotel Trópico*, 55–59.

33. Bacelar, *Hierarchia das raças*, 135–36. See also Bairros, "Pecados."

34. Risério, *Carnaval Ijexá*, 16. See also Butler, "Afterword: Ginga Bahiana," 167–70.

35. Quoted in Risério, *Carnaval Ijexá*, 19. Such politics of identity go much further back of course, but carnival was Risério's frame of reference and Bahian carnival did not begin until the late nineteenth century.

36. Risério, *Carnaval Ijexá*, 20. See also Silverstein, "Celebration of Our Lord of the Good End."

37. Risério, *Carnaval Ijexá*, 11; Risério, *História da cidade da Bahia*, 578–79.

38. This bridging conceptualization also informs the work of Butler, "Afterword: Ginga Baiana"; and Guerreiro, "Trilhas do samba-reggae," 122.

39. Risério, *Carnaval Ijexá*, 7, 20–37, 71–75.

40. Butler, "Afterword," 168.

41. For a negative reaction from segments of the dominant class to the founding of Ilê Aiyê, see Silva, "História de lutas negras," 278–81.

42. Queiroz, "Evolução do sistema institucional público," chap. 5; Risério, *História da cidade da Bahia*, 581–82.

43. Salvador sought to attract exchange students from the southeast to "experience the city in its music, on its beaches, in its Candomblé, in its folklore, in its history, in its traditions, and in the tenderness of its people." *A Tarde*, 6 October 1972, quoted in Santos, "Mixed-Race Nation," 123.

44. A representative sample of work on ethnic identity, black consciousness, and religious belief systems in the contexts of state formation, uneven modernization, and globalization would include Agier, "Between Affliction and Politics"; Santos, "Mixed-Race Nation"; Sansone, *Blackness without Ethnicity*; Sansone and Santos, *Ritmos em trânsito*; Pinho, *Mama Africa*; Guerreiro, *Trama dos tambores*; Perrone and Dunn, *Brazilian Popular Music*, chaps. 2 and 8–12; McGowan and Pessanha, *Brazilian Sound*, chap. 6; Armstrong, "Bahian Carnival"; Collins, *Revolt of the Saints*. See also Albergaria, "Festas populares baianas"; *A Tarde*, 4 December 2003, "Caderno 1." On the race relations bound up with contemporary policy debates about education and affirmative action, see Reiter, "Inequality and School Reform in Bahia"; and Santos and Queiroz, "Sistema de Cotas." Sansi-Roca suggests that the association of Candomblé with blackness is being undermined by the gravitation of its grass roots—"masses of poor, black people"—to Pentecostalism; see Sansi-Roca, *Fetishes and Monuments*, 185–93. Selka explores the relationship between evangelical churches and Candomblé in *Religion and Ethnic Identity*, in which he also explores Bahia's religious heterogeneity and the various ways this heterogeneity informs ethnic identity and racial politics in Salvador. See also Selka, "Ethnoreligious Identity Politics in Bahia."

45. Pinho, *Mama Africa*, 198–205.

Glossary

adro: An open space at the front or side of a church, often paved or gated.

afoxé: A carnival association that is either an extension of a *terreiro* or that relies heavily on membership and musical styles of the *terreiros*.

atabaque: narrow conical drums used in Candomblé and other African-Brazilian musical styles, similar to the conga drum.

baiana: An African-Brazilian woman of Candomblé, typically of some standing within her *terreiro*.

babalaô: A male diviner within Yoruban Candomblé tradition.

barraca: A tent, canopy, or similar temporary structure for selling food and drink.

batucada: Both an African-Brazilian carnival association and the percussive samba style associated with it.

batuque: Historically a festive gathering centered around African-Brazilian percussion music, and the type of music associated with the gatherings.

berimbau: A percussion instrument central to setting the rhythms for capoeira, played by striking a wire strung on a bow with a thin stick.

bloco afro: A type of afro-centric carnival association that emerged in the 1970s and embraced African-Bahian cultural heritage.

caboclo: An Indian deity and a tradition within Candomblé that emphasizes the worship of these deities. Also a term for a non-tribal Indian or someone of mixed-race Indian heritage.

canção-praieira: Genre of song by and about the life of coastal fisherman.

cântico: Religious hymn.

capoeira angola: A style of capoeira that emphasizes African roots.

capoeira regional: A style of capoeira that has incorporated aspects from other martial art traditions.

caruru: An African-Bahian dish made from okra considered "holy food" for certain deities within Candomblé. Also a term for a social or spiritual event during which *caruru* is served.

cuíca: A friction drum common to samba played by pulling a thin stick through the drum head.

feitas: Initiates of a Candomblé *terreiro*.

feitiço: A number of charms, spells, or the act of using magic within African-Bahian religions.

figa: A protective amulet worm by people especially within Candomblé.

filha-de-santo (plural, *filhas-de-santo*): A woman initiate within a Candomblé *terreiro*.

galeota: A small- to medium-sized boat, typically with oars and sails.

imagem: A statue or representation of a religious figure.

largo: A square or plaza, often associated with a church.

macumba: Older term for African-Brazilian religion and associated musical styles.

mãe-de-santo: Candomblé priestess. Female leader of a Candomblé *terreiro*.

olhador (plural, *olhadores*): Diviner or seer within Candomblé.

orixá: A deity within Candomblé.

padroeira (male, *padroeiro*): patron saint or protector.

pai-de-santo: Candomblé priest. Male leader of a Candomblé *terreiro*.

pandeiro: A Brazilian tambourine.

piaçava: A palm with fibers suitable for making brooms, weaving, or thatching.

povo-de-santo: The "people of the saint," or those with commitments to Candomblé belief systems and ritual.

rocinha: Small urban plot of fruit trees and/or medicinal herbs.

roda de samba: Small to medium gathering of participants and onlookers for samba music and dance.

santo: Both a Catholic saint and a term used for an *orixá*.

tabuleiro: The tray of a *baiana* vending food in the street.

tamborim (plural, *tamborins*): A small handheld circular drum played with a drumstick.

terreiro: A temple of Candomblé often with adjacent buildings and land.

trio elétrico: During carnival, a vehicle modified to allow musicians to ride in the open air while playing amplified music.

violão de doze cordas: 12-string guitar.

Bibliography

Archival Collections and Libraries Consulted

Arquivo da Irmandade Devoção ao Senhor do Bonfim, Salvador
    Livro de Atas da Devoção ao Senhor do Bonfim, de 1931 a 1977
Arquivo do Instituto Geográfico e Histórico da Bahia, Salvador
Arquivo Histórico Municipal de Salvador
    Caixa Clubes Carnavalescos e Esportivos
    Fundo Prefeitura Orçamento
    Pasta Clubes Carnavalescos
Arquivo Nacional, Rio de Janeiro
    Fundo da Secretaria da Presidência da República
Arquivo Público do Estado da Bahia, Seção Republicana, Salvador
    Secretaria de Segurança Pública
Biblioteca Amadeu Amaral, Museu Folclórico Edison Carneiro, Rio de Janeiro
    Arquivo Edison Carneiro
Biblioteca da Fundação Gregório de Mattos, Salvador
    Recortes
Biblioteca do Instituto Geográfico e Histórico da Bahia, Salvador
Biblioteca Nacional, Rio de Janeiro
    Divisão de Publicações Seriadas
Biblioteca Digital da Fundação Biblioteca Nacional, Brasília
    Digital Sound Archive, bndigital.bn.br/pesquisa.htm/
Biblioteca Pública do Estado da Bahia, Salvador
    Setor de Periódicos
British Library
Centro de Pesquisa e Documentação de História Contemporânea do Brasil, Fundação
    Getúlio Vargas, Rio de Janeiro
    Arquivo Clemente Mariani
    Arquivo Juracy Magalhães
    Arquivo Anísio Teixeira
Fundação Clemente Mariani, CEDIC/Ba, Salvador
    Arquivo Clemente Mariani
Fundação Pierre Verger, Salvador
    Arquivos Pessoais de Pierre Verger

Irmandade da Conceição da Praia, Salvador
Library of Congress, Washington, D.C.
National Archives at College Park, College Park, Maryland
    Record Group 59, General Records of the Department of State
    Record Group 84, Records of the Foreign Service Posts of the Department of State
Public Record Office, Kew, England
    Foreign Office Records
Schomburg Center for Research in Black Culture, New York Public Library, New York, New York
    Papers of Melville and Frances Herskovits
Smithsonian Institution, Washington, D.C.
    Ruth Landes Papers, National Anthropological Archives
UNESCO Archive, Paris
    Race Question and Protection of Minorities
    Statement on Race

Oral History Interviews

Alves, Inail Maria. Interviewed by Scott Ickes. Salvador da Bahia, 18 October 1999.
Assis, Francisco de (Mestre Gigante). Interviewed by Scott Ickes. Salvador da Bahia, 30 September 1999.
Conceição, Antônia de Oliveira. Interviewed by Scott Ickes and Vera Nathália da Silva. Salvador da Bahia, 2 and 11 November 1999.
Conceição, Severiano da. Interviewed by Scott Ickes and Vera Nathália da Silva. Salvador da Bahia, 2 and 11 November 1999.
Cruz, Ermita Pautilha Souza. Interviewed by Scott Ickes. Salvador da Bahia, 23 October 1999.
Leal, Geraldo Costa. Interviewed by Scott Ickes. Salvador da Bahia, 9 November 1999.
Lima Filho, Durval Emilio de Cerqueira. Interviewed by Scott Ickes and Vera Nathália da Silva. Salvador da Bahia, 26 October 1999.
Lopes, Americo de Oliveira. Interviewed by Scott Ickes. Salvador da Bahia, 10 November 1999. No transcript.
Meyer, Delza Valkyria Carvalho. Interviewed by Scott Ickes, Vera Nathália da Silva, and Válter da Silva. Salvador da Bahia, 21 October 1999.
Meyer, Walkyrio Cosenza. Interviewed by Scott Ickes, Vera Nathália da Silva, and Válter da Silva. Salvador da Bahia, 21 October 1999.
Porto, Deôdeto da Silva. Interviewed by Scott Ickes. Salvador da Bahia, 4 November 1999.
Santos, Hilda Dias dos (Mãe Hilda Jitolu). Interview by Scott Ickes. Salvador da Bahia, 25 October 1999.
Santos, João Pereira dos (Mestre João Pequeno). Interviewed by Scott Ickes. Salvador da Bahia, 24 October 1999.
Santos, José Ferreira dos. Interviewed by Scott Ickes and Vera Nathália da Silva. Salvador da Bahia, 4 and 11 November 1999.
Santos, Luisa Luís. Interviewed by Scott Ickes. Salvador da Bahia, 23 October 1999.
Silva, Clarindo da. Interviewed by Scott Ickes. Salvador da Bahia, 3 June 2009.
Silva, José Elísio da. Interviewed by Scott Ickes. Salvador da Bahia, 7 November 1999.

Silva, Luciano José da. Interviewed by Scott Ickes and Vera Nathália da Silva. Salvador da Bahia, 10 November 1999.

Teixeira, Cid. Interviewed by Scott Ickes. Salvador da Bahia, 4 June 2009.

Periodicals and Newspapers

Bahia Tradicional e Moderna (Salvador)
Brasil Novo (Salvador)
Capital (Salvador)
A Cigarra (Rio de Janeiro)
Correio Paulistano (São Paulo)
Crítica (Salvador)
O Cruzeiro (Rio de Janeiro)
Diário da Bahia (Salvador)
Diário de Notícias (Salvador)
Estado da Bahia (Salvador)
Festa (Salvador)
O Globo (Rio de Janeiro)
O Imparcial (Salvador)
Jornal da Bahia (Salvador)
O Momento (Salvador)
Revista Seiva (Salvador)
Samba (Salvador)
Semana Cathólica (Salvador)
A Tarde (Salvador)

Books, Articles, and Dissertations

7 anos que mudaram a Bahia. [Salvador]: Empresa Gráfica da Bahia, 1975.

Abrahams, Roger. "The Language of Festivals: Celebrating the Economy." In *Celebration: Studies in Festivity and Ritual*, edited by Victor Witter Turner, 161–77. Washington, D.C.: Smithsonian Institution Press, 1982.

Adelman, Jeremy. *Colonial Legacies: The Problem of Persistence in Latin American History.* New York: Routledge, 1999.

Agier, Michel. *Anthropologie du carnaval: La ville, la fête et l'Afrique à Bahia.* Marseille: Parenthèses, 2000.

———. "Between Affliction and Politics: A Case Study of Bahian Candomblé." In *Afro-Brazilian Culture and Politics*, edited by Hendrik Kraay, 134–57. London: M. E. Sharpe, 1998.

Albergaria, Roberto. "Festas populares baianas: Pós-modernização ou retradicionalização?" *A Tarde*, 4 December 2003, sec. Caderno 1.

Alberto, Jorge. "Na Bahia de Todos os Santos: A Festa dos Navegantes." *Última Hora*, 8 January 1953.

Alberto, Paulina L. "Para africano ver: African-Bahian Exchanges in the Reinvention of Brazil's Racial Democracy, 1961–63." *Luso-Brazilian Review* 45, no. 1 (2008): 78–117.

———. *Terms of Inclusion: Black Intellectuals in Twentieth-Century Brazil.* Chapel Hill: University of North Carolina Press, 2011.

Albuquerque, Wlamyra Ribeiro de. *Algazarra nas ruas: Comemorações da independência na Bahia, 1889–1923*. Campinas, São Paulo: Editora da UNICAMP, CECULT, FAPESP, 1999.

———. "Esperanças de boaventuras: Construções da África e africanismos na Bahia (1887–1910)." *Estudos Afro-Asiáticos* 24, no. 2 (2002): 215–45.

———. "Patriotas, festeiros, devotos . . . da independência na Bahia (1888–1923)." In *Carnavais e Outras F(r)estas: Ensaios de História Social da Cultura*, edited by Maria Clementina Pereira Cunha, 157–203. Campinas, São Paulo: Editora da UNICAMP, CE-CULT, FAPESP, 2002.

———. "Santos, deuses e heróis nas ruas da Bahia: Identidade cultural na Primeira República." *Afro-Ásia* 18 (1996): 103–24.

Almeida, Renato. "O folclore na sociedade baiana." *Anais do Primeiro Congresso de História da Bahia* 5 (1951): 167–71.

Alves, Isaías. *O dever da juventude na organização nacional*. Rio de Janeiro, 1941.

———. *Educação e brasilidade (idéias fôrcas do estado novo)*. [Rio de Janeiro]: J. Olympio, 1939.

———. *Educação e saúde na Bahia*. Bahia: Bahia Gráfica e Editora, 1939.

———. *Missão nacional e humana da Faculdade de Filosofia: Discurso de inauguração da Faculdade de Filosofia da Bahia em 15 de março de 1943*. Bahia: Imprensa Vitória, 1943.

Alves, Ívia. *Arco e flexa: Contribuição para o estudo do modernismo*. [Salvador]: Fundação Cultural do Estado da Bahia, 1978.

Amado, Adriana Moreira. *Disparate Regional Development in Brazil: A Monetary Production Approach*. Aldershot, UK: Ashgate, 1997.

Amado, Jorge. *Bahia de todos os santos: Guia das ruas e dos mistérios da cidade do Salvador*. São Paulo: Martins, 1961.

———. *Jubiabá*. 5th ed. São Paulo: Martins, 1947.

———. "O Professor Souza Carneiro." *A Tarde*, 20 June 1981.

Amaral, Amadeu. *Tradições populares*. São Paulo: Instituto Progresso, 1948.

Amaral, Aracy A. *Blaise Cendrars no Brasil e os modernistas*. 2nd ed. São Paulo: FAPESP, Editora 34, 1997.

Andrade, Mário de. *Música de feitiçaria no Brasil*. São Paulo: Livraria Martins Editôra, 1963.

Andrade Junio, Nivaldo Vieira de, Maria Rosa de Carvalho Andrade, and Raquel Neimann da Cunha Freire. "Avant-garde na Bahia: Urbanismo, arquitetura e artes plásticas em Salvador nas décadas de 1940 a 1960." Rio de Janeiro, 2009. http://www.docomomo.org.br/seminario%208%20pdfs/060.pdf/.

Andrews, George Reid. *Blackness in the White Nation: A History of Afro-Uruguay*. Chapel Hill: University of North Carolina Press, 2010.

Appelbaum, Nancy P. *Muddied Waters: Race, Region, and Local History in Colombia, 1846–1948*. Durham, N.C.: Duke University Press, 2003.

Apter, Anthony. "Herskovits's Heritage: Rethinking Syncretism in the African Diaspora." In *Syncretism in Religion: A Reader*, edited by Anita M. Leopold and Jeppe S. Jensen, 160–84. London: Equinox, 2004.

Araujo, Ana Lucia. *Public Memory of Slavery: Victims and Perpetrators in the South Atlantic*. Amherst, N.Y.: Cambria Press, 2010.

Araujo, Emanoel. "Odorico Tavares: A minha casa baiana: Sonhos e desejos de um colecionador." In *Odorico Tavares: A minha casa baiana: Sonhos e desejos de um colecionador*, edited by Emanoel Araujo, 15–23. São Paulo: Impr. Oficial do Estado, 2005.

Armstrong, Piers. "Bahian Carnival and Social Carnivalesque in trans-Atlantic Context." *Social Identities* 16, no. 4 (2010): 447–69.

Assis, Nancy Rita Sento Sé de. "Questões de vida e morte na Bahia Republicana." Tese de Mestrado, UFBA, 1996.

Assunção, Matthias Röhrig. *Capoeira: A History of an Afro-Brazilian Martial Art*. London: Routledge, 2005.

Azevedo, Thales de. *As elites de cor: Um estudo de ascensão social*. São Paulo: Companhia Editora Nacional, 1955.

———. "Comportamento verbal e efetivo para com os pretos." In *Ensaios de antropologia social*. Salvador: Publicações de Universidade da Bahia, 1959.

Bacelar, Jeferson. "A Frente negra brasileira na Bahia." *Afro-Ásia* 17 (1996): 73–85.

———. *Galegos no paraíso racial*. Salvador: Centro Editorial e Didático: CEAO, Ianamá, 1994.

———. *Gingas e nós: O jogo do lazer na Bahia*. Salvador: Fundação Casa de Jorge Amado, 1991.

———. *A hierarquia das raças: Negros e brancos em Salvador*. Rio de Janeiro: Pallas, 2001.

———. *Negros e espanhóis: Identidade e ideologia étnica em Salvador*. Salvador-Bahia: Universidade Federal da Bahia, Centro de Estudos Baianos, 1983.

Baer, Werner. *The Brazilian Economy: Growth and Development*. Westport, Conn.: Greenwood, 2001.

Bairros, Luiza. "Pecados no paraíso racial: O negro na força de trabalho da Bahia, 1950–1980." In *Escravidão e invenção da liberdade: Estudos sobre o negro no Brasil*, edited by João José Reis, 289–323. São Paulo: Editora brasiliense, 1988.

Bakhtin, Mikhail Mikhailovich. *Rabelais and His World*. Cambridge, Mass.: MIT Press, 1968.

Barbosa, Juciara Maria Nogueira. "Descompasso: Como e porque o modernismo tardou a chegar na Bahia." In *Quinto encontro de estudos multidisciplinares em cultura*. Salvador, Bahia, 2009. http://www.cult.ufba.br/enecult2009/19289.pdf/.

———. "Imagens de Salvador, por Pierre Verger, na revista *O Cruzeiro*." *Cadernos do MAV* 4, no. 4 (2007).

Barbosa, Luiz Sergio. "A Federação Baiana do Culto Afro-Brasileiro." In *Encontro de nações-de-Candomblé: Salvador-Bahia*. Salvador: Ianamá, UFBA, Centro Estudos Afro-Orientais [e] Centro Editorial e Didático, 1984.

Barickman, Bert Jude. *A Bahian Counterpoint: Sugar, Tobacco, Cassava, and Slavery in the Recôncavo, 1780–1860*. Stanford, Calif.: Stanford University Press, 1998.

Barreiros, Márcia Maria da Silva. "Educação, cultura e lazer das mulheres de elite em Salvador, 1890/1930." Tese de Mestrado, UFBA, 1997.

Bastide, Roger. *O Candomblé da Bahia, rito Nagô*. São Paulo: Companhia Editora Nacional, 1961.

———. "Manifestações de preconceito de cor." In *Relações raciais entre negros e brancos em São Paulo*, edited by Florestan Fernandes and Roger Bastide. São Paulo: Editôra Anhembi, 1955.

Bastos, Carlos. *Carlos Bastos*. Salvador: C. Bastos, 2000.

Bauman, Richard. "Performance and Honor in 13th Century Iceland." *Journal of American Folklore* 99, no. 392 (1986): 131–50.

Bauman, Richard, and Roger D. Abrahams. *"And Other Neighborly Names": Social Process and Cultural Image in Texas Folklore*. Austin: University of Texas Press, 1981.

Beezley, William H., Cheryl English Martin, and William E. French, eds. *Rituals of Rule, Rituals of Resistance: Public Celebrations and Popular Culture in México*. Wilmington, Del.: SR Books, 1994.

Besse, Susan K. *Restructuring Patriarchy: The Modernization of Gender Inequality in Brazil, 1914–1940*. Chapel Hill: University of North Carolina Press, 1996.

Bhabha, Homi K. *The Location of Culture*. London: Routledge, 1994.

Blake, Stanley E. *The Vigorous Core of Our Nationality: Race and Regional Identity in Northeastern Brazil*. Pittsburgh: University of Pittsburgh Press, 2011.

Borges, Dain. *The Family in Bahia, Brazil, 1870–1945*. Stanford, Calif.: Stanford University Press, 1992.

———. "'Puffy, Ugly, Slothful, Inert': Degeneration in Brazilian Social Thought, 1880–1940." *Journal of Latin American Studies* 25, no. 2 (1993): 235–56.

———. "The Recognition of Afro-Brazilian Symbols and Ideas, 1890–1940." *Luso-Brazilian Review* 32 (1994): 59–78.

Borges, Eduardo José Santos. "'Modernidade negociada': Cinema, autonomia política e vanguarda cultural no contexto do desenvolvimentismo Baiano. (1956–1964)." Tese de Mestrado, UFBA, 2003.

Borges, Vavy Pacheco. "Anos trinta e política." *Luso-Brazilian Review* 36, no. 2 (1999): 109–26.

Braga, Júlio Santana. *Na gamela do feitiço: Repressão e resistência nos Candomblés da Bahia*. Salvador: EDUFBA, 1995.

Brandão, Carlos Rodrigues. *A cultura na rua*. Campinas, São Paulo: Papirus Editora, 1989.

Brandão, Darwin. *A cozinha bahiana*. Bahia: Edição da Livraria Universitária, 1948.

Brito, Laurindo de. "Carnaval." *A Tarde*, 25 February 1954.

Britto, Iêda Marques. *Samba na cidade de São Paulo (1900–1930): Um exercício de resistência cultural*. [São Paulo]: FFLCH-USP, 1986.

Brower, Keith H., Earl E. Fitz, and Enrique E. Martinez-Vidal, eds. *Jorge Amado: New Critical Essays*. New York: Routledge, 2001.

Brown, David Hilary. *The Light Inside: Abakuá Society Arts and Cuban Cultural History*. Washington, D.C.: Smithsonian Books, 2003.

Browning, Barbara. *Samba: Resistance in Motion*. Bloomington: Indiana University Press, 1995.

Burke, Peter. "Performing History: The Importance of Occasions." *Rethinking History* 9, no. 1 (March 2005): 35–52.

Burlamaqui, Aníbal. *Ginástica nacional: Capoeiragem metodizada e regrada*. Rio de Janeiro, 1928.

Burton, Richard D. E. *Afro-Creole: Power, Opposition, and Play in the Caribbean*. Ithaca, N.Y.: Cornell University Press, 1997.

Butler, Kim. "Africa in the Reinvention of Nineteenth Century Afro-Bahian Identity." *Slavery & Abolition* 22, no. 1 (n.d.): 135–54.

————. "Afterword: Ginga Baiana, the Politics of Race, Class, Culture, and Power in Salvador, Bahia." In *Afro-Brazilian Culture and Politics: Bahia, 1790s to 1990s*, edited by Hendrik Kraay, 158–75. London: M. E. Sharpe, 1998.

————. *Freedoms Given, Freedoms Won: Afro-Brazilians in Post-Abolition, São Paulo and Salvador*. New Brunswick, N.J.: Rutgers University Press, 1998.

Campos, João da Silva. *Procissões tradicionais da Bahia*. [Salvador]: Secretaria da Educação e Saúde, 1941.

Capoeira, Nestor. *Capoeira: Roots of the Dance-Fight-Game*. Berkeley, Calif.: North Atlantic Books, 2002.

Capone, Stefania. *La quête de l'Afrique dans le Candomblé: Pouvoir et tradition au Brésil*. Paris: Karthala, 1999.

————. "Transatlantic Dialogue: Roger Bastide and the African American Religions." *Journal of Religion in Africa* 37 (2007): 336–70.

Carneiro, Edison. *Candomblés da Bahia*. Bahia: Secretaria de Educação e Saúde, 1948.

————. *Cartas de Édison Carneiro a Artur Ramos: De 4 de janeiro de 1936 a 6 de dezembro de 1938*. Edited by Waldir Freitas Oliveira and Vivaldo da Costa Lima. São Paulo: Corrupio, 1987.

————. "O Congresso Afro-Brasileiro da Bahia." In *Ladinos e crioulos: Estudos sôbre o negro no Brasil*, edited by Edison Carneiro, 98–102. Rio de Janeiro: Civilização Brasileira, 1964.

————. *Folguedos tradicionais*. Rio de Janeiro: Edições FUNARTE/INF, 1982.

————. *Negros Bantus; Notas de etnografia religiosa e de folk-lore*. Rio de Janeiro: Civilização brasileira, 1937.

————. *Religiões negras: Notas de etnografia religiosa; Negros bantos: Notas de etnografia religiosa e de folclore*. Rio de Janeiro: Civilização brasileira, 1991.

————. *A Sabedoria popular*. Rio de Janeiro: Ministério da Educação e Cultura, Instituto Nacional do Livro, 1957.

————. "Samba." *Estado da Bahia*, 2 July 1936.

Carneiro, Edison, and Aydano do Couto Ferraz, eds. *O negro no Brasil, Trabalhos apresentados ao 2° Congresso Afro-Brasileiro, Bahia [11 a 20 De Janeiro De 1937]*. Rio de Janeiro: Civilização brasileira, 1940.

Cartilha Histórica da Bahia. Rio de Janeiro: Editora Cívica, 1973.

Carvalho, Aloísio de, and Luis Guilherme Pontes Tavares. *Apontamentos para a história da imprensa na Bahia*. 2nd ed. Salvador: Academia de Letras da Bahia, 2008.

Carvalho, José Eduardo Freire de. *A devoção do Senhor J. do Bom-Fim e sua história*. Bahia: Typ. de S. Francisco, 1923.

Carvalho, Patrícia Moreira de. "Juracy Magalhães e a construção do juracisismo." Tese de Mestrado, UFBA, 2005.

Cascudo, Luís da Câmara. *Dicionário do folclore brasileiro*. Rio de Janeiro: Instituto Nacional do Livro, Ministério da Educação e Cultura, 1962.

Castillo, Lisa Earl. *Entre a oralidade e a escrita: A etnografia nos candomblés da Bahia*. Salvador: EDUFBA, 2008.

Castillo, Lisa Earl, and Luis Nicolau Parés. "Marcelina da Silva e seu mundo: novos dados para uma historiografia do Candomblé Ketu." *Afro-Ásia* 36 (2007): 111–51.

Castro, José Guilherme da Cunha, ed. *Miguel Santana*. Salvador: EDUFBA, 1996.

Castro, Ruy. *Carmen: Uma biografia*. São Paulo: Companhia das Letras, 2005.

Cavalcanti, Maria Laura Viveiros de Castro. *O rito e o tempo: Ensaios sobre o carnaval*. Rio de Janeiro: Civilização Brasileira, 1999.

Caymmi, Dorival. *Cancioneiro da Bahia*. São Paulo: Martins, 1947.

Caymmi, Stella. *Dorival Caymmi: O mar e o tempo*. São Paulo: Editora 34, 2001.

Chalhoub, Sidney. *Trabalho, lar e botequim: O cotidiano dos trabalhadores no Rio de Janeiro da belle époque*. Campinas, São Paulo: Editora da Unicamp, 2001.

Chasteen, John Charles. *National Rhythms, African Roots: The Deep History of Latin American Popular Dance*. Albuquerque: University of New Mexico Press, 2004.

———. "The Pre-history of Samba: Carnival Dancing in Rio De Janeiro, 1840–1917." *Journal of Latin American Studies* 28, no. 1 (1996): 29–47.

Clay, Vinícius. "O negro em o *Estado da Bahia*: De 1936 a 1938." Tese de Mestrado, Universidade Federal da Bahia (UFBA), 2006.

Collins, John. "Culture, Content, and the Enclosure of Human Being." *Radical History Review* 109 (Winter 2011): 121–35.

———. *The Revolt of the Saints*. Durham, N.C.: Duke University Press. Forthcoming.

Comaroff, John L., and Jean Comaroff. *Ethnography and the Historical Imagination*. Boulder, Colo.: Westview Press, 1992.

———. *Of Revelation and Revolution*. Chicago: University of Chicago Press, 1991.

Costa, Emília Viotti da. *The Brazilian Empire: Myths and Histories*. Chapel Hill: University of North Carolina Press, 2000.

Couto, Edilece Souza. "As lavagens nas festas católicas de Salvador-BA." *Ciências Humanas em Revista* 7, no. 2 (2009).

———. *A puxada do mastro: Transformações históricas da festa de São Sebastião em Olivença (Ilhéus-BA)*. Ilhéus: Editora da Universidade Livre do Mar e da Mata, 2001.

———. *Tempo de festas: Homenagens a Santa Bárbara, Nossa Senhora da Conceição e Sant' Ana em Salvador (1860–1940)*. Salvador: EDUFBA, 2010.

Cruz, Alessandra Carvalho da. "O samba na roda: Samba e cultura popular em Salvador, 1937–1954." Tese de Mestrado, UFBA, 2006.

Cunha, Maria Clementina Pereira. *Carnavais e outras f(r)estas: Ensaios de história social da cultura*. Campinas, São Paulo: Editora da UNICAMP, CECULT, FAPESP, 2002.

———. *Ecos da folia: Uma história social do carnaval carioca entre 1880 e 1920*. [São Paulo]: Companhia das Letras, 2001.

Cunha, Olívia Maria Gomes da. "Do ponto de vista de quem?" *Estudos Históricos* 36 (July 2005): 7–32.

———. "Sua alma em sua palma." In *Repensando o Estado Novo*, edited by Dulce Pandolfi. Rio de Janeiro: Editora da Fundação Getúlio Vargas, 1999.

Curcio-Nagy, Linda Ann. "From Native Icon to City Protectress to Royal Patroness: Ritual, Political Symbolism and the Vírgin of Remedies." *Americas* 52, no. 3 (1996): 367–91.

———. "Giants and Gypsies: Corpus Christi in Colonial Mexico City." In *Rituals of Rule, Rituals of Resistance: Public Celebrations and Popular Culture in Mexico*, edited by William Beezley, Cheryl English Martin, and William E. French. Wilmington, Del.: SR Books, 1994.

———. *The Great Festivals of Colonial Mexico City: Performing Power and Identity*. Albuquerque: University of New Mexico Press, 2004.

Dantas, Beatriz Góis. *Vovó Nagô e papai branco: Usos e abusos da África no Brasil*. Rio de Janeiro: Graal, 1988.

Dantas Neto, Paulo Fábio. *Tradição, autocracia e carisma: A política de Antônio Carlos Magalhães na modernização da Bahia, 1954–1974*. Rio de Janeiro: Editora UFMG, IUPERJ, 2006.

Dávila, Jerry. *Hotel Trópico: Brazil and the Challenge of African Decolonization, 1950–1980*. Durham, N.C.: Duke University Press, 2010.

Davis, Darién J. *Avoiding the Dark: Race and the Forging of National Culture in Modern Brazil*. Aldershot, UK; Brookfield, Vt.: Ashgate, 1999.

Davis, Natalie Zemon. *Society and Culture in Early Modern France: Eight Essays*. Stanford, Calif.: Stanford University Press, 1975.

Deiab. "A mãe-preta na literatura brasileira: A ambiguidade como construção social (1880–1950)." Tese de Mestrado, Universidade de São Paulo, 2007.

Döring, Katharina. "O mundo musical popular em Salvador no início do séc. XX." Salvador, Bahia, September 1999.

———. "O samba de roda do Sembagota: Tradição e contemporaneidade." Tese de Mestrado, UFBA, 2002.

Drewal, Margaret Thompson. "Dancing for Ogun in Yorubaland and in Brazil." In *Africa's Ogun*, edited by Sandra T. Barnes, 199–234. Bloomington: Indiana University Press, 1979.

———. *Yoruba Ritual: Performers, Play, Agency*. Bloomington: Indiana University Press, 1992.

Dunn, Christopher. "Black Rome and the Chocolate City." *Callaloo* 30, no. 3 (2007): 847–61.

Eliade, Mircea. *O Sagrado e o profano: A essência das religiões*. São Paulo: Martins Fontes, 1996.

Esteves, Martha de Abreu. *O império do Divino: Festas religiosas e cultura popular no Rio de Janeiro, 1830–1900*. Editora Nova Fronteira, 1999.

Fabricant, Nicole. "Performing Politics: The Camba Countermovement in Eastern Bolivia." *American Ethnologist* 36, no. 4 (November 2009): 768–83.

Falassi, Alessandro. *Time Out of Time: Essays on the Festival*. Ann Arbor, Mich.: Books on Demand, 1994.

Faria, Thaís Dumêt. "A festa das cadernetas: O conselho penitenciário da Bahia e as teorias criminológicas brasileiras no início do século xx." Tese de Mestrado, Universidade de Brasília, 2007.

Félix, Anísio. *Filhos de Gandhi: A história de um afoxé*. Brazil: S.n, Gráfica Central, 1987.

Ferreira Filho, Alberto Heráclito. "Desafricanizar as ruas: Elites letradas, mulheres pobres e cultura popular em Salvador (1890–1937)." *Afro-Ásia* 21–22 (1998–1999): 239–56.

Fox, Richard Gabriel. *Gandhian Utopia: Experiments with Culture*. Boston: Beacon Press, 1989.

Fraga Filho, Walter. *Encruzilhadas da liberdade: Histórias de escravos e libertos na Bahia, 1870–1910*. Campinas, São Paulo: Editora UNICAMP, 2006.

———. *Mendigos, moleques e vadios na Bahia do século XIX*. São Paulo, Salvador: Editora Hucitec, EDUFBA, 1996.

Frazier, E. Franklin. "The Negro Family in Bahia, Brazil." *American Sociological Review* 7 (1942): 465–78.

Freyre, Gilberto. *Bahia e baianos*. Salvador: Fundação das Artes/Empresa Gráfica da Bahia, 1990.

———. *The Mansions and the Shanties: The Making of Modern Brazil*. New York: Knopf, 1966.

———. *The Masters and the Slaves: A Study in the Development of Brazilian Civilization*. New York: Knopf, 1956.

———. "Prefácio." In *O negro na Bahia*, by Luiz Viana Filho, 7–16. Rio de Janeiro: J. Olympio, 1946.

Fry, Peter. *Para inglês ver: Identidade e política na cultura brasileira*. Rio de Janeiro: Zahar, 1982.

Fry, Peter, Sérgio Carrara, and Ana Luiza Martins-Costa. "Negros e brancos no carnaval da Velha República." In *Escravidão e invenção da liberdade: Estudos sobre o negro no Brasil*, edited by João José Reis, 232–63. São Paulo: Editora brasiliense, 1988.

Fry, Peter, and Olga R. de Moraes von Simson. "*Gallus africanus est*, ou, como Roger Bastide se tornou africano no Brasil." In *Revisitando a terra de contrastes: A atualidade da obra de Roger Bastide*, 31–46. São Paulo: Faculdade de filosofia, letras e ciências humanas, Centro de estudos rurais e urbanos, 1986.

Fryer, Peter. *Rhythms of Resistance: African Musical Heritage in Brazil*. Middletown, Conn.: Wesleyan University Press; Hannover, N.H.: University Press of New England, 2000.

Fuente, Alejandro de la. *A Nation for All: Race, Inequality, and Politics in Twentieth-Century Cuba*. Chapel Hill: University of North Carolina Press, 2001.

Furtado, Celso. *A operação nordeste*. Rio de Janeiro: Ministério da Educação e Cultura, Instituto Superior de Estudos Brasileiros, 1959.

———. "Uma política de desenvolvimento econômico para o nordeste. Documento elaborado pelo GTDN—Grupo de Trabalho Para o Desenvolvimento do Nordeste." Conselho de Desenvolvimento, 1959.

Garcia, Tânia Costa. "A canção popular e as representações do nacional no Brasil dos anos 30." *Revista Questões e Debates* 31 (1999): 67–94.

Gautherot, Marcel, and Lélia Coelho Fota. *Retratos da Bahia: Fotografias*. [São Paulo]: Edições Pinacoteca, 1996.

Geertz, Clifford. *The Interpretation of Cultures: Selected Essays*. New York: Basic Books, 1973.

Giesler, Patric V. "Conceptualizing Religion in Highly Syncretistic Fields: An Analog Ethnography of the Candomblés of Bahia, Brazil." Ph.D. diss., Brandeis University, 1998.

Gilroy, Paul. *The Black Atlantic: Modernity and Double Consciousness*. Cambridge: Harvard University Press, 1993.

Godi, Antônio dos Santos. "De índio a negro, ou o reverso." *Caderno CRH* (suplemento) (1991): 51–70.

Godofredo Filho. "Eva." *O Cruzeiro*, 20 June 1942.

Góes, Fred de. *50 anos do trio elétrico*. Salvador [Brazil]: Editora Corrupio, 2000.

Goldsmith, William W., and Robert Wilson. "Poverty and Distorted Industrialization in the Brazilian Northeast." *World Development* 19, no. 5 (1991): 435–55.

Goldstein, Daniel M. *The Spectacular City: Violence and Performance in Urban Bolivia.* Durham, N.C.: Duke University Press, 2004.

Gomes, João Carlos Teixeira. "Presença do modernismo na Bahia." In *Camões contestador e outros ensaios.* Salvador: Fundação Cultural do Estado da Bahia, 1979.

Gomes, Nilma. "Caminhando com Ruth Landes pela cidade das mulheres." In *Brasil: Afro-Brasileiro,* edited by Maria Nazareth Soares Fonseca and Jussara Santos. Belo Horizonte, Brazil: Autêntica Editora, 2000.

Gomes, Thiago de Melo, and Micol Seigel. "Sabina's Oranges: The Colours of Racial Politics in Rio De Janeiro, 1889–1930." *Journal of Latin American Cultural Studies* 11, no. 1 (2002): 5–28.

Graden, Dale Torston. *From Slavery to Freedom in Brazil: Bahia, 1835–1900.* Albuquerque: University of New Mexico Press, 2006.

Groetelaars, Martien Maria. *Quem é o Senhor do Bonfim?: O significado do Senhor do Bonfim na vida do povo da Bahia.* Petrópolis: Vozes, 1983.

Guerreiro, Almerinda. *A trama dos tambores: A música afro-pop de Salvador.* São Paulo: Grupo Pão de Açúcar: Editora 34, 2000.

Guerreiro, Goli. "As trilhas do samba-reggae: A invenção de um ritmo." *Latin American Music Review* 20, no. 1 (Spring/Summer 1999): 105–40.

Guimarães, Antônio Sérgio A. *Classes, raças e democracia.* São Paulo: Editora 34, 2002.

———. "Cor, classes e status nos estudos de Pierson, Azevedo e Harris na Bahia: 1940–1960." In *Raça, ciência e sociedade,* edited by Marcos Chor Maio and Ricardo Ventura Santos. Rio de Janeiro: Centro Cultural Banco do Brasil: Editora FIOCRUZ, 1996.

———. "A Formação e a crise da hegemonia burguesa na Bahia, 1930–1964." Tese de Mestrado, UFBA, 1982.

———. *Um sonho de classe: Trabalhadores e formação de classe na Bahia dos anos oitenta.* São Paulo: Editora Hucitec, 1998.

Guimarães, Eduardo Alfredo Morais. "Religião popular, festa e o sagrado: Catolicismo popular e afro-brasilidade na festa do Bonfim." Tese de Mestrado, UFBA, 1994.

Guss, David M. *The Festive State: Race, Ethnicity, and Nationalism as Cultural Performance.* Berkeley and Los Angeles: University of California Press, 2000.

Haber, Stephen H. *How Latin America Fell Behind: Essays on the Economic Histories of Brazil and Mexico, 1800–1914.* Stanford, Calif.: Stanford University Press, 1997.

Hagedorn, Katherine J. *Divine Utterances: The Performance of Afro-Cuban Santería.* Washington, D.C.: Smithsonian Institution Press, 2001.

Hanchard, Michael George. *Orpheus and Power: The Movimento Negro of Rio De Janeiro and São Paulo, Brazil, 1945–1988.* Princeton, N.J.: Princeton University Press, 1994.

Harding, Rachel E. *A Refuge in Thunder: Candomblé and Alternative Spaces of Blackness.* Bloomington: Indiana University Press, 2003.

Hasenbalg, Carlos Alfredo. *Discriminação e desigualdades raciais no Brasil.* Rio de Janeiro: Graal, 1979.

Heers, Jacques. *Fêtes des fous et carnavals.* Paris: Fayard, 1983.

Herskovits, Melville J. *Pesquisas Etnológicas Na Bahia.* Bahia: Secretaria de educação e saúde, 1943.

Hertzman, Marc. "Surveillance and Difference: The Making of Samba, Race, and Nation in Brazil (1880s–1970s)." Ph.D. diss., University of Wisconsin, Madison, 2008.

Holanda, Sérgio Buarque de. *Raízes do Brasil: Edição comemorativa 70 anos*. São Paulo: Companhia das Letras, 2006.

Holloway, Thomas. "'A Healthy Terror': Police Repression of Capoeiras in Nineteenth-Century Rio De Janeiro." *Hispanic American Historical Review* 69, no. 4 (1989): 637–76.

Ickes, Scott. "'Adorned with the Mix of Faith and Profanity that Intoxicates the People': The Festival of the Senhor Do Bonfim in Salvador, Bahia, Brazil, 1930–1954." *Bulletin of Latin American Research* 24, no. 2 (2005): 181–200.

———. "Salvador's Transformist Hegemony." Ph.D. diss., University of Maryland, 2003.

Instituto Brasileiro de Geografia e Estatística (IBGE). *Anuário estatístico do Brasil–1973*. Vol. 34. Rio de Janeiro: IBGE, 1973. http://biblioteca.ibge.gov.br/visualizacao/monografias/GEBIS%20-%20RJ/AEB/AEB1973.pdf/.

———. *Características demográficas do Estado da Bahia*. Rio de Janeiro: IBGE, 1949.

Jelin, Elizabeth. "Formas de organização da atividade econômica e estrutura ocupacional." *Estudos CEBRAP*, July 1974.

Kittleson, Roger. *The Practice of Politics in Postcolonial Brazil: Porto Alegre, 1845–1895*. Pittsburgh: University of Pittsburgh Press, 2006.

Knight, Alan. "Weapons and Arches in the Mexican Revolutionary Landscape." In *Everyday Forms of State Formation*, edited by Gilbert Joseph and Daniel Nugent, 24–66. Durham, N.C.: Duke University Press, 1994.

Kraay, Hendrik. "'Cold as the Stone of Which It Must Be Made': Caboclos, Monuments and the Memory of Independence in Bahia, Brazil, 1870–1900." In *Images of Power: Iconography, Culture and the State in Latin America*, edited by Jens Andermann and William Rowe, 165–94. New York: Berghahn Books, 2005.

———, ed. *Afro-Brazilian Culture and Politics: Bahia, 1790s to 1990s*. Armonk, N.Y.: M. E. Sharpe, 1998.

Kurtz, Donald V. "Hegemony and Anthropology: Gramsci, Exegeses, Reinterpretations." *Critique of Anthropology* 16, no. 2 (1996): 103–35.

Laclau, Ernesto, and Chantal Mouffe. *Hegemony and Socialist Strategy: Towards a Radical Democratic Politics*. London: Verso, 2001.

Landes, Ruth. *The City of Women*. Albuquerque: University of New Mexico Press, 1994.

Lara, Silvia Hunold. "Significados cruzados: Um reinado de congos na Bahia setecentista." In *Carnavais e outras f (r)estas: Ensaios de história social da cultura*, edited by Maria Clementina Pereira Cunha, 71–100. Campinas, São Paulo: Editora da UNICAMP, CECULT, FAPESP, 2002.

Leach, Edmund Ronald. *Culture and Communication*. Cambridge: Cambridge University Press, 1976.

Leal, Geraldo da Costa. *Pergunte ao seu avô: Histórias de Salvador, cidade da Bahia*. Salvador: Grafufba, 1996.

Leal, Herundino. "Africanos no Brasil." *A Tarde*, 26 February 1955.

———. "Capoeira." *A Tarde*, 30 June 1956.

Lears, T. J. Jackson. "The Concept of Cultural Hegemony: Problems and Possibilities." *American Historical Review* 90, no. 3 (n.d.): 567–93.

Leite, Rinaldo. "E a Bahia civiliza-se . . . Ideais de civilização e cenas de anti-civilidade em um contexto de modernização urbana, 1912–1916." Tese de Mestrado, UFBA, 1996.

Leopoldi, José Sávio. *Escola de samba: Ritual e sociedade*. Petrópolis: Editora Vozes, 1978.

Lesser, Jeff. *Negotiating National Identity: Immigrants, Minorities, and the Struggle for Ethnicity in Brazil*. Durham, N.C.: Duke University Press, 1999.

———. *Welcoming the Undesirables Brazil and the Jewish Question*. Berkeley and Los Angeles: University of California Press, 1995.

Levine, Robert M. *Brazilian Legacies*. Armonk, N.Y.: M. E. Sharpe, 1997.

———. *Father of the Poor? Vargas and His Era*. Cambridge: Cambridge University Press, 1998.

———. *The Vargas Regime: The Critical Years, 1934–1938*. New York: Columbia University Press, 1970.

Lewis, John Lowell. *Ring of Liberation: Deceptive Discourse in Brazilian Capoeira*. Chicago: University of Chicago Press, 1992.

Lima, Herman. *Roteiro da Bahia*. [Rio de Janeiro]: Ministério da Educação e Saúde, Serviço de Documentação, 1953.

Lima, José. *A festa de Egun e outros ensaios. Resas, meisinhas, mandingas e mandingueiros da Bahia. Vendedores ambulantes de Bahia*. 3rd ed. Rio de Janeiro: Spivak e Kersner, 1955.

Lima, Milton Costa. "Meu carnaval da Bahia." *A Tarde*, 25 February 1954.

Lima, Vivaldo da Costa. "O candomblé da Bahia na década de 1930." *Estudos Avançados* 18, no. 52 (2004): 201–21.

———. "O candomblé da Bahia na década de trinta." In *Cartas de Édison Carneiro a Artur Ramos*, edited by Waldir Freitas Oliveira and Vivaldo da Costa Lima, 37–73. São Paulo: Corrupio, 1987.

———. "A Roma Negra." *Diário de Notícias*, 10 October 1960.

Lody, Raul, and Alex Baradel, eds. *O olhar viajante de Pierre Fatumbí Verger*. Salvador: Fundação Pierre Verger, 2002.

Lody, Raul Giovanni da Motta. *Afoxé*. Rio de Janeiro: Ministério da Educação e Cultura, Departamento de Assuntos Culturais, Fundação Nacional de Arte, Campanha de Defesa do Folclore Brasileiro, 1976.

———. *Eparrei, Bárbara: Fé e festas de largo de São Salvador*. IPHAN, CNFCP, 2004.

Lopes, Nei. *O negro no Rio de Janeiro e sua tradição musical: Partido-alto, calango, chula e outras cantorias*. Rio de Janeiro: Palla, 1992.

Love, Joseph L. "Furtado, Social Science, and History." In *Colonial Legacies: The Problem of Persistence in Latin American History*, edited by Jeremy Adelman, 193–206. New York: Routledge, 1999.

Ludwig, Selma. "Mudanças na vida cultural de Salvador—1950 a 1970." Tese de Mestrado, UFBA, 1982.

Lühning, Angela. "'Acabe com este santo, Pedrito vem aí . . . ' mito e realidade da perseguição policial ao Candomblé baiano entre 1920 e 1942." *Revista USP* 28 (December–February 1995/1996): 194–220.

———. "O compositor Mozart Camargo Guarnieri em Salvador." In *Ritmos em trânsito*, edited by Lívio Sansone. São Paulo: Dynamis Editorial, 1998.

———. "Pierre Fatumbí Verger e sua obra: Homenagem." *Afro-Ásia* 21–22 (1999): 315–64.

———, ed. *Pierre Verger: Repórter fotográfico*. Rio de Janeiro: Bertrand Brasil, 2003.

MacDonell, Diane. *Theories of Discourse: An Introduction*. London: B. Blackwell, 1986.

Machado, Hélio. "Prefácio." In *Formação e evolução étnica da cidade de Salvador*, by Carlos Ott. Salvador: Prefeitura do Salvador, 1955.

Magalhães, Basílio de, and João da Silva Campos. *O folclore no Brasil, com uma coletânea de 81 contos populares*. Rio de Janeiro: Imprensa Nacional, 1939.

Magalhães, Juracy. *Defendendo o meu governo. (Explicações á Bahia a propósito de um livro do Snr. J. J. Seabra)*. Bahia: Tipografia Naval, 1934.

———. *Minhas memórias provisórias*. Edited by Alzira Alves de Abreu. Rio de Janeiro: Civilização Brasileira, 1982.

Mahony, Mary Ann. "Afro-Brazilians, Land Reform, and the Question of Social Mobility in Southern Bahia, 1880–1920." *Luso-Brazilian Review* 34, no. 2 (Winter 1997): 59–79.

———. "The Local and the Global: Internal and External Factors in the Development of Brazil's Cacao Sector." In *Latin America and the Global Economy: A Commodity Chains Perspective*, edited by Steven Topik, Carlos Marichal, and Zephyr Frank. Durham, N.C.: Duke University Press, 2006.

———. "A Past to Do Justice to the Present: Historical Representation, Collective Memory and Elite Rule in Twentieth-Century Southern Bahia, Brazil." In *Reestablishing the Political in Latin American History: A View from the North*, edited by Gilbert Joseph. Durham, N.C.: Duke University Press, 2001.

Mallon, Florencia E. *Peasant and Nation: The Making of Postcolonial Mexico and Peru*. Berkeley and Los Angeles: University of California Press, 1995.

———. "The Promise and Dilemma of Subaltern Studies: Perspectives from Latin American History." *American Historical Review* 99, no. 5 (1994): 1491–1515.

———. "Reflections on the Ruins: Everyday Forms of State Formation in Nineteenth-Century Mexico." In *Everyday Forms of State Formation*, edited by Gilbert Joseph and Daniel Nugent, 69–106. Durham, N.C.: Duke University Press, 1994.

Mariani, Clemente. "Análise do problema econômico Baiano." *Planejamento* 5, no. 4 (October–December 1977): 55–121.

Mariano, Agnes. *A invenção da baianidade*. São Paulo: Annablume, 2009.

Marinho, Josaphat. "Otávio Mangabeira: Líder político." In *Um praticante da democracia, Otávio Mangabeira*, 133–40. Salvador: Conselho Estadual de Cultura da Bahia, 1980.

Martins, Wilson. *The Modernist Idea: A Critical Survey of Brazilian Writing in the Twentieth Century*. New York: New York University Press, 1970.

Matory, James Lorand. *Black Atlantic Religion: Tradition, Transnationalism, and Matriarchy in the Afro-Brazilian Candomblé*. Princeton, N.J.: Princeton University Press, 2005.

———. "The English Professors of Brazil." *Comparative Studies in Society and History* 41, no. 1 (1999): 72–103.

Matos, Cláudia. *Acertei no milhar: Malandragem e samba no tempo de Getúlio*. Rio de Janeiro: Paz e Terra, 1982.

Matta, Roberto da. *Carnivals, Rogues, and Heroes: An Interpretation of the Brazilian Dilemma*. Notre Dame, Ind.: University of Notre Dame Press, 1991.

McCann, Bryan. *Hello, Hello Brazil: Popular Music in the Making of Modern Brazil*. Durham, N.C.: Duke University Press, 2004.

McGowan, Chris, and Ricardo Pessanha. *The Brazilian Sound: Samba, Bossa Nova, and the Popular Music of Brazil*. Philadelphia: Temple University Press, 2009.

Meade, Teresa A. *"Civilizing" Rio: Reform and Resistance in a Brazilian City, 1889–1930.* University Park, Pa.: Pennsylvania State University Press, 1997.

Medeiros, Jarbas. *Ideologia autoritária no Brasil, 1930–1945.* Rio de Janeiro: Editora da Fundação Getúlio Vargas, 1978.

Mello Moraes, Alexandre José de. *Festas e tradições populares do Brasil.* Rio de Janeiro: Fauchon e cia, 1895. http://hdl.handle.net/2027/nnc1.1000205060/.

Mendoza, Zoila S. *Shaping Society through Dance: Mestizo Ritual Performance in the Peruvian Andes.* Chicago: University of Chicago Press, 2000.

Métraux, Alfred. "An Inquiry into Race Relations in Brazil." *Courier,* September 1952.

Metz, Jerry Dennis. "*Alegria*: The Rise of Brazil's 'Carnival of Popular Participation,' Salvador da Bahia, 1950–2000s." Ph.D. diss., University of Maryland, College Park. Forthcoming.

Mielche, Hakon. *From Santos to Bahia.* (*Fra Santos til Bahia.*) Translated by M. A. Michael. London: William Hodge, 1948.

Monteiro, Antônio. "A procissão folclórica da lavagem do Bonfim." *A Tarde Suplemento,* 18 January 1969.

———. "Propagadores da tradição." *O Globo,* 6 January 1955.

Moore, Robin. *Nationalizing Blackness: Afrocubanismo and Artistic Revolution in Havana, 1920–1940.* Pittsburgh: University of Pittsburgh Press, 1997.

Morales, Anamaria. "O afoxé filhos de Gandhi pede paz." In *Escravidão e invenção da liberdade: Estudos sobre o negro no Brasil,* edited by João José Reis, 264–74. São Paulo: Editora brasiliense, 1988.

Morand, Paul. *Oeuvres.* Paris: Flammarion, 1981.

Mouffe, Chantal. "Hegemony and Ideology in Gramsci." In *Gramsci and Marxist Theory,* edited by Chantal Mouffe. London: Routledge and Kegan, 1979.

Moura, Jair. *Capoeira: A luta regional baiana.* Salvador: Divisão de Folclore, Departamento de Assuntos Culturais, Secretaria Municipal de Educação e Cultura, Prefeitura Municipal de Salvador, 1979.

Moura, Milton. "O carnaval como engenho e representação consensual da sociedade baiana." *Caderno CRH* 24/25 (January 1996): 171–92.

———. "Um mapa político do carnaval: Reflexão a partir do caso de Salvador." *Orbis* 4 (September 2002). http://www.orbis.ufba.br/artigo10.htm/.

Moura, Roberto. *Tia Ciata e a pequena África no Rio de Janeiro.* Rio de Janeiro: FUNARTE, Instituto Nacional de Música, Divisão de Música Popular, 1983.

Nájera-Ramírez, Olga. *La Fiesta De Los Tastoanes: Critical Encounters in Mexican Festival Performance.* Albuquerque: University of New Mexico Press, 1998.

Nájera-Ramírez, Olga, Norma Elia Cantú, and Brenda M. Romero, eds. *Dancing across Borders: Danzas y Bailes Mexicanos.* Urbana: University of Illinois Press, 2009.

Nascimento, Abdias do. "A sociologia desaculturada." *O Jornal,* 13 October 1954.

Nascimento, Karina Rêgo. "Movimento *Caderno da Bahia*—1948–1951." Tese de Mestrado, UFBA, 1999.

Neves, Erivaldo Fagundes. "Invasão em Salvador." Tese de Mestrado, PUC, 1985.

Nina Rodrigues, Raymundo. *O animismo fetichista dos negros baianos.* Salvador: P555 Edições, 2005.

———. *Os africanos no Brasil.* São Paulo: Companhia Editora Nacional, 1977.

Nishida, Mieko. *Slavery and Identity: Ethnicity, Gender, and Race in Salvador, Brazil, 1808–1888.* Bloomington: Indiana University Press, 2003.

Nóbrega, Cida, and Regina Echeverria. *Mãe Menininha do Gantois: Uma biografia.* Salvador: Corrupio; Rio de Janeiro: Ediouro, 2006.

———. *Verger: Um retrato em preto e branco.* Salvador: Corrupio, 2002.

Oliveira, Francisco de. *O elo perdido: Classe e identidade de classe.* São Paulo: Editora brasiliense, 1987.

Oliveira, Gilson. "Agostinho de Silva e o Centro de Estudos Afro-Orientais." Tese de Mestrado, Universidade de São Paulo, 2010.

Oliveira, Lucia Lippi, Monica Pimenta Velloso, and Angela de Castro Gomes, eds. *Estado Novo: Ideologia e poder.* Rio de Janeiro: Zahar, 1982.

Oliveira, Waldir Freitas. "Os estudos africanistas na Bahia dos anos 30." In *Cartas de Édison Carneiro a Artur Ramos,* edited by Vivaldo da Costa Lima and Waldir Freitas Oliveira, 23–35. São Paulo: Corrupio, 1987.

Oliven, Ruben George. *Tradition Matters: Modern Gaúcho Identity in Brazil.* New York: Columbia University Press, 1996.

Ortiz, Renato. *A consciência fragmentada: Ensaios de cultura popular e religião.* Rio de Janeiro: Paz e Terra, 1980.

Osorio, Alejandra. "The King in Lima: Simulacra, Ritual, and Rule in Seventeenth-Century Peru." *Hispanic American Historical Review* 84, no. 3 (2004): 447–74.

Ott, Carlos. *Formação e evolução étnica da cidade do Salvador; o folclore bahiano.* Salvador: Tip. Manú, 1955.

Owensby, Brian Philip. *Intimate Ironies: Modernity and the Making of Middle-Class Lives in Brazil.* Stanford, Calif.: Stanford University Press, 1999.

Paiva, Ruy Miller. "The Development of Brazilian Agriculture, 1945–1960." *Journal of Farm Economics* 43, no. 5 (December 1962): 1092–1100.

Pandolfi, Dulce Chaves. *Repensando o Estado Novo.* Rio de Janeiro: Editora FGV, 1999.

Pang, Eul-Soo. *Bahia in the First Brazilian Republic: Coronelismo and Oligarchies, 1889–1934.* Gainesville: University Press of Florida, 1979.

Paraiso, Juarez. "Entrevista Juarez Paraiso." *Revista da Bahia,* no. 40. Secretaria de Cultura. Fundação Cultural do Estado da Bahia. 2004. http://www.fundacaocultural.ba.gov.br/04/revista%20da%20bahia/Artes%20Plasticas/entre.htm/.

Parés, Luis Nicolau. "The Birth of the Yoruba Hegemony in Post-abolition Candomblé." *Journal de la Société des Américanistes* 91, no. 1 (2005): 139–59.

———. "The Jeje in the Tambor de Mina of Maranhão and in the Candomblé of Bahia." *Slavery & Abolition* 22, no. 1 (2001): 91–115.

———. "The 'Nagoization' Process in Bahian Candomblé." In *The Yoruba Diaspora in the Atlantic World,* edited by Toyin Falola and Matt Childs, 185–298. Bloomington: Indiana University Press, 2005.

Peixoto, Afrânio. *Breviário da Bahia.* 2nd ed. [Rio de Janeiro]: Livraria Agir, 1946.

Pereira, Leonardo Affonso de Miranda. *O carnaval das letras.* Rio de Janeiro: Prefeitura da Cidade do Rio de Janeiro, Secretaria Municipal de Cultura, Departamento Geral de Documentação e Informação Cultural, Divisão de Editoração, 1994.

Perrone, Charles A., and Christopher Dunn, eds. *Brazilian Popular Music and Globalization.* Gainesville: University Press of Florida, 2001.

Pierson, Donald. *Negroes in Brazil: A Study of Race Contact at Bahia*. Chicago: University of Chicago Press, 1942.

Pinho, José Wanderley Araujo de. *Mensagem—Relatório*. Salvador: Imprensa Oficial, 1948.

Pinho, Patricia de Santana. *Mama Africa: Reinventing Blackness in Bahia*. Durham, N.C.: Duke University Press, 2010.

Pires, Antônio. "Movimentos da cultura afro-brasileira: A formação histórica da capoeira contemporânea (1890–1950)." Ph.D. diss., Universidade Estadual de Campinas, 2001.

Prado, Caio. *The Colonial Background of Modern Brazil*. Berkeley and Los Angeles: University of California Press, 1969.

Prandi, J. Reginaldo. *Os candomblés de São Paulo*. São Paulo: Editora Hucitec, 1991.

———. *Mitologia dos orixás*. São Paulo: Companhia das Letras, 2001.

———. *Segredos guardados: Orixás na alma brasileira*. São Paulo: Companhia das Letras, 2005.

Prefeitura Municipal do Salvador. *Roteiro Turístico da cidade do Salvador*. Salvador: Impr. da Organização brasileira de edições culturas, 1952.

Programa de recuperação econômica da Bahia. Salvador: Edições da Comissão de Planejamento Econômico, 1958.

Queiroz, Lúcia Maria Aquino de. "A evolução do sistema institucional público do turismo baiano." *Bahia: Análise & Dados* 11, no. 2 (Setember 2001).

———. "Gestão pública e a competitividade de cidades turísticas: A experiência da cidade do Salvador." Ph.D. diss., Universitat de Barcelona, 2005.

Queiroz, Maria Isaura Pereira de. *Carnaval brasileiro: O vívido e o mito*. São Paulo: Editora Brasiliense, 1992.

Querino, Manuel. *A Bahia de outrora*. Salvador: Livraria Progresso Editora, 1955.

———. *A raça africana e os seus costumes*. Salvador: Progresso, 1955.

Ramos, Arthur. *O folclore negro no Brasil*. Rio de Janeiro: Civilização Brasileira, 1936.

Ramos, Frances L. *Identity, Ritual and Power in Colonial Puebla*. Tucson: University of Arizona Press, 2012.

Raphael, Alison. "Samba and Social Control: Popular Culture and Racial Democracy in Rio De Janeiro." Ph.D. diss., Columbia University, 1980.

———. "Samba Schools in Brazil." *International Journal of Oral History* 10, no. 3 (1989): 256–69.

Rego, Waldeloir. *Capoeira angola: Ensaio sócio-etnográfico*. Rio de Janeiro: Gráf. Lux, 1968.

Reis, João José. *Death Is a Festival: Funeral Rites and Rebellion in Nineteenth-Century Brazil*. Chapel Hill: University of North Carolina Press, 2003.

———. *Domingos Sodré, um sacerdote africano: Escravidão, liberdade e candomblé na Bahia do século XIX*. São Paulo: Companhia das Letras, 2008.

———. *Slave Rebellion in Brazil: The Muslim Uprising of 1835 in Bahia*. Baltimore: Johns Hopkins University Press, 1993.

———. "Tambores e temores: A festa negra na Bahia na primeira metade do século XIX." In *Carnavais e outras f (r)estas: Ensaios de história social da cultura*, edited by Maria Clementina Pereira Cunha, 101–47. Campinas, São Paulo: Editora da UNICAMP, CECULT, FAPESP, 2002.

Reis, João José, and Eduardo da Silva. *Negociação e conflito: A resistência negra no Brasil escravista*. São Paulo: Companhia das Letras, 1989.

Reis, João José, and Beatriz Galloti Mamigonian. "Nagô and Mina: The Yoruba Diaspora in Brazil." In *The Yoruba Diaspora in the Atlantic World*, edited by Toyin Falola and Matt Childs, 77–110. Bloomington: Indiana University Press, 2005.

Reis, Letícia de Souza. "Mestre Bimba e Mestre Pastinha." In *Artes do corpo*, edited by Vagner Gonçalves da Silva. São Paulo: Selo Negro, 2004.

———. *O mundo de pernas para o ar: A capoeira no Brasil*. São Paulo: Publisher Brasil, 1997.

Reis, Meire Lúcia Alves dos. "Cor da notícia: Discurso sobre o negro na imprensa baiana—1888–1937." Tese de Mestrado, UFBA, 2000.

Reiter, Bernd. "Inequality and School Reform in Bahia, Brazil." *International Review of Education* 55, no. 4 (2009): 345–65.

Riggio, Milla Cozart. *Carnival: Culture in Action—The Trinidad Experience*. New York: Routledge, 2004.

Rio, João do. *As religiões no Rio*. Rio de Janeiro: Editora Nova Aguilar, 1976.

Risério, Antonio. *Avant-garde na Bahia*. São Paulo: Instituto Lina Bo e P. M. Bardi, 1995.

———. "Carnaval, as Cores Da Mudança." *Afro-Ásia* 16 (1995).

———. *Carnaval Ijexá*. Bahia: Corrupio, 1981.

———. *Caymmi: Uma utopia de lugar*. São Paulo: Editora Perspectiva; [Salvador]: CO-PENE, 1993.

———. *Uma história da cidade da Bahia*. Rio de Janeiro: Versal, 2004.

Rocha, Carlos Eduardo da. "As influências africanas nas artes da Bahia." *Revista do Instituto Geográfico e Histórico da Bahia* 91 (1994).

———. "Odorico Tavares: Incentivador cultural." In *Odorico Tavares: A minha casa bahiana: Sonhos e desejos de um colecionador*, edited by Emanoel Araujo, 143–49. São Paulo: Impr. Oficial do Estado, 2005.

Rolim, Iara. "Primeiras imagens: Pierre Verger entre burgueses e infreqüentáveis." Ph.D. diss., Universidade de São Paulo, 2009.

Romo, Anadelia A. *Brazil's Living Museum: Race, Reform, and Tradition in Bahia*. Chapel Hill: University of North Carolina Press, 2010.

———. "Race and Reform in Bahia: Primary Education 1888–1964." Ph.D. diss., Harvard University, 2004.

———. "Rethinking Race and Culture in Brazil's First Afro-Brazilian Congress." *Journal of Latin American Studies* 39, no. 1 (2007): 31–54.

Rosado, Abdon, Jafé Teixeira Borges, and Ubiratan Castro de Araújo. *Salvador era assim: Memórias da cidade*. Salvador: Instituto Geográfico e Histórico da Bahia, 1999.

Roseberry, William. "Hegemony and the Language of Contention." In *Everyday Forms of State Formation*, edited by Gilbert Joseph and Daniel Nugent, 355–66. Durham, N.C.: Duke University Press, 1994.

Rowe, William, and Vivian Schelling. *Memory and Modernity: Popular Culture in Latin America*. London: Verso, 1991.

Sampaio, Consuelo Novais. *Os partidos políticos da Bahia na Primeira República: Uma política de acomodação*. Salvador: UFBA, Núcleo de Publicações do Centro Editorial e Didático, 1978.

———. *Poder e representação: O legislativo da Bahia na Segunda República, 1930–1937*. Salvador: Assembléia Legislativa da Bahia, 1992.

Sampaio, Nelson de Souza. "O governador Otávio Mangabeira." In *Um praticante da democracia, Otávio Mangabeira*, 117–32. Salvador: Conselho Estadual de Cultura da Bahia, 1980.

Sandroni, Carlos. *Feitiço decente: Transformações do samba no Rio de Janeiro, 1917–1933*. Rio de Janeiro: Jorge Zahar, Editora UFRJ, 2001.

Sansi-Roca, Roger. *Fetishes and Monuments: Afro-Brazilian Art and Culture in the Twentieth Century*. New York: Berghahn Books, 2007.

Sansone, Lívio. *Blackness without Ethnicity: Constructing Race in Brazil*. New York: Palgrave MacMillan, 2003.

Sansone, Lívio, and Jocélio Teles dos Santos, eds. *Ritmos em trânsito: Sócio-antropologia da música baiana*. São Paulo: Dynamis Editorial, 1998.

Santana, Carla de. "Caleidoscópio: percurso intelectual e a estréia de Heron de Alencar como crítico literário no jornal *A Tarde* (1947–1952)." Tese de Mestrado, UFBA, 2003.

Santana, Jussilene. "Odorico Tavares: O mago das letras." *Memórias da Bahia II, UCSAL*, 9 November 2003.

Santana, Mariely Cabral de. *Alma e festa de uma cidade: Devoção e construção da Colina do Bonfim*. EDUFBA, 2009.

Santana, Nélia de. "A prostituição feminina em Salvador (1900–1940)." Tese de doutoramento, UFBA, 1996.

Santos, Deoscóredes Maximiliano dos. *Axé Opô Afonjá: Notícia histórica de um terreiro de santo da Bahia*. Rio de Janeiro: Instituto Brasileiro de Estudos Afro-Asiáticos, 1962.

———. *Yorubá tal qual se fala*. Bahia: Livraria Moderna, 1950.

Santos, Jocélio Teles dos. "Divertimentos estrondosos: Batuques e sambas no século XIX." In *Ritmos em trânsito: Sócio-antropologia da música baiana*, 15–38. São Paulo: Dynamis Editorial, 1998.

———. "A Mixed-Race Nation: Afro-Brazilians and Cultural Policy in Bahia, 1970–1990." In *Afro-Brazilian Culture and Politics*, edited by Hendrik Kraay, 117–33. London: M. E. Sharpe, 1998.

———. *O poder da cultura e a cultura no poder: Disputa simbólica da herança cultural negra no Brasil*. Salvador: EDUFBA, 2005.

Santos, Jocélio Teles dos, and Delcele Mascarenhas Queiroz. "Sistema de Cotas: Um multiculturalismo brasileiro?" *Ciencia e cultura* 59, no. 2 (June 2007).

Santos, Luis Paulino dos. "Um Dia Na Rampa." 1959. YouTube video. http://www.youtube.com/watch?v=KmJ-ny_bEcM/. Accessed 24 June 2012.

Santos, Mário Augusto da Silva. "Os caixeiros da Bahia." Tese de Mestrado, UFBA, 1974.

———. "Sobrevivências e tensões sociais." Tese de doutoramento, Universidade de São Paulo, 1982.

Santos, Milton. *O centro da cidade do Salvador: Estudo de geografia urbana*. Salvador: Publicações da Universidade, 1959.

Santos, Ruy. "Prefácio." In *Minha vida pública na Bahia*, by Juracy Magalhães, 3–83. Rio de Janeiro: Livraria Jose Olympio Editora, 1957.

Sayer, Derek. "Everyday Forms of State Formation: Some Dissident Remarks on 'Hegemony.'" In *Everyday Forms of State Formation*, edited by Gilbert Joseph and Daniel Nugent, 367–77. Durham, N.C.: Duke University Press, 1994.

Scaldaferri, Sante. *Os primórdios da arte moderna na Bahia: Depoimentos, textos e con-*

siderações em torno de José Tertuliano Guimarães e outros artistas. Salvador: Fundação Casa de Jorge Amado, 1998.

Schechner, Richard. "Carnival (Theory) After Bakhtin." In Carnival: Culture in Action—The Trinidad Experience, edited by Milla Cozart Riggio, 3–11. London: Routledge, 2004.

Schwarcz, Lilia Moritz. O espetáculo das raças: Cientistas, instituições e questão racial no Brasil, 1870–1930. São Paulo: Companhia das Letras, 1993.

Schwartz, Stuart B. Sugar Plantations in the Formation of Brazilian Society: Bahia, 1550–1835. Cambridge: Cambridge University Press, 1985.

Scott, James C. Domination and the Arts of Resistance: Hidden Transcripts. New Haven, Conn.: Yale University Press, 1990.

———. Weapons of the Weak: Everyday Forms of Peasant Resistance. New Haven, Conn.: Yale University Press, 1985.

Selka, Stephen. Religion and the Politics of Ethnic Identity in Bahia, Brazil. Gainesville: University Press of Florida, 2007.

Selka, Stephen L. "Ethnoreligious Identity Politics in Bahia, Brazil." Latin American Perspectives 32, no. 1 (January 2005): 72–94.

Serra, Ordep. Rumores de festa: O sagrado e o profano na Bahia. Salvador: EDUFBA, 2000.

Severiano, Jairo. Getúlio Vargas e a música popular. Rio de Janeiro: Editora da Fundação Getúlio Vargas, 1983.

Silva, Augusto Álvaro da Silva. "Carta Pastoral." Revista Eclesiástica da Bahia XLII, no. 3 (1950).

Silva, Jônatas C. da. "História de lutas negras: Memórias do surgimento do movimento negro na Bahia." In Escravidão e invenção da liberdade: Estudos sobre o negro no Brasil, edited by João José Reis, 275–88. São Paulo: Editora brasiliense, 1988.

Silva, José Calasans Brandão da. Édison Carneiro e o folclore baiano. Salvador: Centro de Estudos Afro-Orientais da UFBA, 1980.

Silva, José Luiz Foresti Werneck da, and Francisco José Calazans Falcon, eds. O feixe e o prisma: Uma revisão do Estado Novo. Rio de Janeiro: J. Zahar, 1991.

Silva, Maria Beatriz Nizza da. "O sagrado e o profano nas festas do Brasil colonial" (n.d.).

Silva, Paulo Santos. Âncoras de tradição: Luta política, intelectuais e construção do discurso histórico na Bahia, 1930–1949. Salvador: EDUFBA, 2000.

Silverstein, Leni. "The Celebration of Our Lord of the Good End: Changing State, Church, and Afro-Brazilian Relations in Bahia." In The Brazilian Puzzle: Culture on the Borderlands of the Western World, edited by David J. Hess and Roberto da Matta. New York: Columbia University Press, 1995.

Simson, Olga Rodrigues de Moraes von. "Espaço urbano e folguedo carnavalesco no Brasil: Uma visão ao longo do tempo." Cadernos do Centro de Estudos Rurais e Urbanos 15, no. 1a (August 1981).

Singer, Milton B. Traditional India: Structure and Change. Philadelphia, American Folklore Society, 1959.

Skidmore, Thomas E. Black into White: Race and Nationality in Brazilian Thought. New York: Oxford University Press, 1974.

———. Politics in Brazil, 1930–1964: An Experiment in Democracy. New York: Oxford University Press, 2007.

Smith, Robert J. The Art of the Festival, as Exemplified by the Fiesta to the Patroness of

Otuzco, La Virgen de la Puerta. Lawrence: Department of Anthropology, University of Kansas, 1975.

Smith, T. Lynn. *Brazil: People and Institutions.* Baton Rouge: Louisiana State University Press, 1963.

Soares, Lélia Gontijo. *Mário de Andrade e a Sociedade de Etnografia e Folclore, no Departamento de Cultura do Município de São Paulo, 1936–1939.* Rio de Janeiro: FUNARTE, Instituto Nacional do Folclore; São Paulo: Secretaria Municipal de Cultura, 1983.

Soares, Mariza de Carvalho. *Devotos da cor: Identidade étnica, religiosidade e escravidão no Rio de Janeiro, século XVIII.* Rio de Janeiro: Civilização Brasileira, 2000.

Sodré, Muniz. *Mestre Bimba: Corpo de mandinga.* Rio de Janeiro: Manati, 2002.

———. *Samba: O dono do corpo.* Rio de Janeiro: Editora Codecri, 1979.

———. *O Terreiro e a cidade: A forma social negro-brasileira.* Petrópolis: Vozes, 1988.

Soihet, Rachel. *A subversão pelo riso: Estudos sobre o carnaval carioca da Belle Époque ao tempo de Vargas.* Rio de Janeiro: Fundação Getúlio Vargas Editora, 1998.

Souza, George Evergton Sales. "Entre o religioso e o político: Uma história do Círculo Operário da Bahia." Tese de Mestrado, UFBA, 1996.

Stam, Robert. "Carnival, Politics and Brazilian Culture." *Studies in Latin American Popular Culture* 7 (1988): 255–64.

Tacca, Fernando de. *Imagens do sagrado: Entre* Paris Match *e* O Cruzeiro. Campinas, São Paulo: Editora Unicamp, 2009.

Tak, Herman. *South Italian Festivals: A Local History of Ritual and Change.* Amsterdam: Amsterdam University Press, 2000.

Talmon-Chvaicer, Maya. *The Hidden History of Capoeira: A Collision of Cultures in the Brazilian Battle Dance.* Austin: University of Texas Press, 2008.

Tavares, Cláudio. "As rodas de samba na Bahia." *Estado da Bahia,* 29 March 1949.

Tavares, Cláudio, and Pierre Verger. "Afoxé, Ritmo bárbaro da Bahia." *O Cruzeiro,* 29 May 1948.

———. "Capoeira mata um!" *O Cruzeiro,* 10 January 1948.

———. "Roda de samba." *A Cigarra,* April 1949.

Tavares, Odorico. *Bahia: Imagens da terra e do povo.* Rio de Janeiro: Olympio, 1951.

———. *Conceição da Praia.* Desenhos de Carybé. Coleção Recôncavo 6. Salvador: Livraria Progresso Editora, 1955.

———. "Conceição da Praia." In *Conceição da Praia.* Desenhos de Carybé. Coleção Recôncavo 6. Salvador: Livraria Progresso Editora, 1955.

———. *Festa do Bonfim.* Desenhos de Carybé. Coleção Recôncavo 5. Salvador: Livraria Progresso, 1955.

———. "A Festa do Bonfim de mestre Carybé." In *Festa do Bonfim.* Desenhos de Carybé. Coleção Recôncavo 5. Salvador: Livraria Progresso, 1955.

Tavares, Odorico, Jorge Amado, and Carybé. *Discurso de um cidadão do Salvador, e alguns conselhos para conhecer a Bahia.* Rio de Janeiro: Editora Civilização Brasileira, 1961.

Tavares, Odorico, Emanoel Araújo, Galeria de Arte do SESI (São Paulo, Brasil), and Museu Afro Brasil. *Odorico Tavares: A minha casa baiana: Sonhos e desejos de um colecionador.* São Paulo: Impr. Oficial do Estado, 2005.

Tavares, Odorico, and Pierre Verger. "Atlas carrega seu mundo." *O Cruzeiro,* 5 April 1947.

———. "Caymmi na Bahia." *O Cruzeiro,* 17 May 1947.

——. "O ciclo do Bonfim." *O Cruzeiro*, 22 March 1947.

——. "Conceição da Praia." *O Cruzeiro*, 31 May 1947.

——. "Cosme e Damião: Os santos mabaças." *Cruzeiro*, 18 November 1950.

——. "A cozinha da Bahia." *Cruzeiro*, 2 December 1950.

——. "Decadência e morte da lavagem do Bonfim." *Cruzeiro*, 23 June 1951.

——. "A escultura afro-brasileira na Bahia." *Cruzeiro*, 14 April 1951.

——. "Itinerário das feiras da Bahia." *Cruzeiro*, 15 February 1947.

——. "Lagoa do Abaeté." *Cruzeiro*, 12 November 1949.

——. "Mataripe." *Cruzeiro*, 25 November 1950.

——. "Pancetti e os mares da Bahia." *Cruzeiro*, 11 November 1950.

——. "A pesca do xaréu." *Cruzeiro*, 18 October 1947.

——. "Rafael, o pintor." *Cruzeiro*, 6 January 1951.

——. "O reino de Yemanjá." *Cruzeiro*, 26 April 1947.

——. "Revolução na Bahia." *Cruzeiro*, 7 July 1951.

——. "Saveiros do Recôncavo." *Cruzeiro*, 30 November 1946.

——. "Trovadores da Bahia." *Cruzeiro*, 26 October 1946.

Taylor, Diana. *Disappearing Acts: Spectacles of Gender and Nationalism in Argentina's "Dirty War."* Durham, N.C.: Duke University Press, 1997.

Teixeira, Cid. "Prefácio." In *Filhos de Gandhi: A história de um afoxé*, edited by Anísio Félix. [Brazil]: Gráfica Central, 1987.

Telles, Edward Eric. *Race in Another America: The Significance of Skin Color in Brazil.* Princeton, N.J.: Princeton University Press, 2004.

Thomas, Deborah A. *Modern Blackness: Nationalism, Globalization, and the Politics of Culture in Jamaica.* Durham, N.C.: Duke University Press, 2004.

Tosta Filho, Ignácio. *Secção B do Volume II do Plano de Ação Econômica para o Estado da Bahia.* Bahia: Instituto de Cacau da Bahia, 1948.

Tourinho, Eduardo. *Alma e corpo da Bahia.* 2nd ed. Rio de Janeiro: Pongetti, 1953.

Travassos, Elizabeth. *Modernismo e música brasileira.* Rio de Janeiro: Jorge Zahar, 2000.

Tupy, Dulce. *Carnavais de guerra: O nacionalismo no Samba.* Rio de Janeiro: ASB Arte Gráfica e Editora, 1985.

Turner, Victor. *The Anthropology of Performance.* New York: PAJ Publications, 1986.

——. *Celebration, Studies in Festivity and Ritual.* Washington, D.C.: Smithsonian Institution Press, 1982.

——. *The Ritual Process: Structure and Anti-Structure.* Chicago: Aldine, 1969.

Turner, Victor, and Edith L. B. Turner. *Image and Pilgrimage in Christian Culture: Anthropological Perspectives.* New York: Columbia University Press, 1978.

Twine, France Widdance. *Racism in a Racial Democracy: The Maintenance of White Supremacy in Brazil.* New Brunswick, N.J.: Rutgers University Press, 1997.

"Utopian Pauper." *Time Magazine*, 12 September 1960.

Valladares, José. *Artes maiores e menores: Seleção de crônicas de arte, 1951–1956.* [Salvador]: Universidade da Bahia, 1957.

——. *Bêabá da Bahia: Guia turístico.* Salvador: Livraria Turista, Livraria Progresso, 1951.

——. "Belas artes na Bahia de hoje." In *Álbum comemorativo da cidade de Salvador.* São Paulo: Habitat Editora, 1954.

——. *Dominicais: Seleção de crônicas de arte, 1948–1950.* Salvador: Artes Gráficas, 1948.

——. "Introdução." In *Casos e coisas da Bahia*, by Antônio Vianna. Salvador: Secretaria de Educação e Saúde, 1950.

Valladares, José, and Carybé. *O torça da bahiana.* [Salvador]: K. Paulo Hebeisen, 1952.

Valle Silva, Nelson do. "The High Cost of Not Being White in Brazil." In *Race, Class and Power in Brazil,* edited by Pierre-Michel Fontaine, 42–55. Los Angeles: Center for Afro-American Studies, UCLA, 1985.

Vaughan, Mary K. *Cultural Politics in Revolution: Teachers, Peasants, and Schools in Mexico, 1930–1940.* Tucson: University of Arizona Press, 1997.

Verger, Pierre. *50 anos de fotografia.* Salvador: Corrupio, 1982.

———. *Fluxo e refluxo do tráfico de escravos entre o golfo do Benin e a Bahia de Todos os Santos, dos séculos XVII a XIX.* São Paulo: Editora Corrupio, 1987.

———. *Retratos da Bahia.* Salvador: Corrupio, 2002.

Verger, Pierre, and Roger Bastide. *Verger—Bastide: Dimensões de uma amizade.* Edited by Angela E. Lühning. Rio de Janeiro: Bertrand Brasil, 2002.

Verger, Pierre, Jean Loup Pivin, and Pascal Martin Saint Léon. *Pierre Verger: Le Messager = the Go-Between: Photographies 1932–1962.* Paris: Editions Revue Noire; New York: DAP, 1996.

Viana Filho, Luiz. *O negro na Bahia.* Rio de Janeiro: J. Olympio, 1946.

Vianna, Angela Ramalho, Guaraci Adeodato Alves de Souza, and Vilmar Faria. *Bahia de todos os pobres.* Petrópolis: Editora Vozes, 1980.

Vianna, Antônio. *Casos e coisas da Bahia.* Salvador: Secretaria de educação e saúde, 1950.

Vianna, Hermano. *The Mystery of Samba: Popular Music and National Identity in Brazil.* Chapel Hill: University of North Carolina Press, 1999.

Vianna, Hildegardes. *A Bahia já foi assim (crônicas de costumes).* Salvador: Editora Itapuã, 1973.

———. *A cozinha bahiana: Seu folclore, suas receitas.* Bahia: [Fundação Gonçalo Moniz], 1955.

———. "Do entrudo ao carnaval na Bahia." *Revista Brasileira de Folclore* 13 (September–December 1965).

———. *Festas de santos e santos festejados.* Salvador: Livraria Progresso Editora, 1960.

———. "Noite de Reis na Bahia." *Revista da Bahia* 38 (n.d.). http://www.fundacaocultural.ba.gov.br/04/revista%20da%20bahia/Folguedos/noite.htm/.

Vieira, Luiz Renato. "A capoeiragem disciplinada: Estado e cultura popular no tempo de Vargas." *História e Perspectivas,* no. 7 (1992): 111–32.

Vieira, Nelson. "Testimonial Fiction and Historical Allegory: Racial and Political Repression in Jorge Amado's Brazil." *Latin American Literary Review* 17, no. 34 (December 1989): 6–23.

Vieira Filho, Rafael Rodrigues. "A africanização do carnaval de Salvador, Bahia: A recriação do espaço carnavalesco (1876–1930)." Ph.D. diss., Universidade de São Paulo, 1995.

Vilhena, Luís Rodolfo. *Projeto e missão: O movimento folclórico brasileiro, 1947–1964.* Rio de Janeiro: Fundação Getúlio Vargas Editora: Ministério da Cultura, FUNARTE, 1997.

Wade, Peter. *Blackness and Race Mixture: The Dynamics of Racial Identity in Colombia.* Baltimore: Johns Hopkins University Press, 1995.

———. *Music, Race and Nation: Música Tropical in Colombia.* Chicago: University of Chicago Press, 2000.

Waters, Anita M. *Race, Class, and Political Symbols: Rastafari and Reggae in Jamaican Politics.* New Brunswick, N.J.: Transaction Books, 1985.

Weinstein, Barbara. *For Social Peace in Brazil: Industrialists and the Remaking of the Working Class in São Paulo, 1920–1964*. Chapel Hill: UNC Press Books, 1996.

———. "Racializing Regional Difference: São Paulo vs. Brazil, 1932." In *Race and Nation in Modern Latin America*, edited by Nancy Appelbaum, Anne Macpherson, and Karin Rosemblatt, 237–62. Chapel Hill: University of North Carolina Press, 2003.

Williams, Brackette F. *Stains on My Name, War in My Veins: Guyana and the Politics of Cultural Struggle*. Durham, N.C.: Duke University Press, 1991.

Williams, Daryle. *Culture Wars in Brazil: The First Vargas Regime, 1930–1945*. Durham, N.C.: Duke University Press, 2001.

Williams, Raymond. *Marxism and Literature*. Oxford: Oxford University Press, 1977.

Wolfe, Joel. "'Father of the Poor' or 'Mother of the Rich'?: Getúlio Vargas, Industrial Workers, and Constructions of Class, Gender, and Populism in Sao Paulo, 1930–1954." *Radical History Review* 58 (Winter 1994): 88–111.

———. "The Faustian Bargain Not Made: Getúlio Vargas and Brazil's Industrial Workers, 1930–1945." *Luso-Brazilian Review* 31, no. 2 (n.d.): 77–95.

Woodard, James. *A Place in Politics: São Paulo, Brazil, from Seigneurial Republicanism to Regionalist Revolt*. Durham, N.C.: Duke University Press, 2009.

Zweig, Stefan. *Brazil: Land of the Future*. London: Cassell, 1942.

Index

Page numbers in italics refer to illustrations

Scott Ickes is assistant professor of history at the University of South Florida.

*   *   *

The University Press of Florida is the scholarly publishing agency for the State University System of Florida, comprising Florida A&M University, Florida Atlantic University, Florida Gulf Coast University, Florida International University, Florida State University, New College of Florida, University of Central Florida, University of Florida, University of North Florida, University of South Florida, and University of West Florida.